The Ultimate Guide to

FREE-MOTION QUILTING

with Angela Walters

TIPS, TECHNIQUES & 104 DESIGNS

Angela Walters

Publisher: Amy Barrett-Daffin

Creative Director: Gailen Runge

Senior Editor: Roxane Cerda

Editors: Madison Moore, Liz Aneloski, Karla Menaugh, and Phyllis Elving

Technical Editors: Priscilla Read, Sadhana Wray, Linda Johnson, Mary E. Flynn, and Ann Haley

Cover/Book Designer: April Mostek

Production Coordinators: Zinnia Heinzmann, Tim Manibusan, Jenny Davis, Jessica Jenkins, and Joe Edge

Production Editors: S. Michele Fry, Joanna Burgarino, Jessica Brotman, Nicole Rolandelli, Jennifer Warren, Jeanie German, and Alice Mace Nakanishi

Illustrators: Aliza Shalit, Wendy Mathson, and Eric Sears

Photography Coordinator: Rachel Ackley

Photography by Christina Carty-Francis, Diane Pedersen, Lucy Glover, and Nissa Brehmer for C&T Publishing, unless otherwise noted

Published by Stash Books, an imprint of C&T Publishing, Inc., P.O. Box 1456, Lafayette, CA 94549

Library of Congress Cataloging-in-Publication Data

Names: Walters, Angela, 1979- author.

Title: The ultimate guide to free-motion quilting with Angela Walters : tips, techniques & 104 designs / Angela Walters.

Description: Lafayette, CA : Stash Books, an imprint of C&T Publishing,Inc, [2024] | Summary: "From stunning shots of the quilts and essays on Angela Walter's creative philosophy, to full techniques and a massive library of free-motion quilting designs, this book includes everything you need to quilt like Angela"--Provided by publisher.

Identifiers: LCCN 2023035303 | ISBN 9781644035238 (trade paperback) | ISBN 9781644035245 (ebook)

Subjects: LCSH: Machine quilting. | Quilting--Patterns. | Patchwork--Patterns. | Patchwork quilts. | Shapes. | BISAC: CRAFTS & HOBBIES / Quilts & Quilting | CRAFTS & HOBBIES / Sewing

Classification: LCC TT835 .W356568 2024 | DDC 746.46/041--dc23/eng/20231102

LC record available at https://lccn.loc.gov/2023035303

Printed in China

10 9 8 7 6 5 4 3

CONTENTS

Design Library 114–115

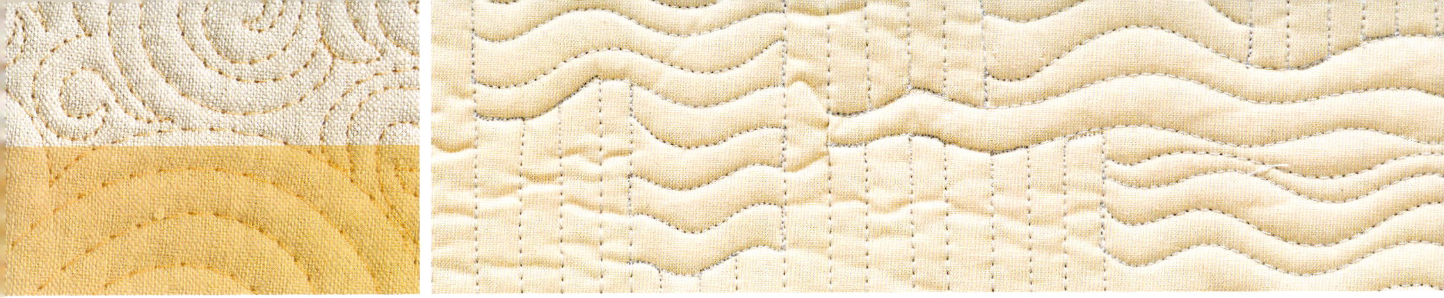

Angela Walters: Quilting is My Therapy

STARTING FROM THE BEGINNING

Have you ever heard of the phrase, "Even a blind squirrel gets a nut sometimes"? It pretty much sums up my quilting career. Like most professionals in the quilting industry, I didn't set out to be a professional quilter. It's not as though that option is in the list of potential careers.

I didn't grow up with family members that quilted, and I was never crafty—well, at least in the sense of making things. In fact, I failed the sewing machine test in eighth grade home economics ... twice. All I had to do was identify the parts of the sewing machine; I didn't have to actually use it! If I am being honest, the only reason I passed the third time was because the teacher finally took pity on me and helped "suggest" some of the answers. So when I say, "If I can do it, anyone can," you can take me at my word.

Impracticality, designed and quilted by Angela Walters

I didn't actually know what a quilt was until I met my husband, Jeremy. His grandparents started quilting after retirement. It was quite amazing, actually. His grandpa made quilts as a way to entice family members to attend the annual family reunion. He pieced and hand quilted a quilt for every generation. To win one of the quilts, a family member had to attend the reunion and could only win a quilt once. I would soon learn why these rules were so important.

I wasn't even married to Jeremy when I attended my first family reunion. It was there that I got the first glimpse of how coveted these quilts were. If you have ever been to a family gathering where things got tense over, let's say, potato salad, you can imagine what happens when the stakes are as high as a quilt. I won't say that it was violent or anything, but there was a lot of passive-aggressive complaining. "Didn't Aunt Martha already win a quilt?" and "Why does her family always win?" were just a few of the comments made. I remember looking around and thinking, "Geez, people! These are just blankets!" I know now that saying such a thing is sacrilegious in quilting. I just want to show how ignorant I was at the time.

Jeremy didn't win a quilt at the reunion, so on a whim I asked Grandpa to show me how to make one. He assured me that even though I had no sewing experience, I could learn how to do it. One thing I want to point out is that he said, "Yes." He didn't say, "Yes, but you need to make the quilt I want you to make using the fabric I like." He didn't judge my choice of fabric or pattern, which is something I think all quilters should do when sharing their love of quilting.

Grandpa started me off on a nine-patch quilt, and I remember making that first Nine-Patch block vividly. He had a 4″ square template and taught me how to trace the shape onto the fabric, cut it out, and piece my first-ever quilt block. About an hour later, I held up my nine-patch (which wasn't horrible, if I do say so myself). With his eyes gleaming, he exclaimed, "Wonderful job! Now let me show you the easy way." Then he pulled out his rotary cutter and ruler. Thank goodness that he did, because I don't think I would be a quilter today if I had to use templates! That first nine-patch quilt is still on my bed.

So it began: I was addicted to quilting. We hand quilted the first several quilts I made. Grandpa gave me a frame, and he, Jeremy, and I sat side by side and quilted. He would tell us stories and we would have a great time. I wish I had taken pictures during this time, but I was too busy enjoying the moment.

FROM HAND QUILTER TO MACHINE QUILTER

I didn't hate hand quilting, but I didn't love it either. Jeremy and Grandpa were way better at it than I was; I was content to just hang out and pretend to quilt. But one day about two years later, everything changed. While hanging out at his house, Grandpa said, "I think you should get a longarm quilting machine."

I quickly answered, "I think I should too ... what is it?" It turns out he didn't know what one was either, having only seen one from afar at a quilt show. Despite our complete lack of knowledge of quilting machines, Grandpa was undeterred. He ordered some information from a company, and we began looking over the options.

When I found out that the company had a used machine available, I was giddy and ready to make it mine. Jeremy, understandably, was more hesitant. Thankfully, Grandpa interceded and pulled rank, telling him, "If you don't buy her one, I'll buy it for her." What could Jeremy do? Everyone wanted to make Grandpa happy, so if Grandpa said buy a longarm, you bought a longarm.

I'd like to take a moment and point out that this isn't how I would suggest buying any kind of machine, especially one as big as a longarm! But like I said, I was just a blind squirrel. Thankfully it worked out.

To say that we were excited about the longarm would be an understatement. While we waited for my baby to arrive, we tried to figure out how it worked. That's right—not only had I never seen one but I had never even machine quilted. Finally we decided that it must be computerized. Really, how else could it work? It made stars and loopy designs; it was really the only way. I'll wait here while you chuckle at my ignorance. ...

Bauble, designed by Emily Cier; quilted by Angela Walters

I am sure you can imagine the look on my face when the machine was delivered. I quickly realized that not only was it not computerized but I also had to hand-guide the thing. There I was, surrounded by Grandpa, Jeremy, and a few other family members. I had to act as though I wasn't scared out of my mind. The gentleman that set up the machine showed me how to load the machine, how to thread it, and how to quilt a meander. Then ... he was gone.

You may wonder why I didn't just machine quilt on my sewing machine. That answer is simple: we didn't know it was possible. Every day I thank God that we didn't know we could, because there is no way I could have talked Jeremy into buying a longarm otherwise.

Luckily for me, Grandpa suffered from a particular eye condition—he never saw an ugly quilt top. If it had at least two pieces of fabric sewed together, he was going to buy it. Whether at a flea market, a thrift store, or an auction, if he saw a "quilt top," he was going to get it. It didn't matter who got in front of his motorized scooter. He was going to run them over in pursuit of the treasure. By the time I received my quilting machine, he had amassed a stack of at least 30 quilt tops. They were real "beauties": hand-pieced, double-knit grandmother's flower garden quilt tops. (Just in case you can't tell, I am being sarcastic.)

Once the machine was set up and the technician left, I took off the practice quilt sandwich and loaded my first quilt top. Even though it had been only a few hours since the technician had left, I wasn't scared. I figured I couldn't make these quilt tops look any worse! I didn't realize it then, but I was beginning the next phase of my quilting "career."

I could lie to you and say that machine quilting came effortlessly to me. I could imply that the machine glided as though it were an extension of my body. But that wouldn't be true. Since I was self-taught, I had an idiot for a teacher. I made so many mistakes! For one, I loaded a quilt back that was too short for the quilt top. Not realizing this until I got to the end of the quilt, I did the only rational thing. I cut the last border off of the quilt. I can see myself giving the quilt to Grandpa afterward and saying, "Sorry it's not quite right; the backing was just too small." Grandpa, the sweetest and most encouraging person I knew, simply replied, "It's perfect!"

So it continued. I quilted Grandpa's quilt tops, butchering most of them. No matter what, he would always tell me that they were the best quilts ever. That was the key element to my success. I didn't have YouTube or free tutorials; Grandpa was the only quilter I knew. He said I was the best ever, and I believed it. I am so thankful that I didn't have anything to compare myself to. I didn't have to drool over pictures of other people's quilting. I wasn't bombarded with Instagram pictures of gorgeous designs. I was blissfully ignorant that anyone else in the world was quilting, and I just enjoyed the process of learning how to machine quilt.

I quilted the whole stack of quilts and presented Grandpa with the bill of $130. It may not seem like enough for 30-plus quilts, but since I ruined most of them and it was because of him that I had the machine, I decided it was fair enough.

Space Dust, designed by Tula Pink; quilted by Angela Walters

GOING PRO

After I finished Grandpa's quilts and the few quilt tops that I had hanging around, I realized I had nothing else to machine quilt. So I had two options: I could piece more quilt tops, or I could become a "professional" quilter and quilt other people's. Now, if the last section could be called "How Not to Buy a Quilting Machine," this section would be "How Not to Go into Business." Same blind squirrel, another nut.

Not surprisingly, I decided to go into business for myself. In my opinion, the less piecing I had to do the better. After convincing Jeremy that I was indeed serious, I hopped on the computer and went to Ask.com to figure out how to start a machine-quilting business. (That was before Google; that's how long it's been.) One website suggested joining a local quilt guild. Hmm ... brilliant! Up to that point, I didn't know any other quilters besides Grandpa. Joining a group seemed a bit scary, but since I didn't worry about looking silly, I jumped right in.

I attended my first local quilt guild meeting after deciding to go into business. I even had some very lame business cards made up just in case. That very first meeting had two significant results. I realized that, at 24, I was a lot younger than the average quilter and that quilt guilds held their own quilt shows. So I did what anyone else would do—I volunteered to be a vendor at the show. I did this despite never having gone to a quilt show ... ever ... in my life. What was the worst that could happen?

Butterfly, designed by Tula Pink; quilted by Angela Walters

Flower Pops, designed by Alex Anderson; quilted by Angela Walters

I'll tell you the worst thing that could happen. You could show up as a vendor. You could bring your quilt (one quilt!) and business cards. You could set them up on the table and have a seat, then slowly start to realize that other vendors are driving trailer loads up to the back loading dock. You could feel a chill as you realize how unprepared and pathetic you might look sitting there, by yourself, in your empty booth. But knowing it's too late, all you can do is smile and hope for the best. Which is exactly what happened. I sat there all weekend, met a few great people, and gave out a few business cards, which were taken most likely out of pity. I did get one customer from the show. I'll tell you more about her later.

Ultimately the show was a bust. I could have given up right then, but I didn't. I wanted to see if I could get just one customer. So, I kept attending guild meetings and actually started getting a few customers (much to my surprise). I will never, ever forget getting paid for the first quilt. I held the $35 check up to my hubby and said, "We are going out to dinner!" Just writing about it now brings a smile to my face. I had met the one and only goal I had set for myself.

My business didn't take off like a rocket ship. It was more like a snowball rolling down a hill, starting small and gradually getting bigger. After a couple of years, I had enough business to keep me busy. I loved the fact that I got to work from home and make money doing what I loved. I truly was living the American dream.

GO BIG OR GO HOME

I would have happily continued quilting for my local customers until the end of time. But six years after I first started machine quilting, two things happened that changed the course of my career and my life: meeting Tula Pink and discovering the Modern Quilt Movement.

Remember how I said I got one customer from vending at the quilt show? That one customer was Kathy, and she picked up my card and called me a few months later. She was opening a new quilt shop and was wondering if I would like to quilt the samples. Um ... of course! She quickly became a favorite customer of mine. A few years after opening her shop, she excitedly told me that her daughter was becoming a fabric designer. Kathy introduced us, and I began quilting for her daughter, otherwise known as Tula Pink. Just writing that now gives me chills. That first quilt show, which I did all those years ago, led to me quilting for Tula. So remember—even if something seems like a failure, you never know how it will turn out.

Tula and I like to joke that we are "married" to each other through quilting. The quilts we create together have resulted in my best work. In fact, you might notice that several of the quilts in this book are hers. It was my quilting in her booth that attracted the attention of C&T Publishing and ultimately led to me becoming an author.

Around the same time, I was invited to the first meeting of the Kansas City Modern Quilt Guild. It was there that I found out that there was such a thing as modern quilts, quilt blogs, and younger quilters in general. I was hooked!

If luck is just preparation meeting opportunity, then I sure was lucky. I was at the perfect place at the perfect time. Having been a machine quilter for several years, I had technical skill and an appreciation for traditional quilts. But I also loved the aesthetic of modern quilts. Looking at them, I could imagine so many ways to apply the quilting designs that I already knew.

It wasn't overnight, but I soon realized that I was in a position to take my business to the next level. I started reading books about business and goal setting. I began to get intentional about growing my business and pursuing as many opportunities as possible. Now that this blind squirrel had found her nut, she was going to go as far as she could.

Radiance, designed and quilted by Angela Walters

BACK TO THE FUTURE

One day in my studio, my middle child Cloe said wondrously, "You must have quilted a hundred quilts!" Laughing, I agreed that I had quilted at least a hundred quilts. I truly have no idea how many I have quilted, but I hope to have the opportunity to quilt twice as many.

I'm not sharing my story to tell you how great I am; I'm trying to show you how great you can be. If I can do it, anyone can. Now it's your turn! What "nut" are you looking for? Go out and get it!

Happy Quilting!

Peaks and Valleys, designed by Tula Pink; quilted by Angela Walters

Getting Started

WHAT IS MODERN MACHINE QUILTING?

Quilting looks best when it complements the quilt top. So *modern machine quilting* could also be called *quilting modern quilts*. The quilting is modern because it is used on a modern quilt. This book is full of designs; some may be considered modern, and some may not. It isn't just the designs you use but also the way you use them, that makes the difference.

The modern quilting community is alive and thriving—there is no denying it. If you go online and take a look at the many, many blogs featuring beautiful modern quilts, you can't help but be inspired. But over and over, I see quilters piecing such beautiful quilt tops only to resort to an allover quilting design, unsure of how to quilt it or doubtful about their quilting ability.

As a machine quilter, I see quilting as another layer of art, the very definition of form and function. I often say that quilting is like putting on makeup. Makeup artists don't put blush all over the face; instead they use different types of makeup in different areas of the face. In the same way, we should consider the quilt top when deciding on the quilting designs.

Draw, Draw, Draw

I love to say that 80 percent of quilting is knowing where to go next. (Surely there is a mathematical algorithm to prove this.) When asked how to get better at quilting, I always tell quilters to practice drawing the designs over and over on paper until they are comfortable with the design. Draw a box and fill it with the design you are practicing. By doing this, you will learn how to fill the space evenly and how not to get yourself stuck in a corner.

Don't Be Too Hard on Yourself

When your nose is two inches from the quilt top, you can see every little imperfection. Remember that every little mistake adds character, and you probably won't notice it from a few feet away. When you are finished with the quilt, put it away for a day. When you pull it out the next day, set it across the room and admire it from afar. Chances are, it will look great.

Remember! Practice Makes Perfect

Anything worth doing well takes a lot of practice. One common misconception is that some people instantly know how to machine quilt. But you can ask accomplished machine quilters and they will tell you that it takes a lot of time and practice. So don't get discouraged; keep practicing, and you will get the hang of it.

THE BASIC SUPPLIES

There are so many questions when it comes to machine quilting. Where to start? What to do? With so many options, it can be overwhelming. The most important thing is that you get started! That's why I am going to walk you through this step by step—almost as if I were sitting right next to you, drinking a coffee, and cheering you on. I'm going to share what works for me. Then, as you become more familiar with machine quilting, you can experiment with different notions and tools.

Get Off on the Right Foot

To get started, you need a sewing machine and a free-motion quilting foot. This is the magic tool that makes free-motion quilting possible.

If you aren't sure what to use with your machine, check with your machine's manufacturer. It may be called a darning foot or hopping foot. There are several different types, just pick one and try it out. As you become more comfortable with free-motion quilting, you can try out different options to see what you prefer.

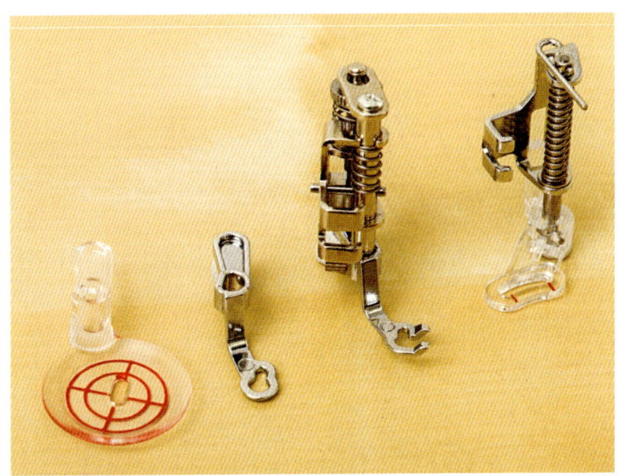

A sampling of free-motion quilting feet

Drop the Feed Dogs

These guys get a break. Normally they move the fabric through while you sew, but since they pull in just one direction, they aren't ideal for free-motion quilting.

If your machine is older or won't let you drop the feed dogs, you can cover them with a Supreme Slider (page 24).

Feed dogs dropped

You may think that you need a special machine to free-motion quilt your own quilt tops, but that isn't the case. Use the machine and the tools you already have and get started. Don't be tricked into thinking you need a longarm quilting machine to machine quilt your own quilts. While it does make quilting easier, it definitely isn't a necessity. All the designs in this book can be quilted using a domestic sewing machine (DSM) or a longarm.

Thread

TYPE

There are so many different types of thread available. I could spend the rest of the book talking just about thread. (Don't worry, I won't.) The two most common types, polyester and cotton, are best for new machine quilters.

Polyester thread tends to be thinner and stronger than cotton thread. It has low lint and tends to blend into the quilt more than cotton.

Cotton thread tends to be a little thicker than polyester, which means you can see where you are going while quilting. It has a little more lint than poly thread but looks amazing on your quilts.

The threads I use the most are So Fine! by Superior Threads (left) and Aurifil cotton (right).

Note

Specialty threads are the bling of quilting! Glitter threads, variegated threads, and glow-in-the-dark threads are just a few examples of specialty threads. Though fun and different, these threads can be finicky to deal with. I suggest trying a small spool before you invest in a large cone.

WEIGHT

The weight of a thread refers to how thick it is—the higher the number, the thinner the thread. Which weight you should use depends on how much you want the quilting to show up.

Starting with a 50-weight (or even a 40-weight) is a good option.

COLOR

This is the fun part; picking out the perfect color thread from the enormous selection available—there is no wrong answer. Pick what you think looks great.

Although I love a range of fun colors, I tend to use neutrals the most. Off-white, light yellow, gray, and tan are my most commonly used quilting threads. When the thread matches the fabric on the quilt top, it helps keep the quilting from overwhelming the quilt.

Batting

Choosing the batting is an important part of the quilt-making process. The good thing is that, as long as you choose a quality batting, there is no wrong answer.

I prefer polyester batting because it has a nice drape and it resists creasing. Cotton batting is also a great option. It has an amazing softness and is perfect for bed quilts. Ultimately, the best option is to try all different kinds of batting and see what you prefer! I like to use Quilters Dream Fusion fusible batting, because it's machine-washable and won't gum up your needle while quilting. Other than being fusible, it's just like regular batting.

Try different kinds of batting and see what kind you prefer.

Needles

Do you need a special needle? The short answer is no. I use the same universal needle for piecing and machine quilting. However, if you are using a specialty thread, or fabric other than cotton, you will probably want to use a different needle. Check the thread manufacturers suggestion for more guidance.

Marking Tools

Some people think that free-motion quilting means that you don't use markings of any kind. This is incorrect. Free-motion quilting refers to the fact that the quilting is hand guided. Using stencils and marking tools will help keep the designs consistent. It is my belief that every quilter, whether a longarmer or those using a DSM, should have an assortment of marking tools.

All of my quilting is free-motion, but sometimes I mark larger motifs on the quilt. I also use registration marks on my quilt. These marks help me ensure that designs are consistent. These are a few of my favorite marking tools:

WATER-SOLUBLE PENS

I will admit that I am a snob when it comes to water-soluble pens. I use only Dritz blue marking pens. I have never had a problem with the marks not coming out, so I figure, why try anything else? I am very cautious to remove the marks quickly, using only cold water, following the manufacturer's instructions.

CHALK

Chalk is a great way to mark dark fabrics or quilts that I don't want to get wet. Chalk pencils and chalk sticks are great for this purpose.

STENCILS

Stencils are great for quickly marking designs on a quilt. The stencils I use most often are grids for marking registration lines. The registration lines help me keep my designs even. I use a chalk pounce pad to mark the stencils. The pad holds blue or white chalk and can be rubbed over the stencil to quickly mark the design. Stencils are available in all different shapes and sizes. When choosing stencils, make sure they are continuous line or machine-quilting stencils. Hand-quilting stencils have too many starts and stops and will be frustrating.

Optional Supplies

QUILTING RULERS

Machine quilting with rulers is a skill that will grow with you on your free-motion journey. Whether you are a brand new quilter that needs a template to follow, or an established machine quilter that is looking for new design inspiration, you are going to benefit from quilting with rulers.

There are so many rulers on the market, different shapes, different colors, and different features, but try to not let the sheer number of them overwhelm you! Something I say a lot is that not every ruler is for every quilter. Start with a few basic rulers, such as a straight edge or wavy ruler, to help you get the hang of quilting with them. Once that feels comfortable, you can begin playing with all the different, wonderful ruler options that are available. With a little practice, you will be quilting like a ruler ninja!

EXTENDED BASE

If your sewing machine manufacturer makes an extended base, you might want to consider getting one. It provides a bigger surface for the quilt, allowing you to quilt more easily. If you like machine quilting at all, this is the first thing I would suggest purchasing.

SUPREME SLIDER

I think the hardest part of machine quilting is dealing with the weight of the quilt. The Supreme Free-Motion Slider (by Pat LaPierre) is a Teflon sheet that allows you to move the quilt with less drag. I can hardly quilt without one!

GLOVES

Having a good grip on your quilt will help you have more control during the quilting process. I like how they allow me to grab the quilt more easily. Some machine quilters swear by them and some can't stand them.

MODERN MACHINE QUILTING BASICS

The Quilting Design

Now that the stage is set, you are ready to create the most important part of this quilt—the quilting design. It sounds more difficult than it really is. You have a number of options for coming up with designs.

USING A STENCIL

If you need a little help choosing designs, or if you just want some inspiration, consider using stencils. Stencils are easy to mark and come in a range of designs. Just remember that with stencils, what you see is what you get; you can't easily make a stenciled design larger or smaller. Look for continuous-line stencils or machine-quilting stencils. These have designs that can be quilted in a continuous line without starts or stops. There's nothing worse than marking your whole quilt, only to realize that the stencil is a hand-quilting stencil with numerous stopping points!

CREATING YOUR OWN DESIGN

If you can't find exactly what you are looking for in a stencil, try making up your own design. Using a piece of freezer paper, draw a design using a dark marker. This will allow you to "trace" the design onto the quilt top over and over again. Alternatively, you can mark a design directly on the quilt top. Use whichever method is easier for you.

Note 

I like to use freezer paper for drawing my quilting designs. It is thicker than standard drawing paper, so it will hold up to repeated use. And because it comes on a wide roll, you can cut off bigger pieces than the normal 8½″ × 11″ sheets.

The design might be one of these:

- A special word, name, or saying
- A symbol that is meaningful to you—a peace sign or a heart, for example
- A mixture of your favorite quilting designs

These are just ideas to help you get started. Don't limit your own imagination—the possibilities are endless!

If you can't find exactly what you are looking for in a stencil, try making up your own design

TRANSFERRING THE DESIGN

A pounce pad makes marking stencils quick and easy! A pounce pad looks similar to a chalkboard eraser, with loose chalk powder under a cloth-type covering. When the pad is gently brushed over the stencil, the chalk marks the design lines on the quilt. Pounce pads come in white and blue (for white fabrics). The chalk is easy to remove—just brush it off with your hand or lightly iron it. You do have to be careful when using a pounce pad. Because the chalk is so easily removed, moving the quilt top can make it come off. This can leave you without your road map.

Marking tools (page 23) can also work great. The drawback to water-soluble pens is that you need to get the quilt wet to remove the marks, sometimes more than once. This can take away precious quilting time! Also, the marks won't show on busy prints or blue fabrics. Marks made with chalk pencils stay put longer than the chalk in a pounce pad, but using them with a stencil means a lot of sharpening. They come in several different colors, including blue, white, and pink. I especially like these when I need to mark quilts made with busy print fabrics on which my blue water-soluble pens won't show up.

Get Your Quilt Ready

Now that your machine is ready, let's prepare the quilt sandwich. Layer the parts of the quilt and stabilize them, so you can easily move them as one. This is called "basting the quilt" in machine quilting lingo. Properly basting the layers of the quilt will help prevent any tucks on the back and makes the whole process a lot smoother.

Just like the rest of the machine quilting, there are a lot of different ways to baste your quilt sandwich. My favorite way to baste quilts is with fusible batting.

Fusible batting is just like regular batting, except that one side has a thin layer of fusible glue on it that is activated when you iron it. It's quick and I like not having to worry about running into pins while I quilt.

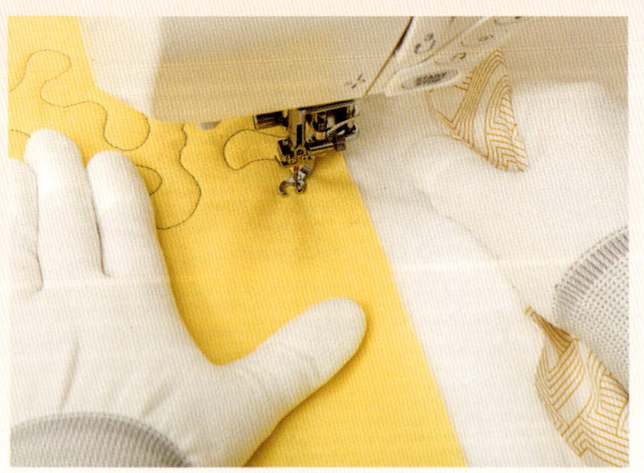

1. Lay the backing face down on a flat surface. Smooth out any wrinkles and try to get the backing as flat as possible. To keep it in place and extra taunt, you can tape the sides down. Just be sure that the tape won't hurt your floor! I like to make my backing a couple inches bigger than the quilt top on all sides. The extra fabric gives me something to hold onto when I am quilting along the edge.

2. Place the fusible batting onto the backing. Quilters Dream Fusion recommends that you lay the batting with the glue side up. (Be sure to follow the instructions on your batting.) Again, smooth the batting making sure there are no bumps or wrinkles.

3. Spread the quilt top on the batting. Smooth it out, getting the top nice and flat. Can you tell that this is important? Trust me, spending a little extra time to ensure that all the layers are nice and flat will prevent frustration when you start quilting. When it comes to machine quilting, the fewer bumps the better.

4. Use a hot, dry iron to iron the top from the center out. Make sure not to touch the iron to the batting. If you do, you will end up with a gooey mess. Don't rush through this step. You want all the fusible glue to melt and adhere the layers together. There you have it, a quilt sandwich that looks good enough to eat ... or at least good enough to quilt. Let's get started!

First Stitches

Woo-hoo! This is it, the moment we have been working up to. Don't be nervous, it's going to be fun.

For now, let's get comfortable with moving the quilt around while machine quilting. Don't worry about anything else right now ... not stitch length or what it looks like. I like to say that worrying about the stitch length when learning how to quilt is like writing a novel while you are learning your letters. It's something we will learn ... just not right now. For the best results, in the very beginning, start with a smaller quilt project. In my classes, I have students bring a fat quarter quilt sandwich. It's perfect for letting you get comfortable with the machine and moving the fabric, without having to deal with the drag of a large quilt.

STEP 1

1. Place the quilt sandwich under the needle. One of the benefits of quilting on a sewing machine is that you can start wherever you like. Most of the time, I start in the center of the quilt. The reasoning is purely psychological. I know that the quilt will never be harder to move than it is at that moment. But that's just what works for me, start wherever you want.

STEP 2

Secure the beginning of the line of stitching by taking a few small stitches in place. I try to start my line of quilting in a seam or on a busier print. It helps to hide the stitches.

1. Lower the foot.

2. Make one stitch, leaving the needle in the up position.

3. Holding onto the "tail" of the top thread, raise the foot and move the quilt sandwich over slightly. The bobbin thread should pull up.

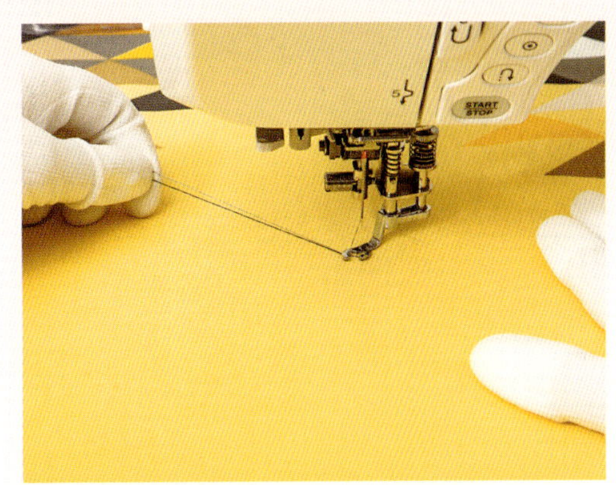

4. Hold both the top thread and the bobbin thread. Move the quilt so the needle is directly over where the bobbin thread is coming up.

5. Quilt a few small stitches in place to secure the quilting.

STEP 3

Start quilting.

1. Press the pedal down and start quilting. Try quilting your name, moving around, whatever. At this point just try getting used to moving the fabric.

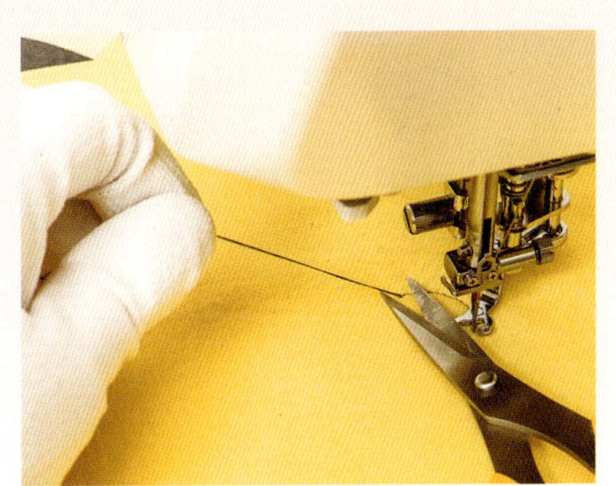

2. Once you have quilted a couple of inches, stop, then trim off the tail threads from your securing stitches. Get in the habit of doing this now to prevent the threads from accidentally getting stuck in the stitches.

3. Keep moving the fabric around as you begin to be comfortable with the whole process. Here's where I get a little "new age-y." As you quilt, try to close your brain off to quilting. Don't judge how you are doing, don't worry about the stitch length or anything else. Instead, try to think of nothing, or of anything else. If possible, try to enjoy just moving your hands around. This is machine quilting at its most basic and I think it's awesomely fun.

STEP 4

Secure the end of the line of stitching by taking a few small stitches in place. You can just cut the threads, or you can bring the bobbin thread up to the top. It takes a couple extra steps, but it prevents having any loose threads on the back. Either way is completely fine! Here's how I like to secure the end of the line of quilting when I am finished.

1. Take a few tiny stitches in place. Use the hand wheel or a needle up/down button when making the stitches that secure the quilting. You don't want to use the pedal because you may take too many. We don't want any fingers harmed when quilting.

2. Raise the needle and the foot.

3. Move the quilt sandwich over to one side and grab the top thread.

4. Bring the quilt back so that the needle is over the point where the thread comes out of the quilt top. Loop the top thread around your finger.

5. Raise the foot and move the quilt over, so the bobbin thread comes up.

6. Trim both threads, so they are flush with the quilt top.

Now take that sample and frame it! It's your first machine-quilted sample (or at least one of your first attempts). You are doing your best quilting right now, be proud of it. By the time you have worked your way through the book, you will have already improved.

Stitching in the Ditch

What's the point of quilting in-the-ditch if no one is going to see it anyway? I am so glad you asked! Stitching along the seam lines stabilizes a quilt and keeps the seams straight and even. It also makes the quilt lie nice and flat.

Different quilters have different approaches to stitching in-the-ditch. I like to stitch in-the-ditch around the quilting area first and then fill it in with my quilting designs, whereas others like to quilt the designs first and then stitch around the seams. In my opinion, the order doesn't matter, as long as you do it.

The good news is that you don't have to stitch in every seam of a quilt top. Most often, I only stitch in-the-ditch around areas that repeat the same quilting design. For instance, when quilting the block in the photograph below, made up of several small squares, I didn't stitch around every seam. I only stitched in-the-ditch around the white squares that were quilted with a design different from all the others. Since the rest of the squares were quilted with the same swirl design, I didn't stitch along those seams.

GETTING IN THE DITCH

When stitching in-the-ditch, it sure does help to have a "ditch" to stitch in. The ditch is formed when the seam allowance is carefully pressed to one side, creating a high side and a low side. You will quilt along the low side—the side without the seam allowances. Quilting in-the-ditch makes the low side a little lower, so that the high side overhangs the low side and the stitches will be almost hidden. Pressing correctly will help you out immensely down the line. When you are quilting along the seam, the difference between the higher and lower sides will make it easier to stay in-the-ditch.

A well-ironed seam is the key to success.

A seam that isn't pressed properly makes stitching in-the-ditch harder because the bulk of the fabric will fall right under the stitching.

WHAT ABOUT PRESSING THE SEAM OPEN?

There are two sides to every discussion, and this one is no different. Some quilters prefer to press their seams open, which does help the quilt to lie flat. But in my experience, it's easier to stitch in the seam when there's a low area. Also, if you iron the seam open and then quilt along the seam, you will be stitching only on thread. But this is just my opinion. Do whatever works best for you!

Frequently Asked Questions (FAQs)

WHERE SHOULD MY HANDS GO?

You will have the most control of your quilting when you hands are on either side of the needle, about 3 or 4 inches away. As you quilt, be sure to reposition your hands often. Forgetting to reposition my hands is my worst habit. I will be quilting along and realize that my hands are way over to one side. It's hard to have good control when your hands aren't in the proper place.

HOW FAST SHOULD I QUILT?

It depends. (I know it isn't probably the answer you want). The best speed is one that isn't so slow that you can critique the job you're doing while you're doing it, but not a speed so fast that you feel out of control. The speed you use will change as you get more comfortable with quilting, so don't be afraid to change the settings.

Your sewing machine may come with a stitch regulator, which means that it will speed up or slow down depending on how fast you move the quilt sandwich. If your machine has one, you don't have to worry about what speed to use.

In the beginning, adjust your needle speed (if your machine has one) to a speed that allows you to put your foot pedal all the way down. (Unless you have a stitch regulator.) Not having to think about the position of your foot gives your mind one less thing to worry about.

If your stitches are too large, speed up the machine. If they are too small, slow the speed.

Make the speed of the machine fit the movement of your hands, not the other way around.

ACK! SHOULD I BE MAKING THE STITCHES ALL THE SAME LENGTH?

Consistent stitch length comes with practice. The more comfortable you become with a particular machine quilting design, the easier it will be to keep the stitch length consistent. Worrying about it right now will only drive you crazy.

HOW SHOULD I SIT AT THE MACHINE?

Make sure that your chair and table is the right height for you. You don't want to be hunched over or reaching up, it will hurt your back.

WHAT SHOULD I DO IF THE BOBBIN RUNS OUT?

Ahhh ... the dreaded empty bobbin. It always seems to run out just when you are getting into your quilting groove. When the bobbin runs out, I start by trimming any loose threads. When I start the new line of quilting, I overlap it by an inch or so. It helps secure the stitching.

WHY IS THE TENSION OFF ON MY QUILTING?

If all of the quilting has poor tension, it may mean that you need to adjust the tension of the thread on the machine. If it is intermittently messing up, it could be that you aren't moving at a consistent speed. As you get more comfortable with a design, you may notice that the tension improves.

Proper Tension

There is no denying that tension is one of the most frustrating parts of machine quilting. If you find your tension is off, here are a few steps to take.

1. Rethread the machine. This is the absolute first thing that I do when problems arise. You don't want to adjust the tension, only to find that the machine wasn't threaded correctly.

2. Check for fuzz or lint in the bobbin or thread path.

3. Change the needle. A dull needle can affect the tension the quilting. Either try a new needle or a different type of needle.

4. Make sure that the thread is quality thread. Again, the thread that works for piecing isn't necessarily good for machine quilting.

Practicing

As much as I hate to say it, there is only one way to get better at machine quilting ... practice.

You can read books, look at tutorials, and watch videos, but ultimately you need to actually quilt. Before you shut the book and use it as a doorstop, I have some good news. It doesn't take as much practice as you might think. You don't need to practice a lot, you just need to practice productively.

PRODUCTIVE PRACTICE

1. Pick one thing to improve.

Each time you quilt, whether on a quilt or just a practice piece, pick one thing you want to improve. (Yes, only one thing.) Trying to improve everything at once is a surefire way to overwhelm yourself or become discouraged. You could work on:

- Keeping the stitch length consistent
- Getting comfortable with the basic shape of the design
- Finding the perfect speed
- Not cussing while quilting (Hey, it doesn't matter what your goal is, just that you have one!)

2. Once you have identified your one thing, start quilting, focusing only on that thing.

3. Assess how you did.

When you are finished, look it over and see how you did. But here's the trick, try not to assess while quilting. Wait until you are finished and look over the whole area you quilted, not just up close.

4. Celebrate the successes.

Look for what you did right. When I was first learning how to machine quilt, something I would tell myself often was, "Well, it's not as crappy as last time."

5. Refine and repeat.

If there are areas that need improvement, make a mental note of what you could do differently and work on it again next time. What I really want you to remember is this, be self-aware without judgment. Talk to yourself as though you are talking to a friend about their quilting.

6. Track your progress.

Having a visual reminder of your improvement will keep you motivated and encouraged. If you are working on practice samples, put the date next to the quilting. I promise, you'll see improvement after even just a few practice sessions.

7. Enjoy the process.

Having a visual reminder of your improvement will keep you motivated and encouraged. If you are working on practice samples, put the date next to the quilting. I promise, you'll see improvement after even just a few practice sessions.

Mistakes

While quilting you might make a mistake. (Not that I think you would make a mistake, you look very smart ... this is just a hypothetical situation.)

This mistake is very noticeable when it's by itself. In fact, you might be tempted to take it out. But instead of ripping out the stitches, keep quilting. Once the mistake is surrounded by quilting, it is far less noticeable.

Can you imagine how much less noticeable it would be if I was using a thread color that matched the fabric? The moral of the story is, when you make a mistake, don't rip it out. Just throw more quilting around it. At least, that's what I do.

Ways to Use Quilting

QUILTING ADDS MOVEMENT

Quilting can help create a sense of movement and is one of the easiest ways to add an extra element of artistry to a quilt. It not only moves the viewer's eyes along the quilt surface, but it also makes the quilt more dynamic and interesting.

Moonrise: Pieced and machine quilted by Angela Walters

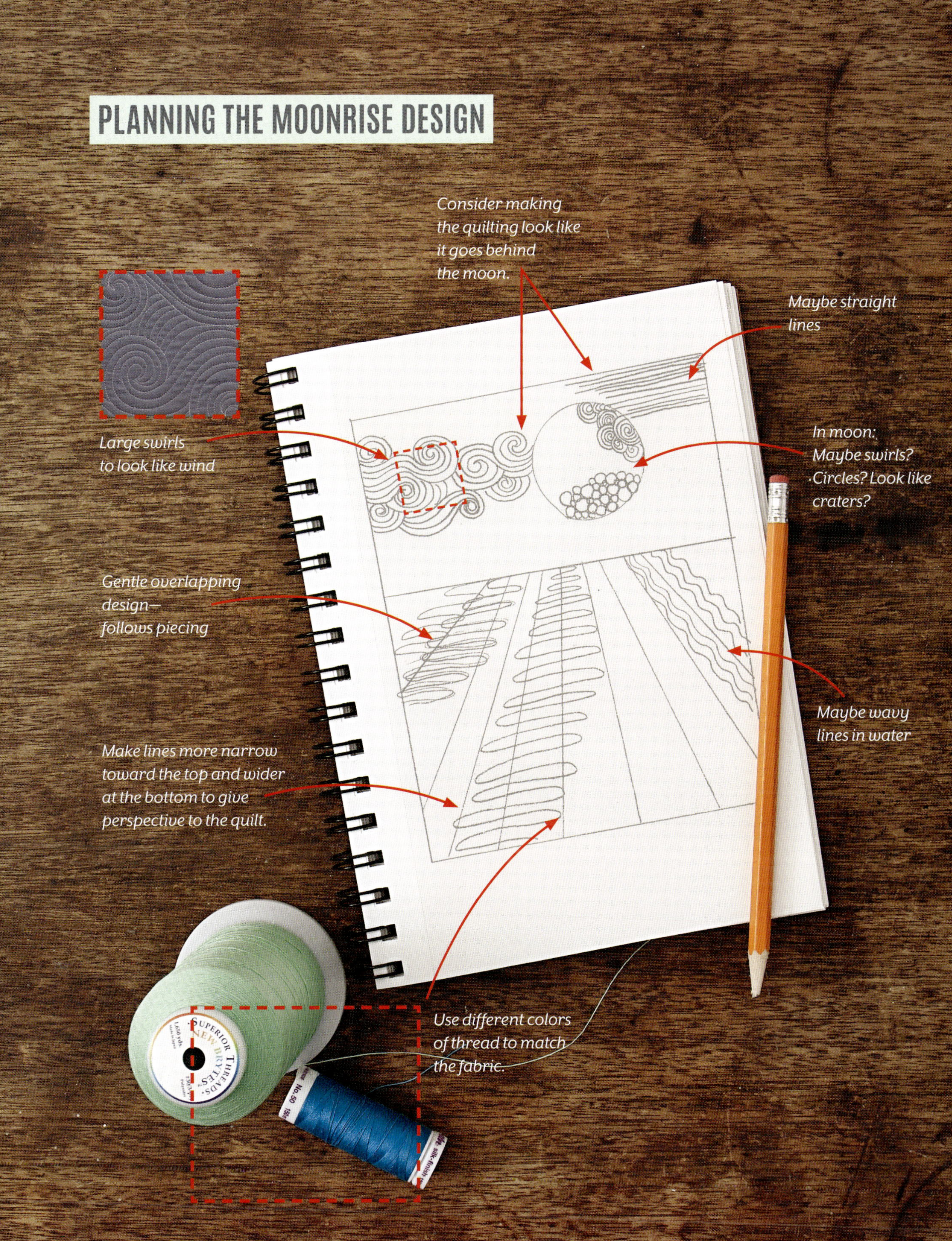
PLANNING THE MOONRISE DESIGN
Consider making the quilting look like it goes behind the moon.
Maybe straight lines
Large swirls to look like wind
In moon: Maybe swirls? Circles? Look like craters?
Gentle overlapping design—follows piecing
Maybe wavy lines in water
Make lines more narrow toward the top and wider at the bottom to give perspective to the quilt.
Use different colors of thread to match the fabric.

Realistic Movement

If you have a recognizable image on your quilt top, such as a car or a kite, using quilting to add movement will make it look even more realistic. To make a car look like it is moving across the quilt, for example, add swirls to suggest smoke or wind behind the car. A kite that is flying high would need wind, so stitch swirls to represent the wind. Don't feel as though you have to make every part of a quilt look as though it's moving. Consider adding just a little movement to a part of the quilt. The Shooting Stars quilt, below, has four stars—but to make just one of them look like a shooting star, I added some wavy lines from the star in the upper right to the edge of the quilt. This helps give the appearance of movement without being overwhelming.

Pieced and quilted by Angela Walters

Other Kinds of Movement

Sometimes you may want to use quilting to add movement to a quilt that is more abstract. In Megapixel, at left, the colors flow in a wavy pattern. I knew that quilting an allover design wouldn't help emphasize the quilt's movement. Instead, I quilted lines that loosely followed the flow of the colors.

First I drew a few guidelines on the quilt to mark how I thought the colors flowed. Then I echo-quilted these lines again and again. In areas where the stitching intersected, I simply filled in with more lines, echoing the top and bottom areas.

Choosing the Right Designs

When choosing quilting designs, remember that any kind of design that moves the viewer's eye across the quilt will work for adding movement—swirly designs, wavy lines, and even straight lines. Experiment with different designs and different ways to use them.

Quilting Example: Moonrise

I used quilting designs to create two different types of movement in Moonrise for the sky and the water.

QUILTING THE SKY

In the sky portion, I quilted wavy lines to represent wind. Elongated swirls that look as if they overlap can suggest wind, water, or even hair! To ensure that the quilting would be visible for illustration purposes, I used a thread color slightly lighter than the quilt top, but thread that matches exactly would actually be best for this design.

To quilt the moon, several design options are available. Circles to look like craters or a large swirl would really make the moon shine on this quilt!

Moonrise: Pieced and machine quilted by Angela Walters

QUILTING THE WATER

When quilting the water portion of this quilt, I used several different colors of thread. I chose threads that blended with each fabric color. The gentle back-and-forth quilting design starts out narrow at the top of the quilt and becomes wider at the bottom.

Even though I matched the thread to the quilt top, I purposely avoided staying within each color strip, instead allowing the quilting to overlap into the other sections. I think it looks like the water is overlapping—much as it would in real life.

QUILTING ADDS DEPTH AND DIMENSION

Adding depth and dimension helps make a quilt more realistic and more dynamic. When a block looks as though it is lying on top of a quilting design, it gives the feeling of depth, creating the illusion that the block is in the foreground and the quilting is in the background.

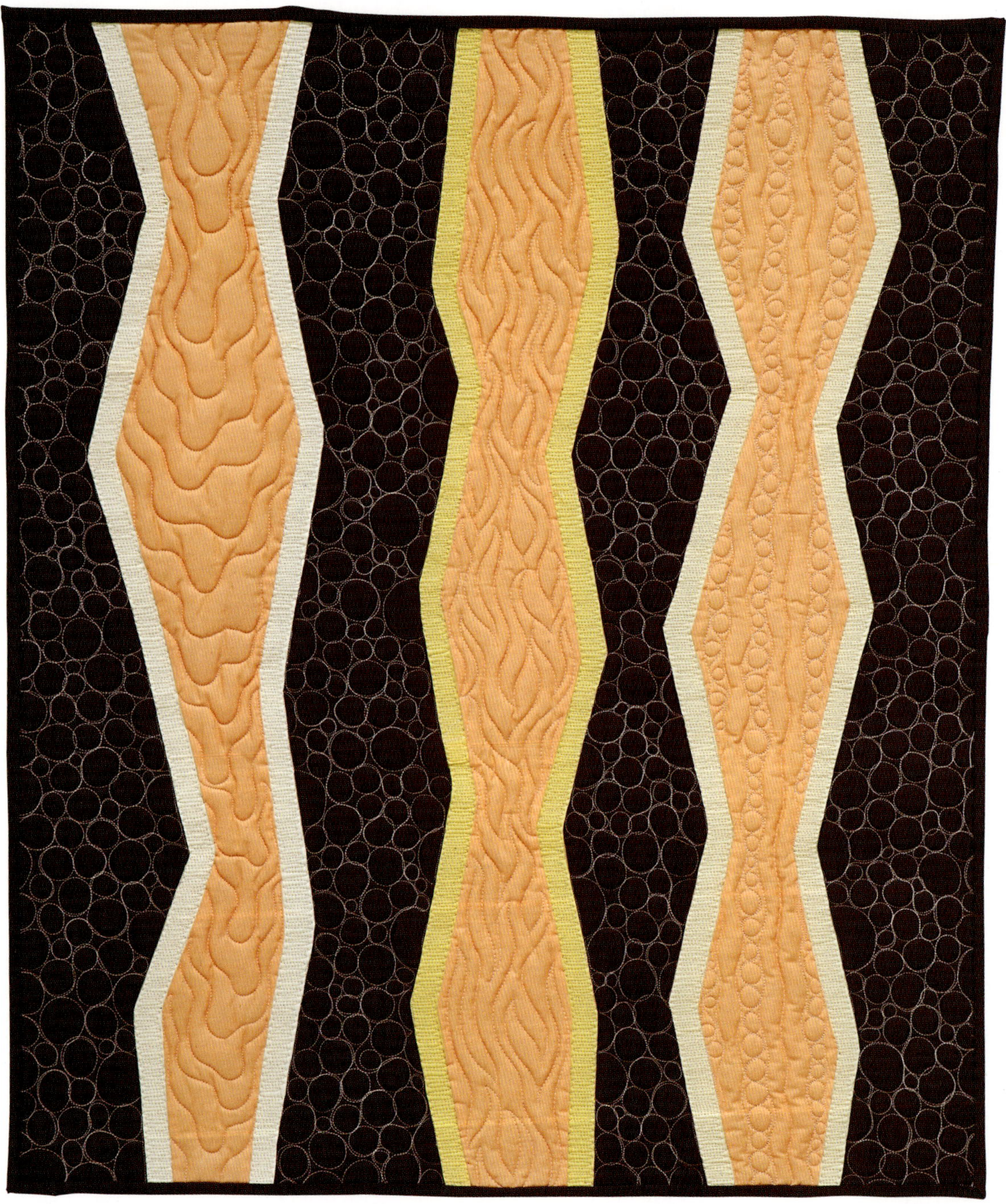

Lava Lamp: Pieced and machine quilted by Angela Walters

PLANNING THE LAVA LAMP DESIGN

Traveling to Add Depth

To make designs look as if they extend behind parts of a quilt, you need to travel. Traveling is simply stitching along a seam or other part of the quilt to move to a different area. Another benefit of traveling is that it allows you to keep the quilting designs the same size, rather than trying to squeeze in a complete design between sections.

In the quilt shown below, the quilted circles look as though they are going behind a block. When quilting around the blocks, I quilted half-circles that touched the block. Then I traveled along the block to start the next design.

Seeing Squares is a great example of the use of this technique. I quilted wavy lines across the entire quilt except for a few squares. When I got to a square that I wanted to appear to be floating on top of the quilt, I traveled along the seam for approximately ½″ and then stitched back in the opposite direction. This makes the quilting seem to go behind the square. As a result, a few portions of the quilt top really pop out, adding interest to the whole composition. It isn't hard to do and actually makes for quick quilting!

Designed and pieced by Shea Henderson

Adding Depth Within Blocks

You don't necessarily have to make the quilting look as if it's going behind a block to add depth to a quilt. In the example of the carpenter block at right, I used quilting to make some parts seem to go under other portions within the block itself.

Quilting the block was as easy as quilting the same back-and-forth design, just going in different directions. I tried to imagine what the pieces would look like if they were woven together. The result is a look of depth within the block.

Some quilting designs, such as concentric circles and tiles, already look as if they are lying on top of one another. They give the illusion of depth all on their own. Try using them in background areas to help add depth to a quilt.

Carpenter block: Look for ways to add depth within a block. Pieced by Georgieanna Martin.

Quilting Example: Lava Lamp

The only thing more fun than making the Lava Lamp quilt top was quilting it. I got in a groovy mood to create depth!

QUILTING THE BACKGROUND

To establish the brown fabric as the background in this quilt, I wanted a lot of dense quilting on the brown sections. I chose to use bubble quilting, not only to help squish down the background but also to give the look of bubbles in a lava lamp.

To add depth, I quilted the bubbles to look as though they continue behind the orange and yellow pieces, adding to the feeling of depth in the quilt.

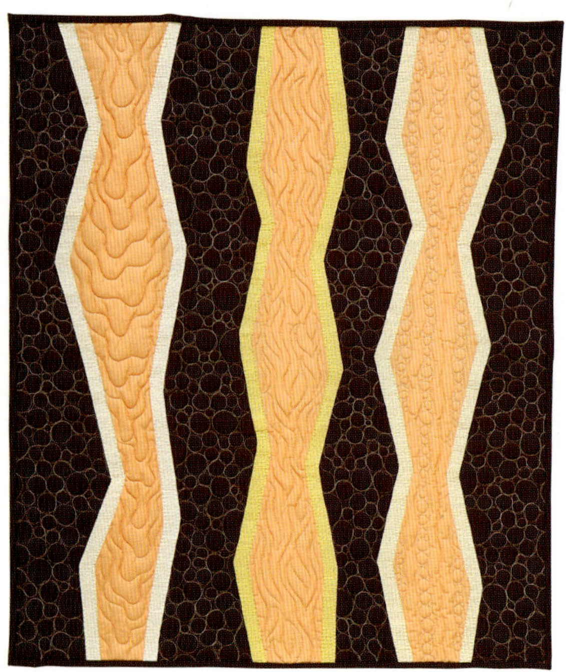

Lava Lamp: Pieced and machine quilted by Angela Walters

QUILTING THE ORANGE SECTIONS

I wanted the orange parts of the quilt top to look like blobs of lava floating in a lava lamp, so I used designs that were flowy and less dense than the background stitching. In one of the orange sections, I quilted vertical wavy lines. To add more interest, I filled in between some of the wavy lines with small circles.

In the yellow strips, I quilted dense back-and-forth lines. I wanted this quilting to separate the orange and brown sections. It defines the orange and yellow sections without taking attention away from the quilt top as a whole.

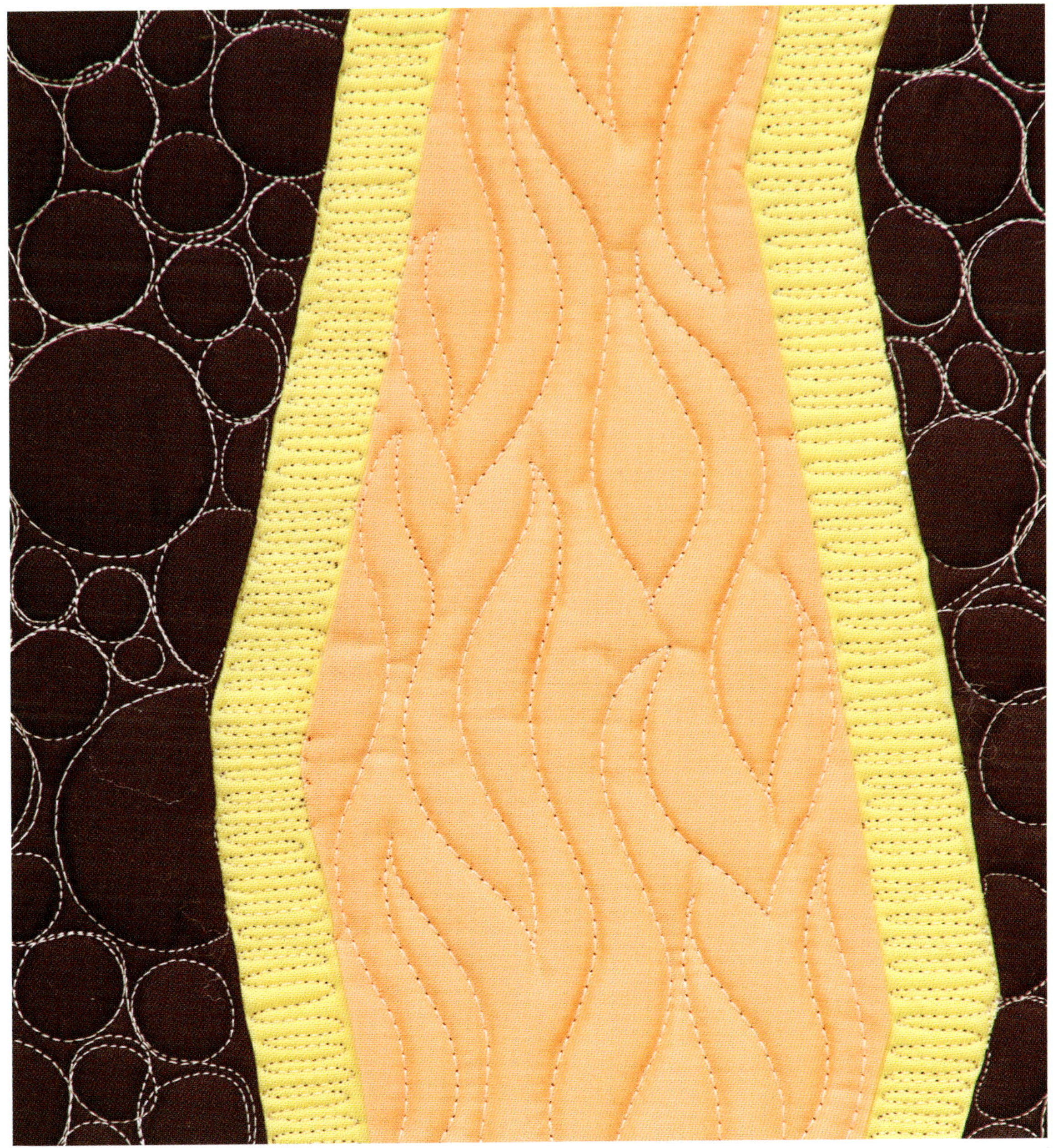

QUILTING ADDS DETAIL

Quilting to add detail isn't the same thing as thread painting, in which the whole design is composed of thread. Instead, it refers to using quilting to add details to an existing pattern.

Adding details is an easy and fun way to quilt. The designs are already there—you just need to decide what details you want to add.

Spools: Pieced by and machine quilted by Angela Walters

PLANNING THE SPOOLS DESIGN

Quilt centers of spools with different colors of thread in a back-and-forth line.

Or quilt zigzag lines.

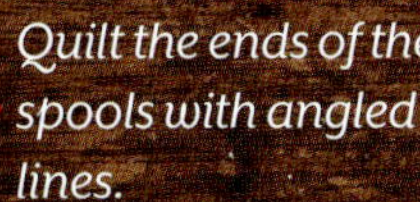

Quilt the ends of the spools with angled lines.

Maybe a geometric pattern

Or you can try quilting the ends of the spools with a combination of different lines.

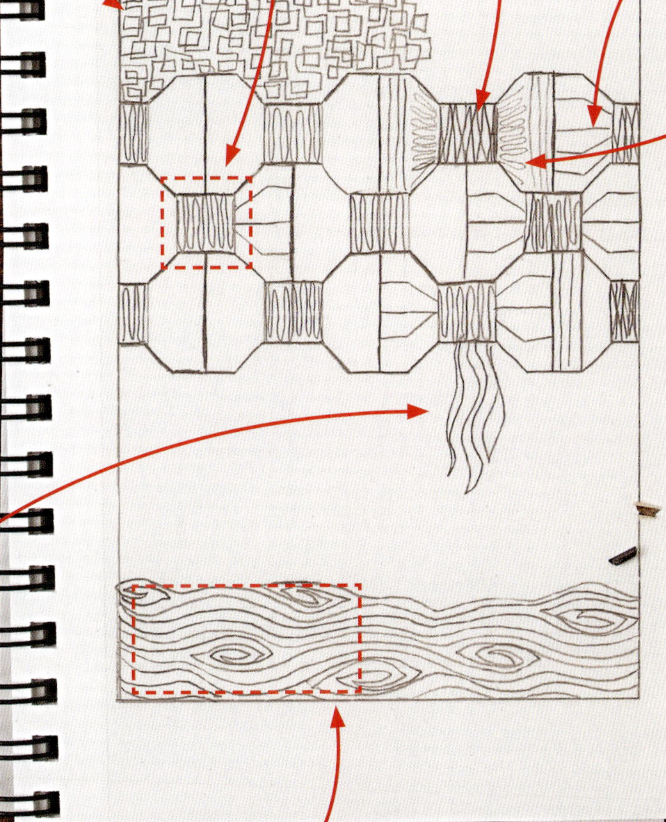

For fun, maybe try quilting "threads" hanging off the spool.

Quilt wood grain in the background.

It's All in the Details

Quilting isn't just for holding a quilt together; it's for doing so much more to enhance the quilt. It can add a bit of realism to a quilt and make the whole quilting process more fun.

The details don't have to be obvious, or even noticeable. They can be something that's only noticeable upon closer inspection. You don't want to become so focused on quilting the details that you lose track of the rest of the quilt. Just do what comes easily and naturally, and then move on.

Details Change the Look of a Quilt

Sometimes adding details can change the look of the quilt altogether. For instance, if a quilt top features circles, you might add petals to make them look like flowers. Or perhaps you want to quilt the circles to look like suns, so you add sunrays with your quilting. The trick is not to limit your imagination but to have fun with it.

Details Help Define the Pattern

Sometimes adding quilting detail can define the pattern of the quilt and make it more noticeable. In the quilt below, using a mod alphabet pattern to spell out the word quilt creates an abstract-looking design. But to help show that the blocks are actually letters and not just random blocks, I quilted the letter in the center of each block. Adding the details helps make the pattern easier to see.

Quilting helps define the abstract letters.

Based on quilt pattern by Tula Pink.

Details Make It More Realistic

On a quilt that depicts an object—such as a flower or a tree—adding quilting details can make that object look more realistic. Coming up with quilting ideas is as easy as paying attention to how things look in real life.

The amount of detail that you can add is endless. For the house block sample at right, I stitched in all the details that I could think of—shingles in the roof, picket fences in the background, windows on the house, flowers and trees in the background, and lots more.

Quilting Example: Spools

Because I envisioned the interlocking blocks as spools of thread, I knew I wanted to quilt them to look like that. My own thread rack is filled with all sorts of fun colors, so I decided to quilt the spools in bright colors. I quilted lines to look like thread across the middle part of each spool.

When I get going on a quilting theme, I have a hard time veering away from it! So when it came time to choose the quilting design for the background of this quilt, I went with a wood-grain design reminiscent of my wooden thread holder.

Spools: Pieced by Kathy Limpic and machine quilted by Angela Walters

Background quilting

QUILTING MAKES THE QUILT

Sometimes the quilting wants to be more than just another layer of art or the last thought. Sometimes it wants to be the star of the quilt.

Quilting as the Main Focus

Sometimes I just have to work backward! I like to come up with a quilting design and then make a quilt to fit the design. This shows off the quilting in all its glory. When the quilting is what makes the quilt, a lot more thought needs to go into the designs—no boring meanders here!

Mod Wholecloth Quilt: Pieced and machine quilted by Angela Walters

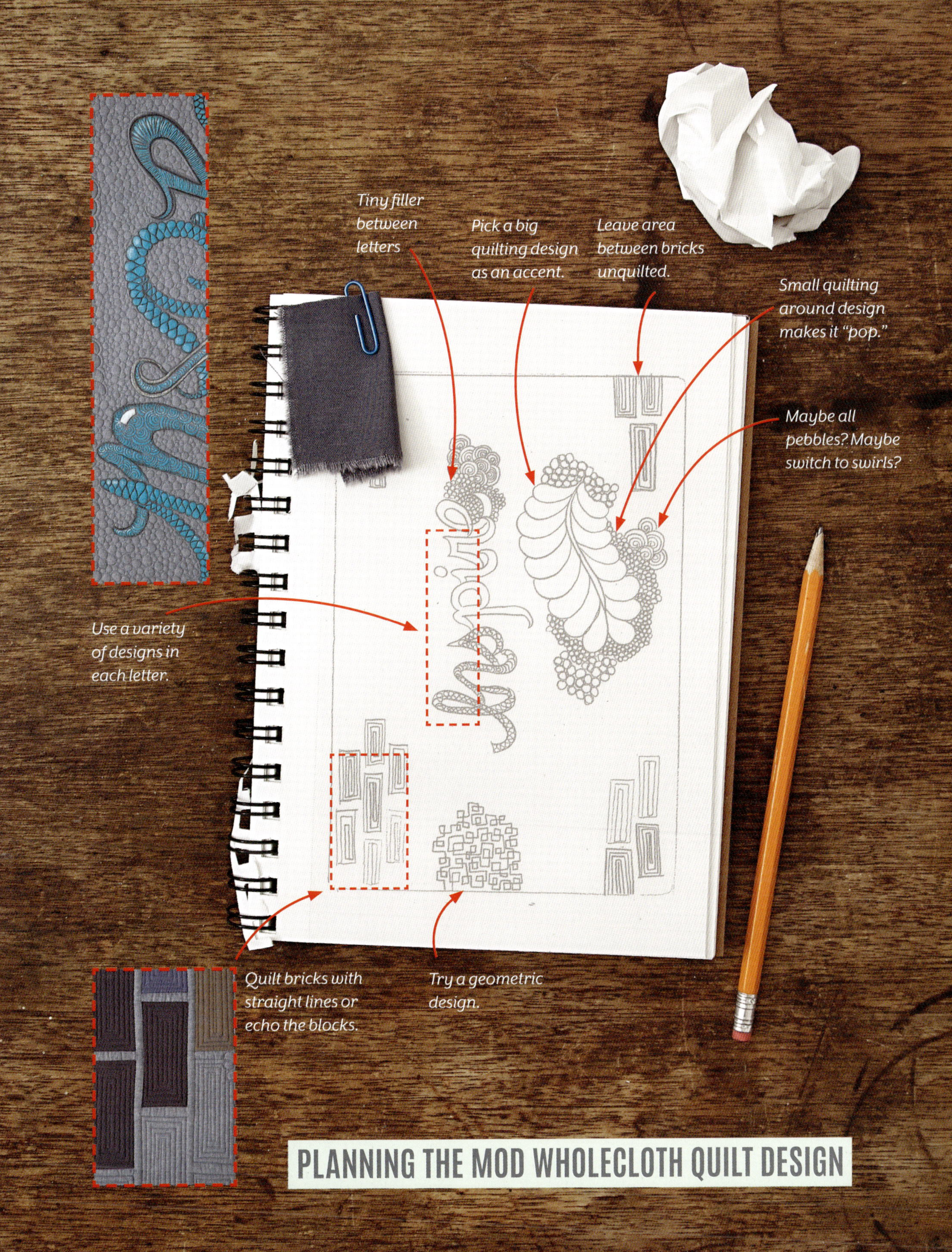
Tiny filler between letters
Pick a big quilting design as an accent.
Leave area between bricks unquilted.
Small quilting around design makes it "pop."
Maybe all pebbles? Maybe switch to swirls?
Use a variety of designs in each letter.
Quilt bricks with straight lines or echo the blocks.
Try a geometric design.
Inspire
PLANNING THE MOD WHOLECLOTH QUILT DESIGN

A Wholecloth Quilt with a Modern Twist

A traditional wholecloth quilt top is one that's made of a plain piece of fabric, usually white or light-colored, with the quilting being the focus and the only design. Wholecloth quilts date back to the 1800s and were considered works of art. Women would spend years making elaborate wholecloth quilts of this type. Quilting a solid piece of fabric isn't the only option, of course. The quilting can still have the starring role if the quilt top is pieced. But to ensure that your quilting isn't upstaged, consider making a quilt top with minimal piecing or with fabrics that read as solids. This will ensure that your hard work will be seen!

Quilted by Jeanne Rumans

A Reversible Quilt

Some quilts are made with busy fabrics that don't show the quilting at all. Instead of just quilting an allover design, switch the quilt around. Quilt an intricate design that will show on the back. *Voilà!* You will have a two-sided quilt.

Making Your Quilting Show

Of course, if the quilting is going to be the star, you need to be able to see it! Consider the following factors to make sure that your hard work will be seen.

CHOOSING THE RIGHT THREAD

Before you start quilting, you need to decide how prominent you want the quilting to be. You may want to use a thread that blends so that the design isn't glaring. If you want the quilting to be more visible, use thread that's a shade or two lighter or darker than the fabric. Be careful to not use thread that contrasts too much, or every bump and bobble in the quilting will be very visible!

TO PUFF OR NOT TO PUFF?

Consider using a batting with a higher loft to help show off your quilting. I'm not talking about a high-loft batting, but one that has just a little bit of puff to it. A puffier batting will help emphasize the difference between dense and less dense areas of quilting.

Sometimes I opt for two layers of batting instead of using a puffier batting. I like to use a thinner poly batting as the base and a batting with slightly higher loft on top. This adds a little more stiffness to the quilt, but it really makes the quilting pop!

Quilt front

Quilt back

Quilting Example: Mod Wholecloth Quilt

This quilt is a great example of designing a quilt backward—starting with an idea for a quilting design and then making a quilt around it. The quilting was inspired by graffiti that I saw on a train. The letters were so bright and vibrant that I just knew I wanted to recreate the same look on a quilt. The quilt top gives a hint of a brick wall, and the quilting forms the graffiti that adorns the wall.

Mod Wholecloth Quilt: Pieced and machine quilted by Angela Walters

MARKING THE DESIGN

Once I decided on my word, *inspire*, I drew it on a sheet of paper. I tried to make it look a little like graffiti by scrunching the letters together and making them overlap. When I was happy with the way it looked, I took it to a print shop and had it enlarged to the size I wanted. You could just draw your design larger and save yourself the time it takes to go to the print shop, but I find that drawing smaller is easier for me. Do whatever works for you!

I don't have a lightbox, so I taped the paper to a window. Then I taped the quilt top over it. With the sun shining through, I was able to trace the design through the dark fabric of the quilt top. I wanted the quilting for my *Mod Wholecloth Quilt* to achieve two goals: I wanted to reinforce the look of a brick wall, and I wanted to make the word *inspire* really stand out.

QUILTING THE BACKGROUND

Within the individual "bricks," I quilted straight lines echoing from the outside toward the inside. I left the spaces between the bricks unquilted, to replicate the mortar. In some places, I also quilted a bubble design to look as though it was spilling over the brick.

QUILTING THE LETTERS

As I quilted around the letters in the word, I filled in each letter with a different quilting design. I knew that I would be painting the letters later with Shiva Paintstiks, so I wanted to add a lot of texture.

Around the letters, I densely quilted little circles. Because I was using two layers of batting, I knew the tiny quilting around the letters would make them pop out even more!

I stitched a different design in each of the letters.

Embellishing the Quilt

I don't usually embellish my quilts, but I really, really wanted the quilting to accentuate the look of spray-painted graffiti. So after the quilt was quilted and bound, I painted the letters with Shiva Paintstiks. I love the way the paint makes the letters look like the graffiti that inspired the quilt in the first place.

QUILTING PROVIDES CONTRAST

Quilting can be a powerful tool. When used correctly, it can define a pattern and add contrast. But used incorrectly, it can detract from the quilt top. This chapter is the result of many, many of my own trials and errors in quilting. When I use the word contrast, I am referring to opposite elements. You can use opposite densities, colors, and designs to create or enhance contrast in a quilt. It's as simple as picking opposites!

Fire and Ice: Pieced and machine quilted by Angela Walters

PLANNING THE DESIGN FOR FIRE AND ICE

Quilting to Create Contrast

In a quilt made out of fabrics that are similar in value, the piecing may tend to blend together. Quilting can help define the pattern of the quilt by adding contrast between the different sections.

To provide contrast on the quilt pictured below, I quilted the darker part using a dense, swirly design. In the lighter areas, I quilted an opposite design of straight lines that follow the piecing pattern.

Quilting can help define the quilt pattern.

Quilting to Emphasize Existing Contrast

Quilting can help define a quilt pattern by adding contrast, but it can also take away from a quilt that already has good contrast. On a quilt with distinct contrasting colors, an allover quilting design can be distracting.

Most often the best choice is to use different thread colors to match the different parts of the quilt top. At the very least, try to find a thread color that blends with much of the entire quilt.

Take, for instance, the contrast quilt pictured below. This quilt already has a lot of contrast, making the quilt pattern easy to see. Instead of quilting an allover pattern, I opted to quilt different designs in each section.

Contrast within Quilting Designs

Lack of contrast in the piecing isn't the only thing you need to look for. If you are quilting motifs, you want to have enough contrast in the quilting that the motifs will show up.

To demonstrate what I mean, I quilted the same design twice using different amounts of contrast. The first photo shows a quilting design that doesn't have enough contrast. The filler quilting around the central motif is almost the same size as the motif itself, making the main design difficult to see.

In the next photo, the motif is much easier to see because of better contrast between the quilting designs.

Not only did I echo-stitch around the design to give some space between the motif and the filler, but I also made the filler stitching smaller than that of the motif. This helps the eye pick out the design much more easily.

Also, I quilted the main design in a slightly darker color in the second example. The contrast in color helps the motif stand out. This may seem like a lot to consider when you are quilting, but it's definitely worth it! If you are going to take the time to quilt a design, you want to make sure that your quilting stands out.

The quilting motif blends in because of a lack of contrast with the filler stitching.

Smaller designs surrounding the central motif make it more prominent.

How to Create Contrast

When trying to create the most contrast between quilting designs, consider the following:

- **Color:** Use slightly differing colors of thread to provide contrast.
- **Density:** Make one design bigger than the other to automatically help the two designs stand apart.
- **Design:** Juxtapose different designs to create contrast—straight lines next to curvier designs, for example.

Consider using different quilting designs in different sections.

Quilting Example: Fire and Ice

This quilt is all about contrast, and the quilting is no different. When selecting the quilting designs, I knew I wanted to have contrast in the types of designs as well as in the color of thread. The result is a quilt that has contrast on every level!

Fire and Ice: Pieced and machine quilted by Angela Walters

QUILTING THE STARS

Within each star, I quilted the same designs with thread that matches the fabric. But the quilting that extends out from the star is a whole different story.

The molten-hot orange star has a swirl design radiating out from each side. The design starts small but grows larger as it gets farther from the block. I used a light orange thread just a few shades darker than the tan background. I wanted just a little contrast; too dark a thread would have detracted from the block.

The ice-cold blue star has piercing straight lines radiating out from the block. As with the orange block, the lines are a little closer together at the beginning and then spread apart as they travel outward. This time I used a pale blue thread to add just a touch of contrast.

I don't often mark my quilt tops, but this quilt is one that I marked. Using a ruler, I drew straight lines radiating out from the stars. These lines acted as guides to keep my quilting design on track.

QUILTING THE BACKGROUND

Because I wanted to make sure that the main quilting would show up, I quilted the background with a smaller swirl design. I also used a thread that matches the background fabric. Because I can never leave well enough alone, I threw some fun details in the background quilting: I quilted three shooting stars (to represent my children) and stars in two of the corners. It is a space-themed quilt, after all!

QUILTING ADDS TEXTURE

What is it about quilting that beckons you to come up and feel it with your fingers? It's one thing to practice the designs on paper, but it's a whole different thing to see them come to life on the quilt. The texture that quilting contributes is what gives the quilt such a finished look.

Using the quilting to create texture is a way of adding another layer of art to a quilt. All you have to do is to be mindful of the designs that you are using.

What Is Texture?

Texture, another element of art, can be used to describe either the way a quilt actually feels when you touch it or how it visually "feels" when you look at it. I love the idea of a quilt's visual feel—quilting that adds so much texture you can almost feel it just by looking at the quilt.

Great texture happens when you don't notice the quilting. Instead, you see the slight shadow and depth that the stitches give to the quilt top.

Basket Case: Pieced by Mary Workman and Jessica Harrison, and machine quilted by Angela Walters

PLANNING THE DESIGN FOR BASKET CASE

Tight back-and-forth lines add a lot of texture.

Maybe try a paisley quilting design.

Keep spacing consistent.

Try several of your favorite designs in the blocks.

Pick a consistent background design and use matching thread to add texture.

Tips for Great Texture

Quilting, by its nature, adds texture to a quilt; the following tips will help you make the most of that texture.

- Concentrate on solid and near-solid fabrics. When a quilt includes large areas of solid fabric, use a quilting design that adds texture. Since quilting doesn't show up as well on patterned fabrics, seek out the solid parts of the quilt so that your quilting will produce a lot of texture.
- Use matching thread. If the thread contrasts with the quilt top too much, a person will see the quilting rather than the texture. Consider using a thinner thread, too. The more a thread blends in, the better. Remember, great texture happens when the quilting "disappears" and the shadow of the quilting shows.
- Use a consistent design. If a design has a lot of variation in spacing, the design becomes the focus. Use dense quilting designs to play up texture—the more quilting, the more texture. If a design has a lot of open space, that open space will become the focus.
- Think of designs in terms of a texture. When choosing designs, think about the kind of texture you want to add to the quilt. Do you want linear texture, swirly texture, pointy texture? Considering this question will help you decide on the perfect quilting design.
- Vary the design to add texture. Texture isn't the same as an allover design. Simply quilting one design, whether it's an allover pattern or a custom design, won't necessarily add the texture you want. Use designs that change the texture, even just a little bit, in parts of your quilt to create more interest.

What Does Texture Look Like?

Defining texture is kind of like defining love. It's hard to explain, but you know it when you see it! So to help illustrate it, I heavily quilted the left side of a quilt block, creating amazing texture, and I less intricately quilted the other half, creating just so-so texture. Of course, how you decide to quilt is a matter of taste and the statement you want to make, but the goal is to have great texture.

On the left side of the block, I used matching thread and designs that are dense and consistent. The designs in each section are even and not distracting.

On the right side of the block, however, I used thread that didn't match as well and quilted designs that weren't as dense. I think the right side of the block looks great—there's definitely nothing wrong with it—but it doesn't have the textural quality that the other side has.

Quilting Example: Basket Case

The choice of solid fabric for this quilt was not an accident! I wanted to be sure that the texture that quilting adds could be seen.

QUILTING THE BACKGROUND

Because dense quilting patterns seem to provide the best texture, I used a variation of the concentric circle design for the background area. The only difference is the spacing of the rings. I alternated between ⅛˝ and ¼˝ between the rings. If you had been in the room while I was quilting, you would have heard me reminding myself out loud, "Close, far, close, far ..."

To add the most texture, I used matching thread and tried to keep the designs consistent.

QUILTING THE BLOCKS

Within the blue sections, I used a thin thread that blends in. I quilted two different designs, each of them adding a different texture. I think the design that looks like building blocks adds the most texture.

Basket Case: Pieced by Mary Workman and Jessica Harrison, and machine quilted by Angela Walters

QUILTING ADDS COLOR

I spend so much time matching thread colors to quilt tops that sometimes I overlook the fact that quilting can actually add color to a quilt. But every once in a while I come across a quilt that is just begging for brightly colored thread. In this section I'll show you different ways to add color to such quilts. So pull out your craziest threads and get ready for some colorific quilting!

Before we start, I want to clarify. I'm not talking here about thread painting. Thread painting is when a quilter uses only thread to make a design. Quilts that include thread painting are obviously stunning. But the purpose of this chapter is to show how you can use thread colors to enhance the quilt pattern.

Spin Doctor: Pieced and machine quilted by Angela Walters

PLANNING THE SPIN DOCTOR DESIGN
Try a variety of designs and thread colors—the more the better!
Use matching thread so as not to distract from piecing.
Super-sized swirls are an option.
Large amount of negative space means you can experiment with fun designs.
Maybe alternating designs?
Try designs in different sizes.
Try extending the quilting beyond the wedge.
Combine designs.

Making a Thread Book

When you are an avid thread collector, like me, it can be hard to remember exactly how the thread will look when actually quilted on a quilt top. I have several thread cards handy, but sometimes they aren't much help.

What I have done is to make a thread book—a quilted sampler of different threads and colors. The great thing about having an actual quilted sample is that I can see exactly what the thread will look like when it's quilted. No more guesswork or painful unquilting!

Making a thread book is super easy and well worth it. On a white or light-colored fabric, draw squares with a water-soluble marker. Quilt within each box using a different thread. Write the thread information on the back of each square to help you remember which thread you used on each square.

Carefully cut apart the quilted squares on the lines you drew. Stack the squares on top of each other and sew along one of the edges to make a book. Keep it next to your sewing machine or quilting machine to use as a reference for selecting thread. Making a thread book is a great way to practice different free-motion quilting designs!

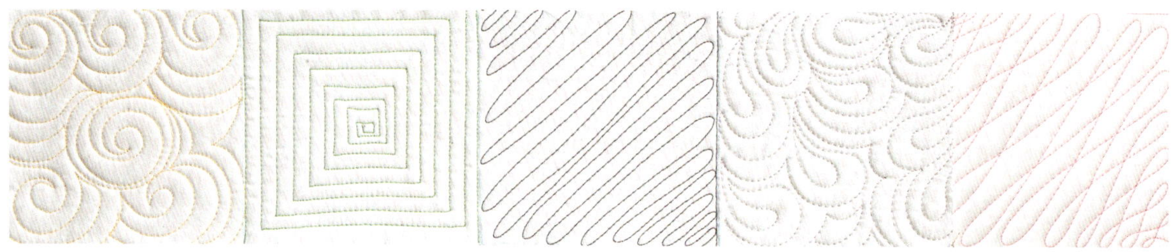

Putting Color to Work

You can use colorful quilting to do any or all of the following:

- Add interest to a quilt. As I've said about a million times, matching thread is my favorite! But every so often I see a quilt that could use a pop of color. You can use color to draw attention to an area or to balance a quilt that has a lot of color in one section but not in the rest of the quilt.
- Change the quilt's appearance. Sometimes I piece an entire quilt, only to find that one fabric doesn't quite work in the quilt. Thread color can help camouflage those "problem" spots."
- Create a different look. When using quilting to add color to a quilt, you don't have to use a lot of color. Just a little bit, used the right way, can give a whole different look to a quilt. In the case of the checkerboard quilt at right, a little strategically placed color added a great deal.

With various orange shades on one side and green shades on the other, I thought the center of the quilt could use a little color as well. So I whipped out my brightest orange and green threads and added a checkerboard pattern. Even though the quilting changes the look of the quilt, it still doesn't overwhelm the bold colors on the sides.

Of course, this is just one example of how to add color to a quilt pattern with quilting. The possibilities are limitless!

Try More Than One Color

If you really want to add color and make the quilting pop, consider using more than one color of thread. This is especially effective with contrasting colors.

The sample pictured below is a great example of using more than a single thread color on a quilt. I quilted a swirly design with two different thread colors. The bright threads stand out against the black background, really helping to showcase the quilting. But to keep the color from being overwhelming, I quilted around the pieced designs with thread that matched the fabric.

But Don't Go Crazy

Using a contrasting thread to add color doesn't mean that you have to use it everywhere. A contrasting thread color looks best when used thoughtfully and sparingly.

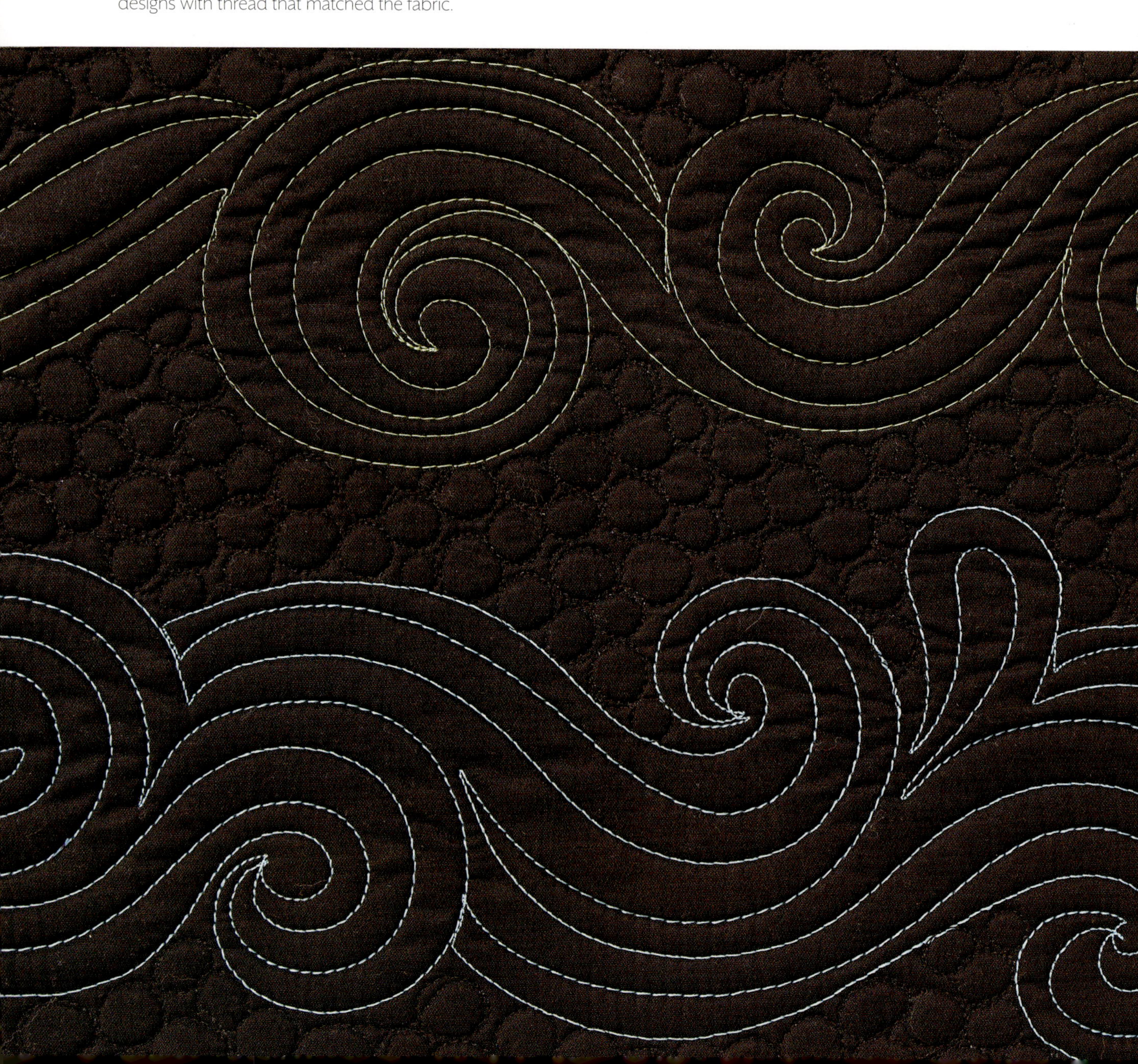

Quilting Example: Spin Doctor

Quilting the *Spin Doctor* quilt offered me a great opportunity to use all the colorful threads that I seem to collect but never use!

QUILTING THE WEDGES

Because this quilt is made of gray and black fabrics, I used different-colored threads to add my own "spin." Before I started, I chose a few different designs to use in the wedges and a few different thread colors. Because the stitching was going to be very noticeable on this quilt, I picked quilting designs with which I felt quite comfortable.

For the designs, I stuck to some of my favorites—wishbones, arcs, swirls, and wavy lines. I specifically chose designs that could easily fit the shape of the wedges. All of these designs use the edges of the pieces as a guide.

For the black circle in the center of the quilt, I quilted a large swirl in matching thread. I wanted something simple that wouldn't detract from the rest of the quilt.

Spin Doctor: Pieced and machine quilted by Angela Walters

QUILTING THE BACKGROUND

Because the center is the dominant portion of the quilt, I didn't want the quilting in the background to distract from it. Actually, I wanted the quilting in the background to draw the viewer's eye to the center. To accomplish that, I quilted gentle wavy lines radiating from the center. And just because I can never leave well enough alone, I added circles between a few of the lines. The result is a design that is interesting but doesn't take away from the overall look of the quilt.

QUILTING GIVES A SENSE OF SCALE

When you want your quilting to be interesting but not overwhelming, consider using it to add scale to your quilt. I'm not talking about scales as in music. I'm talking about scale as a succession of steps or degrees. The same allover quilting design in different sizes, small to large, does the trick.

This technique is easy yet striking, and it will help you take your quilting to a new level. It adds interest to a quilt—especially those large areas of negative space that can be overwhelming—and moves the eye along, drawing attention to the most important parts of the quilt.

Stacked: Pieced by Mary Workman and machine quilted by Angela Walters

PLANNING THE STACKED DESIGN

Quilt each wedge with a different design.

Or quilt each section with one design.

Quilting design smaller to bigger

Blending thread for background

Mark lines to separate different sizes of quilting.

Pick just two designs and alternate.

Experiment with several different designs to get some practice.

Use the same thread in sections or try a fun, colored thread.

Maybe swirls? Most designs work well.

Adding Scale to a Quilt

Perhaps the best thing about using quilting to add scale is that it takes just a little more effort than an ordinary allover design, yet it still contributes a great deal to the artistry of the quilt. Chances are you'll find even more variations than I have suggested here.

FIRST, MARK THE QUILT

Decide how much gradation you want. The more sizes you use, the more variation there will be from the smallest to the largest designs. Roughly divide the quilt into the same number of sections as design sizes. This will help you stay organized, because after you start quilting it is very easy to lose track of what you are doing. Use a blue water-soluble marking pen to label the different sections.

The quilting design can progress in several different ways, as illustrated by the photos below.

Smaller in the middle, larger toward the edges

Smaller on top, larger on the bottom

Smaller in one top corner, larger toward the opposite bottom corner

Smaller in the middle, larger toward the edges

PICK A DESIGN

Almost any allover design works well for this technique. If you can quilt it in many different sizes, then it will work. Circles, swirls, and feathers are just a few examples of successful designs. You can even quilt straight lines that start out being spaced closely together and get farther apart as you proceed.

DRAW A GUIDE

To keep yourself on track, draw the design in each size you'll be using, from smallest to largest, on paper. Keep the designs next to you while you quilt to help you keep the designs the right size.

QUILT IT!

Now use the guide to begin quilting, moving to a new size in each successive section. While you are quilting, it may be hard to see the gradations in scale. But trust me, when you are finished and stand back to view your work, they will definitely be noticeable.

Mixing Two Designs

A different twist on this technique is to start with one quilting design and then gradually turn it into a different design.

Divide the quilt into three sections. The first section will be for the original design, the middle section will be a combination of the two designs, and the third section will be for the second design.

The center section that combines the two different designs allows them to transition gracefully without an abrupt change.

Quilting Example: Stacked

From the smallest block at the top to the biggest block on the bottom, this quilt is all about scale! The quilting is no exception.

QUILTING THE BACKGROUND

Because the quilt was pieced in strips, I already had guidelines for the quilting. This means that I didn't have to mark the quilt to make the design smaller at the top and bigger at the bottom. For this quilt I made my designs smaller on the top and larger on the bottom to mimic the changing scale of the quilt blocks. But I could easily have had the different design sizes go from left to right. Just make guidelines with a water-soluble pen to mark where you want to change sizes.

For the background quilting, I combined two different designs: a swirl and a leaf. First I drew the designs in six different sizes on a piece of paper, from smallest to largest, to use as a guide. I kept the guide next to me as I quilted so that I could be sure my designs remained as consistent as possible. I quilted the smallest design in the first row of the background, the second-smallest design on the second row, and so on, ending with the largest design on the last (bottom) row.

QUILTING THE BLOCKS

For quilting the strips within the blocks, I alternated between a wishbone design and a back-and-forth line. Though these were the designs I used, a number of other patterns would have worked equally well.

Stacked: Pieced by Mary Workman and machine quilted by Angela Walters

Choosing and Adjusting Designs

DECIDING ON QUILT DESIGNS

Feeling stuck? We have all been there—stuck staring at a quilt with no clue how to quilt it. Here are a few tips to help get you going.

Determine whether there is a "background" to the quilt.

If you are quilting a busy quilt with a lot of pieces, it might help to determine whether there is a background that you can quilt with the same design. If so, you will only need to figure out how you want to quilt the shapes in the foreground. When quilting *Mod Bars*, the first thing I did was find the background of the quilt.

After I determined that the gray fabric would be the background, I quilted the same design on all of the gray pieces. Quilting the background of the quilt in the same way helped to emphasize the rest of the piecing. A quilt might not have a background, but when it does, use it to your advantage. See Quilting Background Fillers & Negative Space (page 92).

Mod Bars, 60″ × 75″, designed and pieced by Alissa Haight Carlton; quilted by Angela Walters

Ask yourself, "What is the most important thing about this quilt?

The most important thing about your quilt could be the fabric, the pattern, the piecing, or the fact that it is for a special little boy who will drag it through the mud countless times. When you have established what's most important, you can use the quilting to highlight it.

If the most important thing is the fabric, custom quilt the blocks to feature the fabric. When you want people to notice the quilt pattern first, emphasize the shapes of the pattern. If you know it will get lots of love and washing, quilt it more densely. When you are able to verbalize the main point of the quilt, choosing a design may be easier.

Determine the style of quilting you want.

Think about your favorite quilting designs. Do you prefer swirly, flowery designs? Or are geometric designs your favorite? Deciding on a style of quilting will narrow down the number of designs to choose from.

Start with something.

Sometimes, you have to start quilting to get your creative juices flowing. If you know how you are going to quilt some of it, go ahead and get started. More often than not, inspiration will strike. Many times I have started quilting a certain design only to change my mind.

Look to the quilt for inspiration.

All the inspiration you can ever need is right in front of you. Look at the fabric and the pattern for ideas. You may see a floral design you can use, or perhaps you can quilt shapes that look like the blocks in the quilt. The best quilting complements the quilt top. Taking your quilting designs from the quilt top will definitely complement the quilt.

Sleep on it.

The brain works in mysterious ways. Have you ever had a thought pop in your head at a random time? Quilting inspiration works the same way; so if you can't decide how to quilt it, just take a break. At the very least, it will justify starting a new project!

Close-ups of *Lines and Vines*, 35˝ × 40˝, pieced and quilted by Angela Walters. Wavy lines are used as the background design to set off bold shapes.

Combine designs.

If you can't decide between two designs, try combining them. It may take a little more thought, but chances are you will end up with something that works out perfectly for your quilt. See Combinations (page 280).

Use designs in different ways.

Don't let yourself get stuck thinking that a design can be used only in a certain way. For example, designs that you may consider only for allovers can easily be used to fill borders and sashing. If you are in love with a design but aren't sure it will fit in the area where you need it, tweak it and play with it until it works.

I hope that by now your head is spinning with some new ideas and that you are motivated to move beyond meandering and into custom quilting. But if you take only one thing from this section, remember this: Just do it! Just like anything else, it takes practice, and you can't get better if you never start. Keep trying, keep going, and soon it will be as natural as signing your name.

Swirl combined with back and forth

Concentric circles with wavy lines

Concentric circles with leaves

QUILTING BACKGROUND FILLERS & NEGATIVE SPACE

Background Fillers

It is fun to learn a lot of quilting designs, but honestly, just knowing a few good background filler designs will get you started. In this section, I show you how to quilt several different designs that will work well in different areas of your quilt.

Background filler designs are patterns that work well around other elements of a quilt—for instance, around blocks or other quilting motifs. But the great thing about background filler designs is that you can use them in a few different ways as well.

USE AS ALLOVER DESIGNS & COMBINE DESIGNS

Instead of limiting these designs to backgrounds of your quilt, you can use them all over your quilt. This is especially helpful for quilts that you need to finish quickly! If you can't choose a single design for your quilt, try combining two fillers for a different look.

Laurel: Designed, pieced, and quilted by Angela Walters

TIPS FOR IMPROVING MEANDERS

Meanders or filler designs can be a little challenging, especially when it comes to quilting consistently over the whole quilt. These tips will help make the quilting process a little easier.

Again: Draw!

If you have read any of my previous books, you know that I am an advocate for drawing out designs before you sew. Even though the quilting movement is different from drawing, drawing helps your brain learn where to go next. According to a study that I just made up, 80 percent of quilting is knowing where to go next! After you can draw the design, translating it to the quilting machine is all you have left to learn.

Just Throw Something In

When it comes to actually quilting the designs, let me encourage you to not worry about quilting perfectly. Instead, focus on filling in spaces as consistently as possible. My theory is that a gap in the quilting is more noticeable than an error in the individual design.

Quilting Negative Space

Some modern quilters love to add a lot of negative space to create an interesting quilt. But when the time comes to quilt all that space, it can seem like a daunting task. Instead, think of it as your opportunity to run free and let your imagination roam. Nothing makes me happier than seeing a lot of open space on a quilt. Here are some things to consider when quilting negative space.

BLEND, BLEND, BLEND

It can be very easy for the quilting in negative space to distract from the piecing, especially if you use thread that is a different color. Using a matching thread that blends in will ensure that your quilting will add texture but won't overwhelm the piecing.

MIX UP THE QUILTING DESIGNS

Using the same design in large areas of negative space can make the quilting look boring. To keep it from getting too monotonous, randomly mix in different designs. For instance, if you quilt pebbles on the quilt, add in a couple of swirls to break it up. Using different designs to break up larger quilting areas will create smaller spaces that will seem more manageable.

Almost any design can be used to break up the negative space. You can even use the same design on a bigger scale, as I've done in *Circles*. You are limited only by your imagination.

Circles: 41″ × 55″, pieced and quilted by Angela Walters

When quilting *All Mine*, I combined two different designs to make a larger design, breaking up the negative space and adding more detail. To create the larger design for the lower portion of All Mine, I quilted two rows of brackets and filled in the space between with back and forth.

Quilting the same design in the top portion of the quilt helps to balance the quilting.

All Mine: 51″ × 59″, pieced and quilted by Angela Walters

BE A COPYCAT

One of my favorite ways to quilt negative space is to re-create the shapes within the piecing. The quilting echoes the quilt pattern and helps to create unity in the quilt.

When quilting Techno, I wanted to recreate the colored squares with the quilting. I randomly quilted a few squares and rectangles, being careful not to overdo it with the colored thread. When I finished the colored quilting, I filled in the rest of the area with geometric allover using matching thread. The great thing is that you can customize the amount of quilting. How much or how little you want to add is up to you.

Techno, 58″ × 51″, designed and pieced by Jacquie Gering; quilted by Angela Walters

EXTEND THE PIECING

Sometimes it's possible to extend the piecing into the negative space. This makes the quilting unexpected and a little different. Plus it's just fun to do!

Using the pattern of *Modern Plaid* as my inspiration, I extended the strips into the negative space and quilted it the same as the rest of the block. Extending the piecing into the negative space won't always work. Consider each quilt and evaluate whether you think it will benefit the quilt or detract from the piecing. When used correctly, it is a huge wow factor.

Close up of *Modern Plaid*, 41″ × 56″, designed and pieced by Alissa Haight Carlton; quilted by Angela Walters

Negative Space Designs

For some of the best meander, negative space, and filler designs in this book, check out:

Echoed Pebbles (page 117)

Swirl Meander (page 122)

Swirl Hook Meander (page 133)

Concentric Circles (page 143)

Swirl Chain (page 145)

Loop and Double Loop Swirls (page 148)

Loopy Meander (page 149)

Paisley Meander (page 157)

Geometric Allover (page 164)

Offset Squares (page 165)

Merged Lines (page 167)

Jumbled Lines (page 170)

Tiles (page 188)

Square Flowers (page 200)

Wavy Wavy (page 205)

Signature Design (page 207)

Wavy Serpentine Lines (page 210)

Sunrays (page 218)

Back and Forth Lines (page 224)

Feather Meander (page 234)

Faux Rope (page 238)

Arcs (page 246)

Woven Arcs (page 248)

Allover Leaves (page 260)

Flower Power (page 269)

Wood Grain with Knots (page 275)

Combinations: Allover Designs (page 280)

QUILTING SQUARES

Break up Larger Squares into Smaller Squares

You will find that quite a few of the designs in this book divide blocks into smaller shapes. This makes it easier to manage larger squares or rectangles, especially on a home sewing machine. It can also add complexity to plain squares, resulting in quilting that is fun to look at.

Look at the Whole Quilt

Sometimes it's easier to look at each block as a separate entity. But if you're stumped on which designs to use on your quilt, look at the blocks as part of a bigger picture. Is there a way you can use the quilting designs to pull the blocks all together? Can you quilt designs to form secondary patterns, such as grids, on your quilt? Asking yourself these questions will help you decide on the best designs for your quilt. Can you use different designs within the same block?

QUILTING TRIANGLES

Consider the Size

Try keeping the designs more basic in smaller triangles.

Break It Up

Consider breaking up larger square blocks by quilting two triangle designs. Depending on the quilt pattern, you may also be able to combine smaller triangles to make larger shapes.

Use the Designs for Triangular Shapes within a Block

If your quilt contains Flying Geese, pinwheels, or actually any block with triangular pieces, you can quilt a design on each triangle. This approach really expands your options, from the simplest half-square triangle to complex kaleidoscope blocks. For strong graphic effect, you can plan the stitching direction in the triangle patches so your quilting creates a larger design.

QUILTING CIRCLES

Stitching in the Ditch

I personally like to quilt in the seams around the blocks in a quilt. Even though staying on the curves of a circle can be a bit tricky, I still quilt around them. I love how the quilting sets off the circular shape. But it is not absolutely necessary, so do what works for you!

Branch Out

Many of the designs I have created for squares and hexagons can be used in circle-shaped blocks. The reverse is also true.

Appliqué

A question I am very often asked is whether I like to quilt over appliqué. There's a good chance that you will come across circles that are appliquéd, so knowing how to approach them will help make the quilting go smoothly. As with most everything quilting related, this is a matter of personal preference. When I am quilting a quilt with appliqué (of any shape), I try not to quilt over the top of it. However, if the appliqué is large, I will quilt something on it to help stabilize the quilt. When I do that, I tend to keep the designs fairly simple, so as to not distract from the appliqué. But as I said, that is a personal preference. I am only the expert of my opinion; do what works for you!

QUILTING DIAMONDS

Try the Designs in Different Shaped Blocks

Since diamond-shaped blocks are similar to squares (think of diamonds as evenly wonky squares), diamond designs can be used in a number of different shapes. Try them in squares or rectangles—I think you will find they are easily adaptable.

Divide and Conquer

If you can't find a diamond design that will work for your quilt, you can divide the diamond into two triangles and use a triangle design. Talk about getting more for your money!

Don't Let Diagonal Lines Get You Down

Some of these designs have diagonal lines, which aren't my favorite to quilt. To help make quilting diagonal lines more painless, you can try a few things. When quilting on a home sewing machine, I like to turn the quilt ever so slightly, so I am quilting a straight line. It may not be possible depending on your machine and the size of the quilt, but if you can maneuver it, it will help keep your lines smoother and more fluid.

If you are quilting on a longarm quilting machine, definitely consider using a ruler. No matter how long the diagonal line is, I always have my trusty ruler on hand. No matter what kind of machine you use, relax and just enjoy the process. If a diagonal line isn't perfect, don't worry. Just move on to the next one.

QUILTING HEXAGONS

Get to the Point

I am a huge fan of using the corners (or points) of a block as a guide for the quilting design. So it probably goes without saying that I love the abundance of corners in hexagon-shaped blocks. Choosing quilting designs that go from corner to corner is an easy way to quilt hexagons of all sizes.

Consider Circular Designs

A hexagon is fairly similar in shape to a circle (imagine the points morphing) so if none of the hexagon designs seem right, check out the circles. Almost all of the designs can easily be adapted to fit in hexagon blocks of all sizes. In fact, some square designs would do well in hexagons too!

See the Bigger Picture

When quilting a quilt that consists of several hexagons, see if you can create secondary designs with the placement of the blocks and the quilting. Try arranging the quilting designs to create flowers or grids. Your imagination is the limit!

QUILTING BORDERS

Oh, borders—I tend to have a love-hate relationship with them. Honestly, this is the area of a quilt that is probably my least favorite to quilt! But over the years, I have learned how to manage them and make the process a little easier.

Turning the Corner

When it comes to wrapping the designs around the corner of the border I have a couple of go-to options.

USE A PIVOT POINT

My favorite way of turning the corner uses the inner border corner as a pivot point. Having this point as a reference will help you visualize the turn and wrap it around the corner.

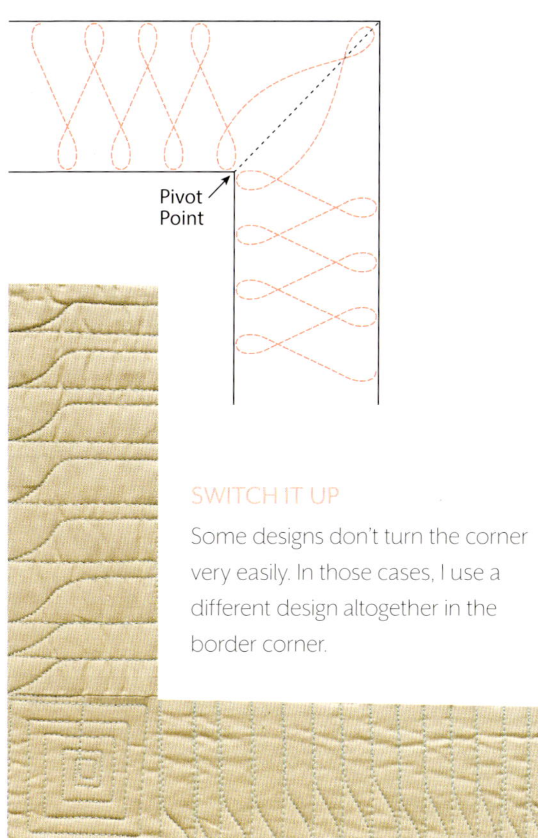

SWITCH IT UP

Some designs don't turn the corner very easily. In those cases, I use a different design altogether in the border corner.

Making Borders More Manageable

If you are still a little hesitant to work on the borders of your quilt, here are a couple of easy options.

MAKE THE CORNERS SPECIAL

Instead of working your way all around the border, you could add a design in the corners, then switch to an allover design in the rest of the border. I love this option because it gives the quilt a custom look but is still easy to stitch! At least it's easier than trying to quilt a continuous design down the entire length of the quilt.

USE SIMILAR DESIGNS

Choosing filler and border designs that are similar will ensure that you don't have to switch between completely different designs. For example, if I opted to use a feather design in the border, I could choose to use a feather meander in the center of the quilt.

Choose a stitching direction that works best for you. I show designs moving from left to right, mostly because I work on a longarm machine and the horizontal direction comes naturally to me. Also, the horizontal orientation works better in a book format. However, the designs can be quilted in a different direction, depending on the type of machine you use and the orientation of the quilt.

Close-up pieced by Ruth Doss and quilted by Angela Walters

Quilting Modern Quilts

This is where the rubber meets the road, or more specifically, where the needle meets the fabric. You have practiced your designs several times and are now ready to apply them to your favorite quilts. But in which quilts should you use them, and how? That is exactly what this section is about. I will show you some common scenarios in modern quilts and discuss different options for quilting them.

Disclaimer: The opinions and ideas contained in this section do not necessarily reflect the opinions of the modern quilting community.

I give the above warning in a tongue-in-cheek sort of way, but it is true. Keep in mind that the tips and suggestions I give here are what have worked for me.

Take what you like, leave what you don't, and just have fun with the process! When I am allowed to decide how to quilt my customers' quilts, I usually rely on my own preferences.

My personal motto is, "Quilt until you have quilted too much—and then quilt some more." I love lots and lots of quilting. Most of the quilts you will see in this section are quilted very densely.

I always want the quilting to complement the piecing, not overpower it—a challenge because of my fondness for dense quilting. To accomplish this, I use matching thread that blends with the quilt top.

QUILTING SQUARE IN A SQUARE QUILTS

When getting ready to quilt Square-in-a-Square quilts, consider a few tips:

Highlight just one part of the blocks.

Even if you want to quilt an allover design on your quilt top, consider doing something different in one area of the blocks. For instance, most Square-in-a-Square blocks have a center square, so consider quilting a different design in the middle. This is one of my favorite things to do.

Pick two different designs and alternate between them.

Deciding on two different designs and using only those will help make the quilting decisions easier. This doesn't take much longer than doing one design but adds a much more custom look to the quilting.

Close-up of *All Mine*: 51″ × 59″, pieced and quilted by Angela Walters

Go crazy with it!

Custom quilting is the hardest yet most rewarding way to quilt this kind of quilt. It takes longer, but your effort will be well worth it. Choose several of your favorite designs, and quilt each portion of the block individually.

Use straight lines.

Even though this book is about free-motion quilting, straight-line quilting definitely holds a special place in my heart. Combining straight lines with more intricate designs adds interest and a touch of drama. Try quilting a variety of designs using straight lines.

Squares: 34″ × 34″, pieced and quilted by Angela Walters. Each block is quilted using a different design.

QUILTING ZIGZAG QUILTS

The close-ups in this section are from *Zigzagged*, designed and pieced by Empty Bobbin Sewing Studios; quilted by Angela Walters.

Take it A Step Further

Some quilters love to use straight lines that follow the shape of the quilt. But you can take it a step further and add more quilting, making those zigzags stand out. Try echoing the zigzag, and then filling in the space between with different designs.

Zigzag with straight lines

After you have quilted the lines, you can fill the area with a different quilting design.

Up and Down or Side to Side?

Even though the majority of zigzag quilts have horizontal zigzags, you are not limited to using only horizontal designs. A number of horizontal and vertical designs work well in these kinds of quilts.

Quilting the Plume Feather on Zigzagged is an example of using a horizontal design. It fills the whole quilting area and helps move your eye across the quilt.

You can also try vertical designs within the zigzags.

A Plume Feather (page 232) is a great example of using a horizontal design when quilting zigzag quilts.

In this example I used the Pulleys design to quilt the zigzag. Because I used the edges of the quilting area as my guide, I was able to keep the design straight.

Create More Zigzags

If the zigzags in the quilt top tend to blend in, try quilting extra lines to help emphasize the horizontal look of the quilt. Doing this breaks the bigger sections into smaller zigzags, reinforcing the horizontal look of the quilt.

For instance, in Field Study, I quilted several horizontal lines that followed the piecing. Then I filled in the spaces between the lines with horizontal designs.

Close-up from *Field Study*: Quilt pattern designed by Tula Pink; pieced by Georgieanna Martin; quilted by Angela Walters.

QUILTING WONKY QUILTS

Wonky Log Cabins

Pick one part of a block, such as the outer ring of a block, and quilt a custom design in only that part of the block. Then, quilt the rest with an allover pattern. Doing this will highlight that area of the quilt but will be fairly easy to quilt.

If you love the look of custom quilting, you may want to do a little more quilting. Consider quilting the outer ring and center of the Log Cabin block with a custom design and filling in the rest with an allover design.

The quilting in *Housing Project* is a prime example of custom quilting. I quilted the center of the block with Pebbles and the outer portion with a Wishbone or Back & Forth.

Housing Project: 48″ × 53″, quilt designs and pieced by Scott Hansen; quilted by Angela Walters.

CUSTOM QUILTING…OR NOT?

Under normal circumstances, I hesitate to quilt each part of the wonky Log Cabin block with a separate design. Usually (I say "usually" because there are always exceptions) wonky Log Cabins are bright, funky, and full of different types of fabrics. Quilting each little piece differently can be overwhelming and make the quilt confusing to look at. To keep that from happening, I like to highlight only a few parts of the block and quilt the rest with an allover design. If you like the idea of custom quilting each of the sections, go for it!

Other Wonky Quilts

Of course wonky doesn't refer only to Log Cabins; it includes any design that is off-center or askew. When quilting any type of wonky shape, choose designs that use the edges of the quilting area as a guide. The result will be quilting that easily fills the random shapes.

When quilting wonky stars, the points of the stars can be random sizes. A Back & Forth design (page 222) is one of my favorite ways to quilt the random shapes.

Close-up of *Wonky Stars*, pieced and quilted by Angela Walters.

Close-up of *Housing Project* (page 107).

QUILTING STRIP QUILTS

Use All Your Favorite Designs

Try quilting a number of different designs on the quilt, one in each strip. Not only will it add variety, but it also will be great practice. Almost any of the Lines & Vines designs work well for strip quilts.

Allover Designs

Allover designs also can work well in strip quilts. Instead of quilting each strip differently, try using allover designs. When quilting *Low Volume*, I picked two quilting designs: Flower Power (page 269) for the white areas and Allover Leaves (page 260) for the rest of the quilt.

Quilting it this way makes the individual strips less noticeable and makes the overall design of the quilt stand out more. Also, using two designs can be quilted as quickly as using one allover design but adds a semi-custom look to the quilt. This may not work in every strip quilt, but it is an option for the right quilt.

Low Volume, 42˝ × 55˝, designed and pieced by Jacquie Gerring; quilted by Angela Walters.

QUILTING BUSY PRINTS

Bold, bright fabrics are one of the things that jump-started the modern quilting trend. When a quilt has a lot of busy fabrics, it can be tempting to automatically quilt a meander on it. Let me encourage you to try some different things.

Use the Fabric as Inspiration

Chances are, you love the fabric in your quilt. So why not emphasize it? Quilting along the designs within the fabric is quick and easy. And most modern fabrics have a lot of designs to choose from. Another bonus—no marking!

Brioche And Baguette, 37″ × 53″, pattern by Modern Quilt Relish; pieced by Georgieanna Martin; quilted by Angela Walters.

Close-ups from
Brioche And Baguette

Close-ups from *Flowers & Chocolate*, designed and pieced by Jenifer Dick; quilted by Angela Walters. Outlining some of the flowers and filling in the rest of the area with an allover design is a great way to quilt modern fabrics.

If you are short on time, quilt around only the elements in the fabric that you like the most. For example, if you happen to love a big flower that is featured, quilt around it and fill in the rest of the area with a different allover design. You can decide how much effort you want to put into it.

Practice Makes Perfect

Because busy prints tend not to show the quilting very well, use those areas as a chance to practice some designs that you aren't completely comfortable with. That way all your bumps and bobbles won't be visible. You can practice worry-free and improve your free-motion quilting. It's a win–win!

Get Funky with It

Quilts made with brighter, bolder fabric can handle quilting that is bolder and funkier as well. So use this as your opportunity to quilt your designs on a bigger scale. Or try using a crazy, funky design you normally wouldn't try. The main thing is to have fun with it!

Design
Library

CIRCLES & SWIRLS

PEBBLES

If we vacuum packed a loopy design until all the circles were stuck together, we would have pebbles. Pebbles are easy to quilt but can be very time consuming—although the effort required is worth it.

Tip

When quilting the pebbles, trace around some of the pebbles an extra time to add more texture to the design.

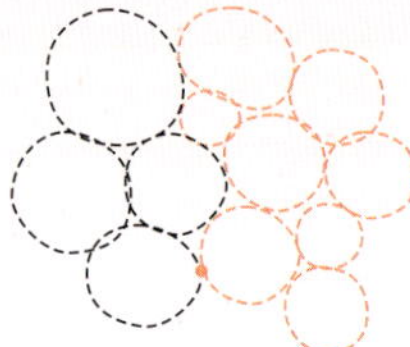

1. Start with a circle.

2. Without stopping, quilt another circle that touches the first one.

3. Continue quilting circle that touch each other until the whole area is filled.

ECHOED PEBBLES

Echoed pebbles can really highlight areas of your quilt. Make the pebbles as large or as small as you like to fit the scale of your quilt.

1. Quilt a circle shape that touches the edge of a block.

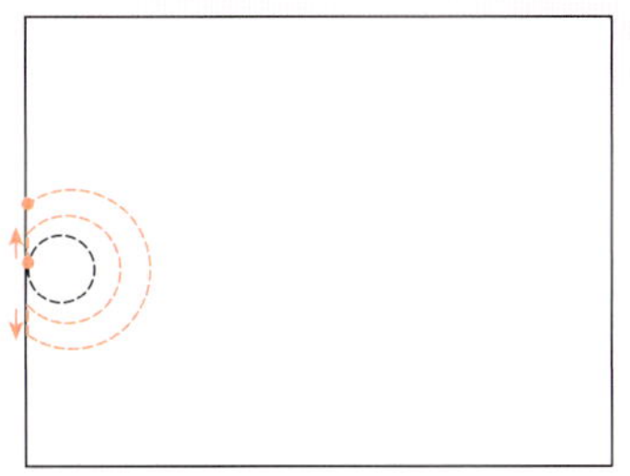

2. Travel along the edge of the block about ¼″ and echo around the circle until you reach the other side. Travel along the edge of the block and echo again.

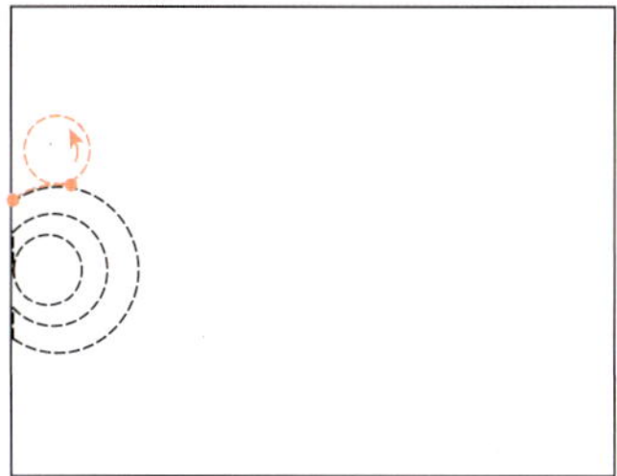

3. Travel along the last echo line about ¼″ and quilt another circle.

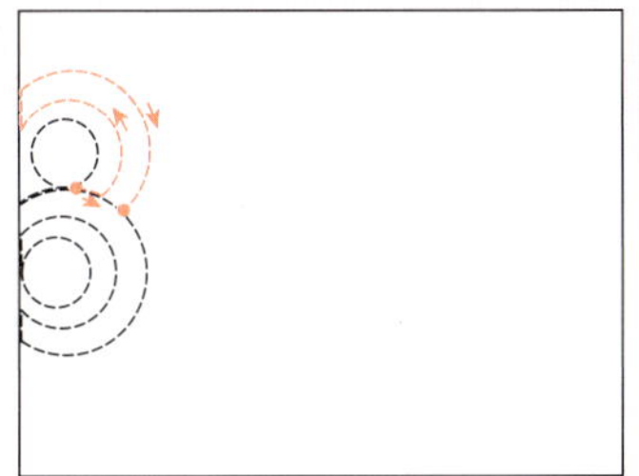

4. Travel and add a few echoes, just as you did on the first pebble.

5. Continue adding pebbles and echo lines until the area is completely filled in.

Tip

It doesn't matter how many times you echo around the circle. Add as many echoes as you wish!

Variations

Add a defined look to each pebble by stitching around it a few times before echoing.

Quilted pebbles require some traveling around the original circle. You could smooth out the travel lines and highlight the circles by stitching around each at least twice before starting the echo lines.

Draw attention to part of the quilt by inserting some regular pebbles.

Since this is a variation of a pebble, you can combine it with regular pebbles for a different look.

CIRCLE 1

When is a circle not a circle? When you use the quilting to give it an offset look. All it takes is a smaller circle and several echoes around it to create an optical illusion that would be a fantastic choice for circles of all sizes.

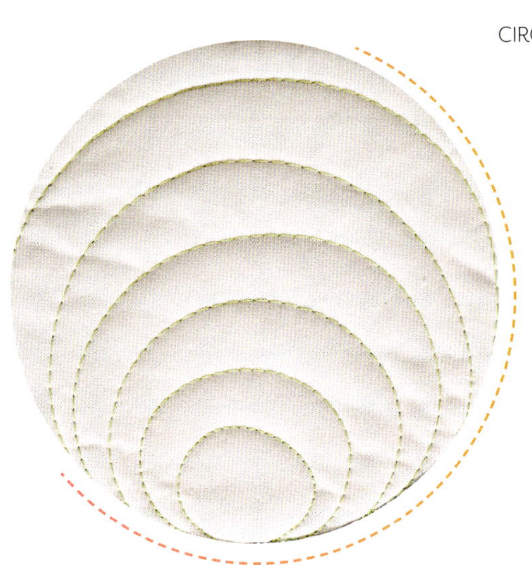

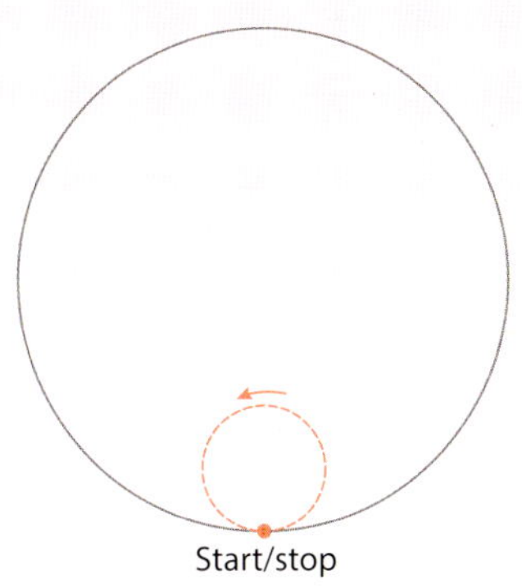

1. Starting at the edge of the circle, quilt a small circle that touches the edge, ending where you started. You can make it as large or as small as you would like.

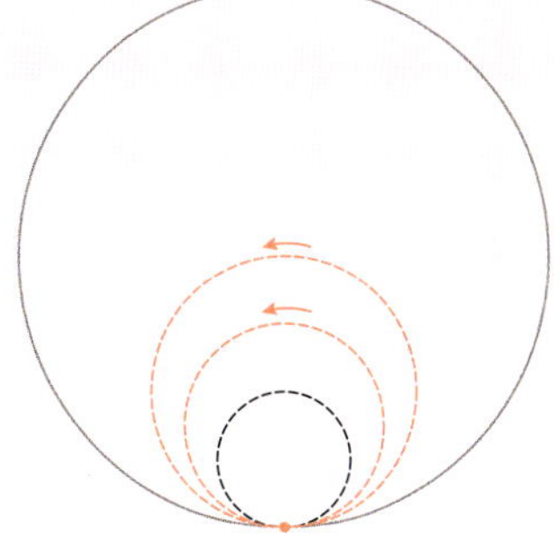

2. Echo around the outside of the circle you just quilted. Make sure the echoed lines are tucked into the edge of the circle block.

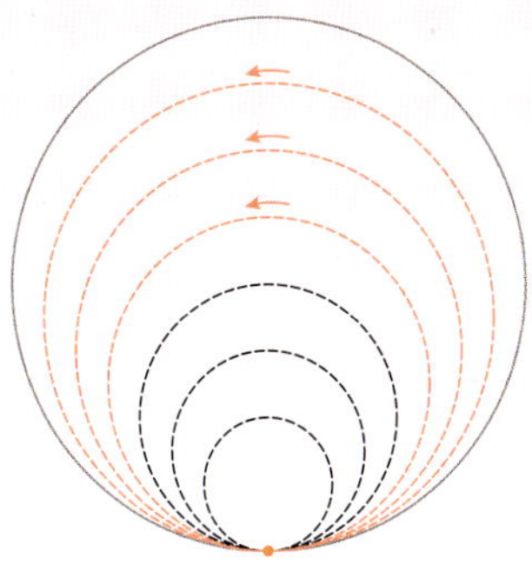

3. Continue echoing until you have filled the whole circle.

Note 

Although I like to quilt my echoed lines about ¼″ apart, you could space them farther apart if you want less dense quilting.

Variation

If your circles need a little more pizzazz, no worries! After quilting the first circle in Step 1, fill inside with the free-motion quilting design of your choice. For me, filling it with tiny circles seems like an obvious choice!

Try adding pebbles inside the smallest circle.

BASIC SWIRL

Swirls are my absolute favorite quilting design. This design is very simple, and all the other swirl designs are based on this shape. The basic swirl is great for filling large areas as an allover design.

1. Start from the edge of the quilting area and quilt a curvy line that curls in on itself.

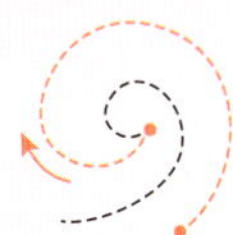

2. Immediately change directions and echo the swirl until you are back to the edge of the quilting area.

After you have quilted the first swirl, you have a choice to make: Depending on where you want to go, you can either echo the first swirl or start a new swirl. In these instructions, I quilted another swirl.

Note

The biggest problem new quilters have with this design is they don't finish the second half of the swirl. Make sure you return to the bottom of the swirl before starting the next one.

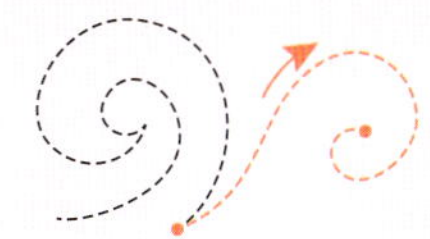

3. From the ending point of the first swirl, quilt the inside of another swirl.

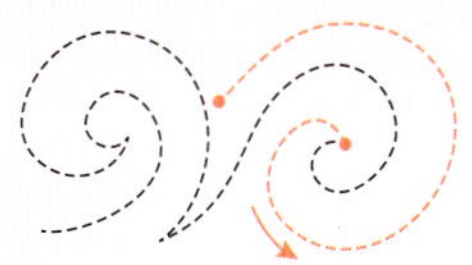

4. Then, echo the outside of the second swirl, just as you did the first, until you reach the edge of the first swirl. It doesn't have to touch, but get it close.

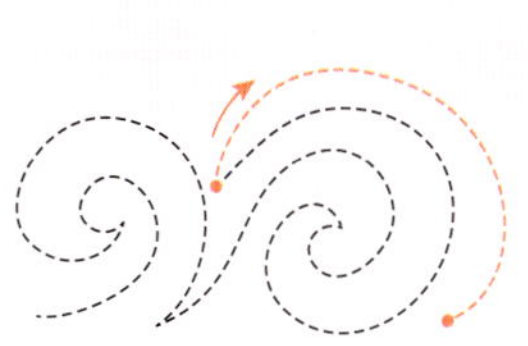

5. Echo the swirl again to move to the other side of the swirl.

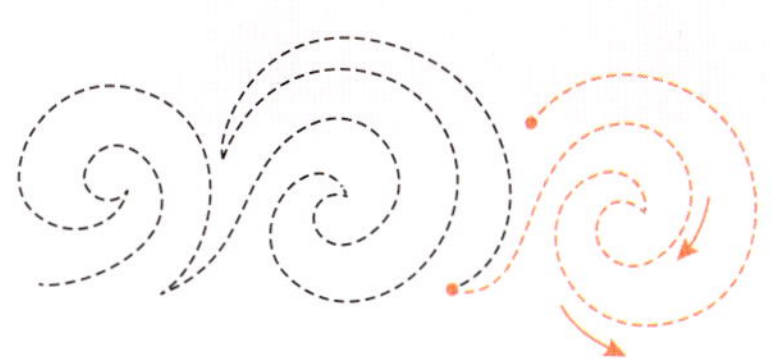

6. Quilt another swirl.

7. Continue quilting swirls and echoing until you fill the whole area.

SWIRL MEANDER

This design incorporates echoing, which is an important skill to learn. Echo quilting allows you to maneuver around an area and helps you learn to change direction with your quilting—both of which are useful skills for future quilting designs

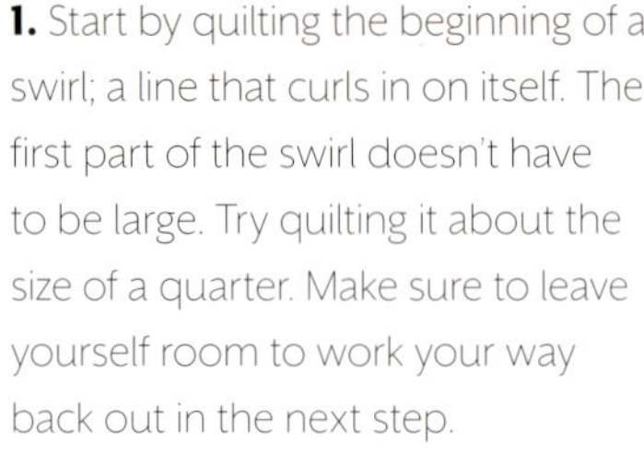

1. Start by quilting the beginning of a swirl; a line that curls in on itself. The first part of the swirl doesn't have to be large. Try quilting it about the size of a quarter. Make sure to leave yourself room to work your way back out in the next step.

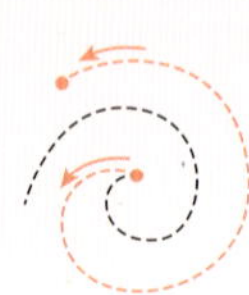

2. Finish the swirl by echoing back around the first line, stopping before you touch anything. There isn't any touching in this design. As soon as you come close to the edge of the area or another swirl, stop and quilt your next swirl.

3. Quilt another little swirl, then echo around it, stopping before you touch the previously quilted swirl.

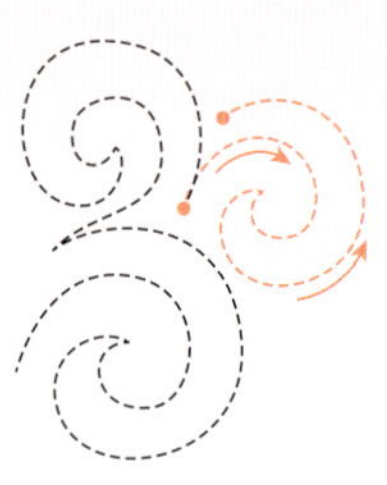

4. Third time's a charm! Quilt another swirl.

Note 

Echoing is quilting the same shape as a prior quilted line, with a space between. Most often, echo quilting is done outside of a design, but can also be quilted inside the design.

Continued on page 124

Tips

- Remember, there is no touching in this design. As you start to approach another swirl or the edge of an area, it's time to change direction.
- Don't forget to finish the swirl. It's the most important part of this design. It won't look horrible; it's just not the look that we are going for. If your swirls start looking like that, don't stop quilting or rip it out. Just keep going, trying to remember to finish the swirls as you go.

If you forget to "finish your swirls," your quilting may look like this.

- You may notice that some of my swirls face down, and some face up. That's how it is supposed to be! The swirls can point in any direction.

Both versions look great! So don't worry about the direction, just quilt a swirl and finish it.

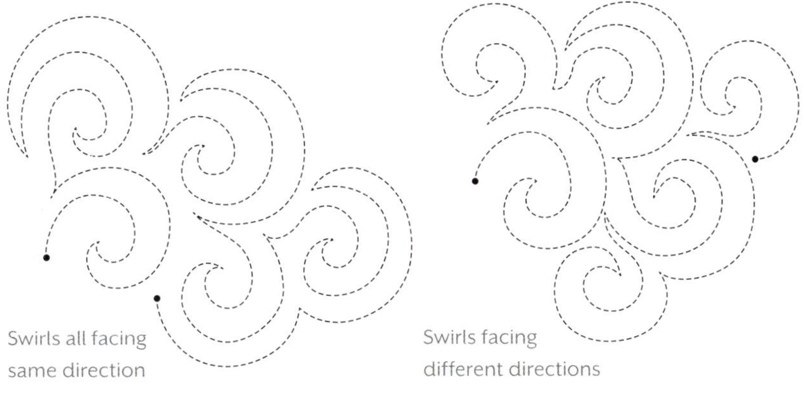

Swirls all facing same direction

Swirls facing different directions

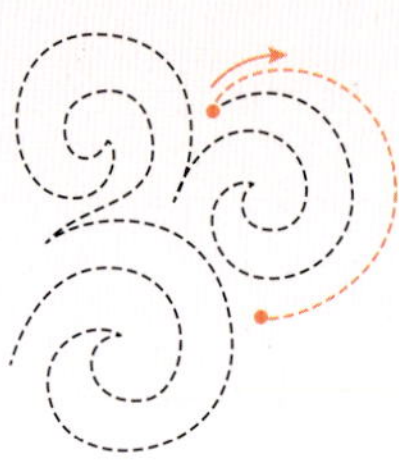

5. Echo the swirl. It's time to include echoing in our design. Echoing around your swirls is the perfect way to maneuver your way around the area. You can echo the swirl you just quilted.

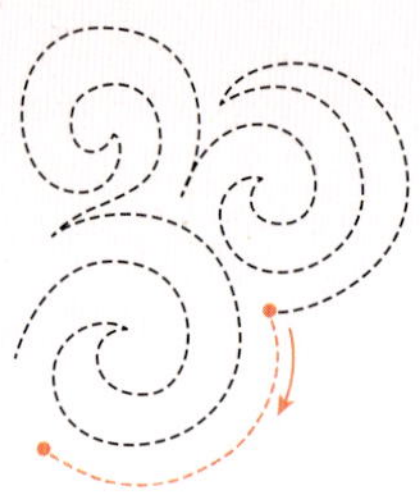

Or you could echo a previously quilted swirl.

Tip

Keeping the spacing of the echo lines the same as the swirls will help them blend in with the rest of the quilting.

6. Continue quilting swirls and echoing.

7. To fill in any corners or small gaps, you can quilt a smaller swirl.

Or you can add more echo lines.

If you get stuck, you can travel along the edge of the areas.

Just like all the other designs, it's more important that it's filled in completely than if it's perfect.

8. When in doubt, echo. You can even echo around the whole group of swirls. This will help you move into areas that you need to fill in.

9. If there isn't enough room to echo around the whole swirl, just go until you run out of room and then change direction.

Continued on next page

10. Keep echoing and swirling until the whole area is filled in.

Tip

There are only two steps to this design—swirl and echo. As you are quilting, if you become confused, just remember to pick one. There is no wrong answer! Breaking a design down to its most basic elements will help keep it from being overwhelming.

Note

Quilting the swirl meander on a smaller scale is a great way to turn an allover design into filler. Filler quilting designs are used to highlight blocks or even other quilting designs.

CIRCLE 1

To me, the most important thing about quilting is to have fun. And I think quilting is fun when it's easy and quick; that's exactly what this design is.

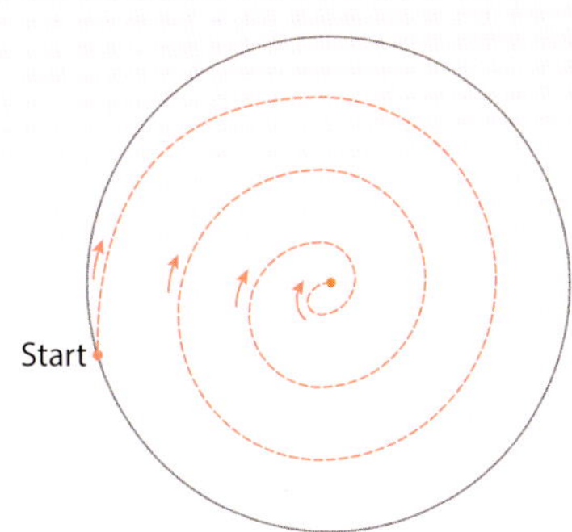

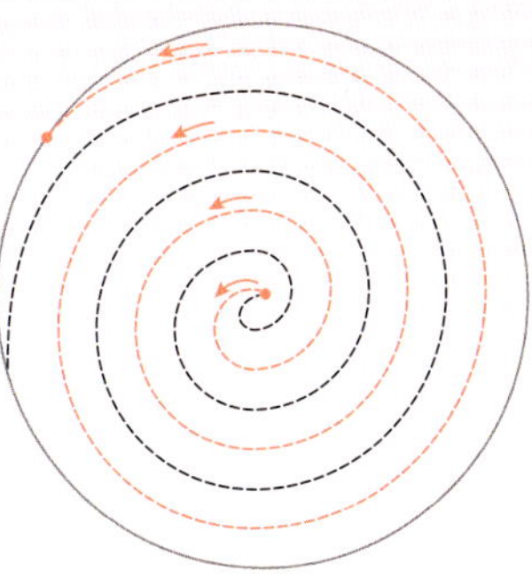

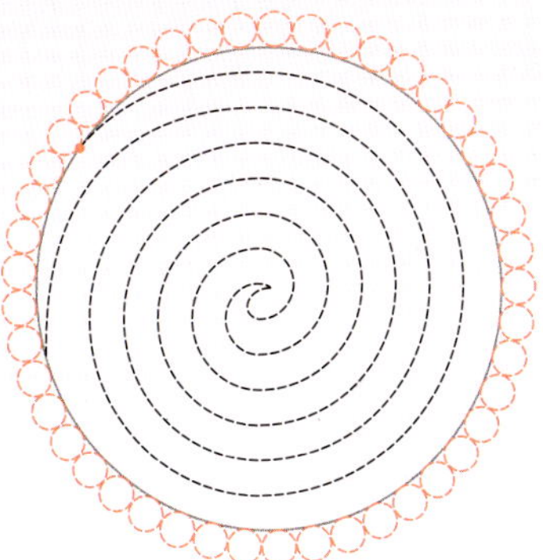

1. Starting from any point on the outside of the circle, quilt a spiral ending in the center of the circle, keeping the lines approximately ½˝ apart.

2. Abruptly change direction and echo your way back out, trying to stay an even distance between the lines of the spiral. Continue until you reach the edge of the circle.

You can extend the quilting outside the block by adding small circles around the perimeter. This detail will add another layer of richness to your quilting.

Note

To help keep the spacing between the lines consistent, I like to use the presser foot as a guide.

CIRCLE 2

This design adds a groovy look to your circle blocks and is great for small or medium circles.

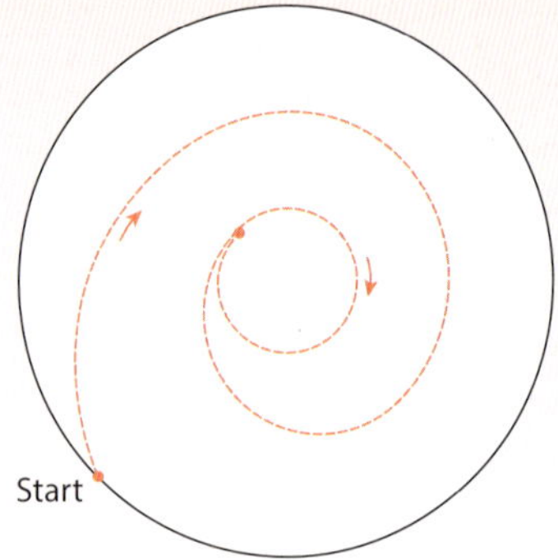

1. Starting from any point on the edge of the circle, quilt a line that curls in toward the center and ends in a circle.

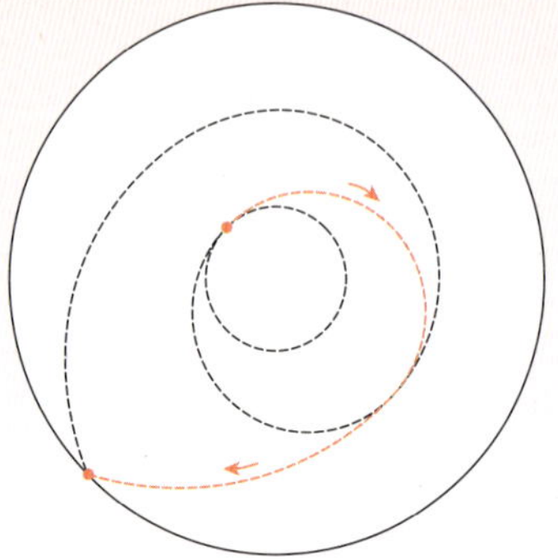

2. Work your way out of the swirl by quilting a line that curls away from the center circle, crossing the line across from it until you reach the outside of the circle.

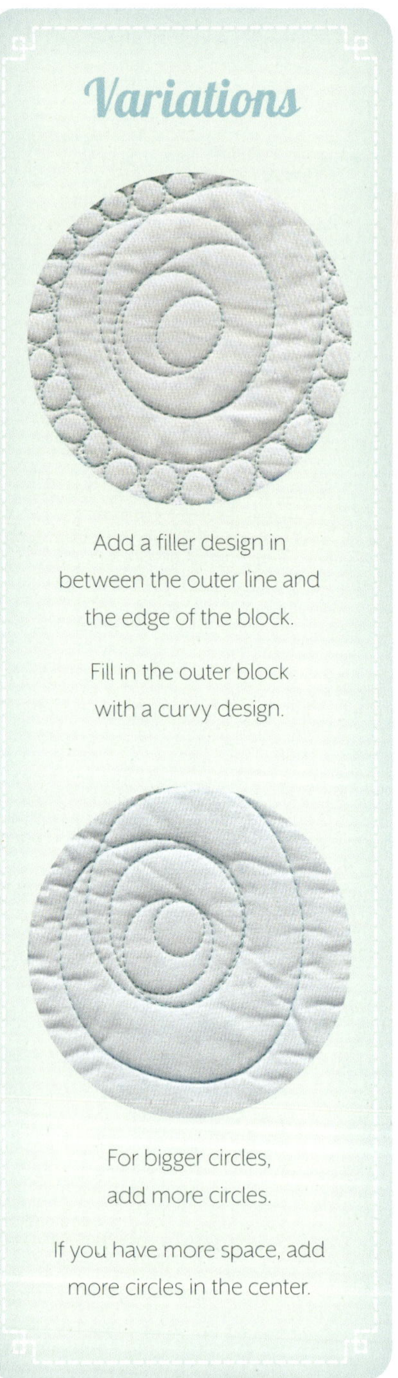

Variations

Add a filler design in between the outer line and the edge of the block.

Fill in the outer block with a curvy design.

For bigger circles, add more circles.

If you have more space, add more circles in the center.

BORDER: NESTED SWIRLS

This design may look complex, but it's mostly echoing. Once you get the hang of it, you will be surprised at how quickly you will be able to quilt the borders of your quilt.

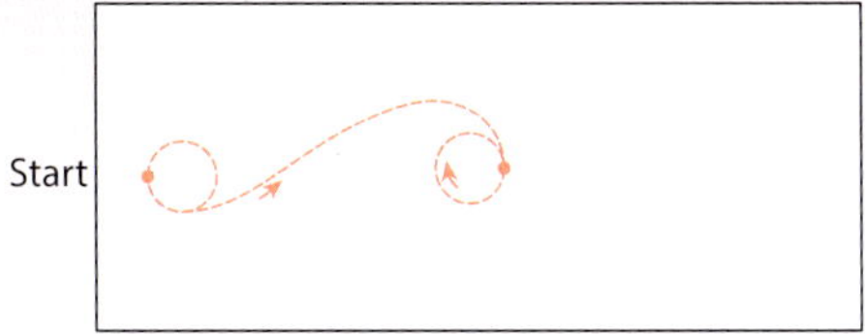

1. In the middle of the border, quilt a circle that moves into an S-shaped line and ends in another circle.

Note

Try to stitch the circles in the middle of the border to keep the design even on both sides.

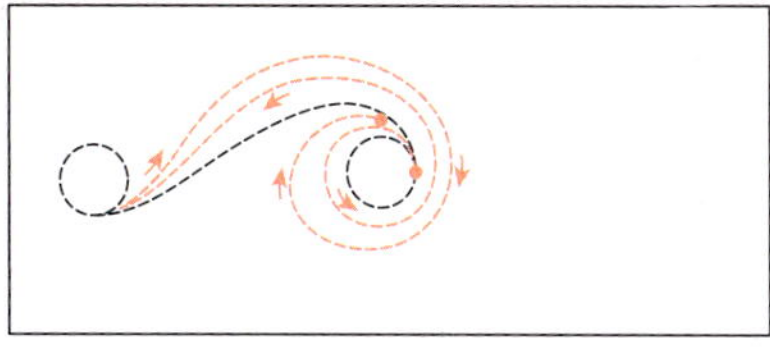

2. Echo around the outside of the line, tucking the end of the line into the first circle. Echo back around to the second circle.

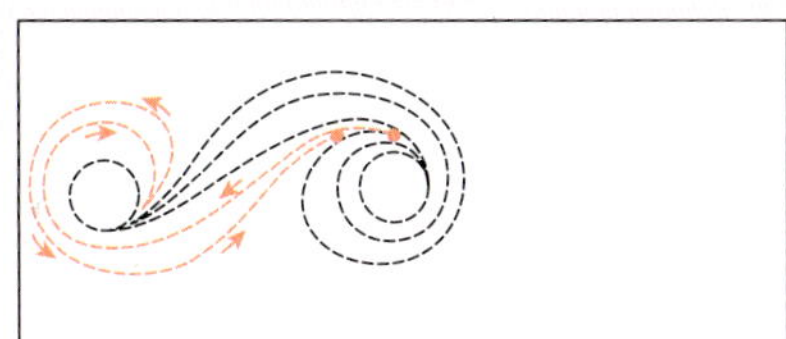

3. Repeat on the inside of the swirl line, echoing to the first circle and back again.

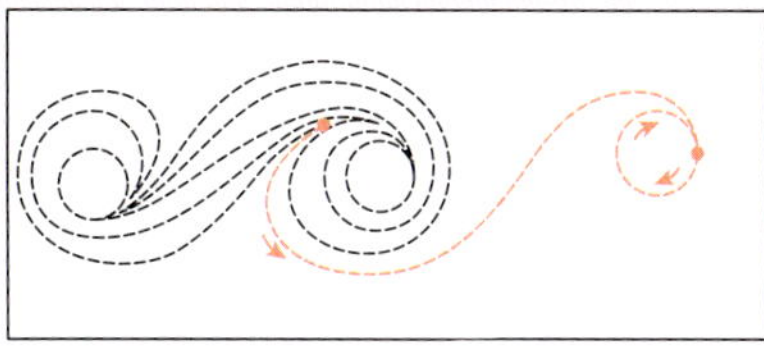

4. Continue by quilting another S-shaped line ending in a circle. Try to keep the circles evenly spaced out, but don't worry too much about it. The echoing around the design will add to the overall texture.

Continued on next page

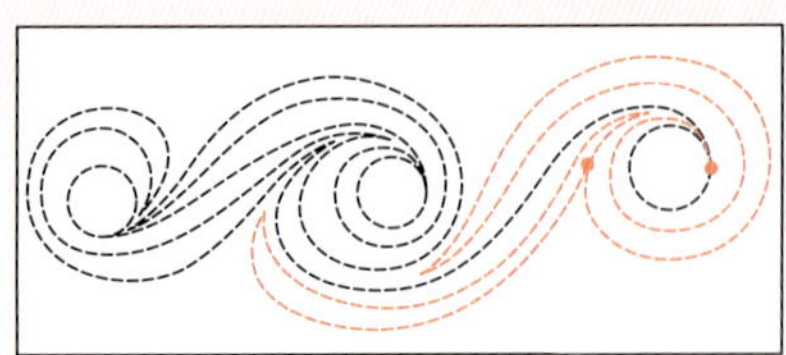

5. Repeat Steps 2 and 3 to echo the line. Continue adding more echoed S lines and circles to fill the border.

Tip 

For wide borders, add more echo lines to help fill in the spaces consistently. Or try some other fillers around the swirled line.

Add echo lines or other fillers around the swirls to fill in space on large borders.

You could also add some paisley shapes as well.

Small paisleys are a charming way to fill in the space.

6. To quilt around the corner, end an S line with a circle in the center of the corner. Echo around the shape as usual, then stitch the next S line in a perpendicular direction to continue quilting the next side.

Wrap the design around the border corner by changing the direction of the new S line.

Variation

For an allover design, quilt this design in rows and fill between them with another design to create a fun, multilayered look.

Make an unusual background filler by quilting the swirls in rows.

SWIRLED HOOK

What makes this design different from Basic Swirl is that we add a small hook. This design is great for more masculine quilts and is helpful when you need a swirl design that can fit into tight spots, such as the points of triangles.

1. Starting from the edge of the quilting area, quilt the inside of a basic swirl.

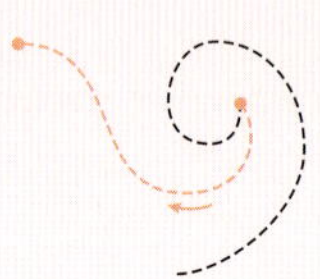

2. Immediately quilt a gentle, curvy line extending out from the center. This "hook" doesn't have to point anywhere in particular; just try to fill in the empty areas evenly.

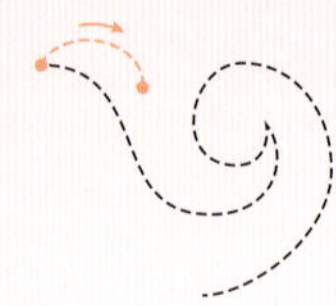

3. Echo the curved line until you are approximately ¼″ from touching the edge of the inner swirl.

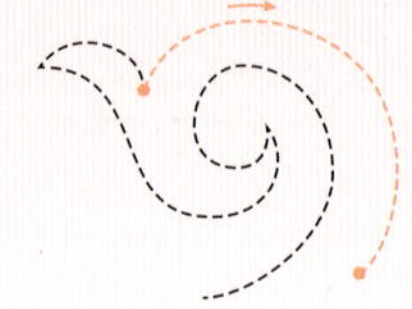

4. From that point, echo the swirl until you reach the beginning of the swirl.

5. You can echo the swirled hook, or immediately quilt another one. Continue until you finish filling the area.

SWIRL HOOK MEANDER

The swirl hook design takes a basic swirl and adds another little step, a hook. It's great for irregular shaped areas or between blocks, and I especially like it for masculine quilts. No matter how you choose to use it, it's definitely a design worth learning.

1. Quilt the beginning of a swirl, just as you did with the swirl meander (page 122).

2. Quilt a serpentine line as a hook extending from the curl. It doesn't matter how long or short the hook is or even how curvy it is. Just quilt an "S" shape that extends from the swirl.

3. Echo the hook back toward the swirl, stopping about ½˝ from the swirl. This is where most quilters get tripped up. You don't have to rethink the design, just echo around what you have already quilted. Sometimes we tend to make the quilting harder than it has to be.

Continued on next page

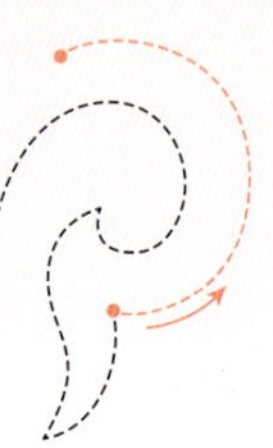

4. Now, echo around the rest of the swirl, stopping before you run into anything. In this step, we are finishing the swirl, just as we did in the swirl meander.

Tip

If echoing around the hook is tripping you up, you can just quilt the hook and then echo around the swirl. Leaving that step out will give you one less thing to think about.

5. Quilt the beginning of another swirl. Just as with the swirl meander, it doesn't matter what direction the swirl faces. Just quilt another swirl close to the previously quilted one.

6. Quilt another hook. Try to keep the serpentine line close to other swirls. It will help prevent gaps in the quilting.

7. Finish the swirl by echoing the hook and then echoing around the swirl.

8. Quilt your next complete swirl hook.

Tip

Echoing is also a great way to deal with the corners of an area. If you can't fit the whole design, just echo the lines you have already quilted until it's filled in. Then, when you have room, you can quilt your next swirl.

9. Echo around a swirl. Just like the swirl design, echoing is an easy way to maneuver your way around the area. You can echo the swirl that you just quilted or even one quilted previously, as I did here.

Continued on next page

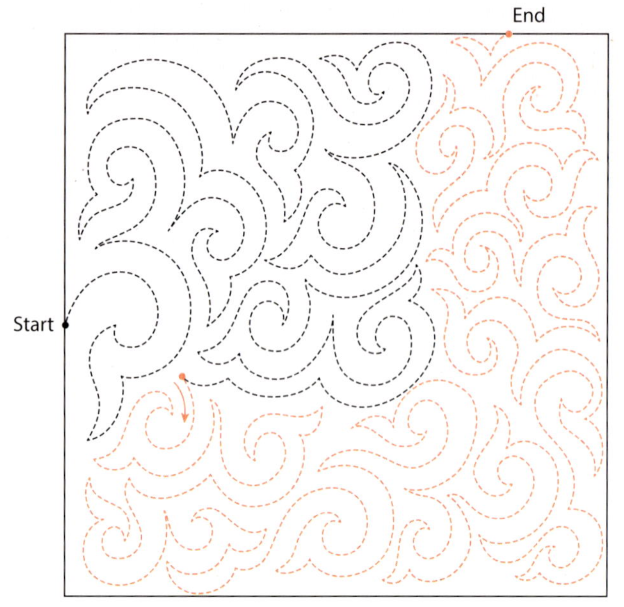

Continue quilting swirl hooks and echoing to fill in the complete area.

Tip

If quilting the hooks in this design seem a little difficult, start by adding a few swirl hooks in among some basic swirls. It will let you practice a little bit without feeling overwhelmed by a new design.

Focus on keeping the spacing consistent. Instead of focusing on the hook or the swirls, pay attention to the spacing between the lines. If the spacing is consistent, it gives the illusion of perfection.

SWIRL HOOK MEANDER AS A BORDER DESIGN

I love using this swirl hook design in borders that are 3″–5″ wide. It's a great way to practice the hook in a more confined space.

Quilting the swirl hook in alternating directions really fills in the area nicely.

DIAMOND 1

When working with smaller blocks, it's usually best to keep the quilting on the simple side. I like to use this design for quilts with a lot of smaller pieces. Not only is it quick and easy, but it also starts and ends in the same spot.

Tip 

You could also use this design in triangle-shaped blocks. The "hooks" of the design are great for reaching into tight spaces.

Continued on next page

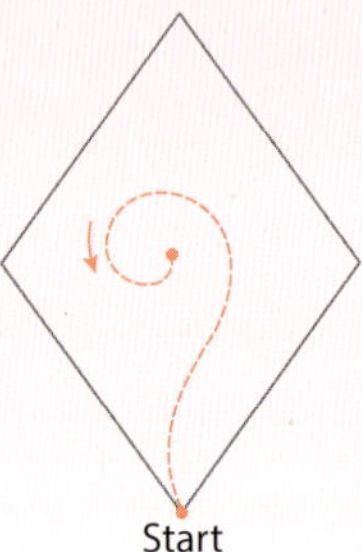

1. From the bottom of the diamond, quilt a swirl in the center of the diamond. Stop in the center of the swirl.

Note 

Make sure to leave space between the edge of the block and the swirl. This will ensure that you have room to complete the design.

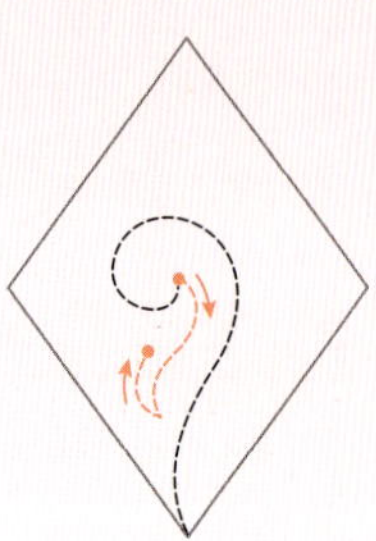

2. From the center, add a hook to the swirl by quilting a serpentine line going toward the bottom of the block. From there, partially echo the line you just quilted, stopping about 1˝ from the swirl.

Variation

If the hooks of this design are throwing you off, omit them and quilt a couple of swirls instead.

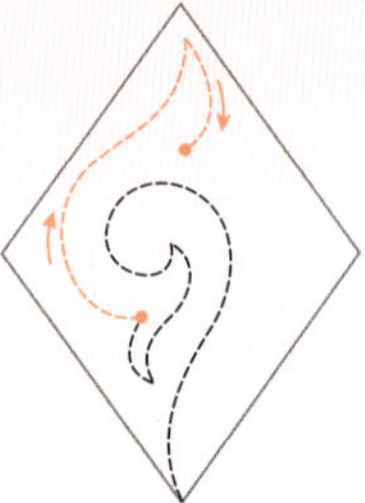

3. Echo around the outside of the swirl, coming to a point just below the top of the block. Quilt a small curve to echo the line you just quilted, stopping about 1˝ from the swirl.

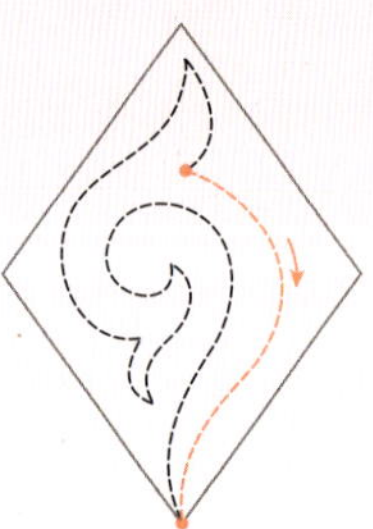

4. To finish the design, echo around the outside of the swirl, returning to the bottom of the block.

BORDER: SWIRL HOOK CHAIN

This is what I call a throwback design. It has been around for a long time and for good reason.

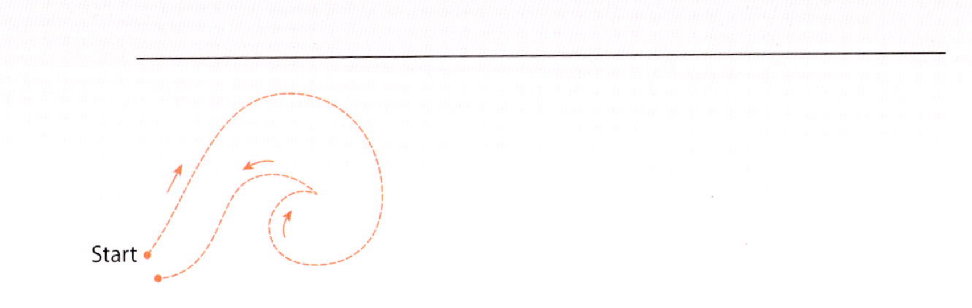

1. Quilt a line that curls in toward the middle of the border. Add a "hook" by quilting a serpentine line that curves back toward the edge of the border.

Continued on next page

2. Echo the hook back toward the swirl, stopping about ¼" from the inside of the swirl. Continue echoing around the outside of the swirl, stopping before the border edge.

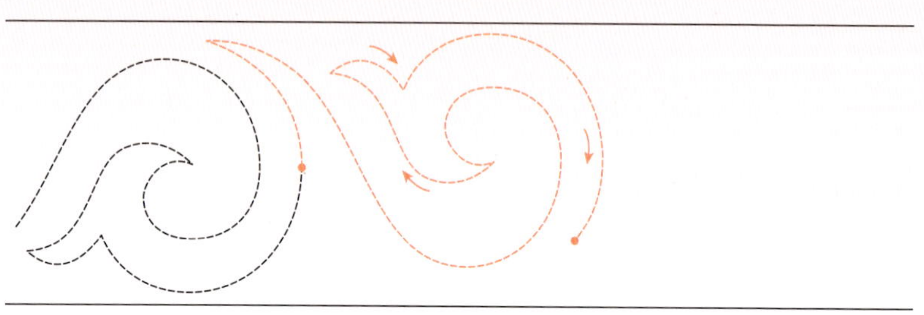

3. Quilt a new swirl facing the opposite direction from the first.

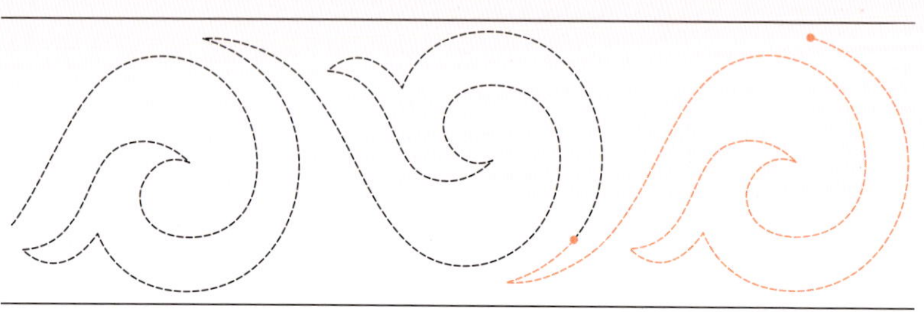

4. Add a hook and echo the swirl as in Steps 1 and 2, ending on the bottom side of the border.

5. Continue quilting swirls in alternate directions, using the hooks and echo quilting to fill in the empty spaces.

CONCENTRIC CIRCLES & SWIRLS

Concentric Circles are the more precise cousins of the Basic Swirl. They like their spacing to be even and consistent. Even though they often frown on looser, uneven swirls, they play well with other designs. Using this motif adds a lot of dense quilting. Use in big, open areas of the quilt—the fewer edges to go around, the better.

Tip

At all times you want your circles to touch the edge of another circle or the edge of the quilting area. This will help ensure that no areas are left unquilted.

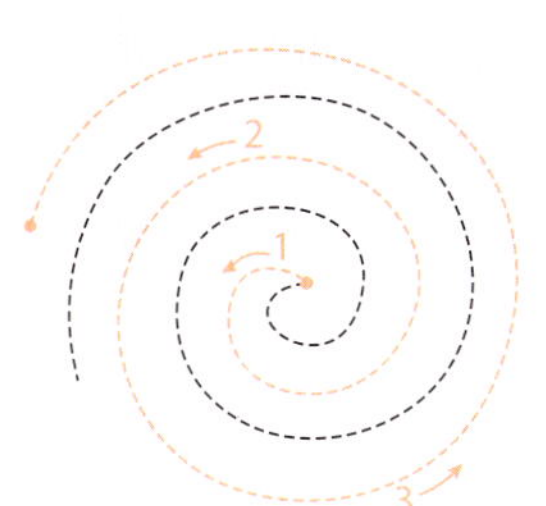

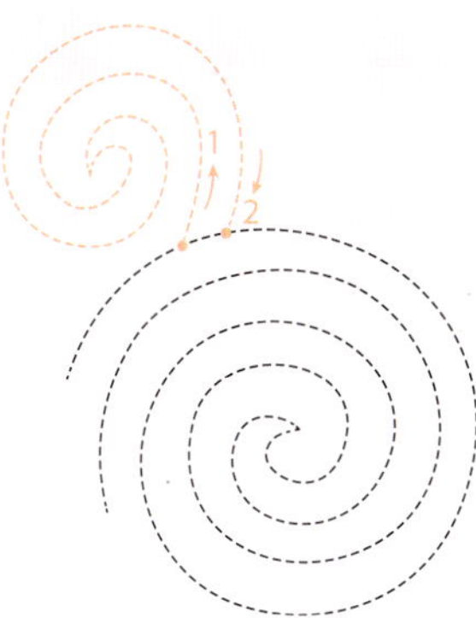

1. Quilt a spiral going inward, trying to keep the distance between the rings about ½″.

2. When you reach the middle of the spiral, stop and quilt back out of the spiral, keeping the stitching between the lines of the spiral. Continue until you are near the starting point of the circle.

3. Congrats! You have quilted your first circle. To add more circles, travel along the edge of the first circle about 1″–2″. Quilt another circle the same as you quilted the first, ending on a line of the first circle.

Continued on next page

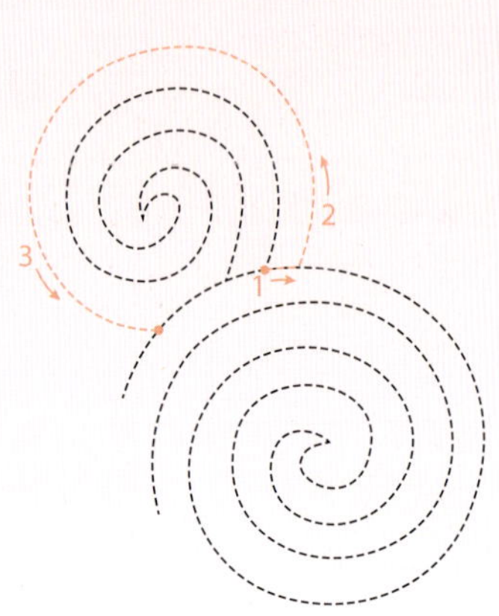

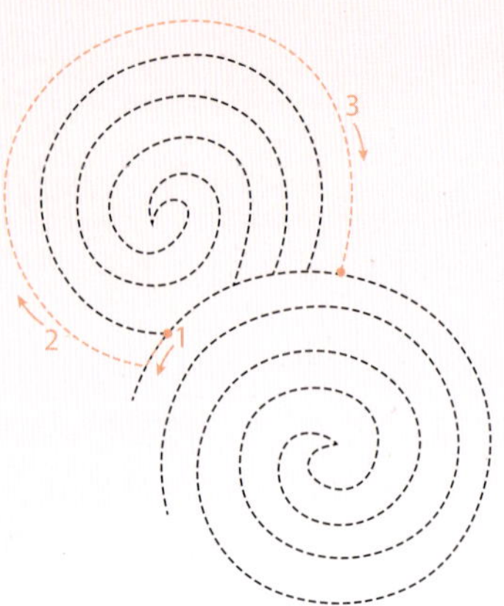

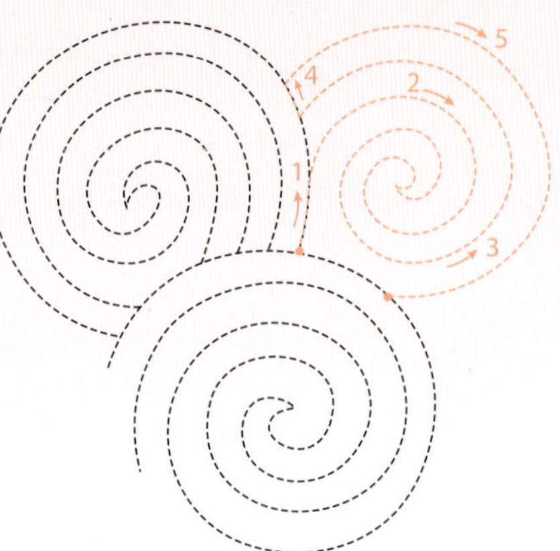

4. Travel along the edge of the first circle about ¼″ and echo the second circle, keeping the spacing about ¼″. You should end up on the other side of the second circle, touching the edge of the first circle.

5. Travel along the edge of the first spiral about ¼″ and add another ring to your second circle.

6. When you decide that the second spiral is the size you want, travel ¼″ along the outer edge and begin another swirl.

Note

By traveling along the edges of the circles, you will give the illusion that circles float on top of one another. It takes a little more time, but the result is well worth it!

7. Continue until you have filled the quilting area.

SWIRL CHAIN

I am a swirl girl at heart. To me, swirls are the ultimate quilting design. you can use them in so many different ways and in so many areas of the quilt. The swirl chain takes the basic swirl and pumps it up a notch. This design looks anything but basic and is perfect for filling large areas of negative space.

Note

Don't be afraid to try out this design! It's basically just quilting elongated swirls in a row.

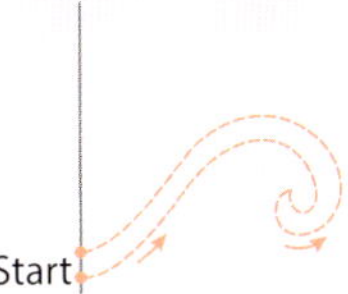

1. Starting from the edge of the quilting area, quilt an elongated swirl and echo back to the edge.

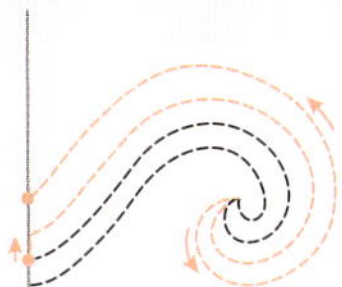

2. Travel up the edge about ¼˝, echo outside the swirl from Step 1, and echo back to return to the edge again.

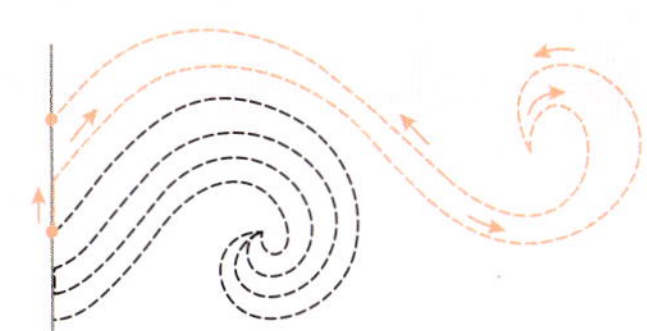

3. Travel up the edge about ¼˝ and quilt an elongated swirl that goes out and above the one you quilted in Steps 1 and 2. Return to the edge.

Note

To help the swirls fit together better, have them point in opposite directions.

Continued on next page

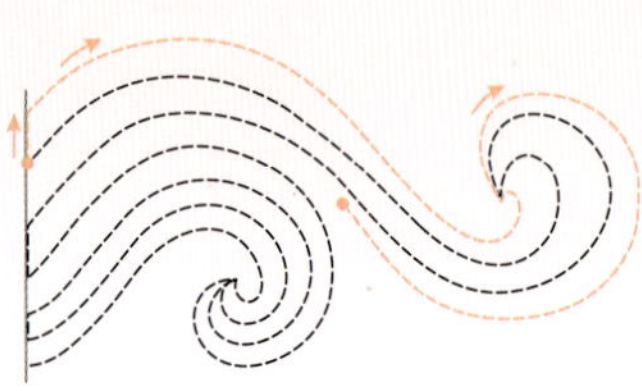

4. Travel up the edge about ¼″ and then echo around the swirl from Step 3 so that you are pausing at the point where the 2 swirls meet.

5. Quilt a teardrop shape and echo it. This is an optional step; you could omit the teardrop if you would like.

6. Quilt the next swirl so it goes under the previous swirl. Echo the previous swirl partly, and then create another swirl, ending at the point where the 2 swirls meet.

7. Add a teardrop and quilt the next swirl as you did in Steps 5 and 6.

8. Continue quilting the swirls until you reach the other side of the quilting area.

Tip

When quilting this design, if you find yourself on the wrong side of the swirl, just echo around it until you get to the desired side. By the time you fill in around the design, you won't even notice the extra lines!

Quilting The Swirl Chain In Negative Space

When using this quilting design in the negative space of your quilt, you can quilt it in a few different ways.

Quilt the swirl chain design in rows and fill in between them with a filler such as swirls. This one adds movement to your quilt but without all the attention going to the swirl chain.

To use the swirl chain design in negative space, quilt them in rows and fill in between with swirls.

Or, if you want the swirl chains to be much more noticeable, try using a smaller filler such as pebbles.

Fill in between rows of the swirl chain with pebbles to really make the swirl chain stand out.

Instead of quilting them in rows, you can use the same components of the swirl chain as an allover design. To do so, quilt the elongated swirls in various directions.

Use the swirl chain as an allover design.

LOOP AND DOUBLE LOOP SWIRLS

Even though Loop & Double Loop Swirls are the first step to Pebbles (next up on our list), they are fun on their own. I like to use this design in small sashing or in larger areas to fill in with quilting that is less dense.

This design is a basic meandering line with a loop thrown in randomly.

1. Starting at any edge of the quilting area, quilt a wavy line with a loop at the end.

2. Without stopping after quilting the loop, continue the wavy, meandering line. Add another loop.

3. Continue the design, winding around in random directions, and filling in the entire area.

Instead of single loops, try quilting double loops to add even more detail to the quilting.

1. Start with a wavy line with a loop at the end.

2. Quilt a second loop circling the first one, ending at the same point.

3. Continue quilting the design until the whole area is quilted.

Tip

You can quilt double loops in a straight row to fill narrow, straight areas.

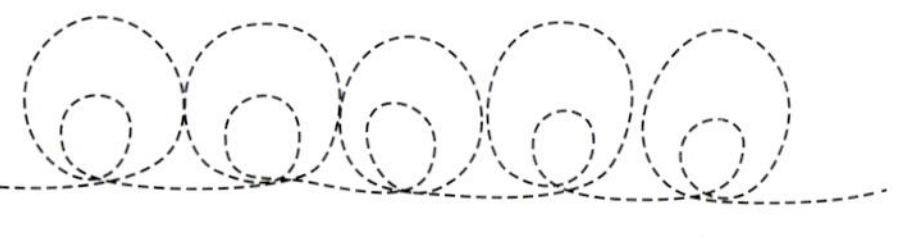

LOOPY MEANDER

The loopy meander uses a meandering line, but with a randomly added small loop. That's all. There's nothing scary about loops, so don't be worried. In fact, I think they are adorable. It's a fun, whimsical design that is great for all kinds of quilts, especially for kids' quilts or novelty quilts.

Quilting the loopy meander will help you get comfortable with moving the fabric in all different directions. This will be helpful as you progress into the other designs.

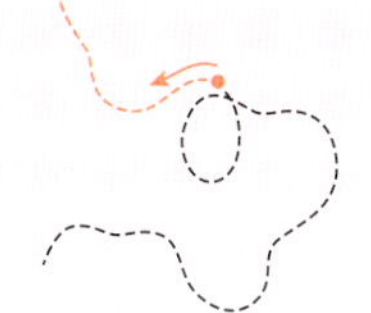

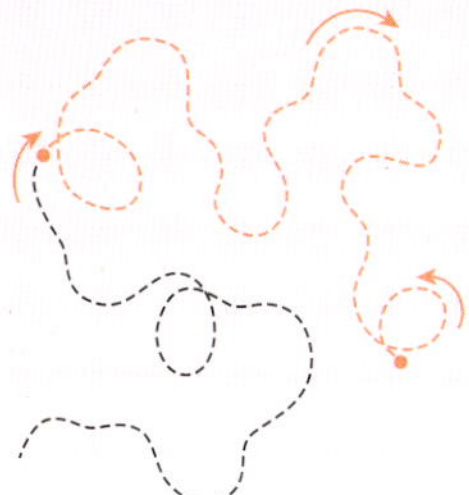

1. Start by quilting the meandering line as shown.

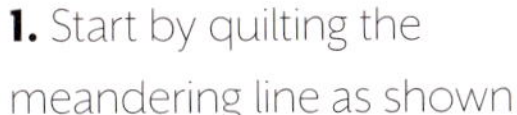

2. At a random moment—whenever you are ready—quilt a loop shape. This loop can happen anywhere in the design.

3. Once the loop is finished, continue on the path of the meandering line. It should look as though, if the loop were removed, the line would still look fine.

4. Continue quilting the meandering line, adding another loop when you are ready. The loops can go in any direction, so don't overthink that part of the design.

Continued on page 151

Tips

- If quilting loops makes you nervous, just add a few throughout the area. Adding them in slowly will help make learning them less overwhelming. Remember, there is no rush. Learn at your own pace.

- When you quilt a loop, you are trying to quilt a circular shape. Please notice that I said "circular," but I could have just as easily said "circle-ish." It doesn't have to be a perfect circle, it can be a teardrop or any other shape you feel like quilting.

The loop can be any size. If you want the loops to be the most noticeable part of the design, quilt them bigger.

If you want the loops to blend in with the meander or not be as noticeable, quilt them smaller. This would be the way to quilt it if you are new to machine quilting and don't want any of the mistakes to be noticeable.

5. Once you are comfortable quilting the loops, try adding more of them to the meander line. Don't forget to quilt the line in all different directions.

6. As you quilt, add as few or as many loops as you like. Make this design fit your preferences.

7. Continue quilting loops and meandering until you fill the area.

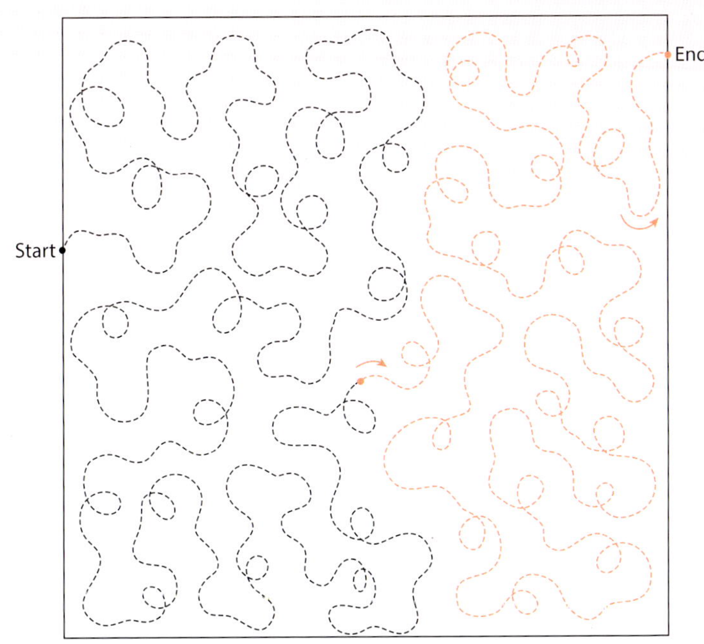

The most important thing is that the area is filled in as completely as possible. No one will notice that your loops aren't perfect. All they will see is the overall texture of the design.

OTHER WAYS TO USE THE LOOPY MEANDER

Once you have mastered the loopy meander, try using it in different ways on your quilts.

As A Border Design

This design is perfect for thinner borders and sashing. This is also a great way to practice quilting loops, if the thought of filling in a whole area seems daunting. You can also change the orientation of the loops or quilt them all facing the same direction.

Loops alternating directions

Loops going the same direction

Add More Loops

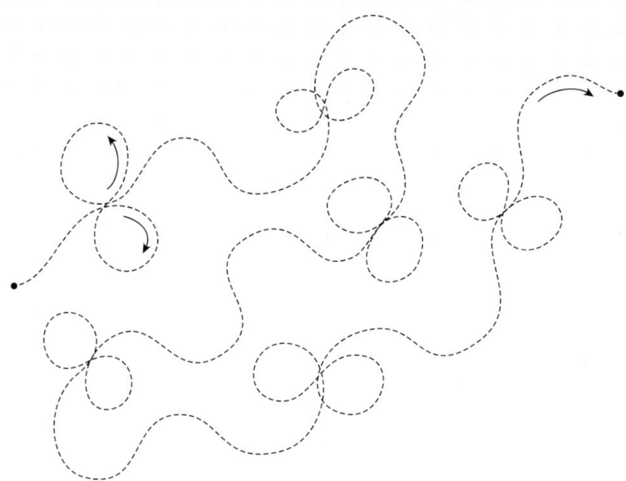

Sometimes, more is better. To make this meander even more loopy, quilt two loops instead of one. I like to quilt it almost like a figure eight.

CIRCLE 1

I love the look of spirals on circle blocks, but sometimes, keeping those curved lines nice and smooth can be a pain. This design takes the basic idea of a spiral and changes it up a bit by incorporating loops. It's great for larger circles and especially easy to quilt. Give it a try!

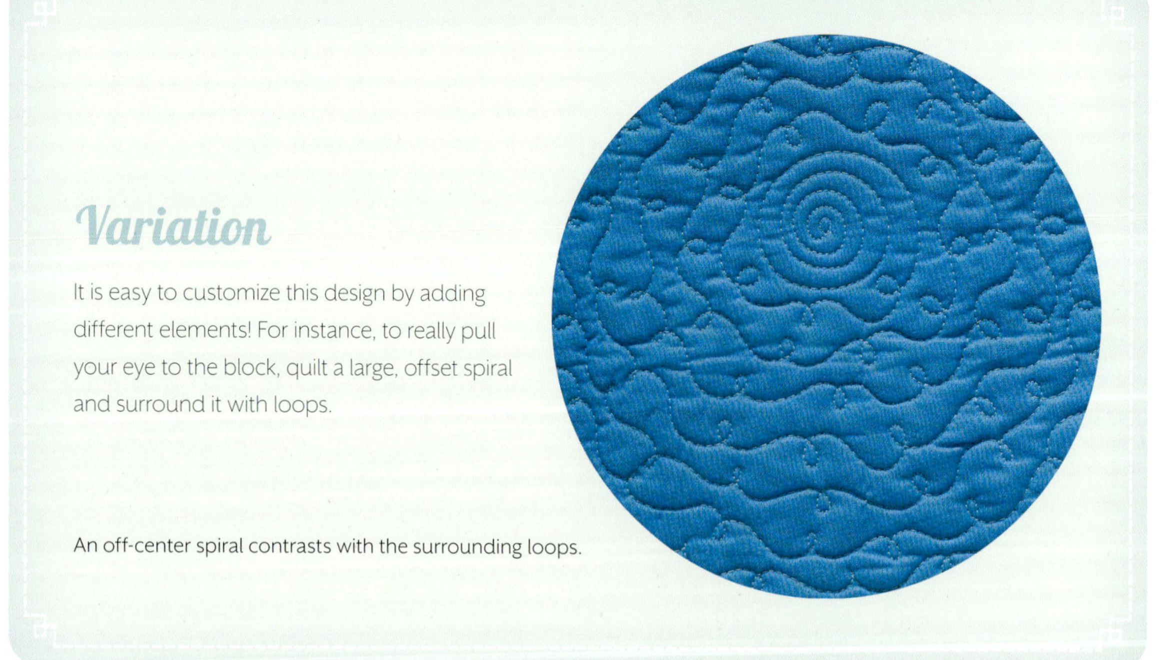

Variation

It is easy to customize this design by adding different elements! For instance, to really pull your eye to the block, quilt a large, offset spiral and surround it with loops.

An off-center spiral contrasts with the surrounding loops.

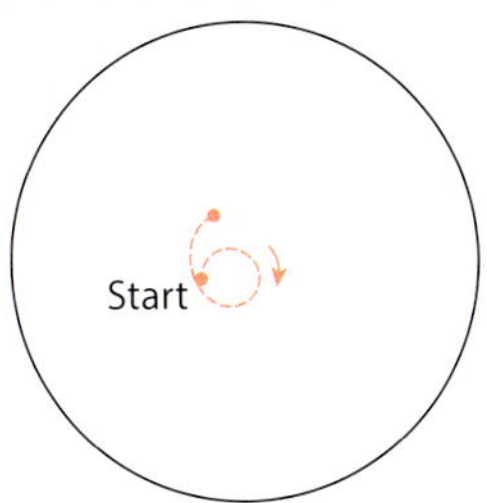

1. Starting from the block center (or somewhat close), quilt a small circle that extends past itself.

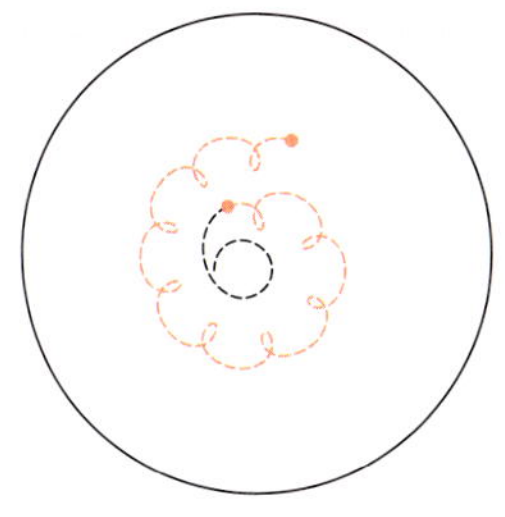

2. Begin quilting loops that wrap around the circle.

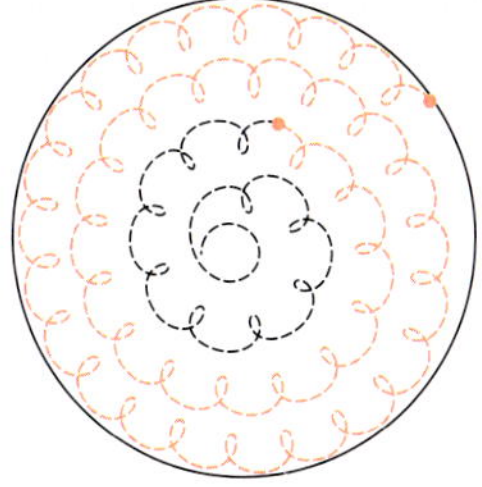

3. Continue quilting loops around and around until you fill in the entire quilt block.

Tip

I like to alternate the direction of the loops, but you could keep them all going the same way if you would like.

Alternating the direction of the loops allows the rows to stick closer together.

PAISLEY

Paisley is another quilting design that is commonly used, but the texture it adds to modern quilts makes it a personal favorite. Paisley might not look like a swirly design, but because the construction is similar, it has been included in this chapter. You can quilt this design larger to use as an allover design or smaller to fill small areas.

1. From the edge of the quilting area, quilt a curved teardrop shape that ends near the beginning point. I like the movement the slightly curved shape gives to the quilting.

2. Echo the shape twice.

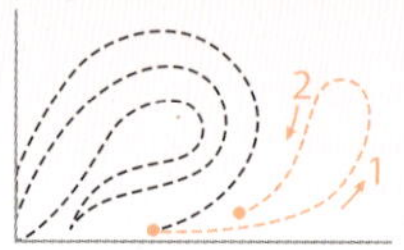

3. Quilt another paisley shape, gently curving it to fit close to the first one.

4. Echo the paisley twice, ending close to the first shape.

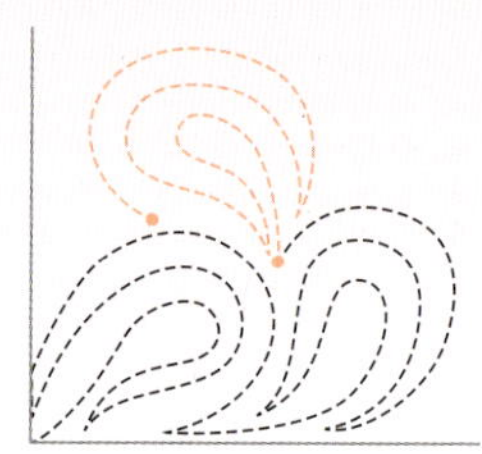

5. Continue quilting the shapes and echoing until you fill the entire area.

Tip 

If you find yourself stuck in an area too small for a paisley shape, echo other paisleys until you fill in the area.

PAISLEY MEANDER

The paisley meander is such a beautiful design and it works on all sorts of quilts. You can use it as an allover design, but it works just as well as a background filler. Try quilting it around blocks, appliqué, or even quilted motifs. With paisleys, changing the direction of the design is key to creating a nice overall texture.

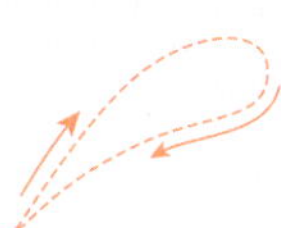

1. Start by quilting a line that goes out and curves back to where you started. It is almost like a teardrop shape. It should be rounded at one end and come to a point at the other.

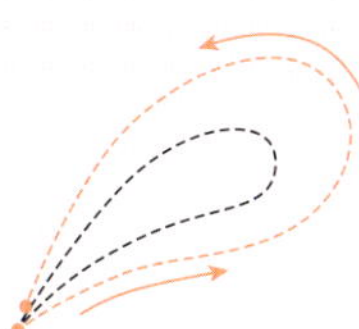

2. Echo around the paisley, going around the curved end and coming back to the pointed end.

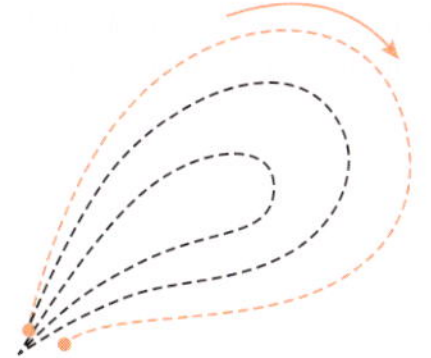

3. Echo a third time. In fact, you can echo the paisley as many times as you would like. The echo lines don't have to perfectly touch at the points, just get them as close as you can.

Note

Your paisleys may be curved like mine, or they may be straighter. Either way is perfect!

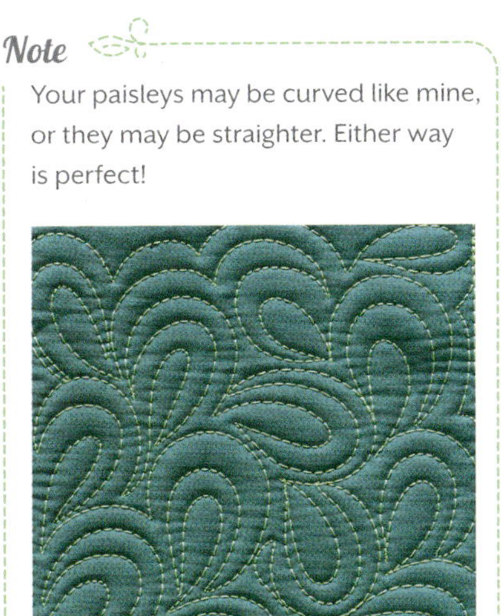

Continued on next page

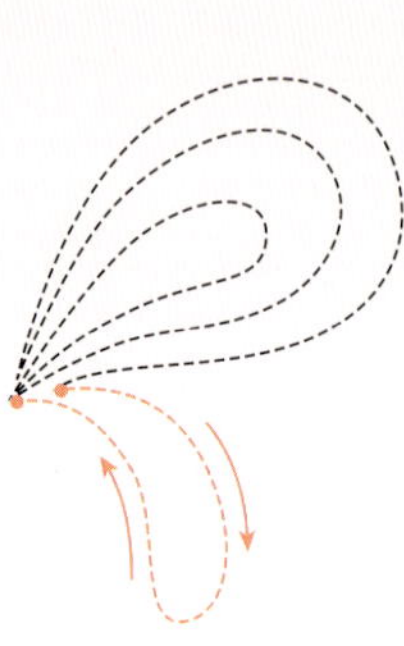

4. Quilt another teardrop shape that extends from the pointed end of the first paisley.

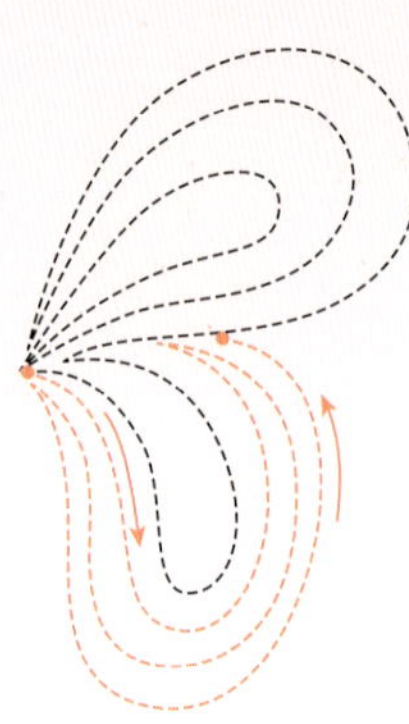

5. Echo the paisley 2 or 3 times.

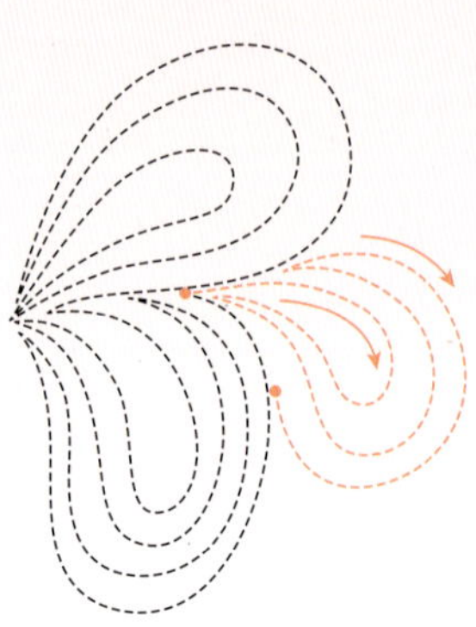

6. Quilt another paisley with the echo lines.

Note 

Notice that you can't always get back to the pointed end of the paisley. That's completely fine. Just get as close as you can and then change direction and echo again.

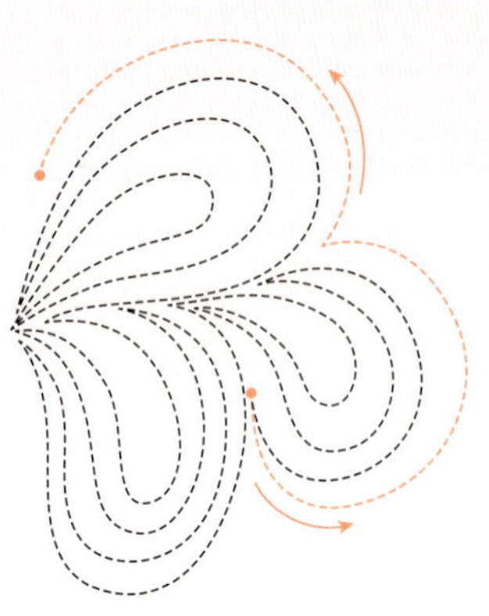

7. If needed, echo around a previously quilted paisley.

Echoing around other paisleys will help you maneuver around the area.

Fill in the area by quilting paisleys and echo lines.

Tips

Things to Consider When Quilting the Paisley Meander

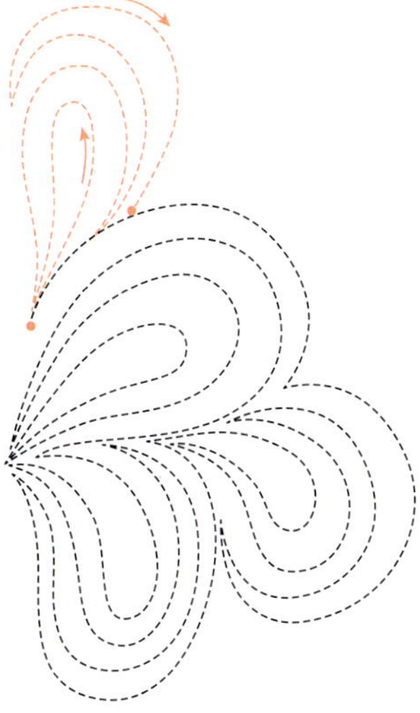

When quilting in the corners and other irregularly shaped areas, be sure to fill the area as much as possible, even if you aren't able to echo around the whole paisley.

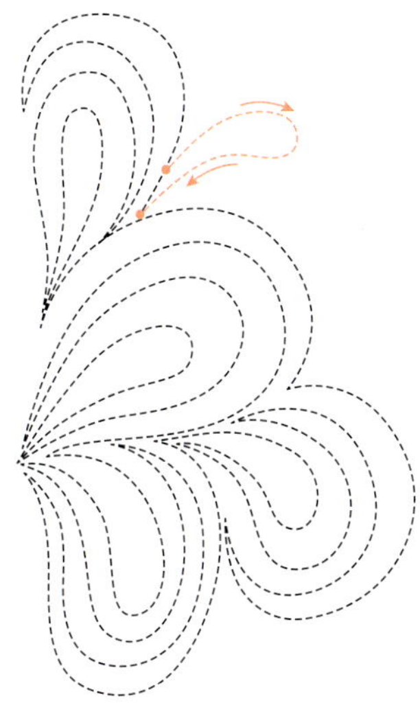

Don't be afraid to extend the first part of the paisley out from the rest of the quilting. Doing that will leave enough space for the echo lines.

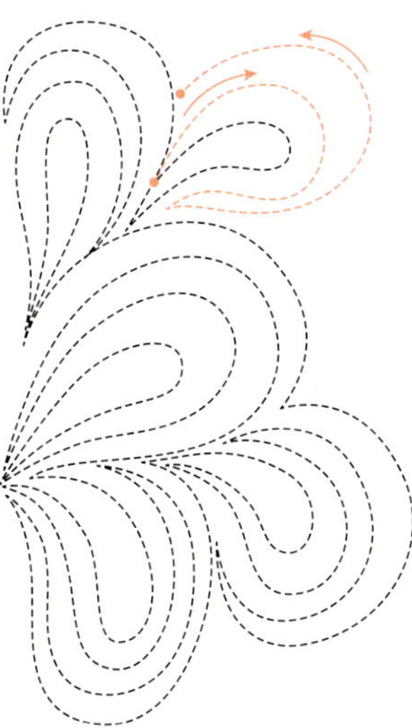

If you get stuck, just quilt your way out. Whether you quilt along another line or squeeze out between lines, it will look fine. I promise, when the whole quilt is finished, you won't even notice it.

There might be times when you find yourself stuck between two paisleys, without room to add another one. If that happens, echo quilt until you fill in the area and move to where you have room to add the next paisley.

Tip continued on next page

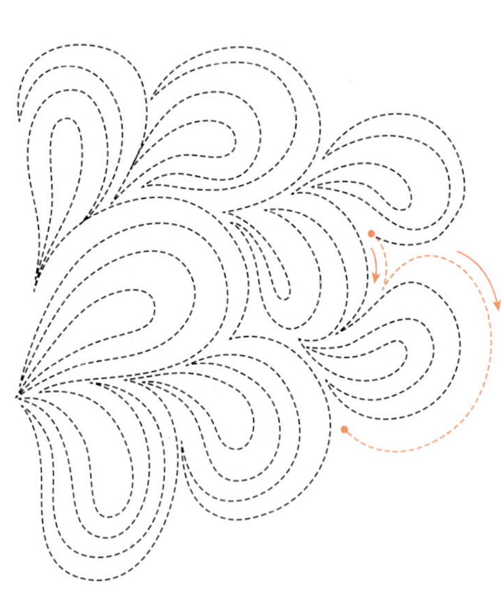

Filling in the space as consistently as possible is probably the most difficult part of any quilting design. A good rule of thumb is that as long as a gap is smaller than the individual design, it won't be noticeable.

Since this gap is smaller than the paisley, I am fine with just leaving it alone. Of course, you could fill it in with more echoes if you prefer.

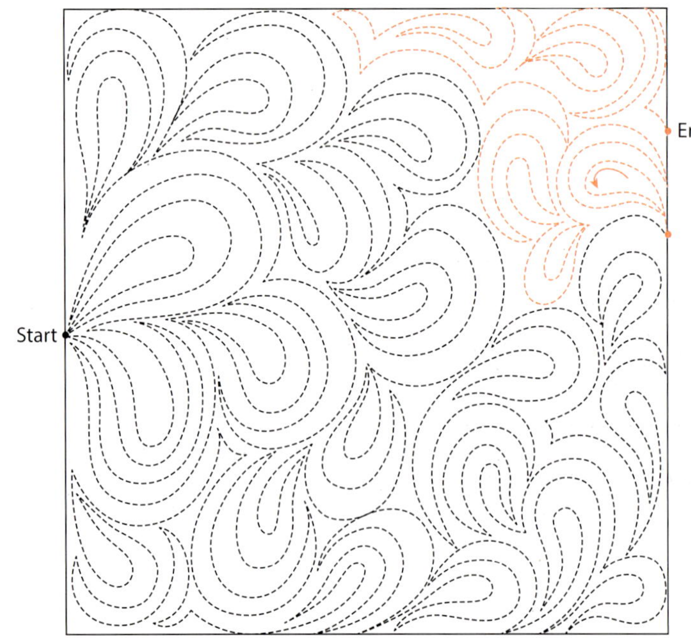

Fill in the area by quilting paisleys and echo lines.

CIRCLE 1

This design starts in the middle of the circle, which means it takes a bit longer to quilt it. But I think the effort is well worth it!

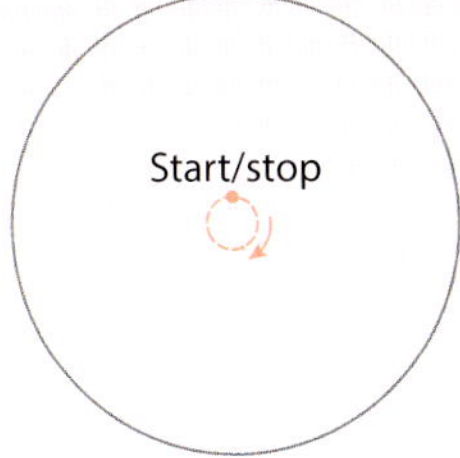

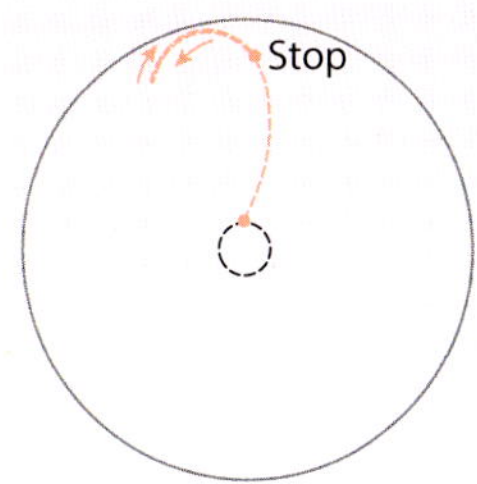

1. Starting slightly above the center of the circle, quilt a small circle. I usually aim for about 1″ wide.

2. Quilt a line with a smoothly rounded top, stopping when the curve starts to head back down. Backtrack along the curve until you are just over the rounded top.

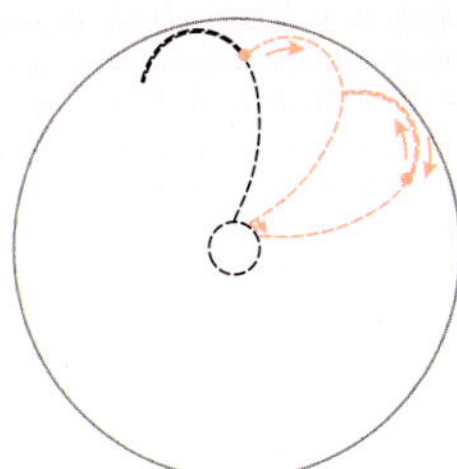

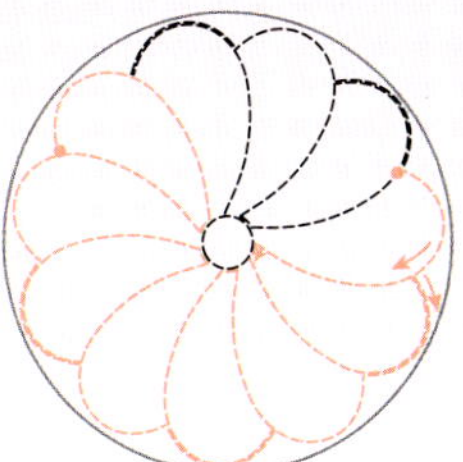

3. Quilt the curved end of the next petal, heading down toward the center circle. Travel along the center circle just a little; then quilt another petal as you did in Step 2.

4. Continue until you have filled the entire circle with petals.

Variation

No matter what you are quilting, echoing is a quick and easy way to spice things up. The same is true with this design! Echoing around the outside of the petals not only adds to this design's floral look, but it also helps fill in larger circles.

SQUARE 1

This design is all about the echoing, making it a really forgiving design. When in doubt, just add more echo lines. The dense quilting is perfect for drawing your eyes to the blocks you want to highlight. It doesn't matter if you are quilting larger or smaller blocks; this design works well in both.

1. Starting from any corner of the block, quilt an elongated swirl that ends toward the center of the block. Echo back to the starting point. I tend to make my swirls look like a question mark.

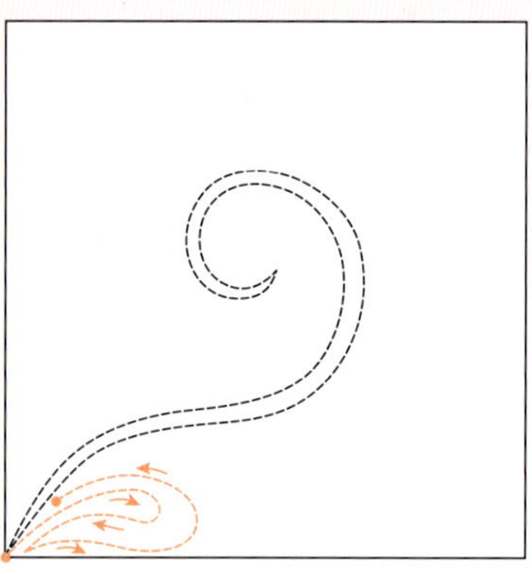

2. At the bottom of the swirl, quilt a paisley shape and echo around it once or twice.

Tip

To make the paisley petals fit the area, quilt them so that they are "merging" into the swirl.

3. Continue working your way around the swirl, quilting paisleys and echoing until you get to the center of the swirl.

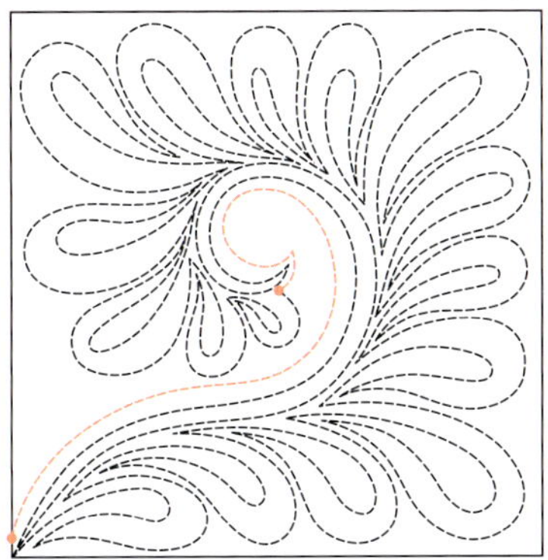

4. Echo along the swirl, returning close to the starting point. This allows you to quickly and easily move on to the next block.

Tip

Remember, the answer is almost always echoing. If the design doesn't fill the area as much as you want or if you find yourself stuck, just echo around the petals.

Variation

Quilt the design in smaller blocks, rotating the placement, to create a repetitive look.

Try quilting the pattern in a set of adjacent blocks.

STRAIGHT LINE QUILTING

GEOMETRIC ALLOVER

This boxy quilting design is great for beginners. You can make the shapes bigger or smaller, depending on how dense you want the quilting to be. Just channel your inner square (or rectangle) and let loose. I am going to show you an example of this design, but it is only to give you an idea of how to quilt it. There is no right or wrong way to make the shapes. Just let the design flow!

1. Starting from the edge of the quilt or a block, quilt a square.

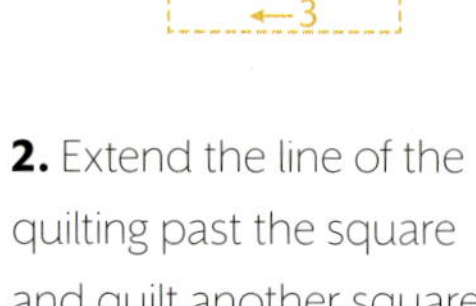

2. Extend the line of the quilting past the square and quilt another square.

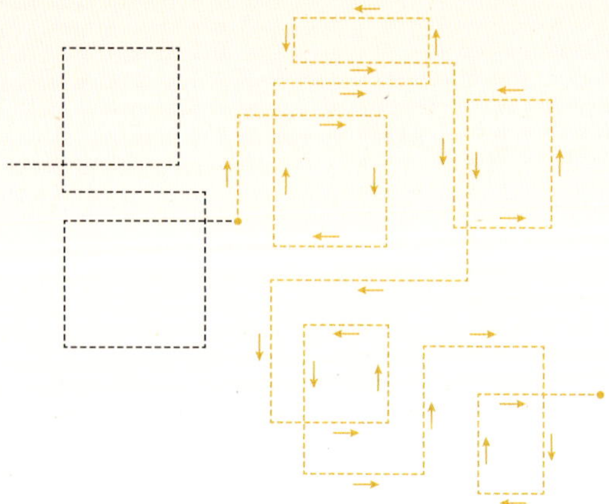

3. Continue quilting squares or rectangles, filling in the whole area.

Tip

Have a plan. Working from left to right, or up and down, can help you fill in spaces without getting trapped in a corner.

OFFSET SQUARES

Want a more geometric look for your quilts? This design is for you! It's best for larger areas of negative space and is easy to quilt. you can make the offset squares as small or as large as you want.

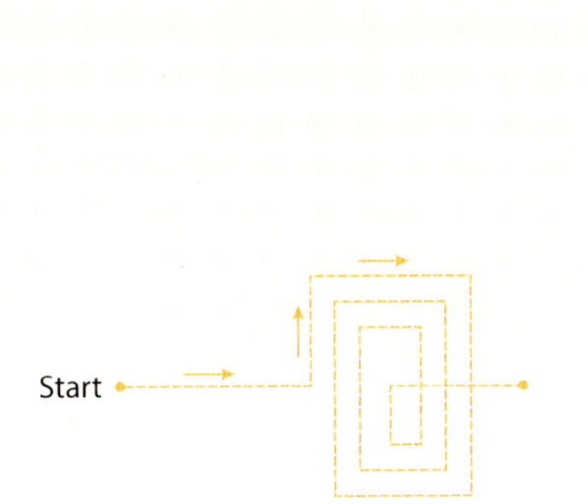

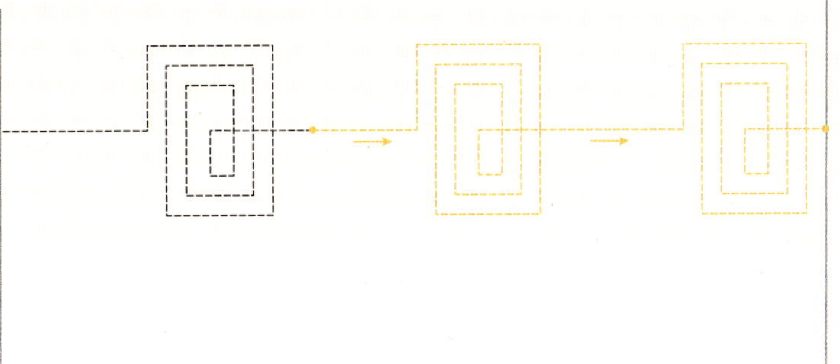

Before starting, let's talk about the square we will be using. Starting from one side, quilt the outside of a box and keep echoing inside until you get to the center. From the center, go across the previously quilted lines so that you'll be in position to quilt the next square.

Now let's learn how to offset the squares and give them a neat, tailored-to-fit look.

1. Working your way across the quilting area, quilt the squares with spaces in between. Try to keep these spaces roughly the same size as the outermost square.

Note

Don't measure the boxes beforehand; just eyeball it! Even if they aren't all the same size, the squares will still look great!

Continued on next page

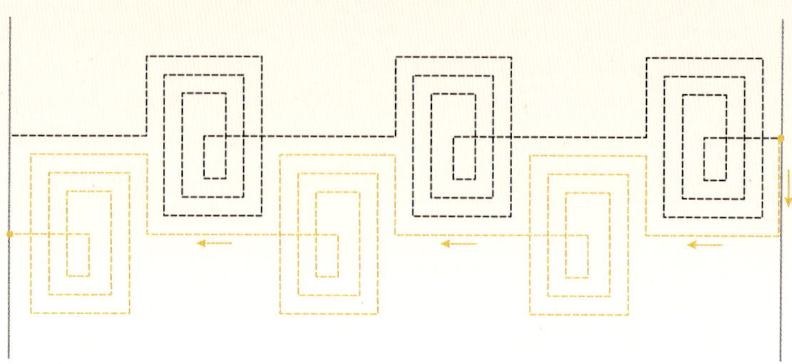

2. Travel down the edge of the quilting area until you are about ½″ below the bottom of the last square. Work back across the quilting area, offsetting this row of squares to fit into the spaces you left as you quilted the previous row.

3. Continue until the whole area is filled.

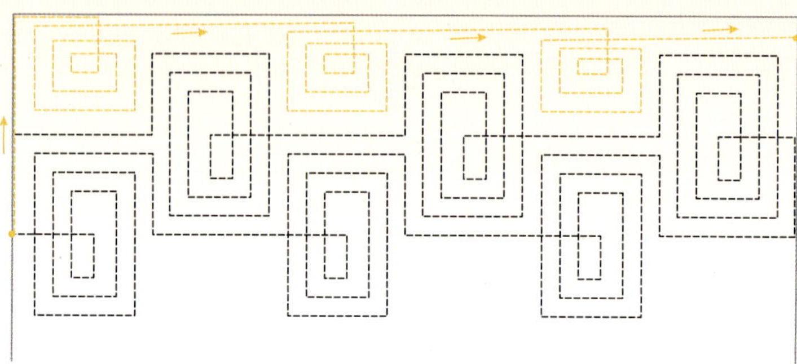

4. When quilting the top and bottom of the quilting area, quilt smaller blocks to fill in the spaces.

More Thoughts ...

If you can't get the spacing quite right, just go with the wonky look.

Don't worry about the ruler! The lines are short enough that you can get them straight without one.

MERGED LINES

Who knew that echoing straight lines would look so interesting? This design adds a simple but groovy look to your quilt. This one works spectacularly in all sizes of negative space or as an allover design. You may be tempted to get out the ruler, but I don't think you will need it. I quilt this design without a ruler, and even though it isn't perfect, the techno vibe makes the "wires" looks great!

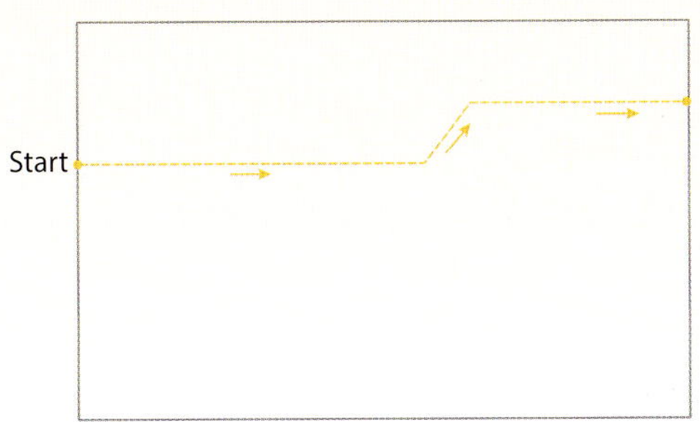

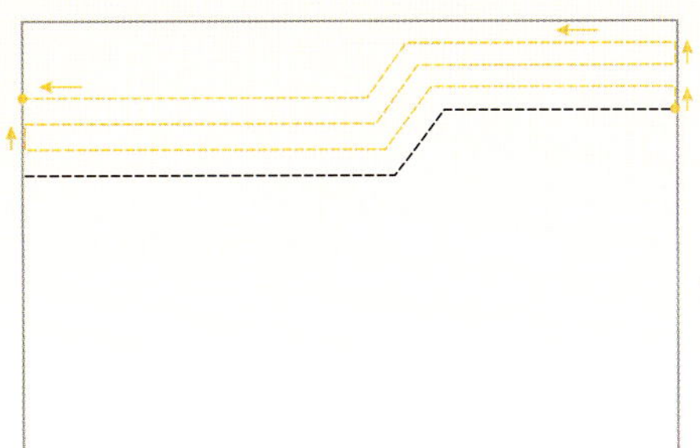

1. Start a few inches from the top of the quilting area and quilt a horizontal line toward the opposite side. At a random point, quilt a diagonal line at about 45° and then continue quilting horizontally until you reach the other side.

2. Before quilting the rest of the quilting area, fill in above the line, by echoing the first line. For this design, I normally echo about ½˝ apart.

Note

The first line of this design starts below the top of the quilting area, so you have enough space.

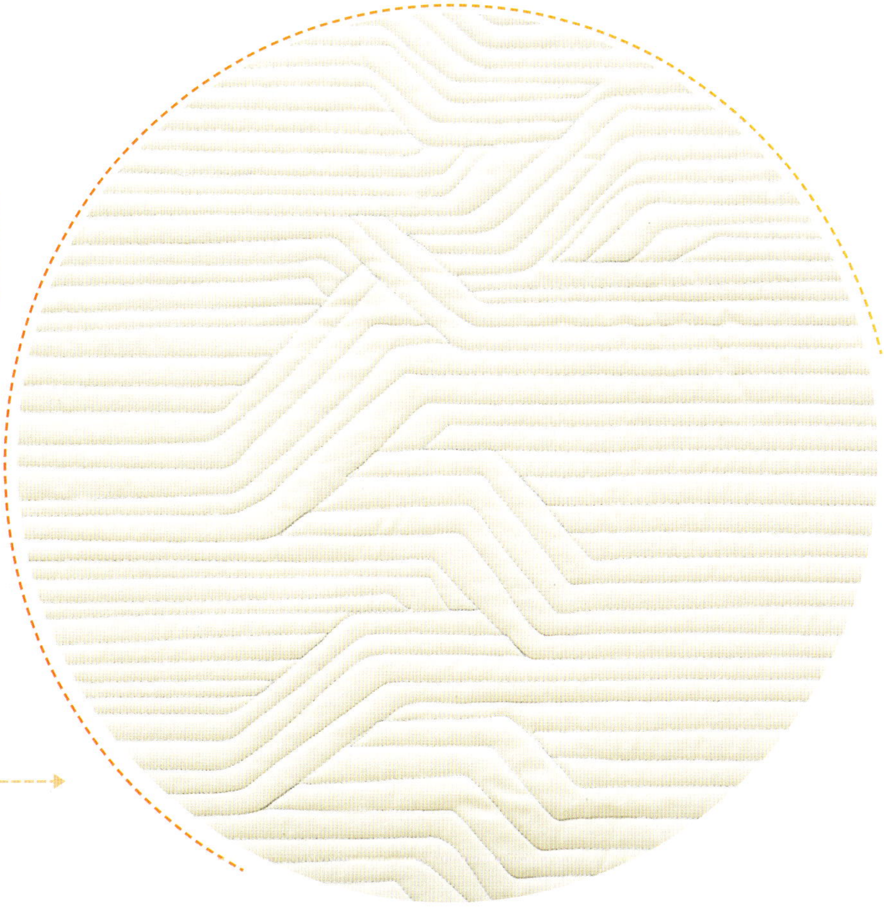

Continued on next page

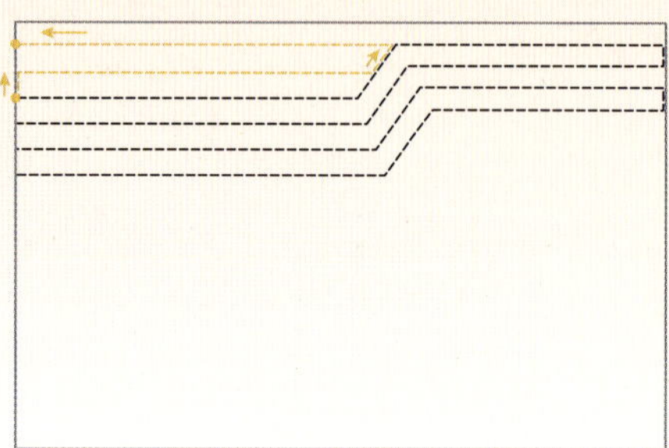

3. You can also echo only a portion of the line. For instance, instead of echoing the diagonal portion of the line, echo just the horizontal part. Travel along the previously quilted diagonal line and return to the edge.

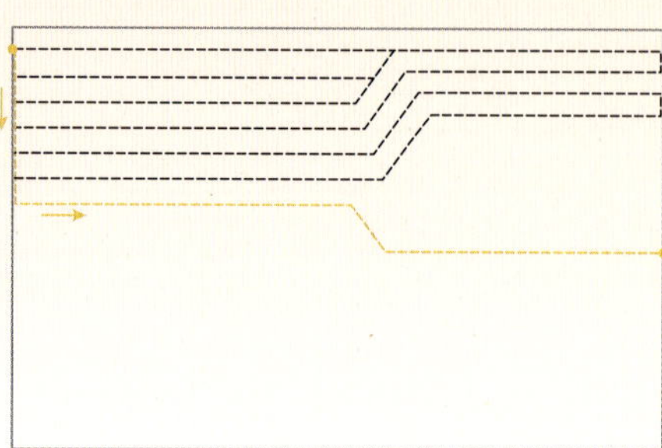

4. Once the top of the area is filled, it's time to quilt the line that will set off the next portion. Travel along the edge so that you are about ½″ below the first line, and quilt another horizontal line, randomly going down at an angle and then continuing horizontally until you reach the edge.

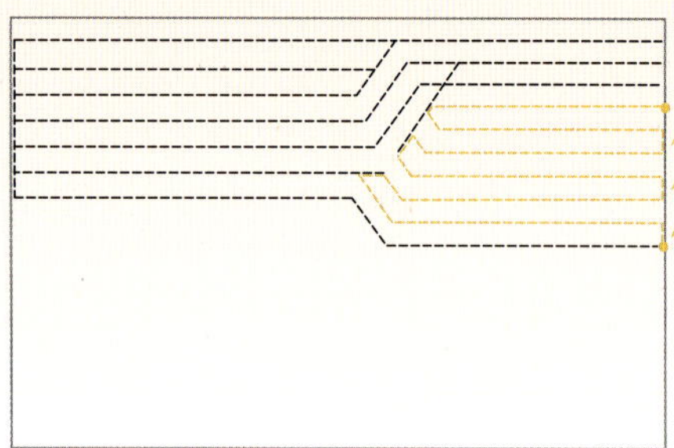

5. Fill in the area between the 2 lines by echoing. Be sure to travel along the edge of the quilting area or previously quilted lines, as shown.

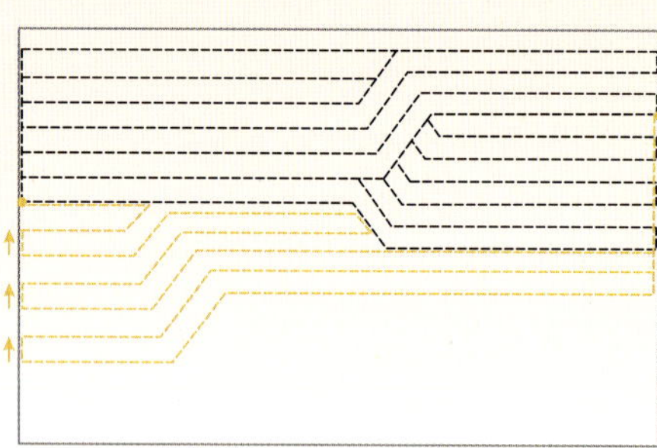

6. After you have filled in the area, travel along the edge of the quilting area and repeat the technique in Steps 1–5.

7. Continue until the quilting area is completely filled.

Variations

This design is so cool exactly as it is, but if you want something a little different, try quilting an easy variation. Instead of echoing the lines that set off this design, try filling the space with a free-motion quilting design, such as swirls.

Create a variation of this design by leaving out some of the echoed lines and quilting a free-motion quilting design, such as swirls.

I am always looking for ways to make designs look fresh—designs that look a little different from anything I've quilted before. If you want to switch things up as well, you can vary the spacing between the lines or place some pebbles between the lines. The only limit is your imagination!

JUMBLED LINES

I like quilting designs that incorporate straight lines; what I don't like is quilting long straight lines over and over again. This design helps keep me from getting bored! alternating the direction of the lines adds a more complex look and is actually easy. No marking involved!

When quilting this design, you are basically dividing up the quilting areas into smaller squares and filling them in.

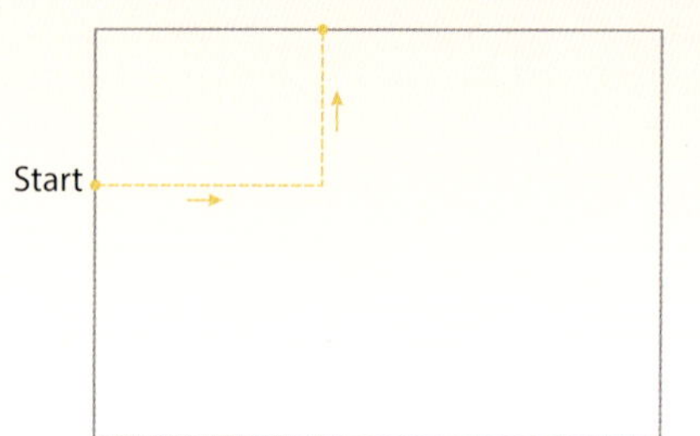

1. Starting from the side of the quilting area, quilt 2 sides of a rectangle.

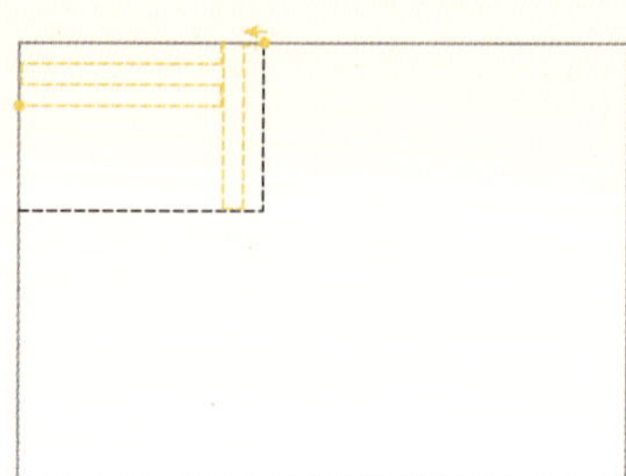

2. Begin filling in the rectangle, alternating between horizontal and vertical lines. Travel along the previously quilted lines.

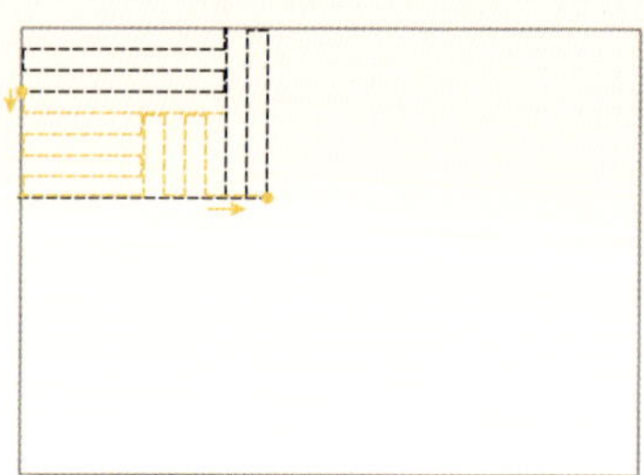

3. Continue until the section is filled. End so that you are at a corner of the rectangle.

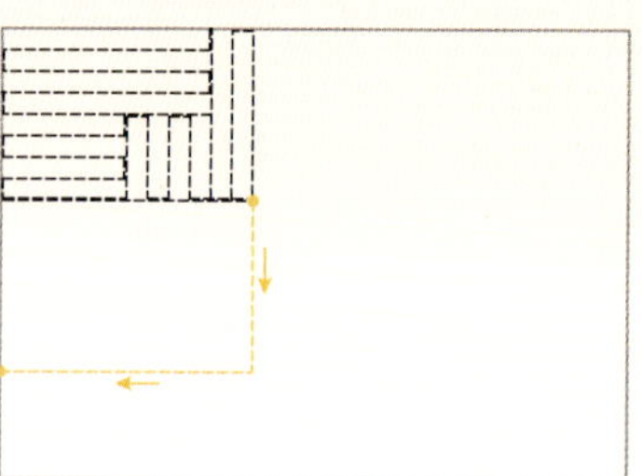

4. Quilt the sides of another rectangle that touches the first one that you quilted.

Tip

If you get stuck, no worries! Just travel along a line of quilting to get where you need to be.

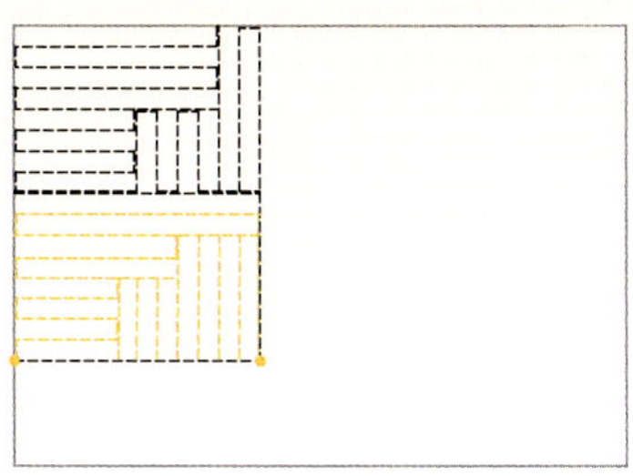

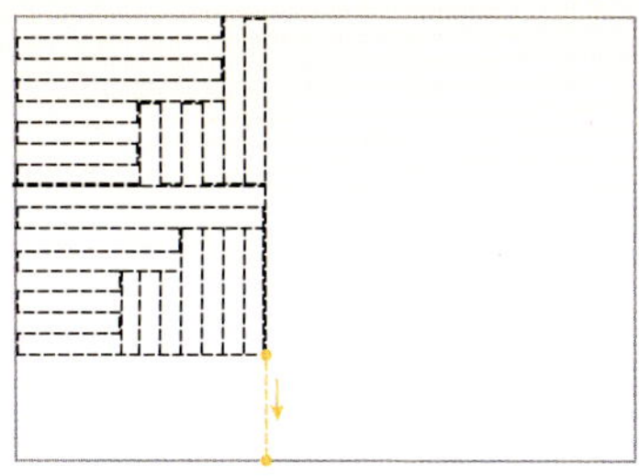

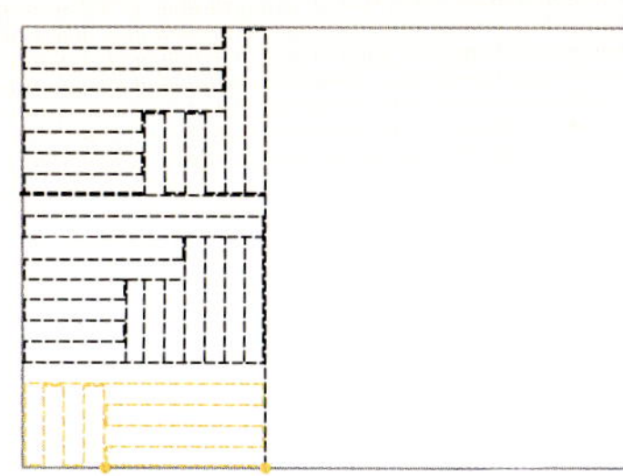

5. Fill in the rectangle by alternating between horizontal and vertical lines, as you did in Step 2.

6. When you get to the bottom of the quilting area, you may need to quilt only one line to create the next section.

Variations

To put a fun twist on this design, try combining straight and wavy lines. Use one type of line for the vertical lines and the other for the horizontal lines.

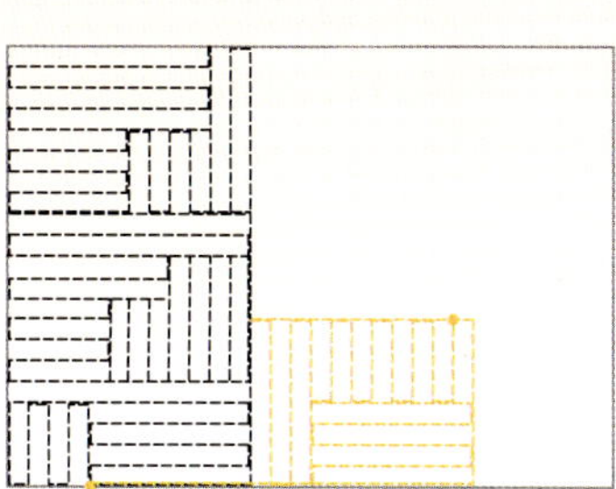

7. Travel along the edge of the quilting area; quilt another rectangle and fill in with lines.

8. Continue until the quilting area is completely filled.

Tips

Quilting Straight Lines

- If using a longarm quilting machine, you may want to use a ruler. But I find that if I am quilting shorter lines, I can usually freehand it.
- Using a matching color of thread will help cover any bumps and wobbles.
- Above all, don't stress. Tensing up won't help you at all!

CIRCLE 1

Inspiration for quilting designs can come from anywhere! This particular design is reminiscent of the traditional churn dash quilt block and is quick and easy to quilt!

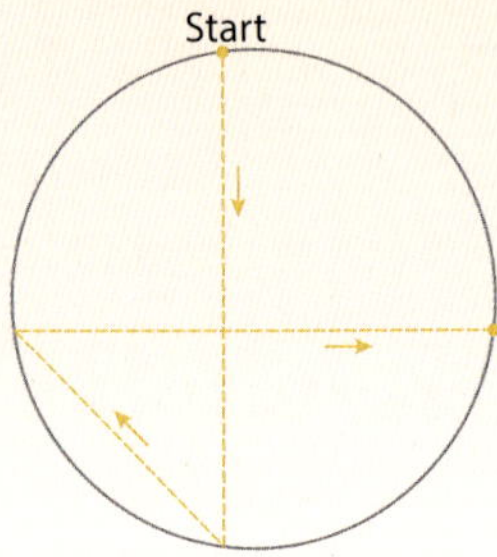

1. Quilt a straight line slightly left of center, from the top to the bottom of the circle. Continue quilting a diagonal line to the left side of the circle, and horizontally to the right side.

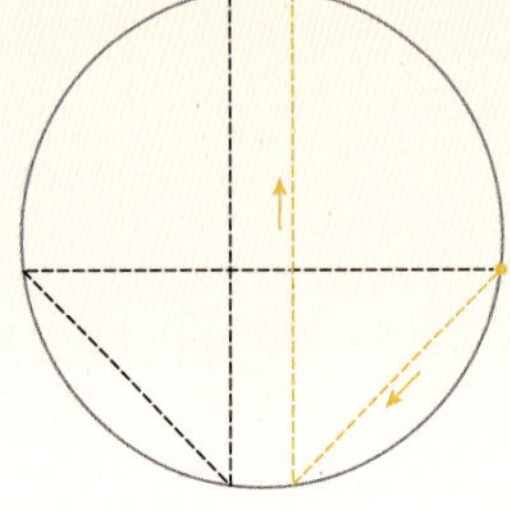

2. Quilt a diagonal line to the bottom of the circle and then straight up to the top of the circle.

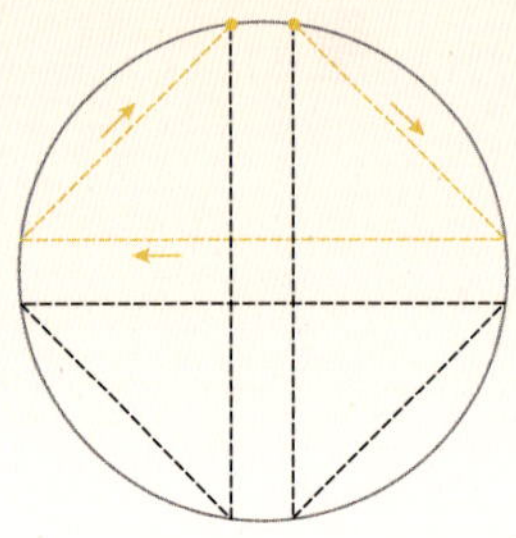

3. Complete the design as shown for the top half.

Note

Even though I demonstrate this design in a circle, you could use it for different shapes, such as a rectangle.

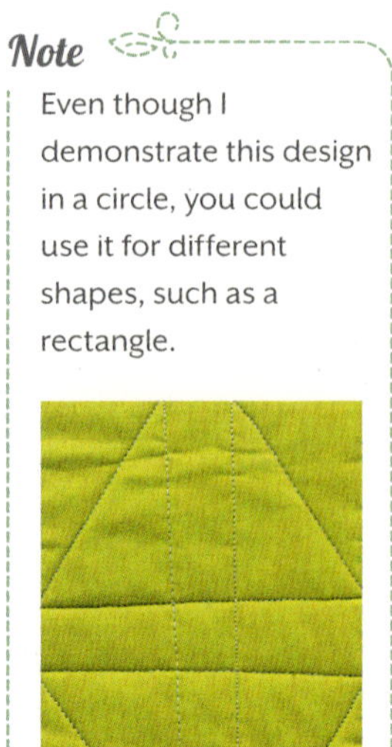

Variations

You might want to add a little bit of "curve" to this quilting design. Replace the straight diagonal lines with curves, creating a subtle repetition with the circular block shape.

Swap the straight diagonal lines with curves that repeat the block shape and create a different look.

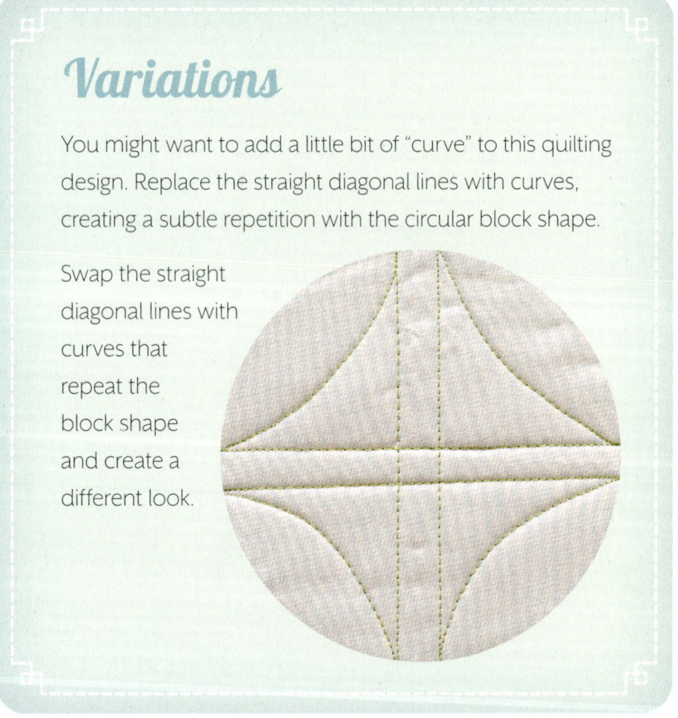

SQUARE 1

This design will give your square quilt blocks a groovy look using only straight lines. it starts from outside the block and ends in the center, which means you'll need to start each block separately. While that is normally against my get-it-done-quickly quilting philosophy, this design is worth the extra effort.

Tip

This design is also handy for quilting rectangles.

Continued on next page

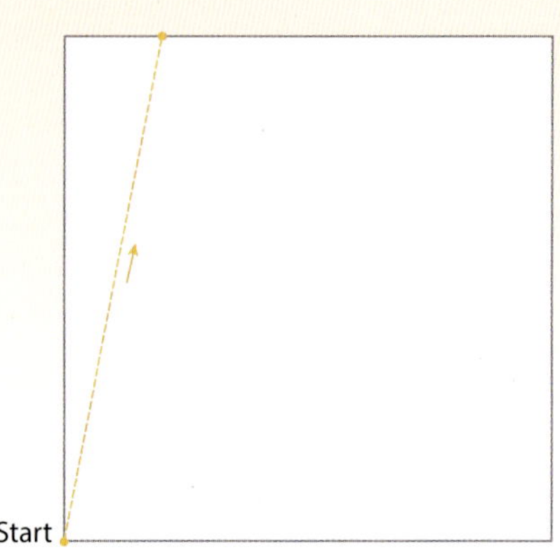

1. Starting from a corner, quilt a straight line ending about 1˝ from the next corner.

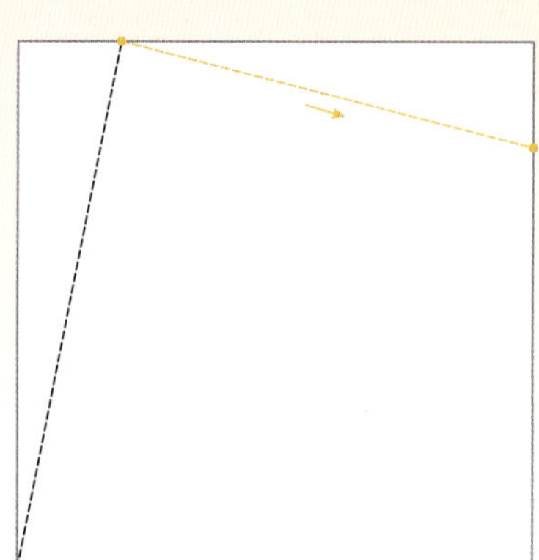

2. Quilt another straight line ending about 1˝ from the next corner.

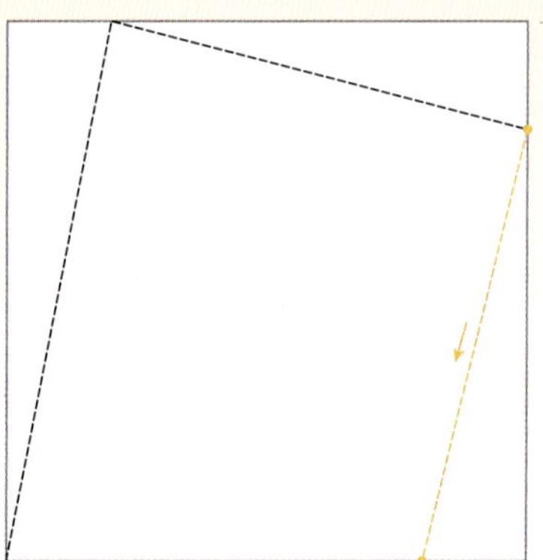

3. Repeat Step 2 to add a third line.

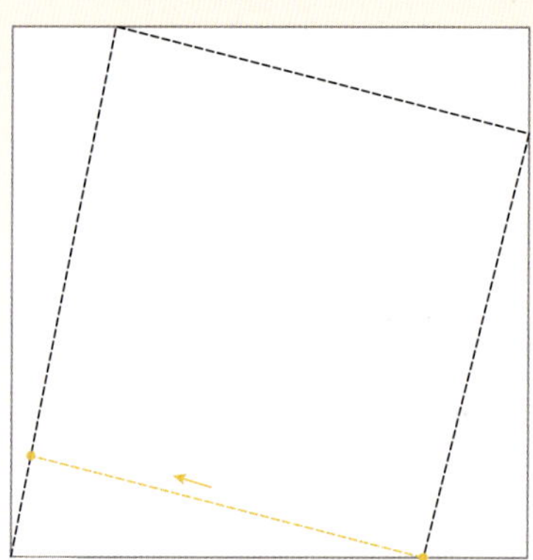

4. Quilt the fourth line just as you did the others, ending on the first line you quilted about 1˝ from the corner.

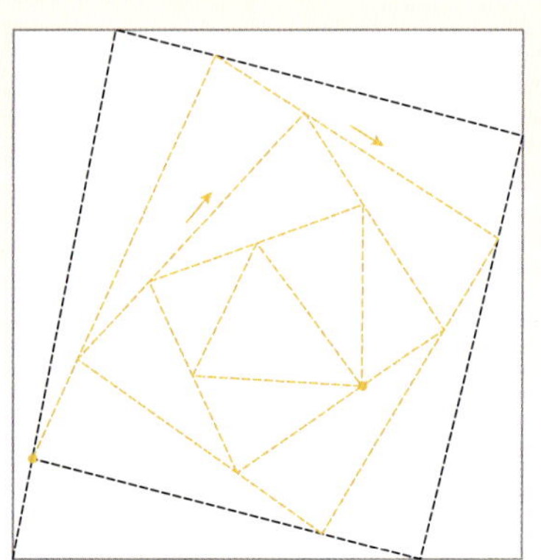

5. Repeat Steps 1–4, quilting your way into the center of the square.

Variations

For larger squares or for denser quilting, you can quilt the lines closer together. Simply move the endpoint closer to the corner, say ¼″ or ½″ from the corner instead of 1″.

Moving the lines closer together will help fill in larger quilt blocks better.

If straight lines aren't your cup of tea, try wavy lines instead.

Trade straight lines for wavy lines for a fun variation.

TRIANGLE 1

Sometimes you will come across a quilt block that could use a little more quilting than normal. If you just so happen to face one of these blocks, this design is for you. it's especially appealing when used in larger triangles, although you could use it for smaller triangles too.

> ***Tip***
> Using a thread color that blends with the fabric helps keep your stitches looking neat and tidy when traveling.

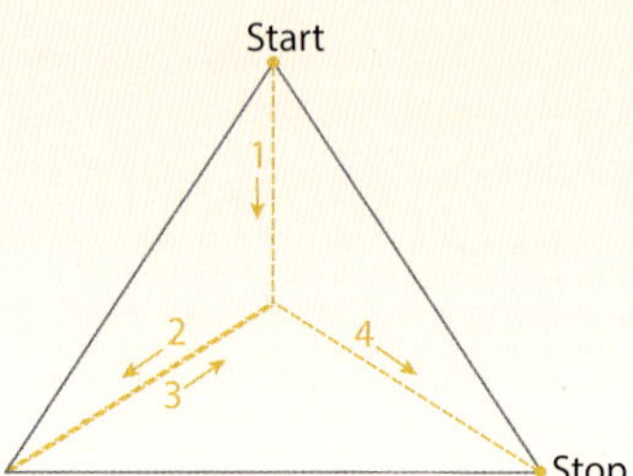

1. From one point of the triangle, quilt a straight line to the center. Quilt a diagonal line to the next point of the triangle and immediately travel back to the center. Quilt a diagonal line down to the third point. You've now formed three inner triangles.

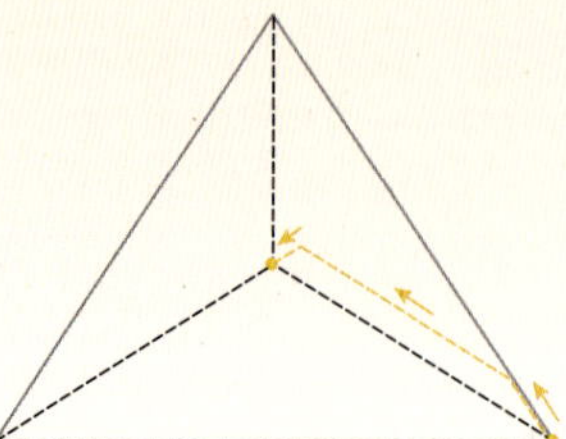

2. Travel along the edge of the triangle ¼˝. Echo one side of an inner triangle, then pivot and quilt a short line to the exact center.

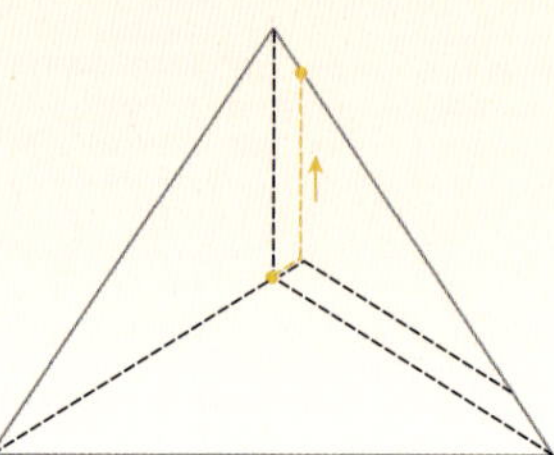

3. From the center, travel back along the short line. Echo along the other side of the inner triangle.

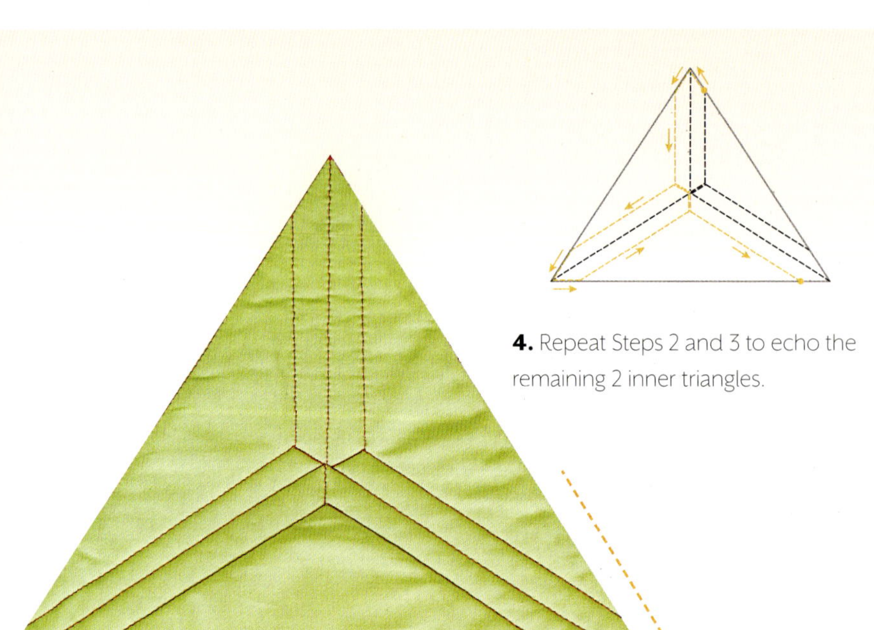

4. Repeat Steps 2 and 3 to echo the remaining 2 inner triangles.

> ***Variation***
> The convenient thing about this quilting design is that the three inner triangles leave space for you to add a meandering design, such as swirls.

TRIANGLE 2

I love using quilting to change the look of a block. This basic design turns a triangle into a hexagon. it can change the whole look of the quilt with just a couple of lines. to get a symmetrical design, use it in equilateral triangles.

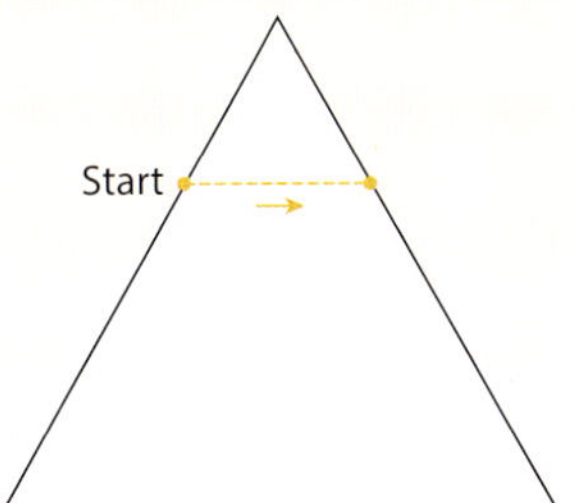

1. Starting about a third of the way down from a corner, quilt a straight line across to the same point on the other side.

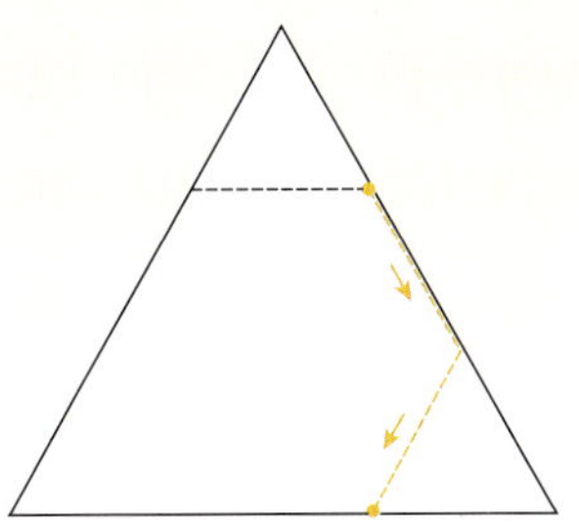

2. Travel along the edge until you are the same distance away from the next corner. Repeat Step 1.

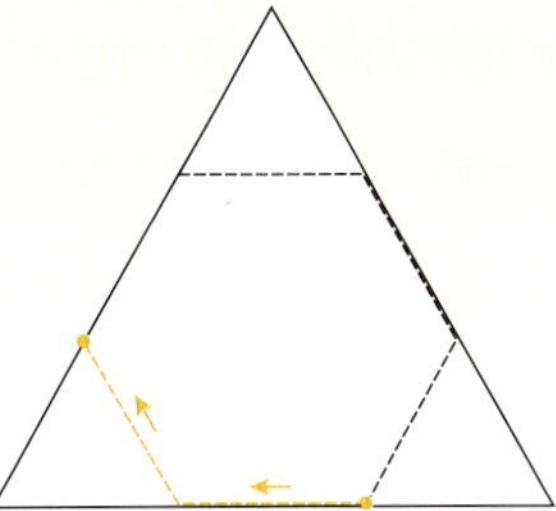

3. Repeat Step 2 with the last corner.

4. Fill in the hexagon shape with the design of your choice.

Variations

You can use any design to fill in the hexagon. In this variation, I used a different hexagon design. If your block is large enough, you can fill in the triangles as well.

Use any hexagon design as a filler.

DIAMOND 1

I always say that echoing is your friend! Echoing the sides of a quilt block is an easy way to make the shape of the block stand out, and this design is a perfect example. Simply echoing opposite edges of the block results in a lattice-like pattern that is perfect for all kinds of quilts.

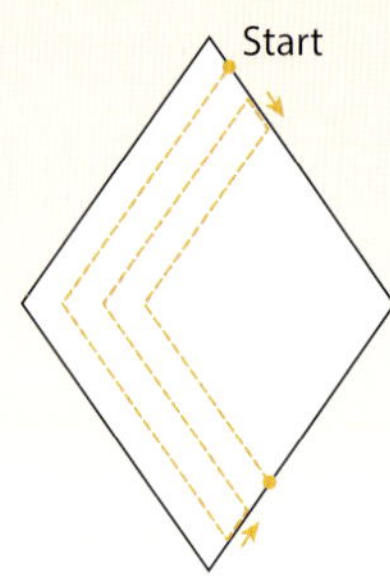

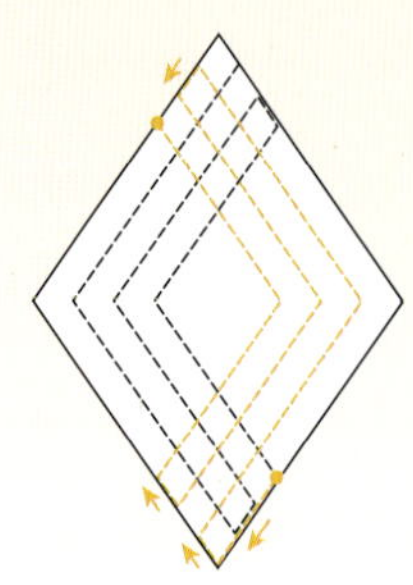

1. Start about ¼″ from the top corner and echo along the left side of the block. Travel along the edge and echo 2 more times.

2. Travel back along the side of the block so that you are about ¼″ on the other side of the starting corner. Repeat Step 1 by echoing the opposite side of the block.

Note

I tend to quilt lines in groups of three, but of course you could do more or less, depending on what works for you.

Variations

You can add a little extra flourish by quilting a design in the center before finishing the last line.

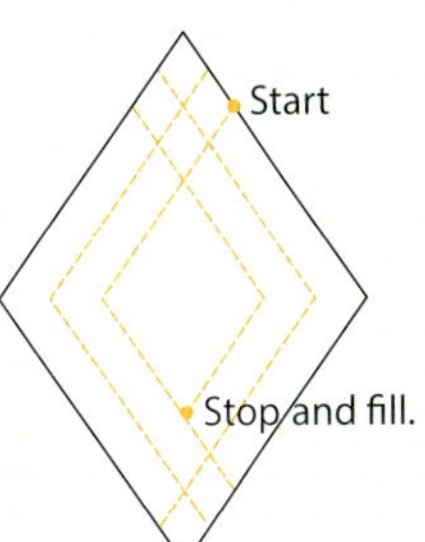

When quilting the last echo line, stop when it touches the first echo line. Fill in square, return to the point, and finish the last line.

Even though I have this design in the diamond section, I really like to use it in outside blocks as well.

Diamond pattern around the points of a star

Of course, this works for any block with sides.

Diamond 1 in a half-square triangle

Diamond 1 in a triangle

HEXAGON 1

This is a simple design that gives the block an elegant look, almost like a jewel. It's a design that I like to use when I want to show off the fabric in the block, or if I want light quilting for any reason.

Check out how eye-catching this design is when used in multiple blocks.

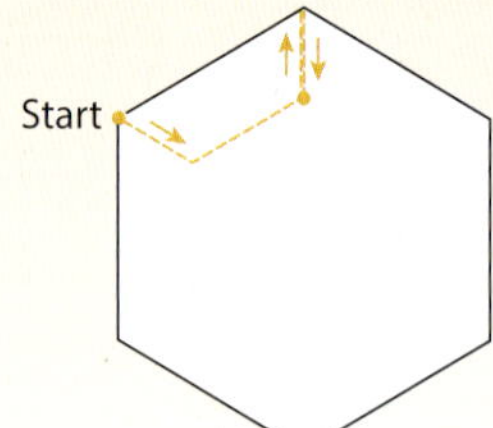

1. From any corner, quilt a 2˝ diagonal line. Turn and echo the side of the block, stopping about 2˝ away from the next corner. Quilt a line up to the corner, then travel back to the last point.

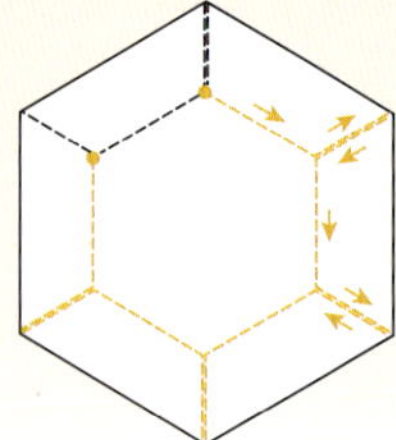

2. Work your way around the block, echoing each side until you end up about 2˝ from the starting corner.

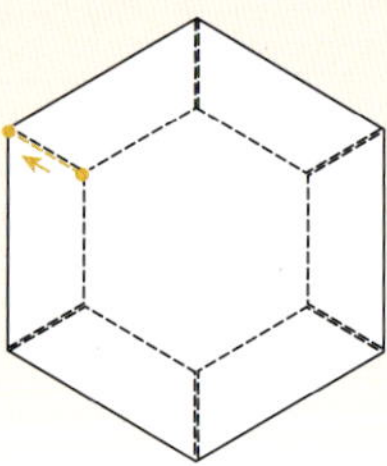

3. Work your way around the block, echoing each side until you end up about 2˝ from the starting corner.

Variations

Before you stitch Step 3, quilt the inner hexagon with a different design.

Add filler quilting to the inner hexagon.

If you don't like traveling along previously stitched lines, leave out every other travel line. You still have an interesting design with half the work.

Omit every other short line between the inner hexagon and the edge of the block.

If you really want to show off your quilting skills, you can quilt it again.

Stitch another hexagon inside the first.

BORDER: TRIANGLES

Give your quilt borders a more geometric, jagged design by quilting triangles along one edge of the quilt. This strong graphic design works best in medium-sized borders. If quilting larger borders, consider throwing in a curvier free-motion quilting design as a filler, to create balance and contrast!

Before starting, decide how wide you want the base of the triangles. using a marking pen, such as a water-soluble marker, make small marks to divide into sections. Or, look for a visual reference on the quilt, such as repeating quilt blocks.

Tip

When quilting diagonal lines on my longarm, I almost always use a ruler. I can't seem to get diagonals nice and smooth without it! If you are quilting this on your sewing machine, try positioning the quilt so you are moving the quilt back and forth.

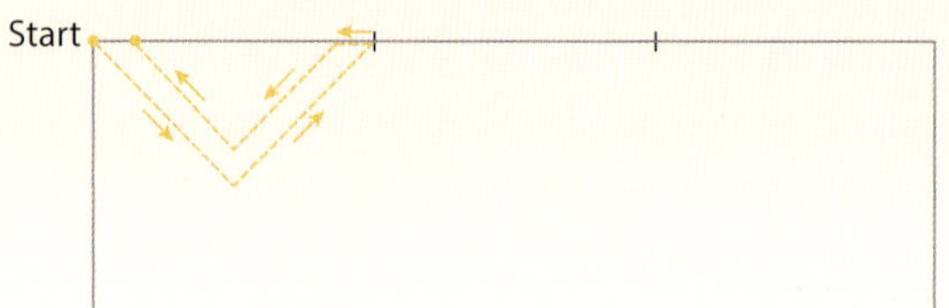

1. Starting from a corner of the border, quilt a diagonal line (roughly 45°) until you are approximately halfway across the border. Quilt diagonally in the opposite direction until you reach a marked point on the top of the border.

Travel along the top of the border about ½˝ and echo the inside of the triangle you just quilted.

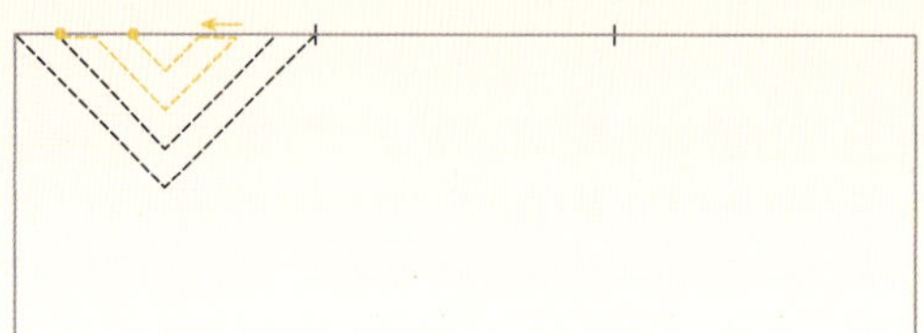

2. Continue traveling and echoing the inside of the triangle until it is filled.

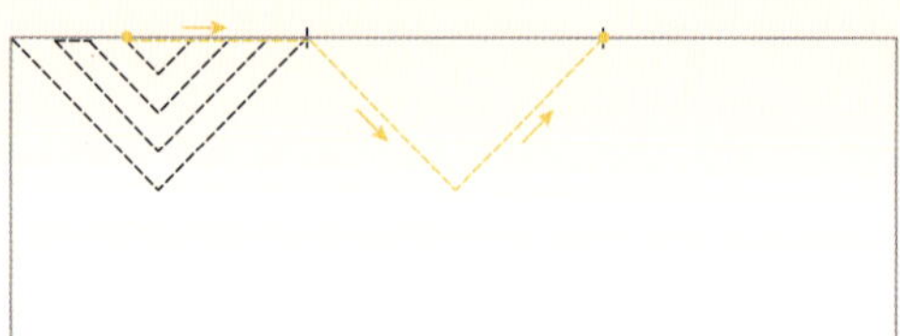

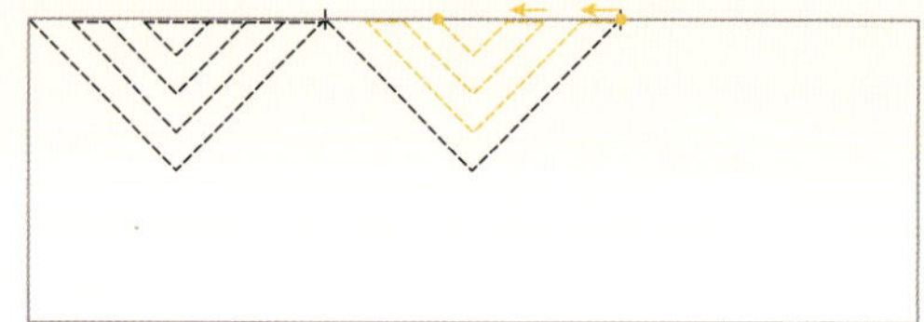

3. Travel along the top of the border until you reach the edge of the first triangle and repeat the technique in Steps 1 and 2 to continue the border.

CORNER OPTIONS

Since most borders wrap around the quilt, you may find that you need to adjust the design so that it fits. You can do this a couple of different ways:

Instead of placing a triangle at the corner, quilt 3 sides of a square.

Quilt the triangles so the end is on the corner.

Variations

If you need the triangles design to have a bit more oomph, try varying the spacing or angles of the triangle. Using a filler design as background for this border will really help the triangles stand out!

BORDER: DOT TO DOT

I couldn't write a section of border designs without having one that uses straight lines! This design uses points on the border to create a complex-looking design. it looks a lot harder than it is, trust me. All you have to do is mark and connect the dots!

Just as you did with the arches quilting design, you will need to do a bit of marking. Divide the border into equal sections using tick marks. For this design, I usually divide it into 2″ or 3″ sections.

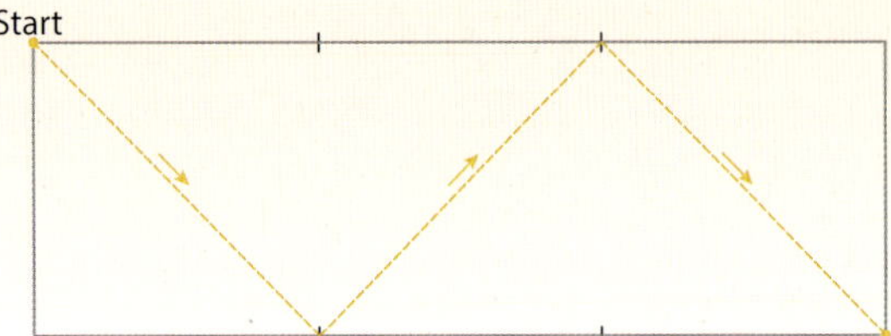

1. Starting from one corner of the border, quilt a diagonal line to the next mark on the bottom edge, and the back up to the next mark. Repeat until you get to the edge of the border.

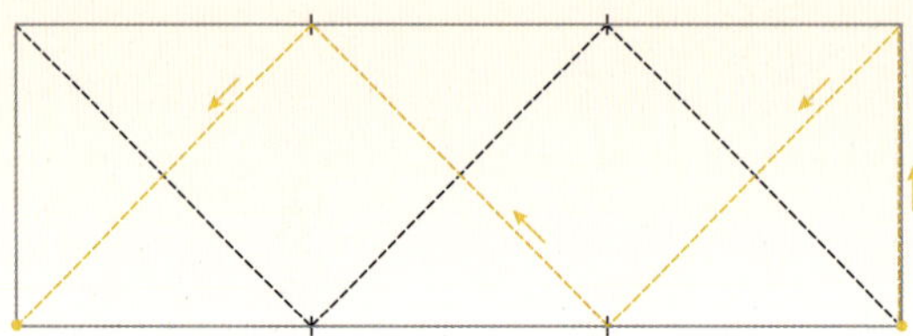

2. Travel along the edge of the border to the top corner, and quilt back to the other side of the border. You will have what looks like a row of X's.

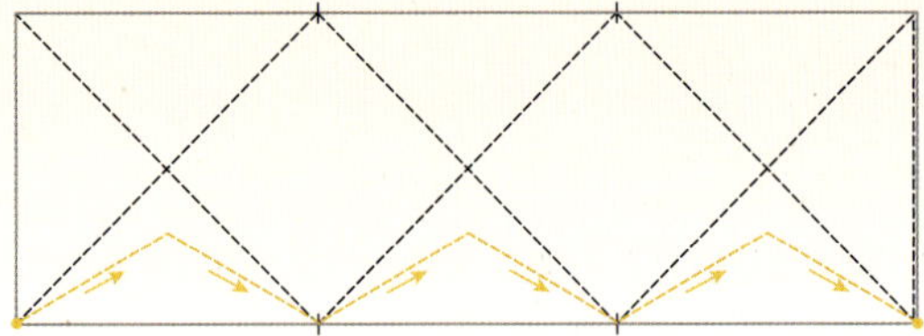

3. Now we are going to fill in the bottom of the X's. Quilt a line diagonally until you are about ½″ from the center of the X, then quilt diagonally to the next mark. Repeat until you have worked your way across the border.

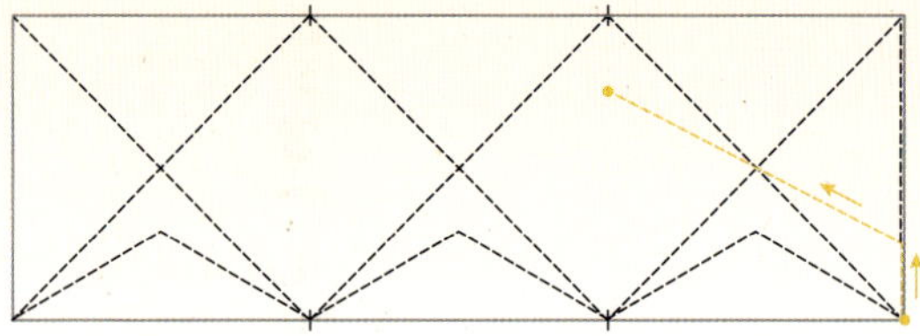

4. Travel along the edge of the border about ½″ and quilt a diagonal line that crosses through the center of the first X, stopping ½″ from the mark at the top of the border.

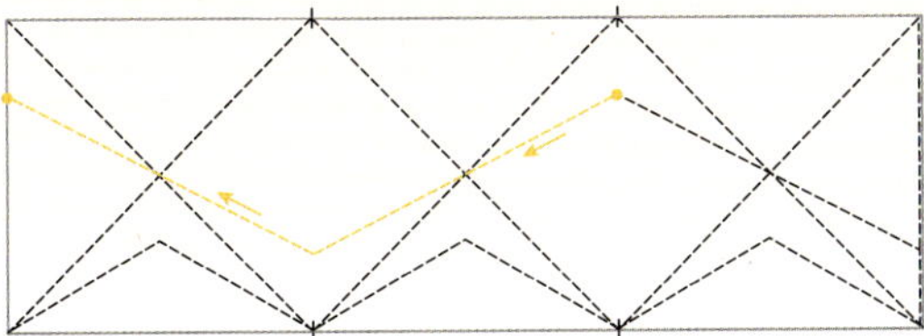

5. Work your way across the border, quilting diagonal lines that cross at the X's.

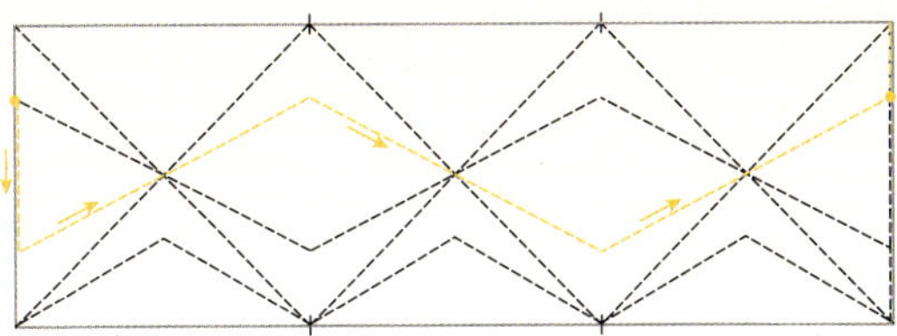

6. Travel down the side of the border until you are about ½″ from the bottom corner of the border; repeat Step 5. Continue until you reach the opposite side of the border.

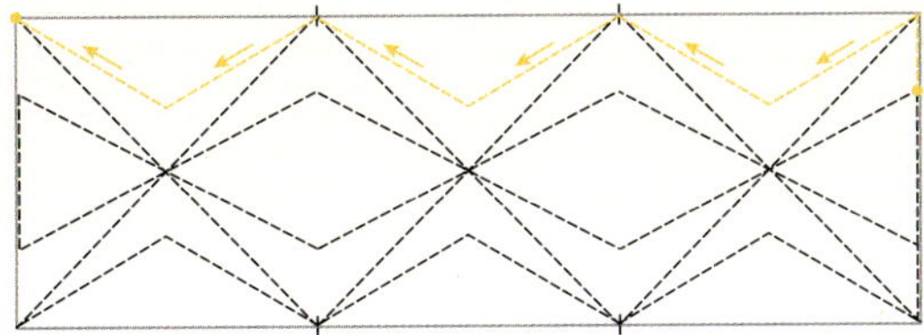

7. Almost done! Travel along the edge of the border until you are at the top corner. Repeat the technique in Step 3, filling in the top of the X's.

Variations

If you are working on a larger border, or are an overachiever, you could add a free-motion quilting design between the shapes you just quilted.

In this example, I used a figure-eight quilting design, but you could try other dense fillers such as pebbles or swirls.

BORDER: TRIANGLE WEDGES

This geometric design is perfect for graphic, modern quilts. You also can try it on large borders of all kinds. It may look complex, but it's actually pretty easy once you get the hang of it!

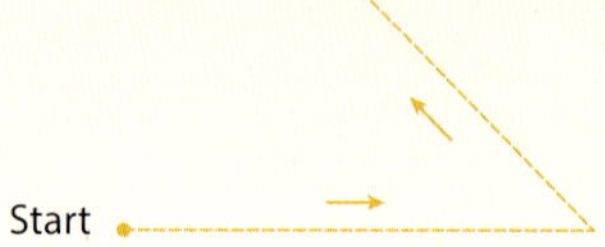

1. Quilt a 3˝–4˝ line parallel to the inside edge of the border. Angle back toward the top of the border, stopping about ¼˝ from the edge.

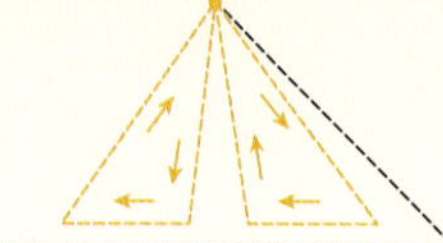

2. Quilt 2 triangle-shaped wedges, both meeting at the same point.

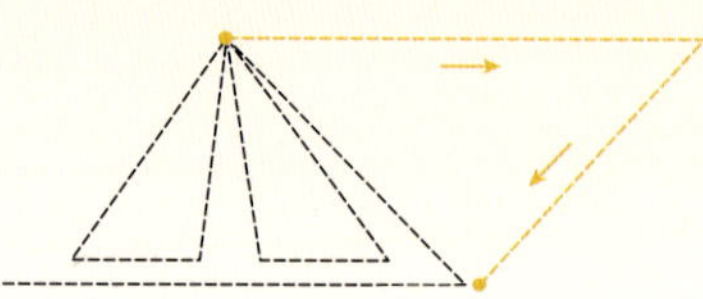

3. Quilt a 3˝–4˝ horizontal line, then angle down toward the other side of the border. Stop about ¼˝–½˝ from the corner of the triangle you quilted in Step 1.

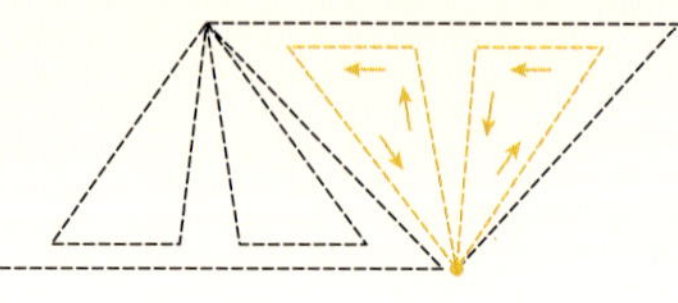

4. Fill in the space by quilting 2 triangle wedges, just as you did in Step 2.

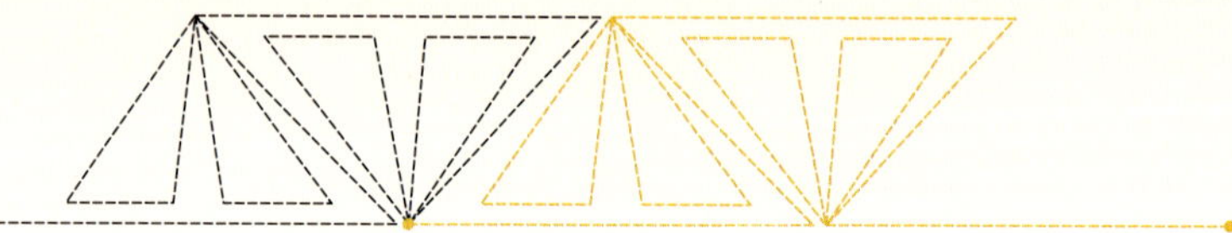

5. Continue working your way along the border, alternating the directions of the triangles and stitching wedges inside each.

6. To turn the corner, rotate the wedges to fit together.

Variation

You could quilt 1 wedge instead of 2 and fill it in with a different machine quilting design.

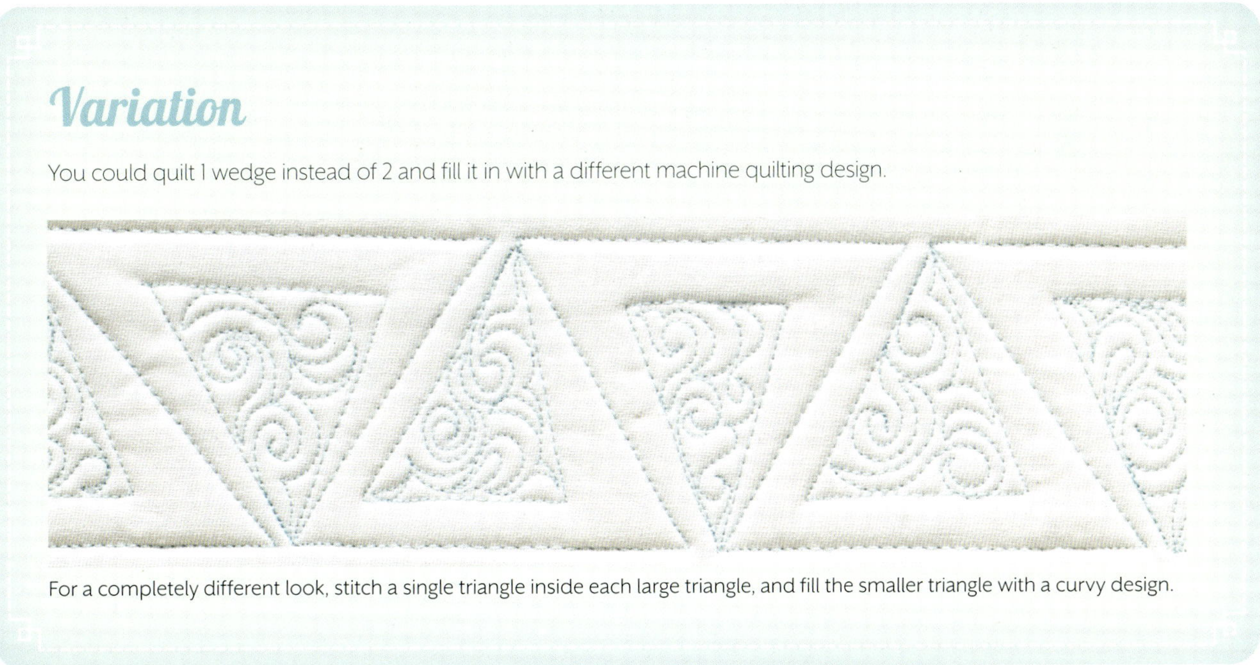

For a completely different look, stitch a single triangle inside each large triangle, and fill the smaller triangle with a curvy design.

TILES

When you really want to add dense quilting to your quilt top, Tiles is the design to use. The combination of rigid borders and swirly insides adds so much texture and can really add some fun to large sections of open space. Even though it is an intermediate design, it is not too difficult. The hardest part is deciding where to place the next tile. After a little practice, you will have it down pat!

Tip

Try quilting a few tiles randomly among a geometric allover design.

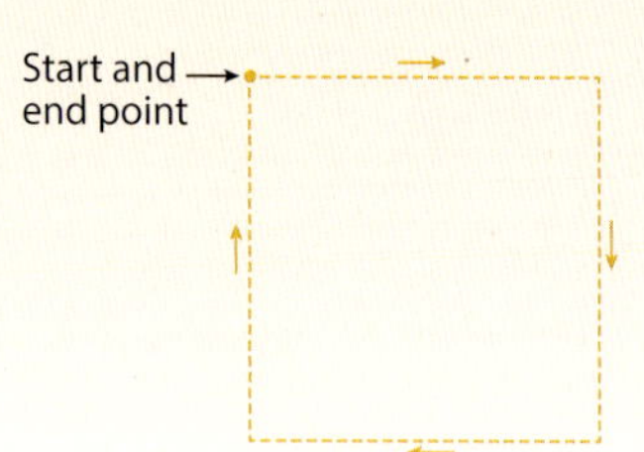

1. From your starting point, quilt a square the size that you desire. If you want denser quilting, make it smaller. If you want less dense quilting, make it larger. For this illustration, the square is 2″. Stop in a corner of the square.

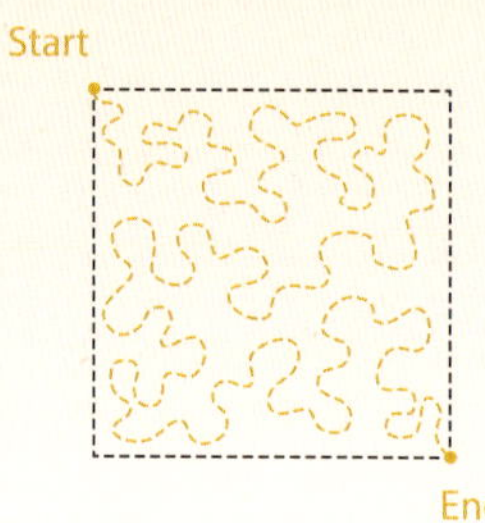

2. From this corner, quilt an allover design, filling the square and ending at another corner of the square.

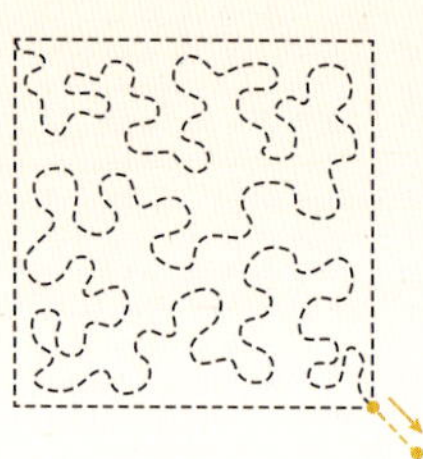

3. From the corner, quilt out diagonally about ¼″.

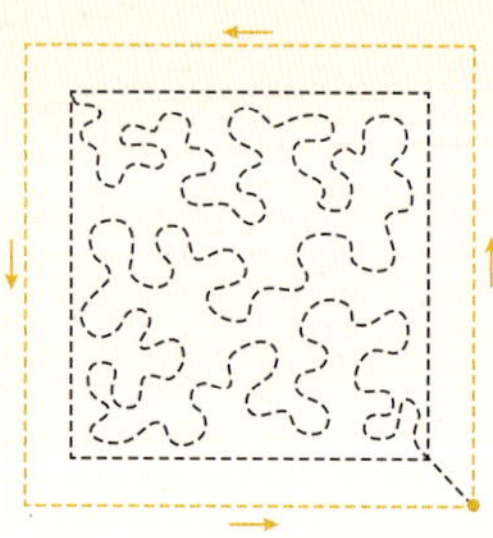

4. Echo the outside of the square. You can space the echo out as close or as far as you would like. I usually space it out ¼″. Stop at the starting point of the echo square. This is the first tile.

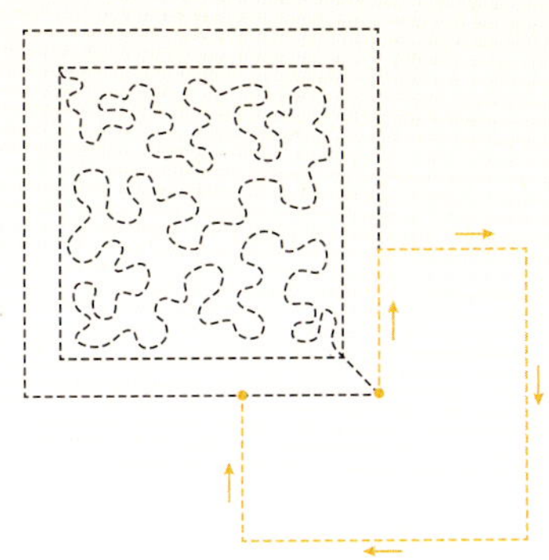

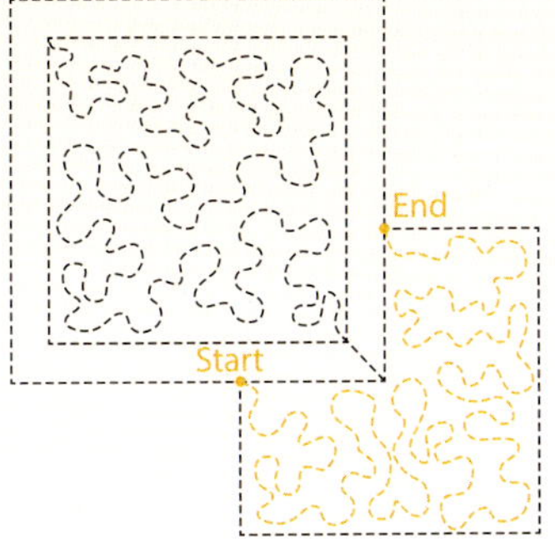

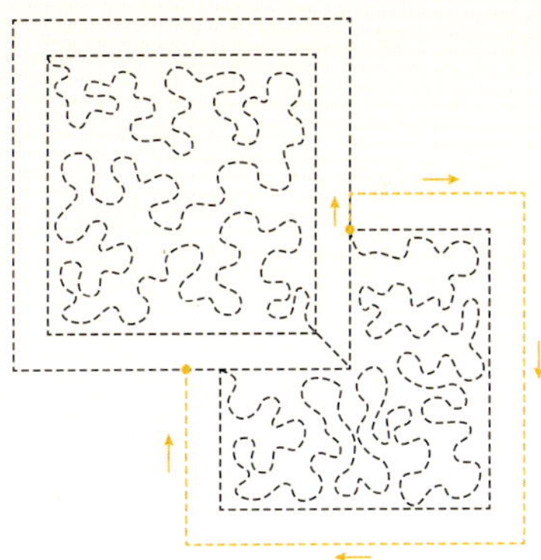

5. Now you will quilt the next tile. From the ending point, travel along the outer line of the first tile approximately 1˝. You are going to start the next tile from this point. Quilt to the right 1˝, making a partial side of the square; quilt 2˝ down; quilt 2˝ left; quilt up 1˝, ending on the side of the first square.

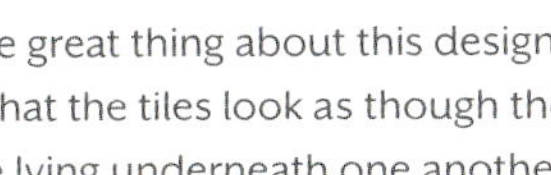

Note

The great thing about this design is that the tiles look as though they are lying underneath one another, giving the illusion of depth.

6. Fill in the second square with the allover design, ending at the point where the square touches the first one.

7. Travel ¼˝ along the edge of the first tile. Echo around the second tile approximately ¼˝.

8. Repeat again and again, filling in the entire area. Don't be afraid to make the tiles different sizes.

Tip

To quilt a modern variation of Tiles, quilt the design with irregular shapes to add a funkier, jagged twist.

SQUARE 1

When choosing quilting designs, I often use elements of the block itself as a part of the design. This particular design echoes two sides of the square and is well suited for medium to larger blocks. I like to use this design for the corner blocks of a larger design. The best part of this design? It is completely customizable, so you can add as many lines as you think it needs, and even change up the spacing.

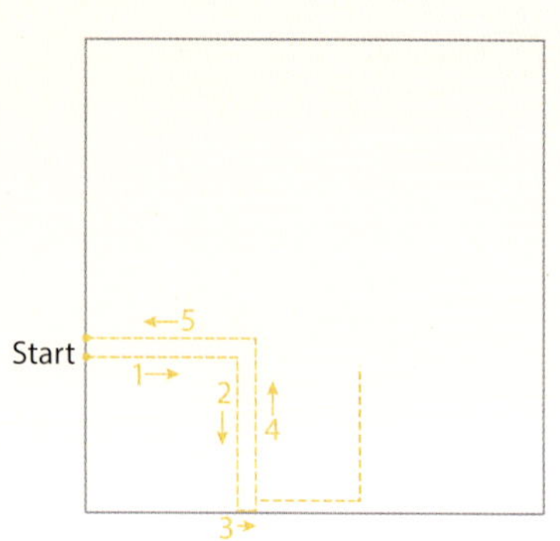

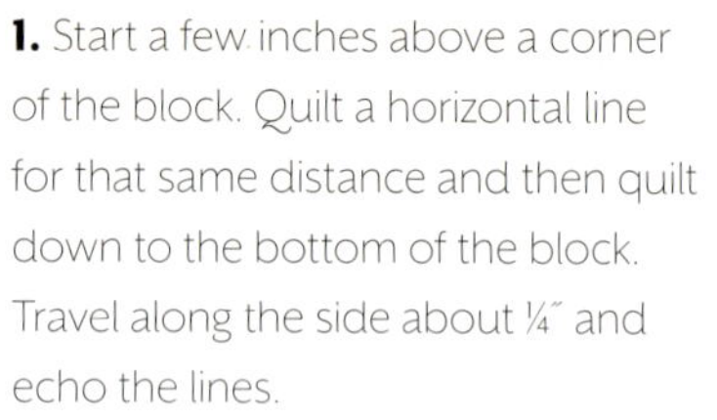

1. Start a few inches above a corner of the block. Quilt a horizontal line for that same distance and then quilt down to the bottom of the block. Travel along the side about ¼″ and echo the lines.

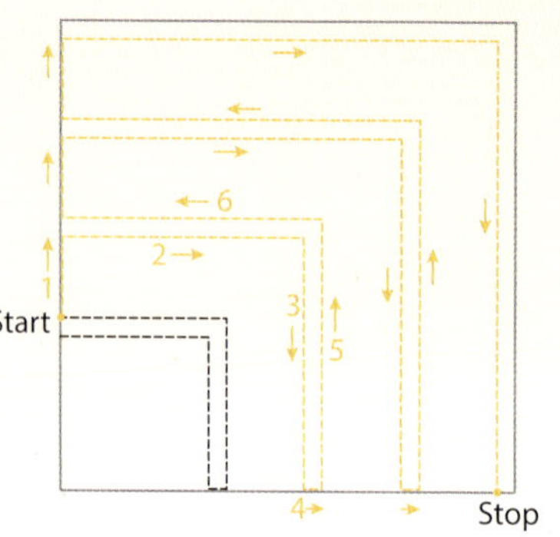

2. Repeat the first step, traveling along the side of the block and quilting straight lines.

Variations

For greater intensity, fill in between the lines with a different quilting design such as back-and-forth lines or pebbles.

Quilt pebbles between the straight lines for a variation of this design.

SQUARE 2

I love dividing blocks into smaller shapes. The smaller areas are a little easier to stitch, and the divisions can create some secondary designs that are really beautiful. This design is best for medium to large blocks and can be changed easily for a variety of looks.

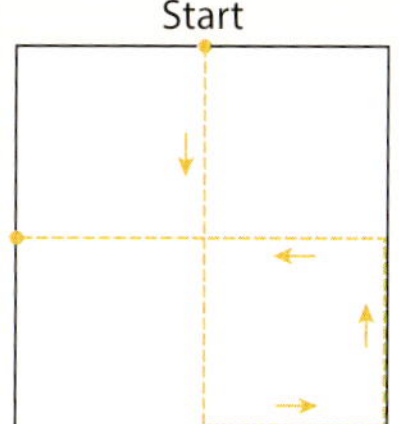

1. Break the block into 4 smaller squares. Quilt a vertical line down the middle of the block. Travel along the edges to the midpoint of the adjacent side and quilt a horizontal line to the opposite side.

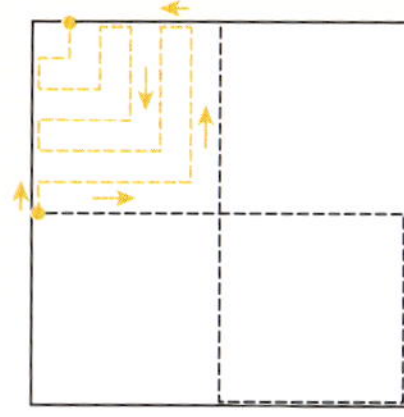

2. Fill in the top left square by echoing the quilting lines, traveling in between lines.

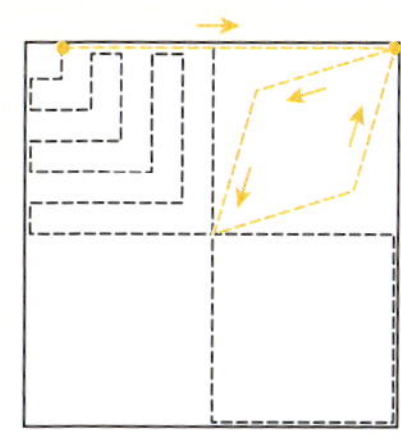

3. Travel along the top edge of the block to the next outer corner, and quilt a diamond-shaped design that touches the center of the block and returns to the starting point.

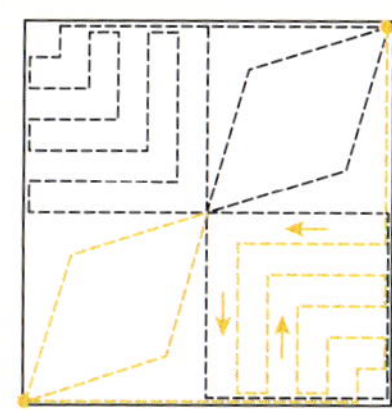

4. Travel along the edge of the block to repeat Steps 2 and 3 in the bottom half of the square.

Variation

Of course you can use different designs in each of the smaller squares, but you also can change up the design as it is. In this example, I added more echo lines inside the diamonds and varied the spacing between the echo lines.

Add more lines and stagger the spacing for a different look.

SQUARE 3

This design actually pulls double duty. it fits perfectly into rectangles and can be mirror-imaged to work in squares as well. It looks a lot more difficult than it actually is and can create some interesting secondary designs.

Tip

If you want to fill in more of the block, try adding a diagonal line at the beginning and end of the design.

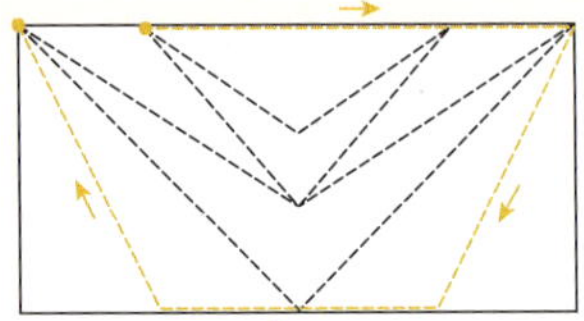

Start and end about equal distance from a corner and the block center for this variation.

1. Starting from any corner, quilt a diagonal line to the center of the opposite side and up to the opposite top corner.

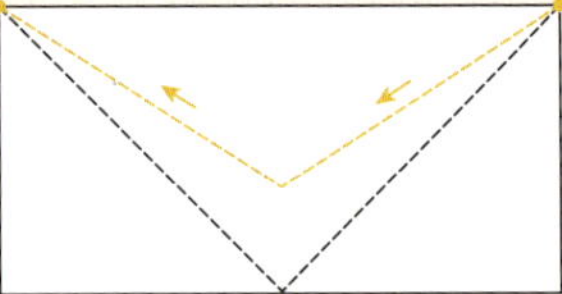

2. Quilt a diagonal line down to about 1˝ above the bottom of the V and back to the first corner.

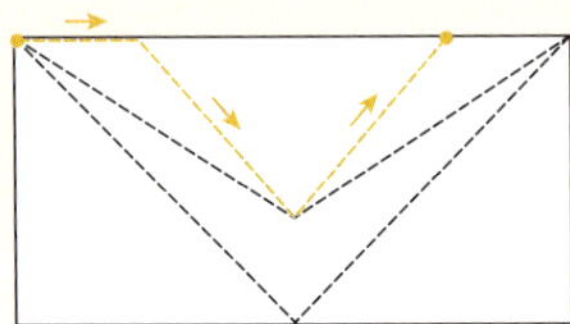

3. Travel along the top edge of the block about 1˝. Quilt another diagonal line to touch the bottom of the V you quilted in Step 2 and back up to about 1˝ inside the opposite corner.

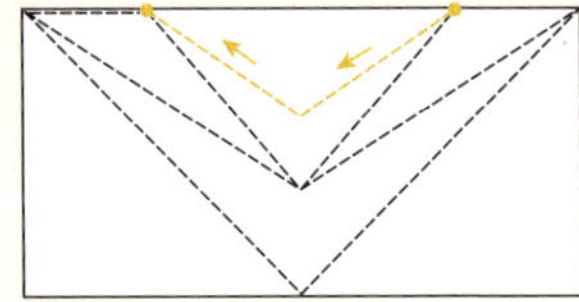

4. Quilt a diagonal line down to about 1˝ above the bottom of the V and back to the starting point of Step 3.

Variations

I love to use this design to frame other blocks. It really helps draw the eye to that area.

You can also use this in differently shaped blocks as well.

Try using this design to frame other blocks.

The Square 3 design in a square block

The Square 3 design in a hexagon block

TRIANGLE 1

If you believe that "less is more," then this design is perfect for you. Simply echoing two sides of the triangular shape is an easy way to quilt triangles of all sizes. I especially like to use this on the triangles in flying geese blocks.

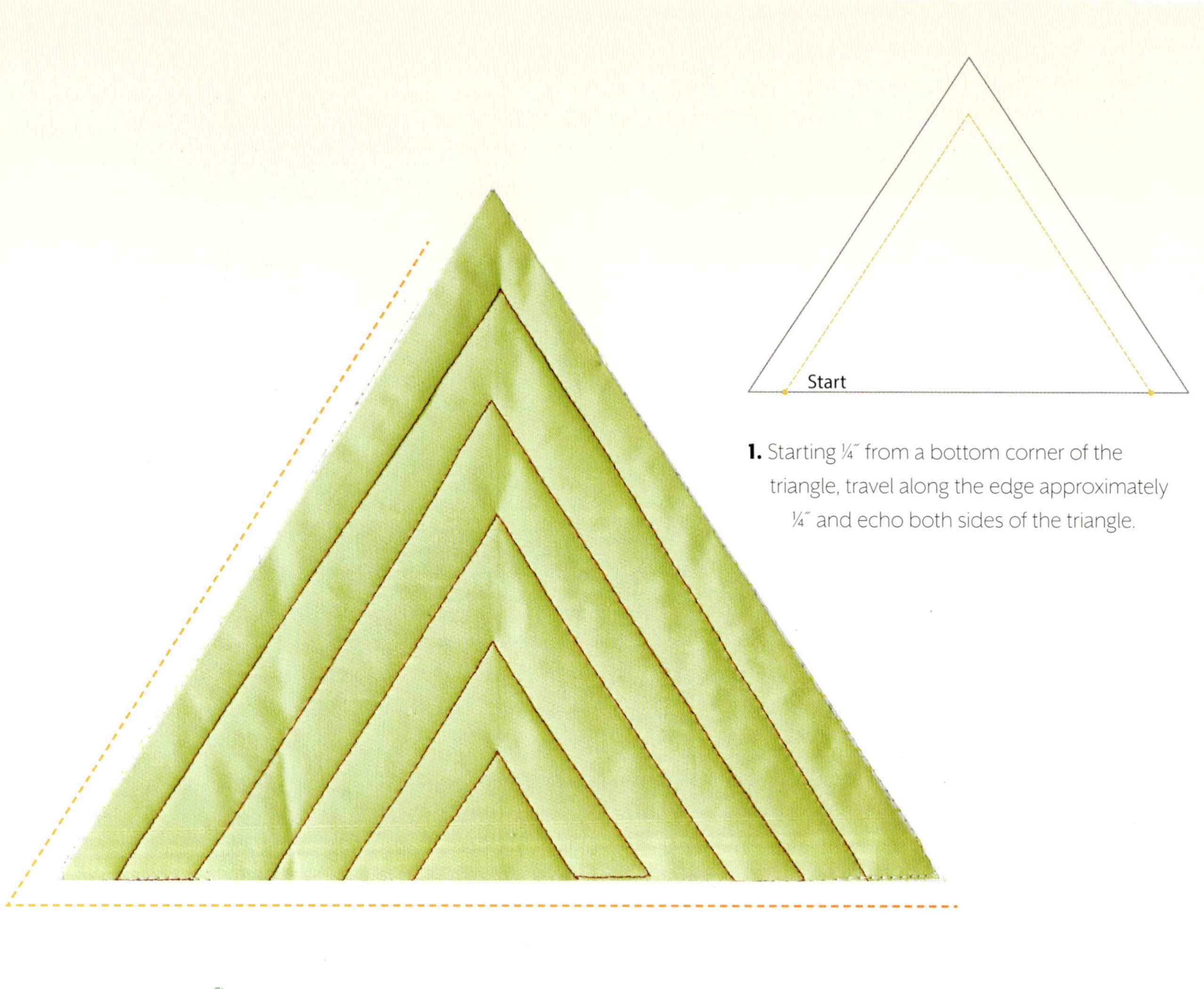

1. Starting ¼″ from a bottom corner of the triangle, travel along the edge approximately ¼″ and echo both sides of the triangle.

Note

Depending on how dense you want the quilting, try spacing the lines closer or farther apart.

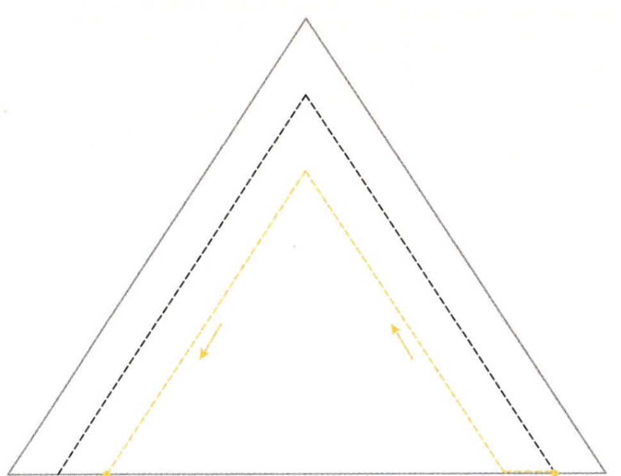

2. Travel ¼˝ toward the inside of the triangle and echo the lines you just quilted.

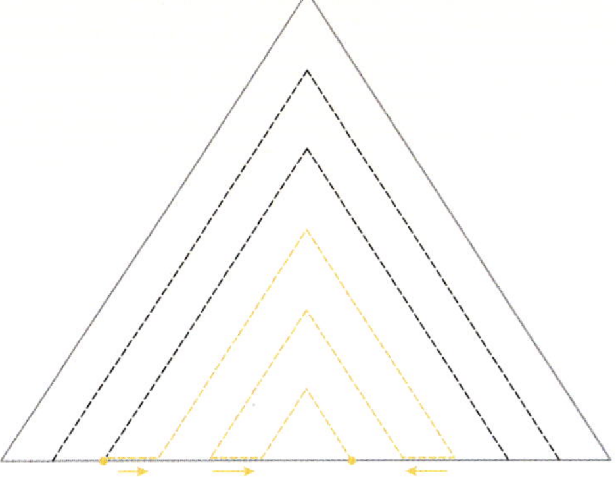

3. Continue quilting lines until the triangle is filled in.

Variations

You don't have to stick with just straight lines. Fill in between random lines with a filler, such as circles, to add extra oomph to your quilt block.

Combine pebbles with the straight lines to give this design a more custom look.

TRIANGLE 2

Combining straight lines with just a little bit of traveling results in a design that adds a look of depth to your quilting. if you aren't a fan of traveling along previously quilted lines, don't worry—it's just a little bit. The result is well worth the extra step. This works in triangles of all shapes and sizes.

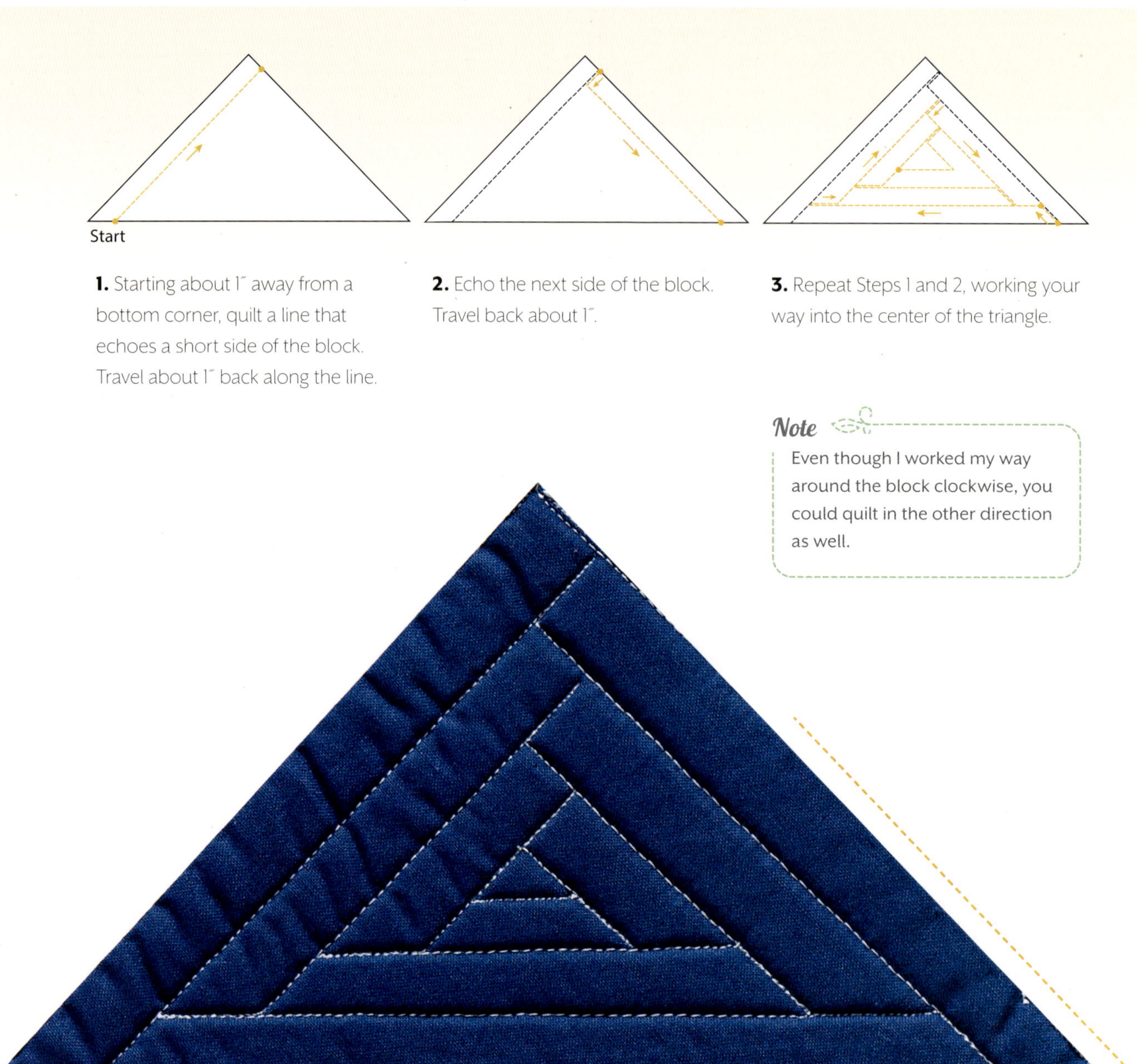

1. Starting about 1˝ away from a bottom corner, quilt a line that echoes a short side of the block. Travel about 1˝ back along the line.

2. Echo the next side of the block. Travel back about 1˝.

3. Repeat Steps 1 and 2, working your way into the center of the triangle.

Note

Even though I worked my way around the block clockwise, you could quilt in the other direction as well.

Variations

Try quilting the lines closer or farther apart, depending on the size of the block. In this example, the lines are about ¼″ apart.

Change the space between lines to fit the size of the block.

You can also get a nice effect by varying the spacing within the block. As I worked my way toward the inside of the block, I quilted the lines closer and closer.

For a different look, vary the spacing between lines.

HEXAGON 1

Diamonds are a quilter's best friend, even when they are part of a hexagon block. This design uses the edge of the block as a reference point, meaning you don't have to mark the design. It is fast and fun to stitch, making it one of my favorites.

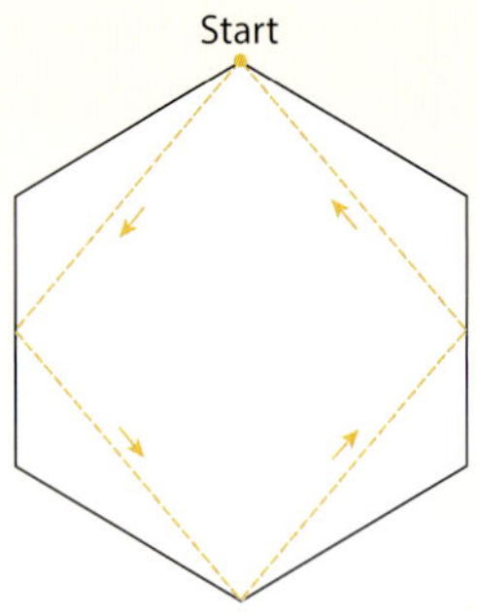

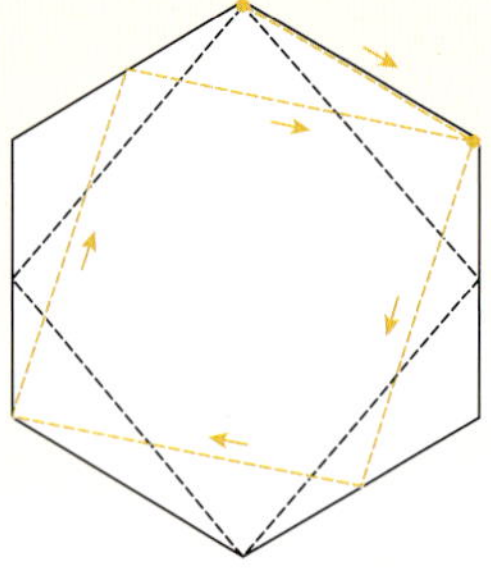

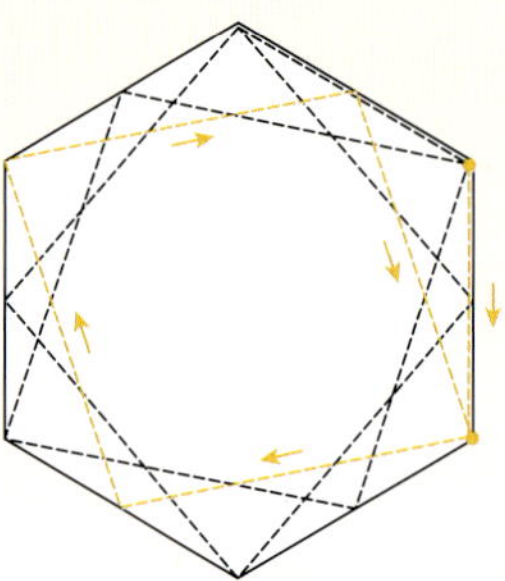

1. From any corner, quilt a line diagonally to the middle of the next side, on to the opposite corner, across to the middle of the next side, and back to the starting point.

2. Travel along the edge of the block to the next corner and repeat Step 1.

3. Travel along to the next corner and repeat Step 1 again. When you finish, you will have quilted into every corner of the hexagon.

Tip 

Once you quilt a few of the lines of this design, it can be hard to figure out where to go next. If you get lost, just pause and take a moment to find the next quilting point.

Note

When you have finished with this design, you will have traveled in the seam of two of the sides. When I am quilting this design on my quilts, I go ahead and finish stitching in the rest of the seams. It not only completes the block but also makes the design end where it started. Of course, you can leave that out if you would like.

Variations

If straight lines aren't your favorite, try curved lines instead.

Before you stitch the last set of lines, add some filler to the center. This is perfect for larger hexagons.

Curved lines create a playful star.

Add a filler before you stitch the final diamond.

SQUARE FLOWERS

If flowers were square, this is what they would look like. With a middle square and boxy petals, this design will add interest and depth to your quilt. This design is best used in large backgrounds where it can bloom. Try quilting several square flowers, or add one or two for visual interest.

Tip

Start away from the edge of the quilt or block; this design starts in the center and works its way outward.

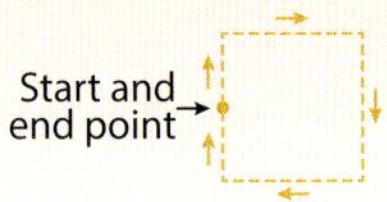

1. Pick your starting point. Quilt up ½˝, to the right 1˝, down 1˝, to the left 1˝, and up ½˝. You are halfway between the top and bottom of the left side. This is the center of the square flower.

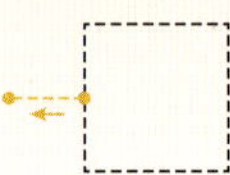

2. Now quilt the square petals. Quilt away from the square ½˝.

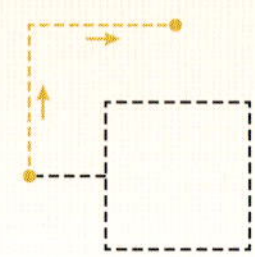

3. Quilt up 1˝ and to the right 1˝.

4. Quilt a line down to the top edge of the square, and then trace it right back up to the top of the line. This is going to form a "petal" of the flower.

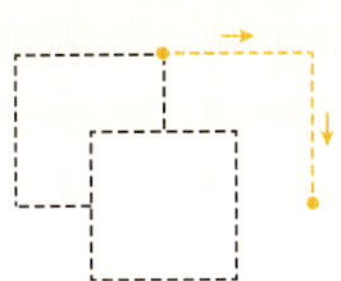

5. Quilt a line 1˝ to the right, past the edge of the square. Quilt a line 1˝ down.

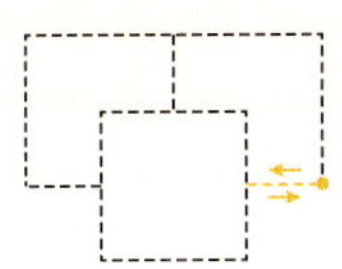

6. Quilt a ½˝ line in to the right edge of the square, and then trace it back out to where you started. You have added the second petal.

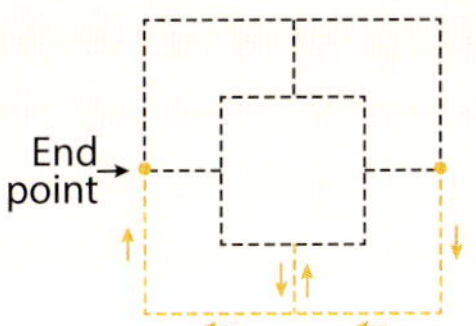

7. Repeat Steps 2–6 around the last 2 sides of the square, ending so that you are touching the first petal. This completes the first layer of petals.

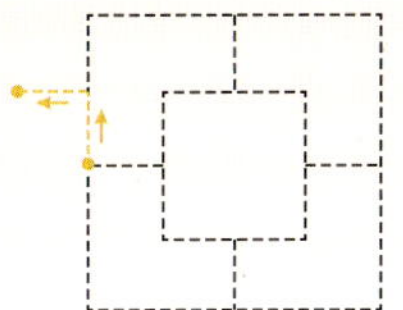

8. Travel along the left side of the petal approximately ½˝ and then quilt a ½˝ line to the left.

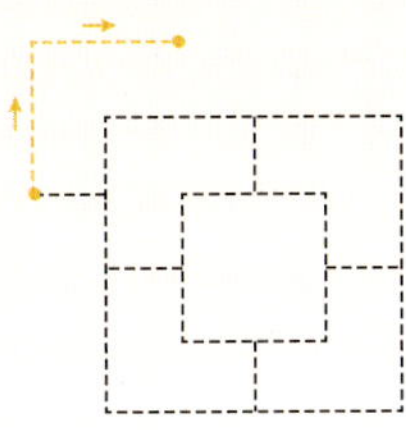

9. Now you will add the next layer of petals. Quilt up 1˝ and to the right 1˝.

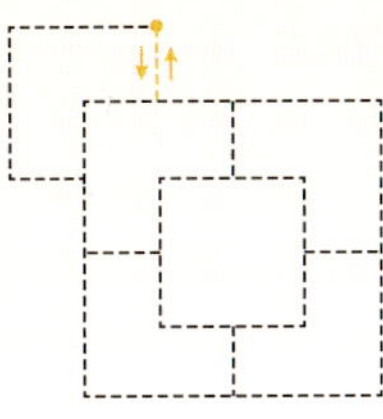

10. Quilt down ½˝ to the top of the petal and trace the line back up to the starting point.

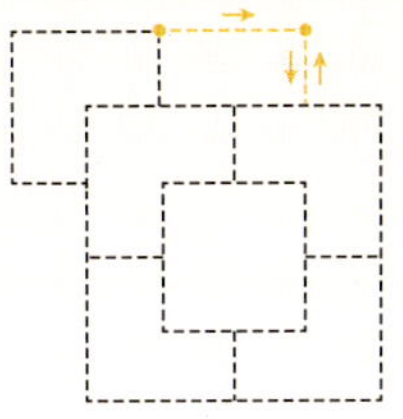

11. Quilt to the right 1˝, then down ½˝, and trace back up the line to where you started.

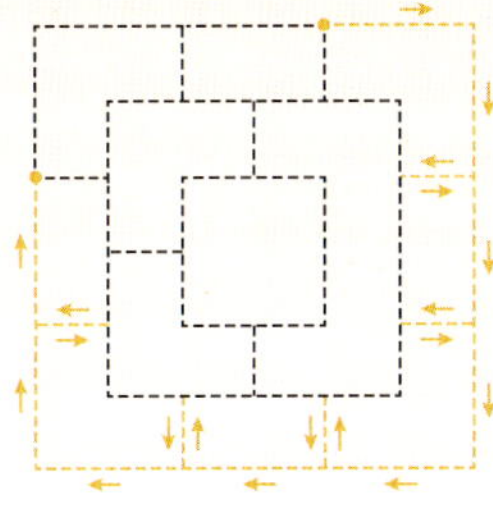

12. Continue around the design until you have reached the desired size. When you are done, end with the last quilting line touching the flower to give a completed look. Tie off the thread and repeat with another flower.

If you are not a fan of starting and stopping, make your flowers bigger by starting with a larger center square and making the petals wider. The overall texture of the design is the same, regardless of the size of the individual flowers.

Tip

Quilt the petals different sizes or make the corners rounded to add an organic feel to the design.

WAVY LINES & VINES

FIGURE 8

This design isn't difficult, but getting the rhythm down was always a little tricky for me. Practice it, and you will get it in no time! This design is one of my favorites for long, thin areas, such as borders. When quilting this design you will use the top and the bottom of the quilting area as your guide.

1. From the bottom corner of the quilting area, quilt an S shape that just barely grazes the top edge of the quilting area.

2. Without stopping, quilt a backward S shape. You want it to curve out and come back in and just barely touch the bottom part of the first S.

3. Once you are almost to the bottom edge, quilt another curve out and back to touch the top curve.

Tip

This design looks the best when there is no space between the curves, the top or the bottom. This can be a little tricky, but it becomes easier with practice.

4. Continue quilting the alternating curves until you reach the end of the quilting area.

TRIANGLE 1

One of my favorite things to do is to use classic quilting designs in unexpected ways. For instance, I like to take designs normally seen in borders and sashings, and use them in quilt blocks. This figure-eight quilting design is a great example of that. Try it in triangles of all sizes.

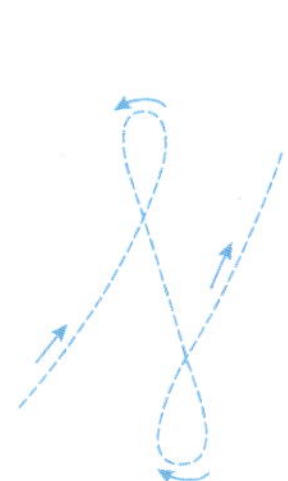

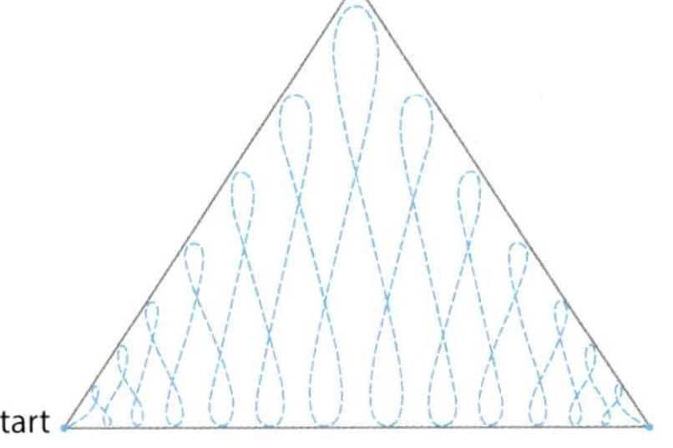

1. Start from one corner and quilt a figure-eight design, filling up the triangle and working toward the opposite corner.

Tip

Use the edges of the block as a guide as you make the figure-eight loops. That will allow the design to stretch and fit perfectly.

Variations

You could definitely use any design that lends itself to different widths. Instead of a figure-eight design, you can use a dense back-and-forth line.

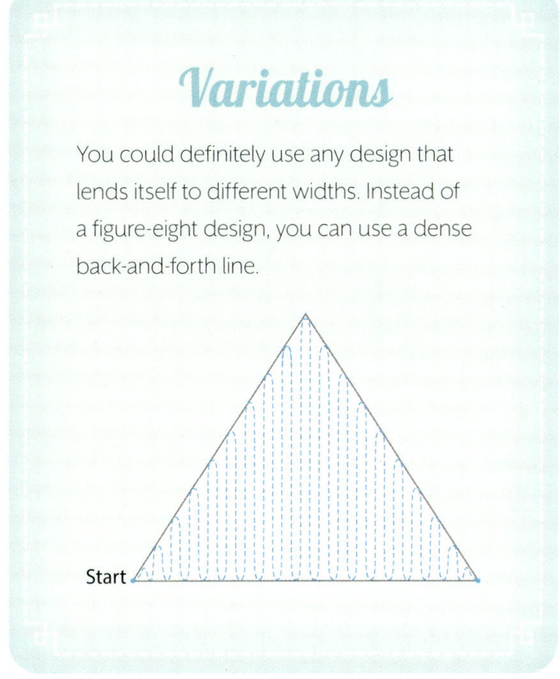

WAVY LINES

Oh, how I love wavy lines! They are one of my all-time favorite designs. You can use them to draw your eyes to a focal point of your quilt or to add movement, whether vertical or horizontal. It seems like every week I am finding more and more uses for this easy, versatile design.

1. For vertical or horizontal wavy lines, determine the top and bottom of your quilting area. Starting at a corner, quilt a gently wavy line to the top.

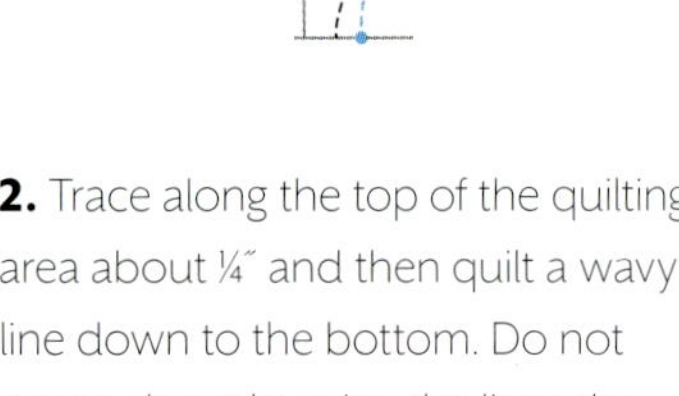

2. Trace along the top of the quilting area about ¼˝ and then quilt a wavy line down to the bottom. Do not worry about keeping the lines the same.

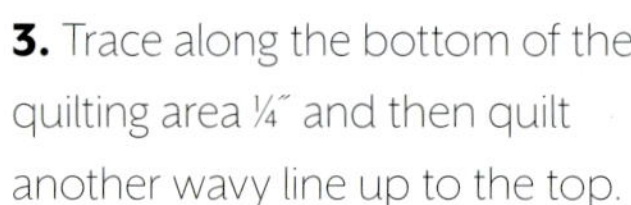

3. Trace along the bottom of the quilting area ¼˝ and then quilt another wavy line up to the top.

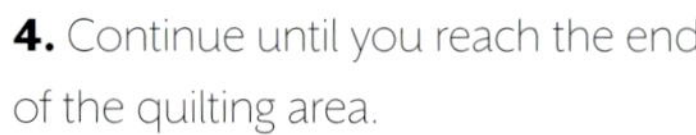

4. Continue until you reach the end of the quilting area.

WAVY WAVY

Wavy Wavy shows that a simple design can add movement and texture to your quilt. It's just an added bonus that it's so easy to quilt. This design is perfect for medium to large areas of negative space or as an allover quilting design.

Note

The instructions are just to teach you the technique. When you are quilting this design, you will find your own rhythm.

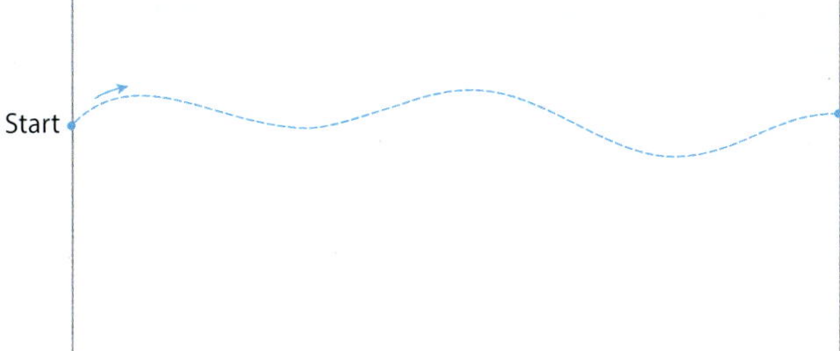

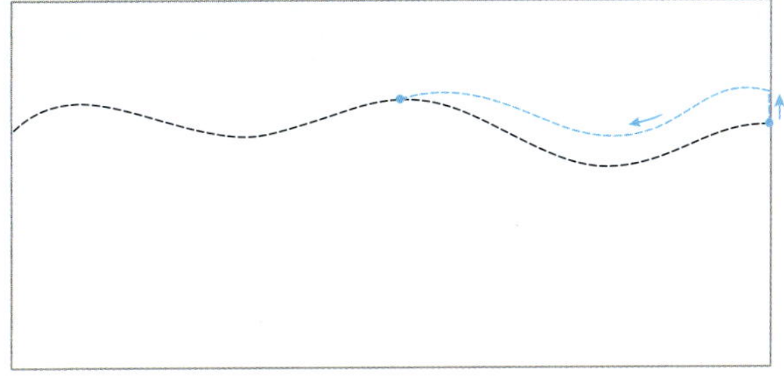

1. Starting a few inches below the top of the quilting area, quilt a gently waving line from one side to the other.

Note

Starting the design a small distance from the top of the quilting area allows you to get a wavy line on which to build the rest of the design.

2. Travel up the edge of the quilting area about ½˝. Quilt a wavy line that echoes the first wavy line. At a random point while echoing, run into the line below.

Note

When you run into the line below, you want the lines to look as if they are merging.

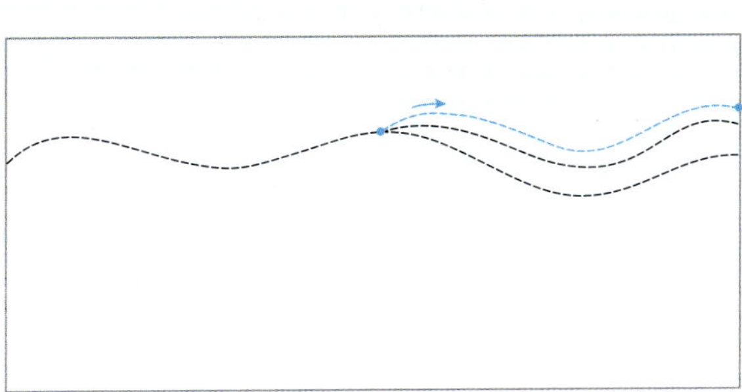

3. Quilt a line echoing back the opposite direction, returning to the edge.

Continued on next page

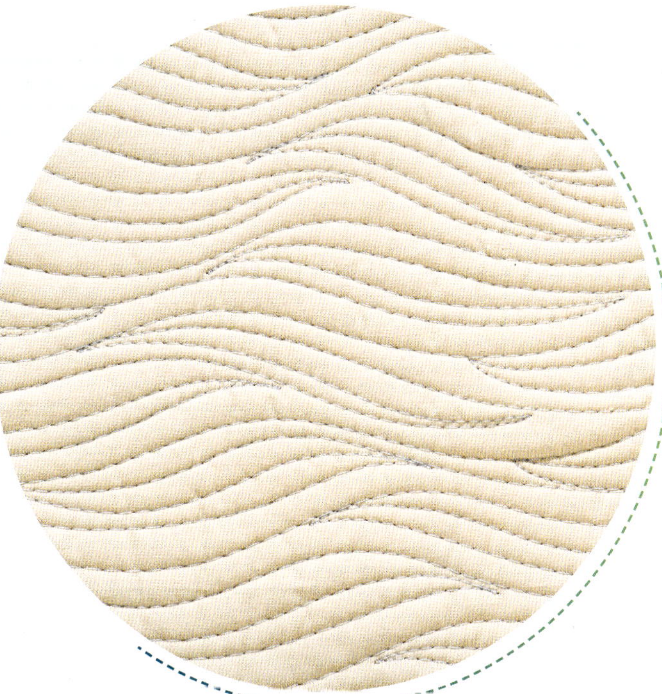

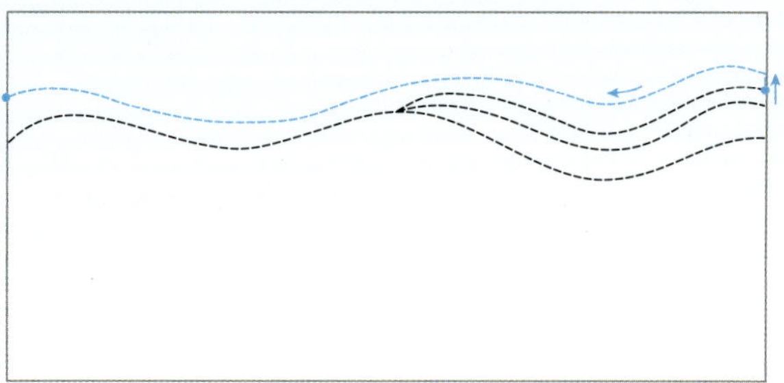

4. Travel up the edge of the quilting area and then echo across to the other edge of the quilting area. Traveling along the edge ensures that your lines will stay somewhat horizontal.

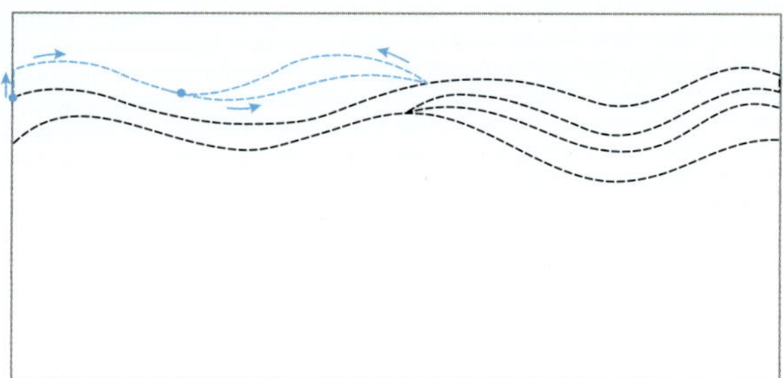

5. Work your way back across the quilt, running into the line below.

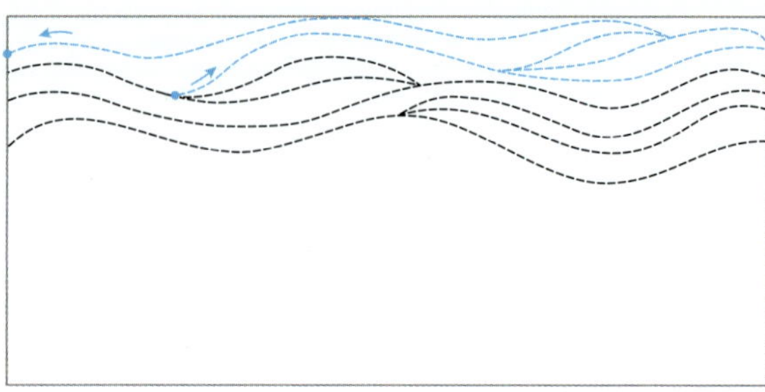

6. Repeat the technique in Steps 1–5, filling in the area.

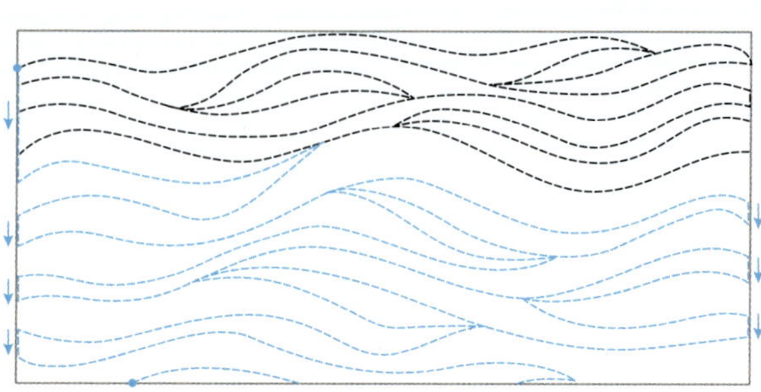

7. Travel down along the edge until you are about ½″ below the first line (from Step 1). Repeat the technique in Steps 1–6 to fill in the quilting area.

Tip

You can add more movement with this design by running into lines more often.

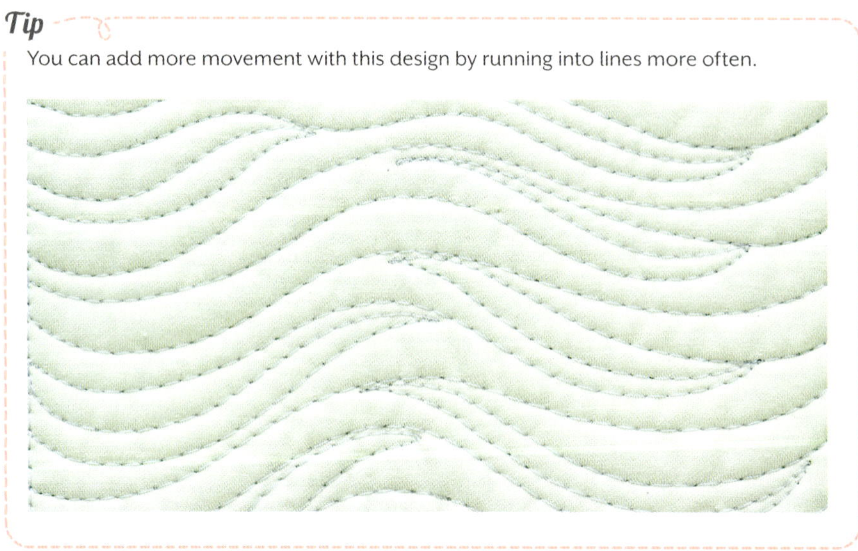

SIGNATURE DESIGN

I love quilting designs that are fast, fun, and require no marking. That includes this signature design! Not only does it add movement to your quilt, but it adds a bit of contrast with the vertical and horizontal lines. I normally use this design in larger areas of negative space, but it can also go in larger blocks or be used as an allover design. no matter how you use it, I'm sure you are going to love it!

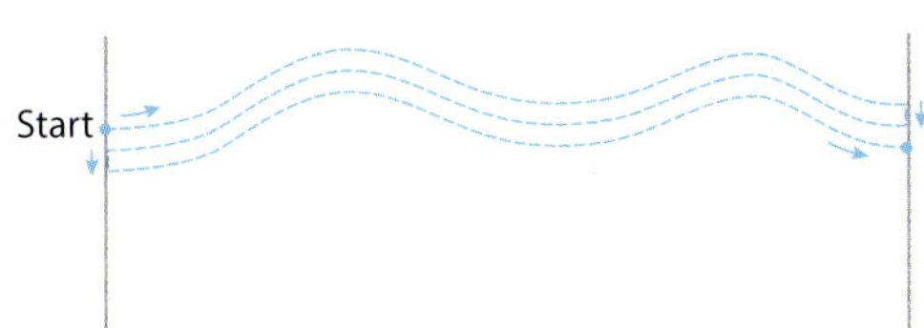

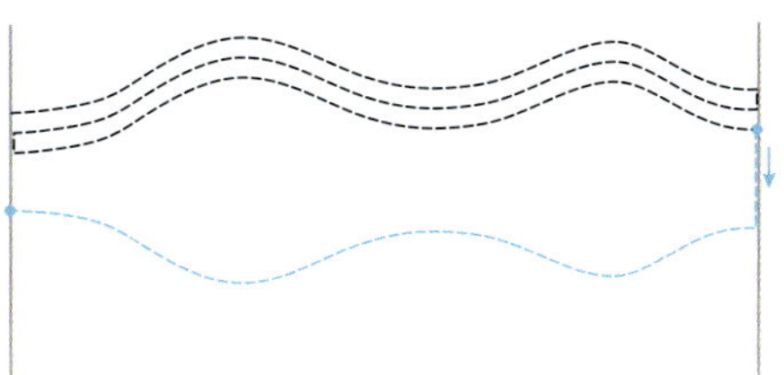

1. Starting at the top of the negative space, quilt a gently waving line to the opposite edge of the quilting area. Travel along the edge approximately ½″ and echo the first line. Repeat one more time until you have 3 wavy lines.

2. Travel down the edge of the quilting area a few inches and quilt a wavy line that is a reflection of the wavy line above.

Note 

I happen to love the number 3, which is why I chose 3 wavy lines, but you could add more or fewer lines.

Note 

Don't stress out if it isn't a perfect reflection; close enough is good enough.

Continued on next page

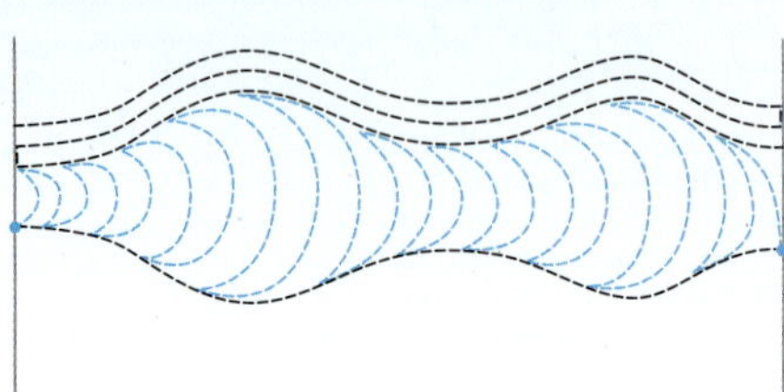

3. Fill in the space between the wave you just quilted and the top set of wavy lines with curved lines, working your way across the area.

Tip

For some help on quilting these curved lines, see one of the triangle designs (Triangle 10). It looks different there, but the quilting technique is the same!

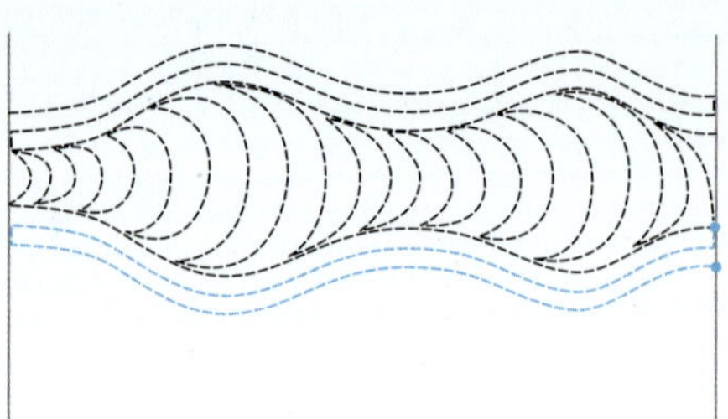

4. Echo the wavy line twice.

Repeat as shown, working your way down and filling in the negative space completely.

Tips

A Few Pointers

- Traveling along the edge of the quilting area will help make sure that wavy lines stay somewhat horizontal.
- When quilting the wavy lines, don't quilt them too wavy. It will be much easier to quilt if you have gently curving lines.
- Don't stress if it isn't perfect; when the whole area is quilted, it will look great. Also, using thread that blends will hide any imperfections.

Variations

Try quilting different variations of this design. There are so many different ways you can tweak it!
Try quilting the curved lines in opposite directions.

Or, try a different filler design between the wavy lines.
The figure-eight or ribbon candy designs are great alternatives.

Quilting the figure-eight quilting design between the wavy lines will give this design a different look.

Try the ribbon candy quilting design between the wavy lines.

WAVY SERPENTINE LINES

This design has an amazing texture that results from combining wavy lines and serpentine lines. It especially looks great when quilted with a thread color that matches the quilt top.

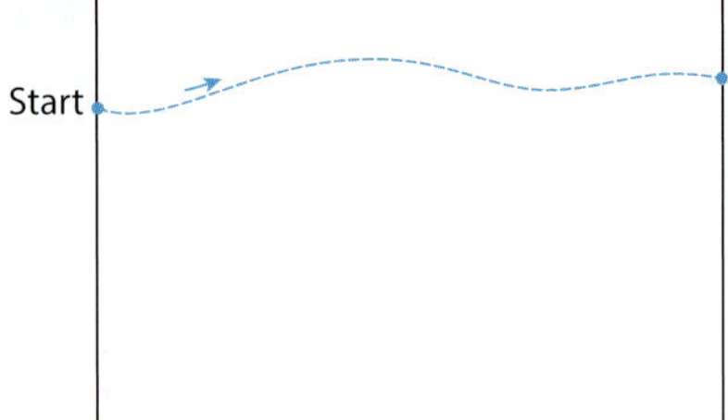

1. Quilt a gently waving line from one side of the quilting area to the opposite side.

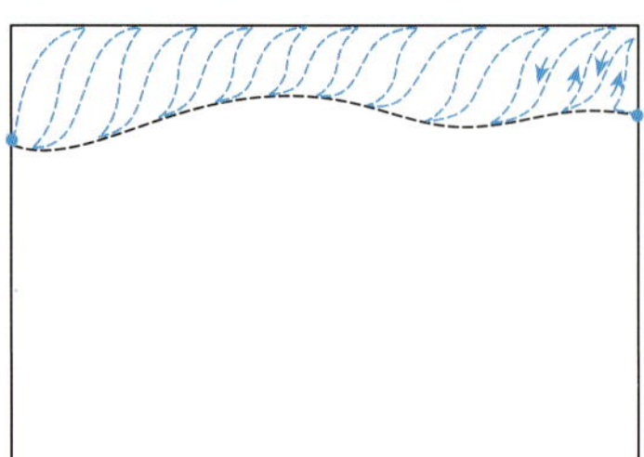

2. Fill above the wavy line by quilting an S-shaped serpentine line, working your way back to the starting point.

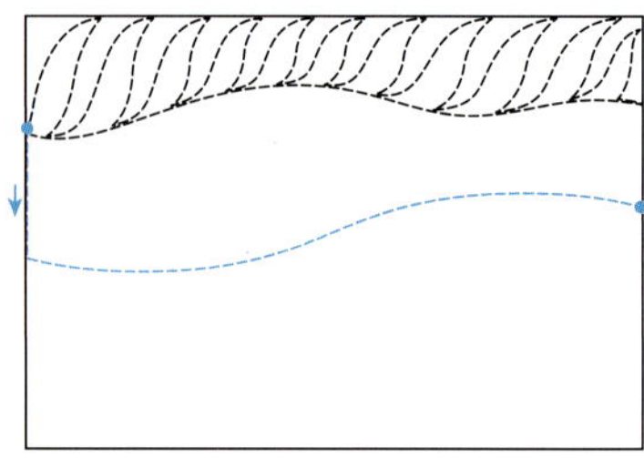

3. Travel along the side of the quilting area a couple of inches and quilt another wavy line to the opposite side.

Note

Don't worry about making the wavy lines echo each other. In fact, I think that this design looks best when the wavy lines are slightly off-kilter and completely different.

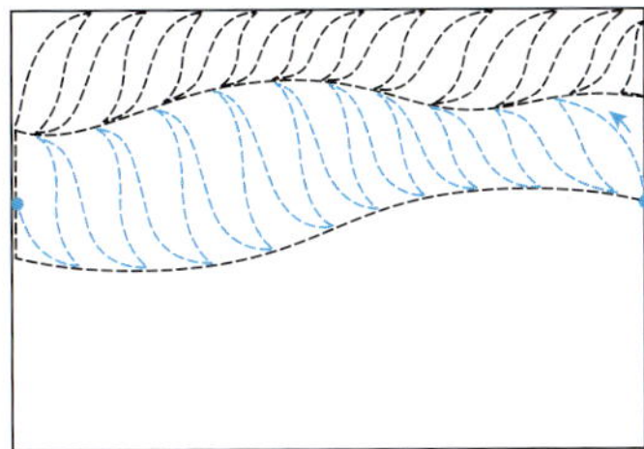

4. Fill above the wavy line with a serpentine line, just as you did in Step 2. Because I am easily amused, I thought it would be fun to stitch my serpentine lines in different directions.

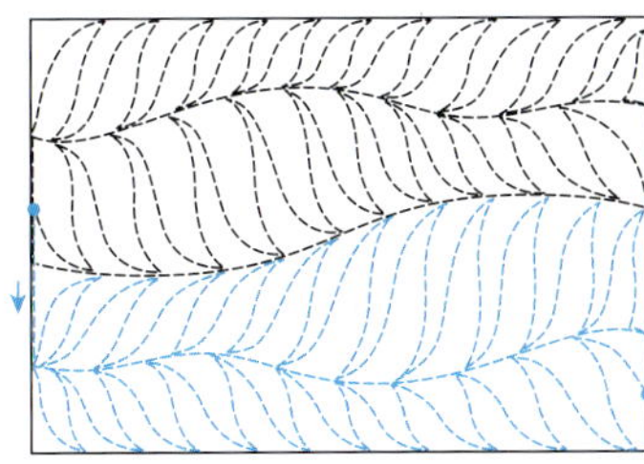

5. Continue working your way down the quilting area, quilting wavy lines and filling in above them.

Variations

Once you have the basic idea of this design, you can experiment with the placement of the wavy lines.

Quilt the serpentine lines at diagonal angles or in other directions.

If the serpentine lines are giving you trouble, try a basic arc as a filler or use any kind of filler that you would like.

Replace the serpentine lines with arc shapes for an easy-to-stitch design.

You could also use a different filler in every other row.

Alternate between fillers to add interest.

DIAMOND 1

This design takes the classic crosshatch quilting lines and gives them a curvy look. I thoroughly enjoy the optical illusion vibe that it has. But then again, I am easily amused! The lines create a strong visual impact not only in diamond blocks; you could also try them in squares, rectangles, and even borders.

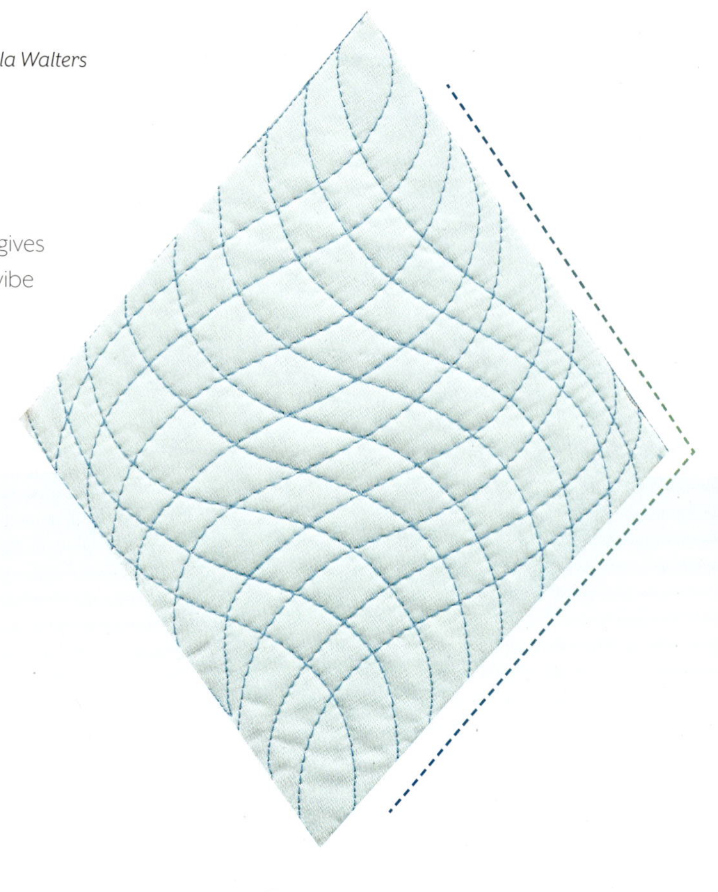

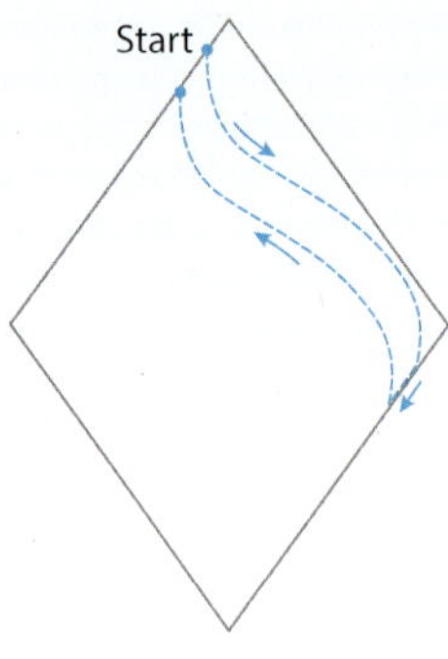

1. Starting about ¼″ from the top point of the block, quilt a serpentine line, ending on the opposite side. Travel along the side of the block and echo the first curve, ending about ¼″ below the starting point.

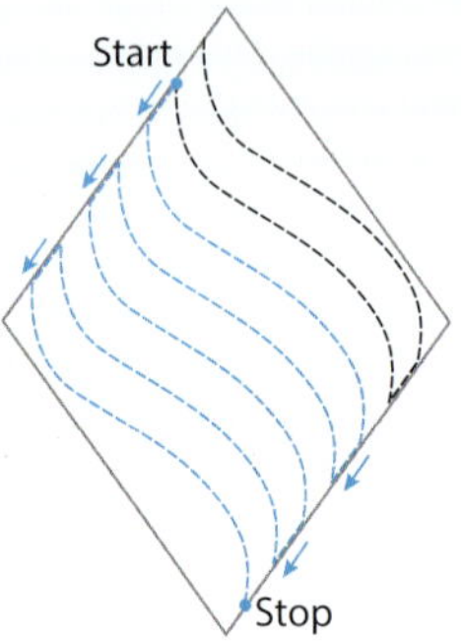

2. Repeat as shown, traveling along the sides of the block and quilting serpentine lines until you reach the bottom of the block.

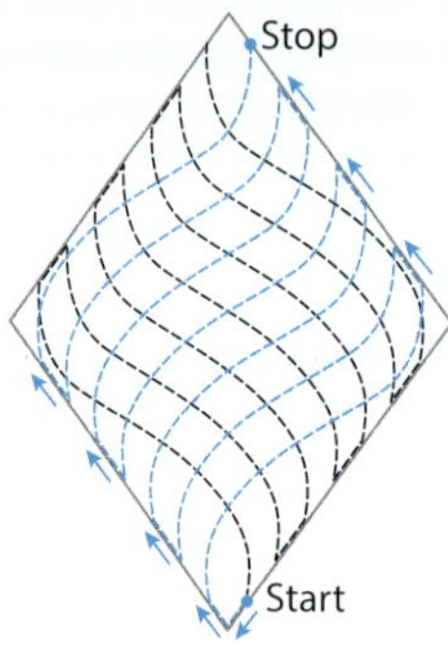

3. Travel along the bottom point of the block until you are on the opposite side of the block. Quilt serpentine lines that diagonally cross the lines already quilted.

Variations

If you need a more geometric look, you can quilt a straight crosshatch design. Just follow Steps 1–3, quilting straight lines instead of serpentine lines.

To quilt the classic crosshatch design, switch out the serpentine lines for straight lines.

HEXAGON 1

The points of a hexagon make perfect reference marks for stitching quilting designs. This quilting design takes full advantage of them, allowing you to quilt quickly without marking!

This design is fun to quilt in rectangles as well.

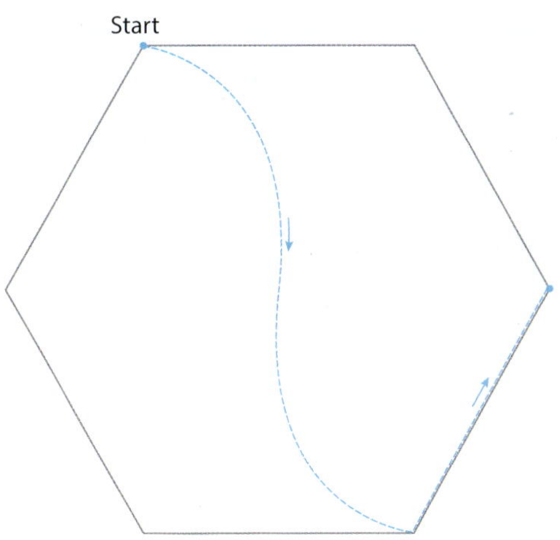

1. From one corner, quilt a serpentine line across to the opposite point. Travel along the edge of the block to the next point.

Continued on next page

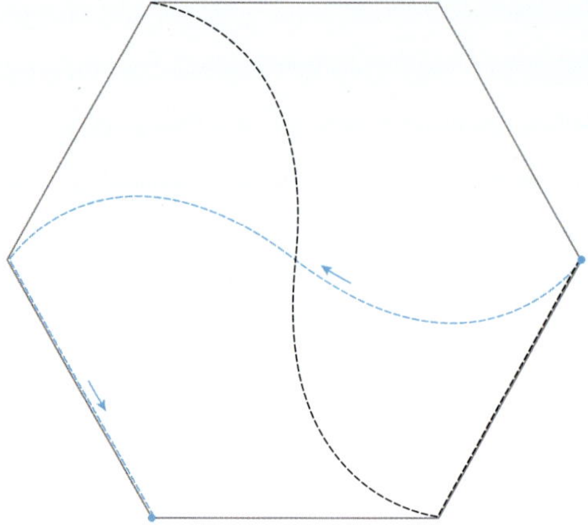

2. Repeat the first step, quilting a serpentine line to the opposite point. Travel to the next point.

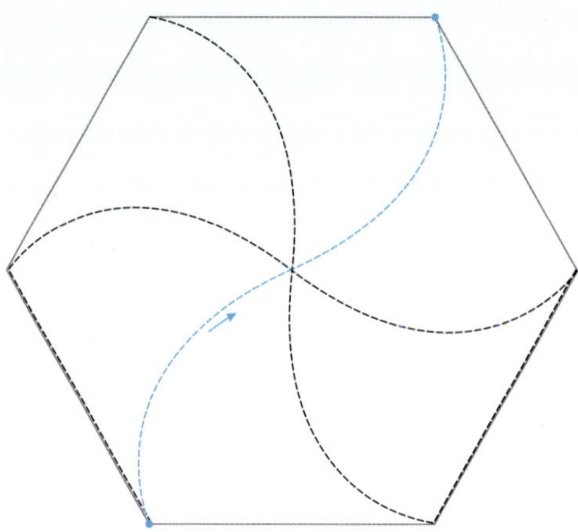

3. Quilt a third serpentine line.

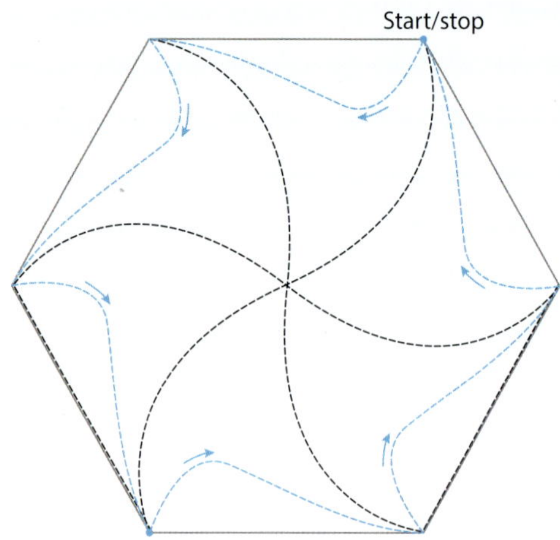

4. From that point, quilt a half heart shape that goes to the next point. To quilt the half heart shape, quilt a line curving out at the beginning and in at the end. Work your way around the block, from point to point, until you arrive at the starting point.

Variations

To give this quilting design a little twist, straighten it out. Replace the serpentine lines with straight lines and replace the half heart shapes with a more symmetrical arc shape. Either way you quilt it, it's going to look great!

Switch out the serpentine lines with straight lines for a variation of this design.

BORDER: WAVY VARIATION

Wavy lines are easy and fast to quilt, but sometimes a quilt needs a little more than just regular wavy lines. This design takes the basic wavy line and alternates the direction to create an interesting visual effect. This design is also quilted in sections, which means you can quilt the border as you make your way down the quilt.

When quilting this design, you definitely don't want to mark the lines. The fluid, organic look of this design is what makes it so great!

Note

This design is in the border section of the book because it goes from edge to edge. But you could use it in larger quilt blocks as well.

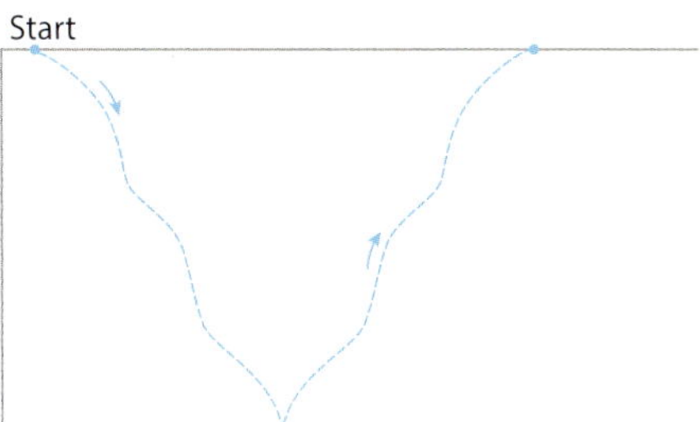

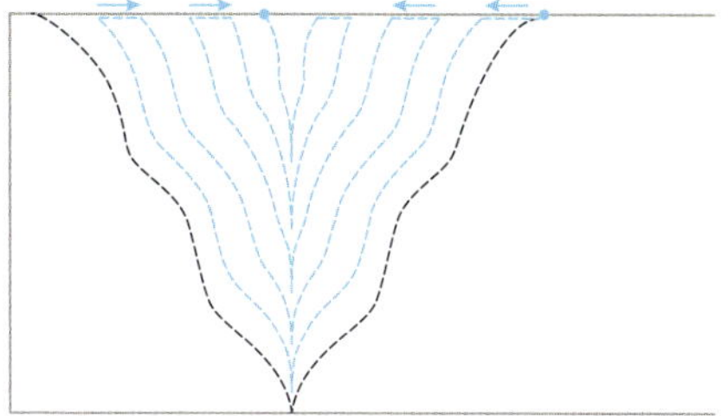

1. From one corner of the border, quilt a gently waving line diagonally until you reach the other side of the border. Quilt back up to the top of the border at an angle.

2. Travel along the top of the border approximately ½″; then echo the inside of the V. Continue traveling and echoing until the space is completely filled.

Note

When echoing the inside of the V shape, quilt the lines so they are almost touching at the points but are about ¼″ to ½″ apart at the edge of the border. This is what gives the design a groovy look!

Continued on next page

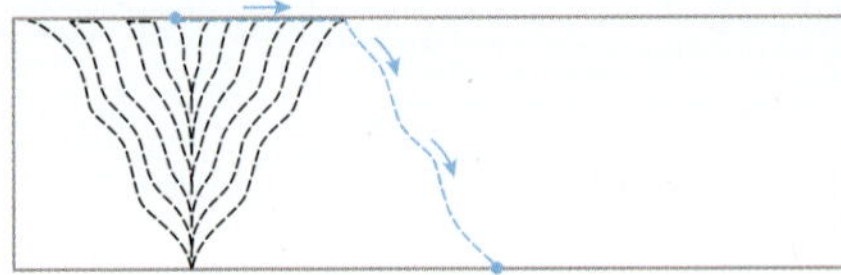

3. When finished with the first V, travel along the edge of the border until you are at the edge of the V. From that point, quilt a diagonal wavy line until it touches the opposite edge of the border.

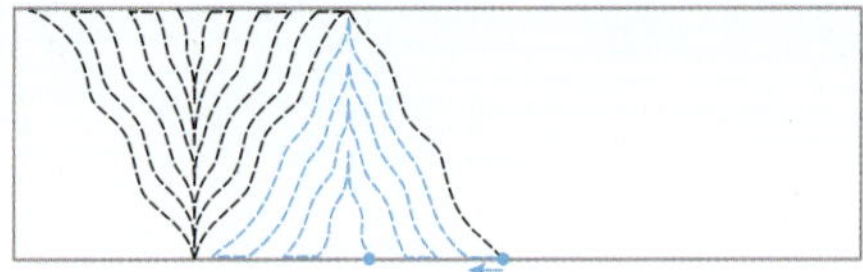

4. Repeat Steps 1 and 2 to fill in the V.

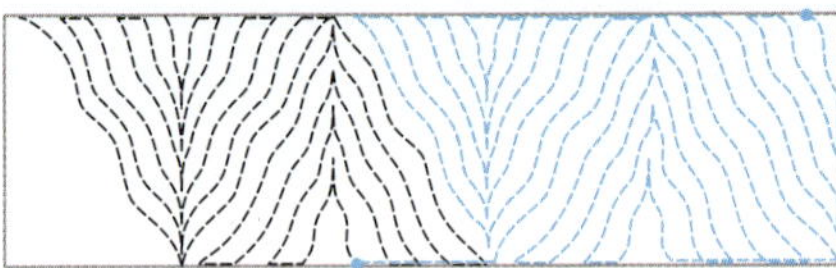

5. Work your way across the border, quilting alternating V shapes and filling them in with the wavy lines.

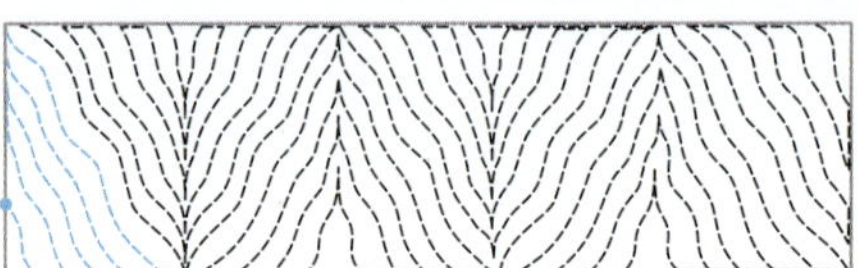

When starting or finishing a border, you will have a half V. Fill those spaces by echoing one side of the V.

This design looks amazing in the corners of a border as well.

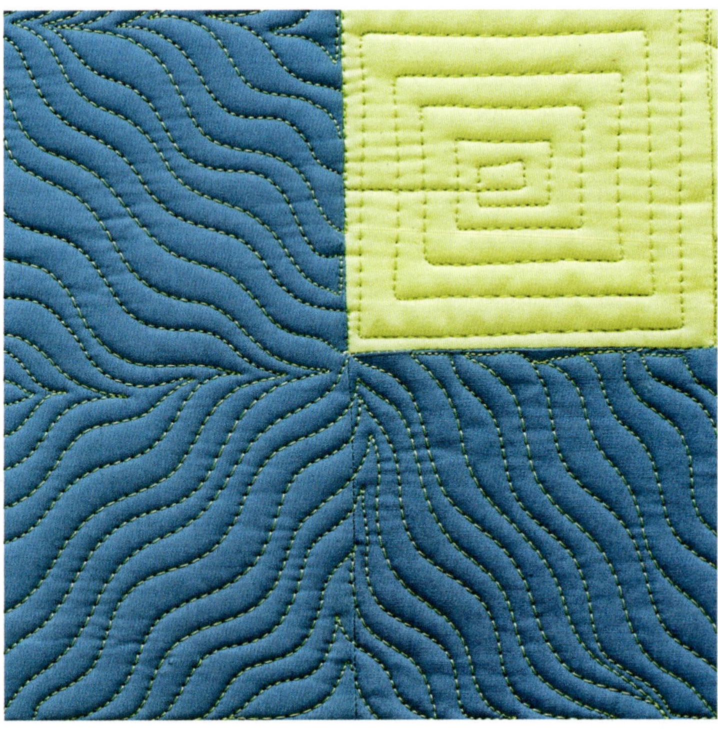

Variations

This design is so fast and fun that you might not need any variations. But just in case, here are a few ideas of how you can give this design a little makeover.

Try quilting the V shapes wider and more spread out.

Instead of keeping the V shapes the same size, vary the widths. Try alternating skinnier and wider V's for an even more organic look.

Try this design in a large square so that each side of the square is the wide part of a V.

SUNRAYS

Wavy lines radiating from the center of the quilt are a modern take on traditional straight-line quilting—without the marking and difficulty of quilting perfectly straight lines. They help draw your attention to the center of the quilt.

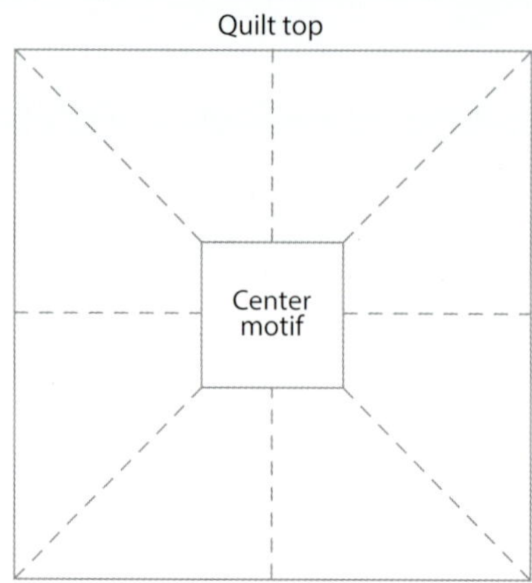

1. Decide on a starting point. I prefer to start on the left and work my way up and around. Mark light registration lines to help you stay on the right angle.

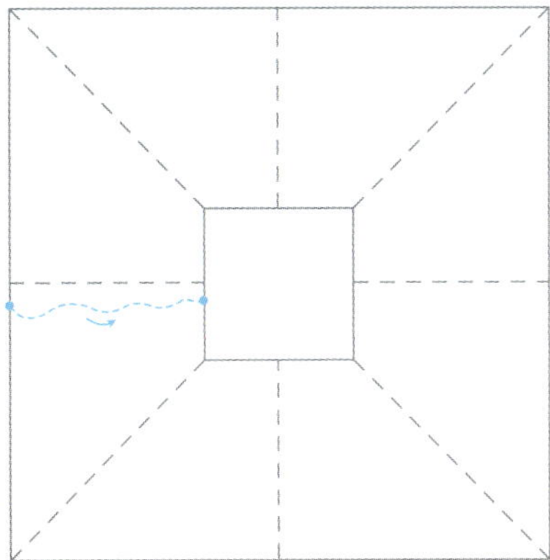

Note

In this illustration, the center of the quilt is a square, but it may be a different shape. The steps are the same; you will just need to take care when tracing along the center.

2. Starting from the edge, quilt a wavy line in toward the center of the quilt. Stop at the edge of the center area.

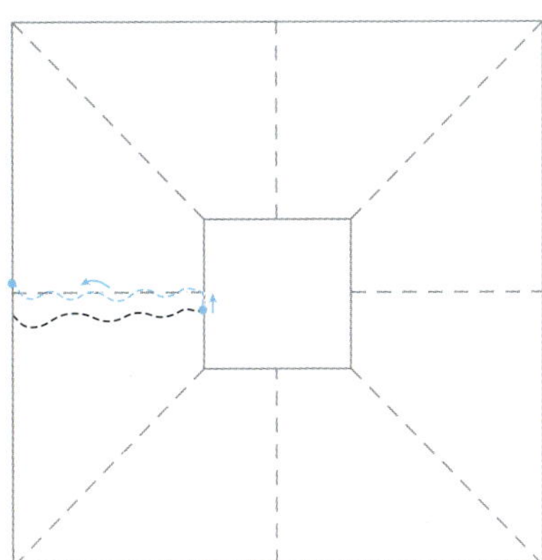

3. Trace up the edge of the quilting area about ¼″ and quilt a wavy line to the outer edge of the quilt, ending about ½″ above the first wavy line. Because they radiate from the center, the wavy lines will be closer in the center of the quilt and farther apart on the outer edge. The registration lines you drew will help you keep them even.

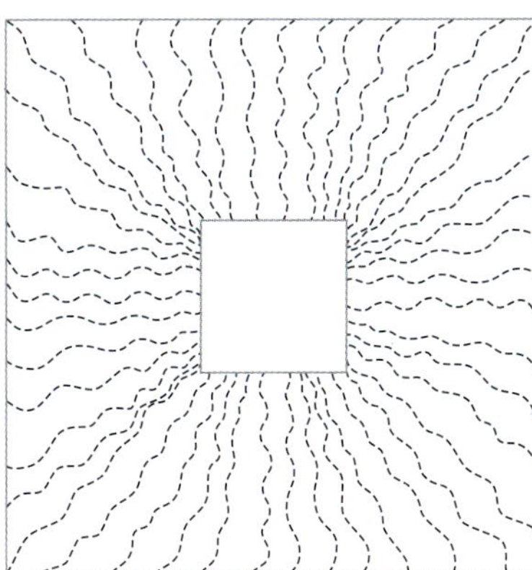

4. Continue quilting wavy lines until you have gone all the way around the quilt.

Modern Variation

Pebbles (page 116) are used with heavy Wavy Lines (page 204) to create a wave.

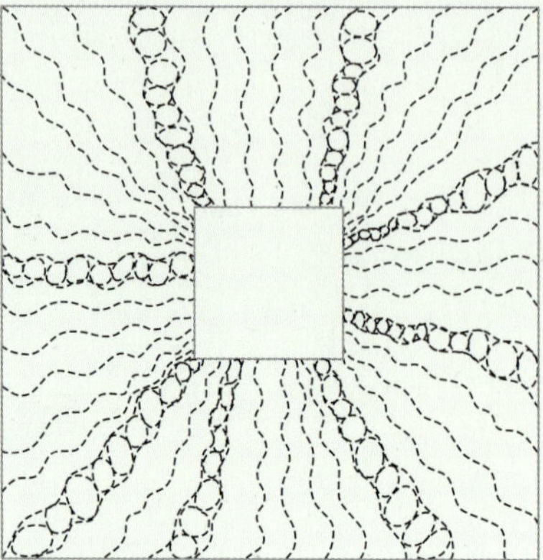

When quilting wavy lines, quilt pebbles between some of the rays. By making the lines of pebbles random, you will add tons of interest to your quilt.

TRIANGLE 1

After all the straight-line designs in this chapter, I knew I had to include something with curves. The pointy shape of a triangle is perfect for a fern quilting design. This design will allow you to easily and evenly fill in triangles of all widths.

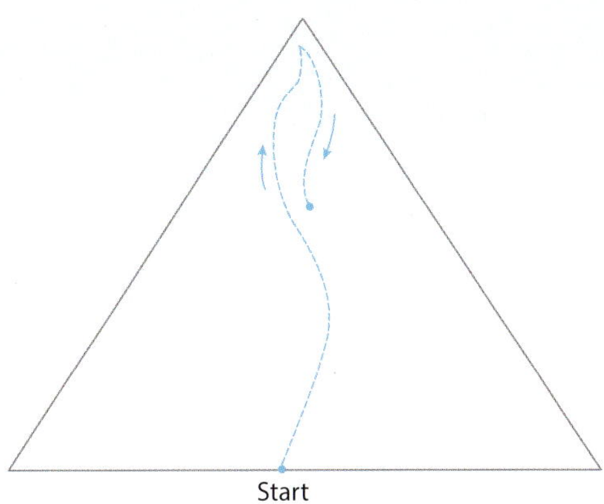

1. Starting from the midpoint of one side, quilt a gentle curve that almost touches the top of the triangle. Quilt a gentle S to form the first side of a petal.

2. Working your way down the spine, quilt petals to fill the area as consistently as possible.

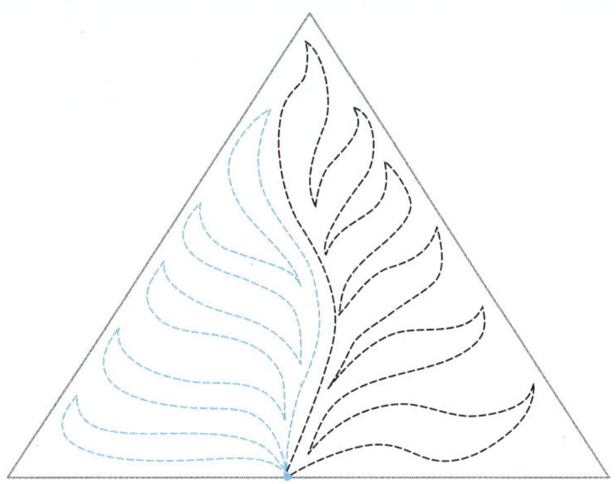

3. Echo up the other side of the spine and quilt petals on the other side of the triangle.

BACK AND FORTH

Probably the easiest quilting design ever, Back & Forth has a stunning impact on any quilt. Use it in wide or skinny areas, long or short areas—any areas! The trick to making this look great is keeping the spacing the same.

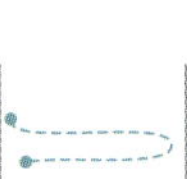

1. Starting from the edge of the area to be quilted, quilt toward the other side. Quilt a U-turn right before you touch the edge, and head back to the first side.

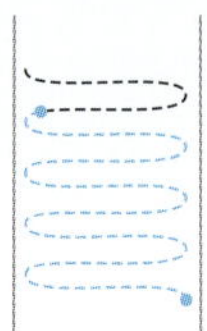

2. Before you reach the left edge, quilt another U-turn, and head back to the opposite edge.

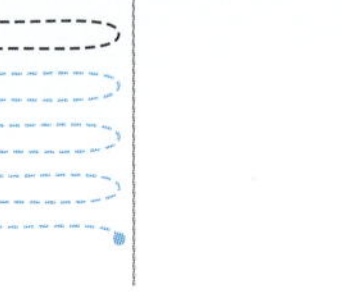

Note

This design looks best when the U-turns don't touch the edges. Try to keep them about ⅛″ away from the edges.

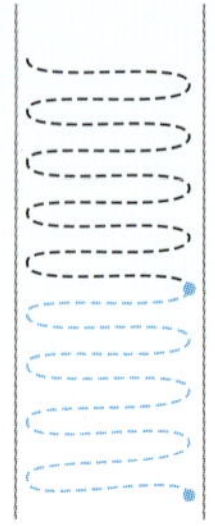

3. Continue to the end of the quilting area.

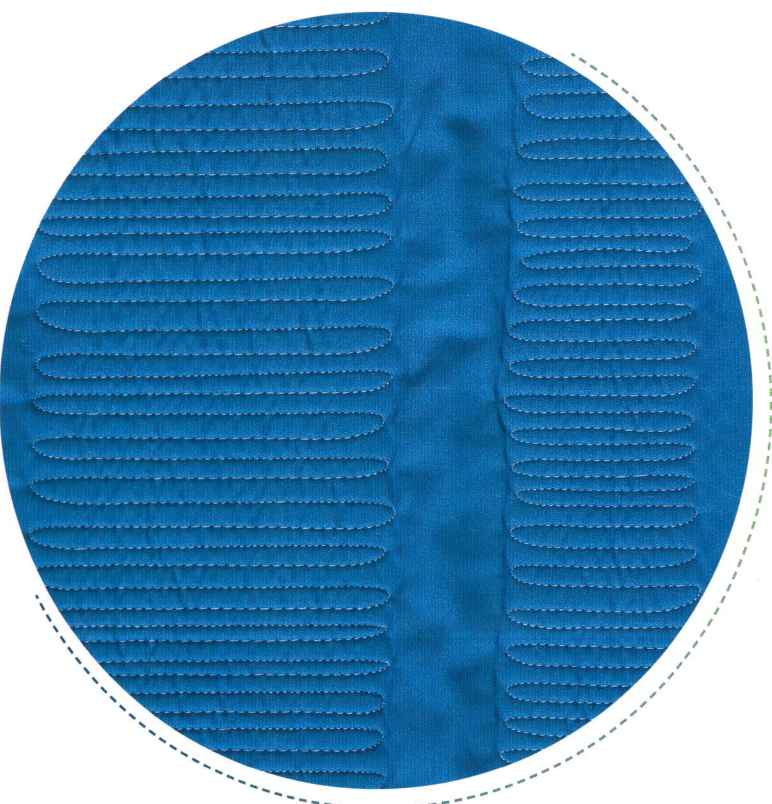

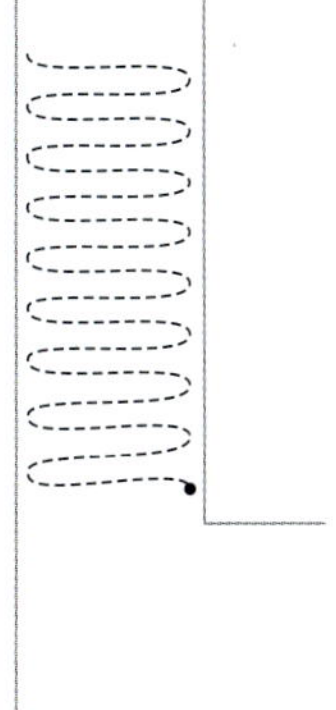

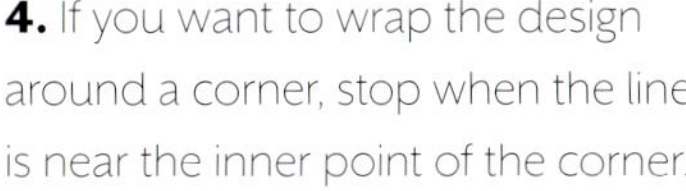

4. If you want to wrap the design around a corner, stop when the line is near the inner point of the corner.

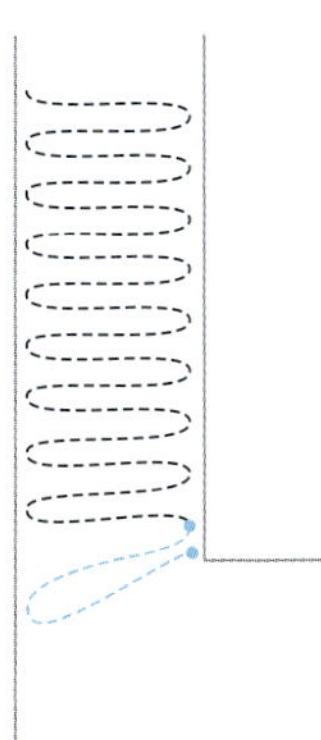

5. Quilt an elongated loop at a slight angle toward the outer edge. Return to the inner corner.

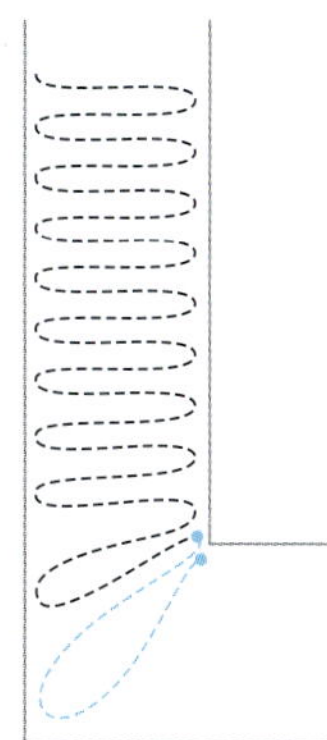

6. Quilt a second elongated loop that lines up with the outer point. Return to the inner corner.

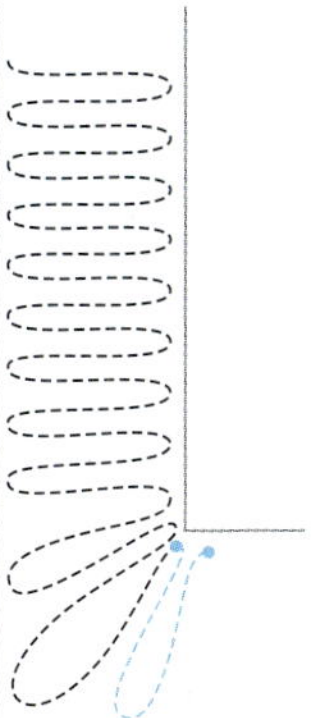

7. Quilt a third loop that is angled toward the bottom edge of the block. Return to the inner corner.

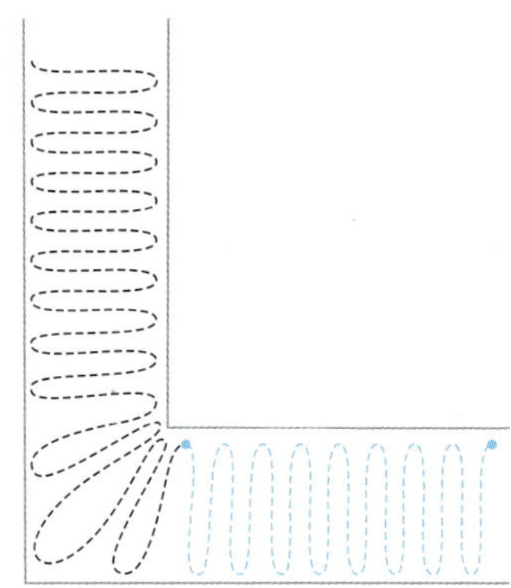

8. Continue quilting the back and forth lines along the bottom of the area.

BACK AND FORTH LINES

I love the look of matchstick quilting: long, densely quilted lines over the whole quilt. This design has the same idea, but the difference is that we are going to break up the design into columns. This can make the quilting more manageable when using a home sewing machine. I also love how the little bits of unquilted area between the columns give the quilt a distinct texture.

This scalable design can be quilted as small or as large as you like. Try it in small areas of negative space or as a quick way to fill up larger areas of negative space. Use the back-and-forth lines around appliquéd blocks or quilting motifs to make them pop! As you can see, there are so many different ways to use it!

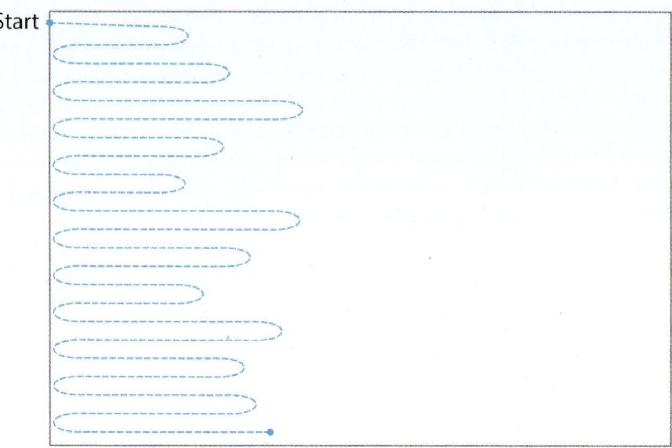

1. Starting in a corner of the quilting area, quilt a column of back-and-forth lines that almost touch the edge but are varying widths. Work your way to the bottom of the quilting area.

Note

Varying the widths of the lines will help the quilting fit together without making the sections so obvious.

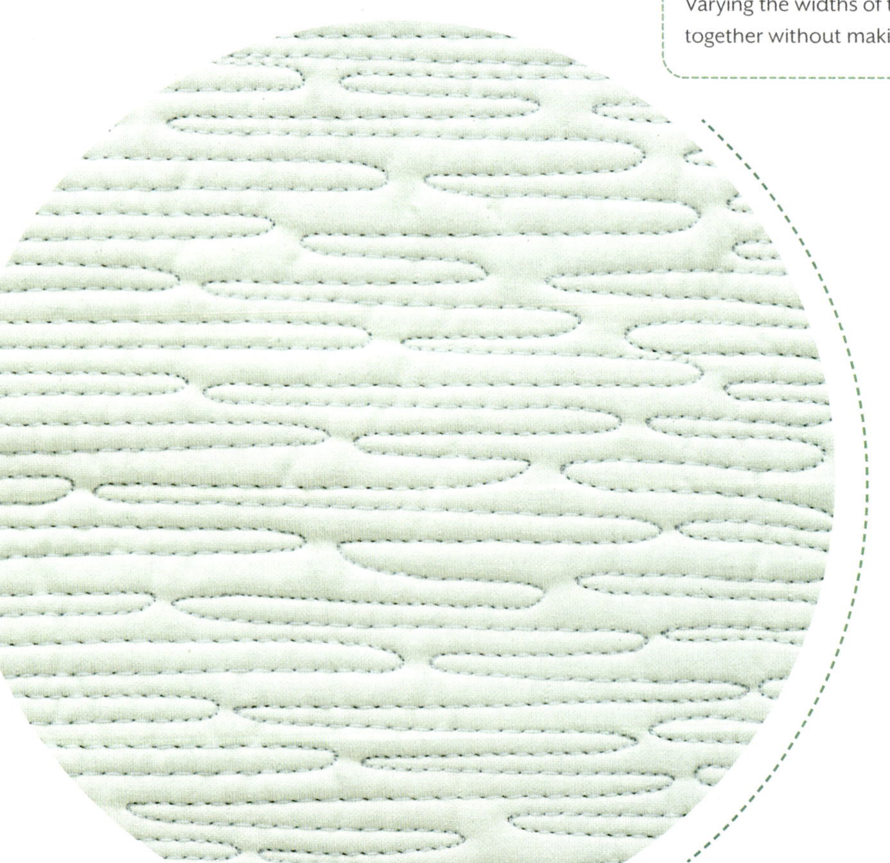

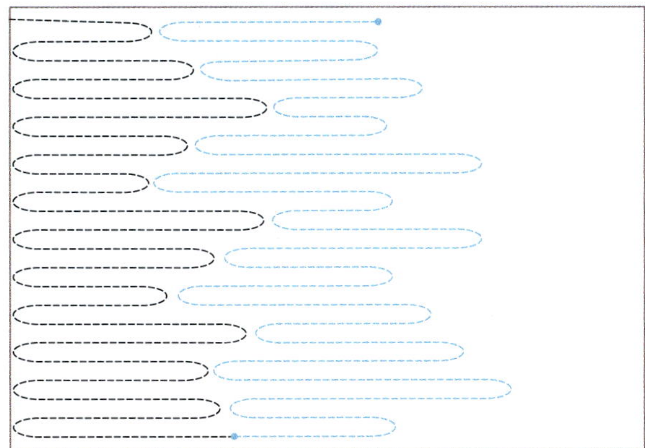

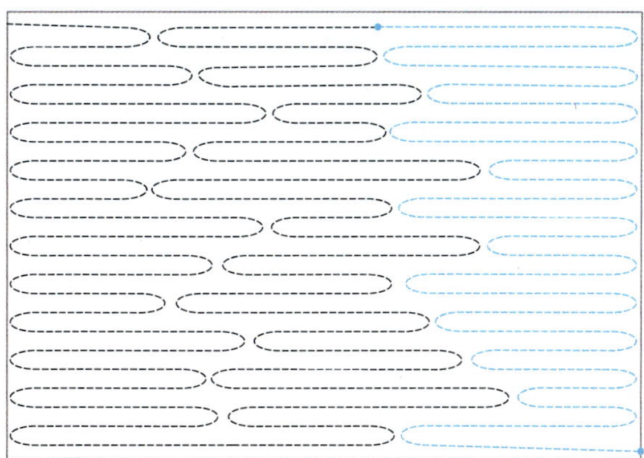

2. At the bottom of the quilting area, begin quilting another column of back-and-forth lines, working your way back up the quilt. Make each of the lines varying widths, but make the lines on one side close to the lines of the previous column.

3. Depending on the size of your quilting area, continue quilting columns of back-and-forth lines. When you get to the edge of the quilting area, quilt the lines so they fit in the remaining space.

Variations

I love the texture that this design adds to a quilt. But if you want to change things up just a bit, try changing directions of the lines. Quilt one area with horizontal lines and quilt the next with vertical back-and-forth lines.

HEXAGON 1

Nothing makes me happier than quilting that adds texture. I especially like this design for tumbling-block quilts, because the directional lines define each face of the tumbling block. The dense back-and-forth lines create texture that invites you to run your fingers over it.

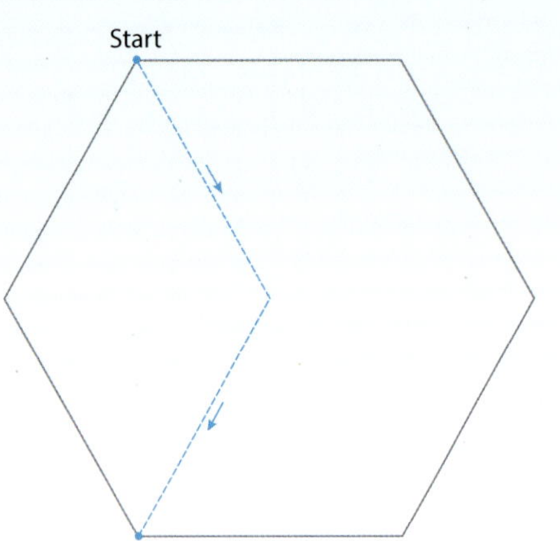

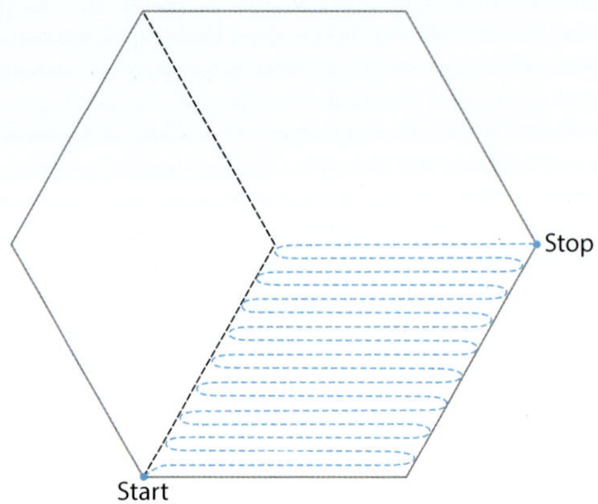

1. From one corner of the hexagon, quilt a line diagonally to the center of the block. Pivot and quilt a straight line to the corner directly below the starting point.

2. Quilt dense lines horizontally from the quilted line to the edge of the block. End so that the last line goes from the center of the block to the corner.

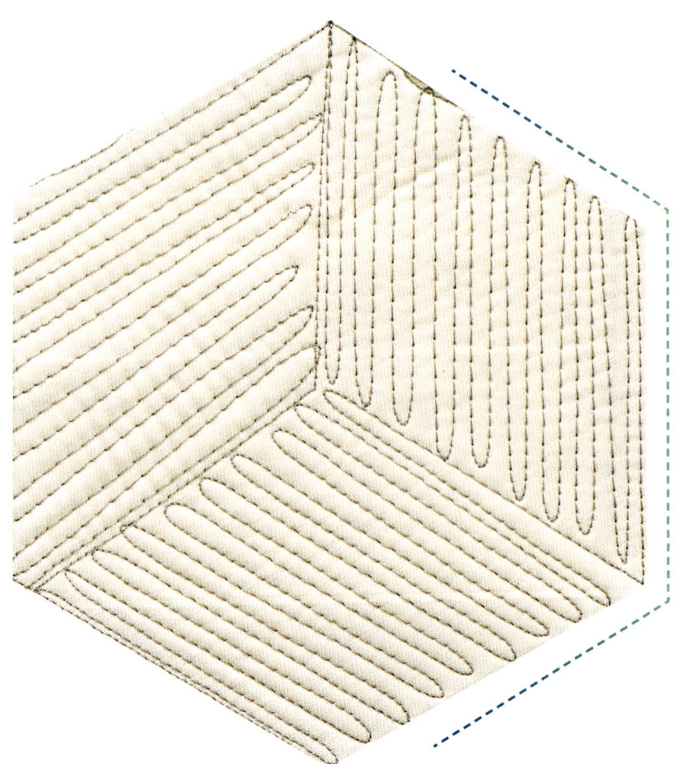

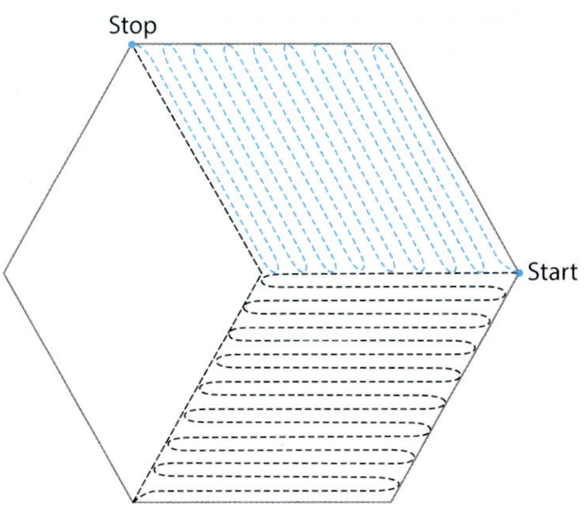

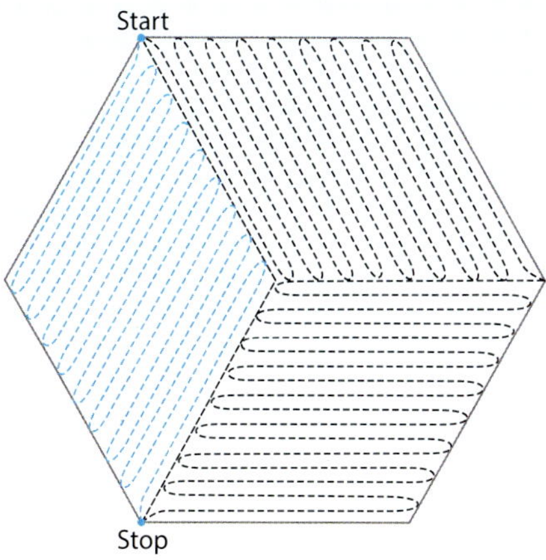

3. From the corner, quilt the same dense back-and-forth lines that you did in Step 2, changing the direction from horizontal to diagonal. End at the top corner of the block.

Tip

Use the edges of the block as a reminder of what direction to quilt the back-and-forth lines.

4. Fill in the last section of the block with the back-and-forth lines, making sure the direction of the diagonal lines follows the sides of the block.

To readily move on to the next block, make sure the stitching ends on the bottom corner of the block instead of the center.

Variations

Quilting all three sections of the block with the same dense quilting provides awesome texture to the quilt. But, if you want to give your block the illusion of depth, quilt one section of the block less densely than the rest. You could also switch out the back-and-forth lines with straight lines that echo the side of the section. The result is quilting that gives your quilt a look of depth.

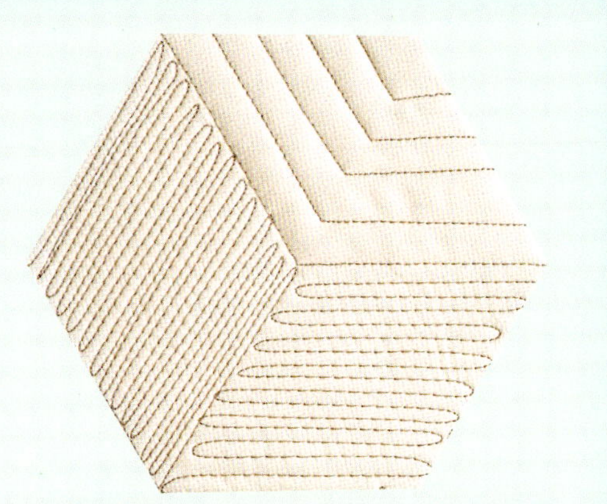

Quilting blocks with designs of different densities will give your block an illusion of depth.

BORDER: DOUBLE WISHBONES

What's better than quilting the wishbone design in your narrow borders and sashing? Twice the wishbones! This design spreads out the basic wishbone design and fills in with a second one.

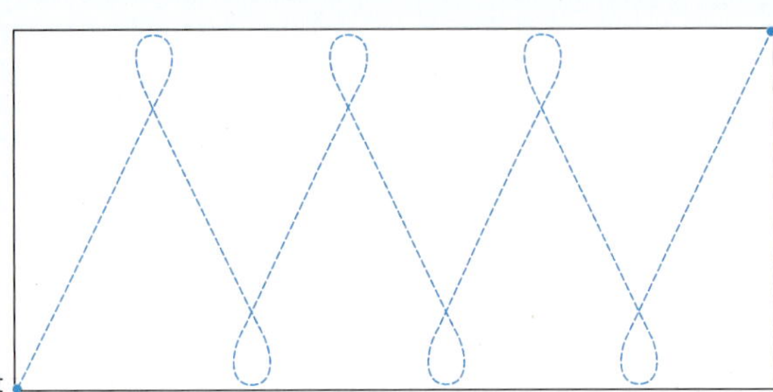

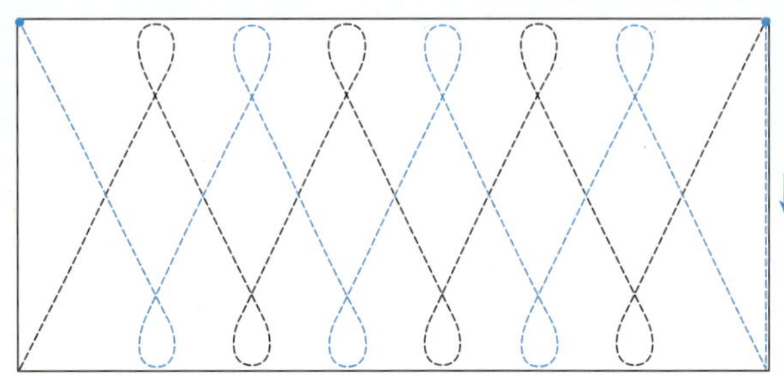

1. Starting on a long side of the border, quilt a wishbone design across the border. Spread the wishbones out about 1˝ or so to leave room for the next step.

2. Work your way back across the border, quilting new wishbones between those you stitched in Step 1.

Turning the corner isn't hard at all. Just pivot around the inner corner.

Quilt a large wishbone in the corner, using the inner corner as a pivot point.

Variation

Make a softer, rounder wishbone design by placing the circles inside the curved lines.

Alter the entire look of the wishbone design by changing the placement of the circles.

BORDER: ANGLED LINES

Great for small, narrow borders, this design is perfect when you aren't sure what to do. It has some traveling, but don't worry if it's not perfect. The quilting will cover up any traveling mistakes!

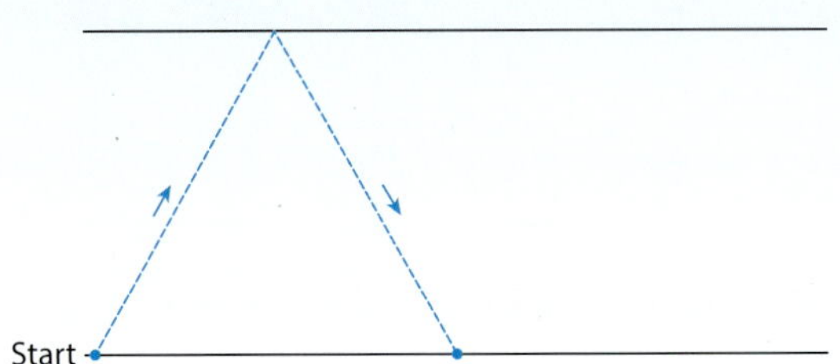

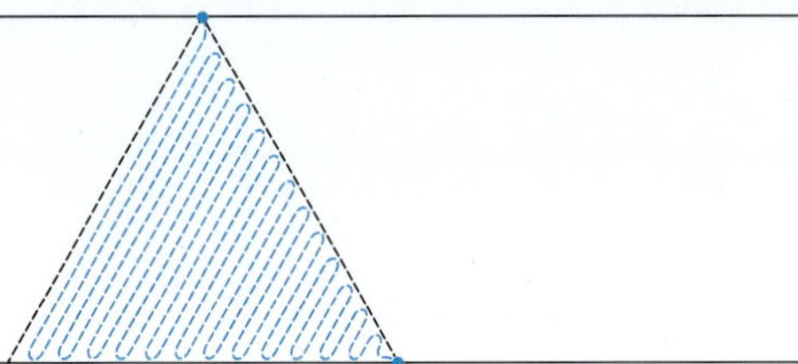

1. Quilt a diagonal line from the inside border to the outer border. Continue stitching another diagonal line back to the inside border.

2. Fill the triangle with a back-and-forth line parallel to 1 of the diagonal lines, ending at the outer edge of the border.

Note

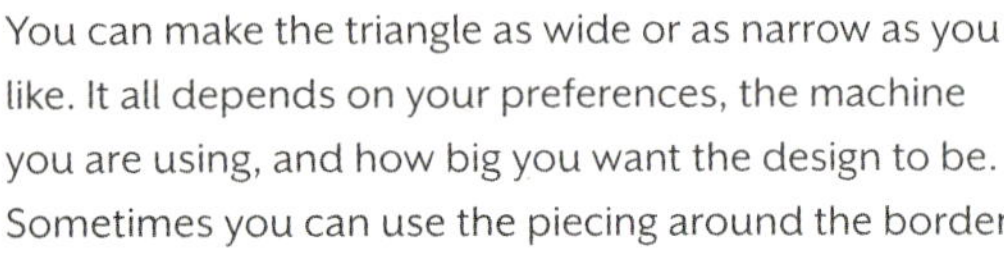

You can make the triangle as wide or as narrow as you like. It all depends on your preferences, the machine you are using, and how big you want the design to be. Sometimes you can use the piecing around the border as guide for spacing out your triangles.

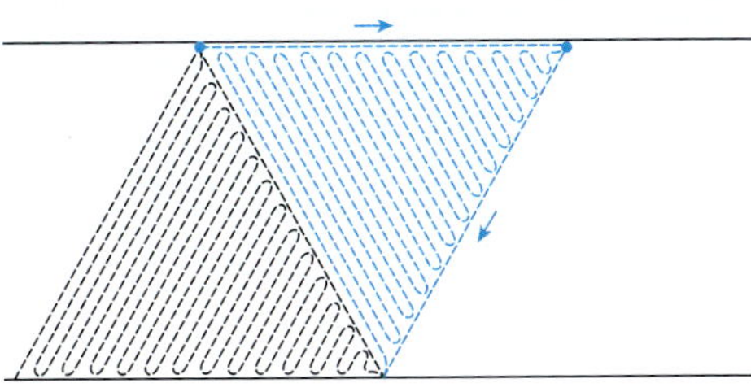

3. Travel along the edge of the border about 2″–3″, then quilt a diagonal line back to the outer point of the first triangle. Fill the new triangle with a back-and-forth line in the opposite direction as the filler in the previous triangle, ending at the tip of the triangle.

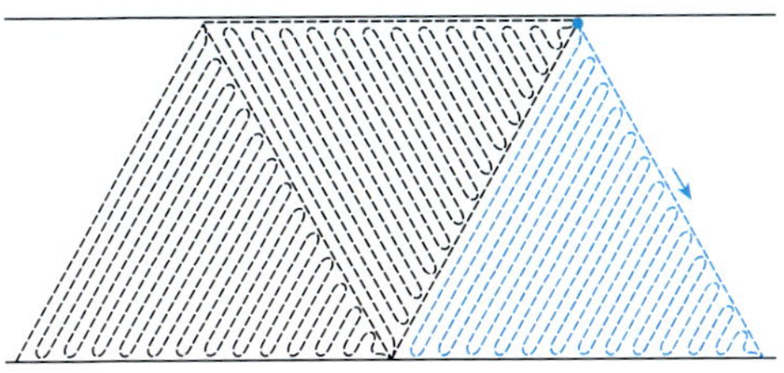

4. Continue to add triangles and fill them in, alternating the direction of the filler stitching in each triangle.

Variations

If you'd like a more open look for your borders, replace the back-and-forth filler with a few zigzag lines.

Widely spaced zigzags create more open space in the border.

Add a strong zigzag line throughout the border by leaving a little gap between the back-and-forth lines and the outer edge of each triangle.

Create a zigzag line by leaving space between the triangle edge and the filler quilting.

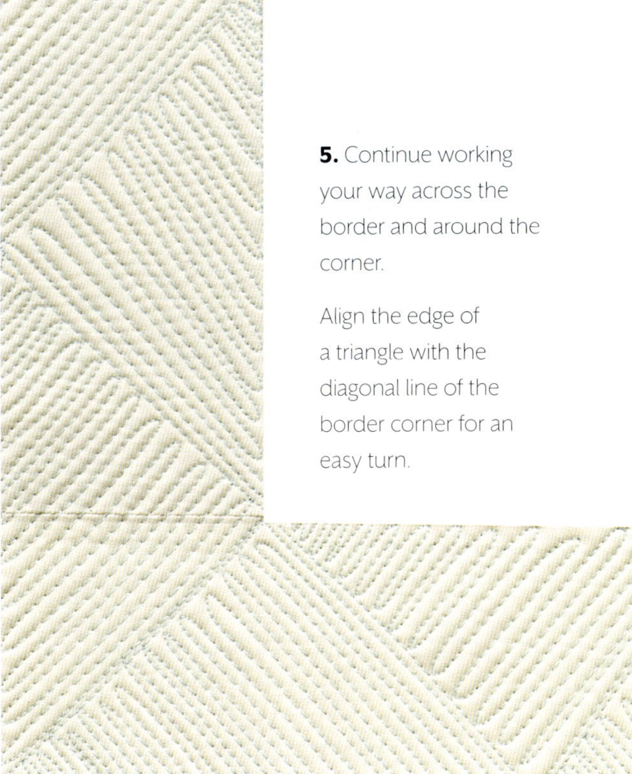

5. Continue working your way across the border and around the corner.

Align the edge of a triangle with the diagonal line of the border corner for an easy turn.

PLUME FEATHER

The Plume Feather is more of a fern, but whatever you call it, it packs a punch! This design can fill irregular shapes of any height or width and is one of my favorite designs. It can fit in any shape or block, but for this illustration, we will be using a triangle.

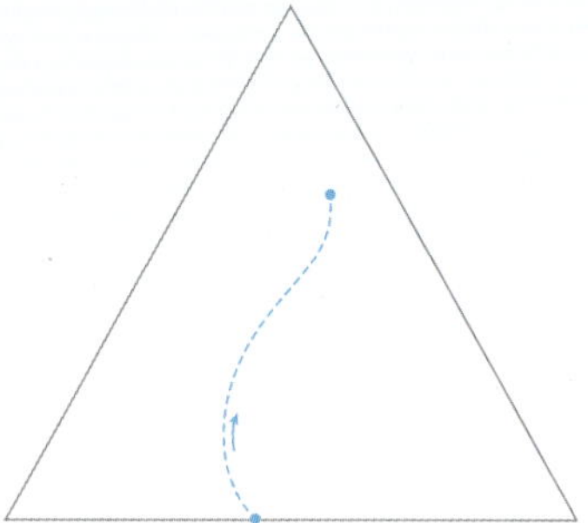

1. From the middle of the bottom edge, quilt a gently curving line toward the top.

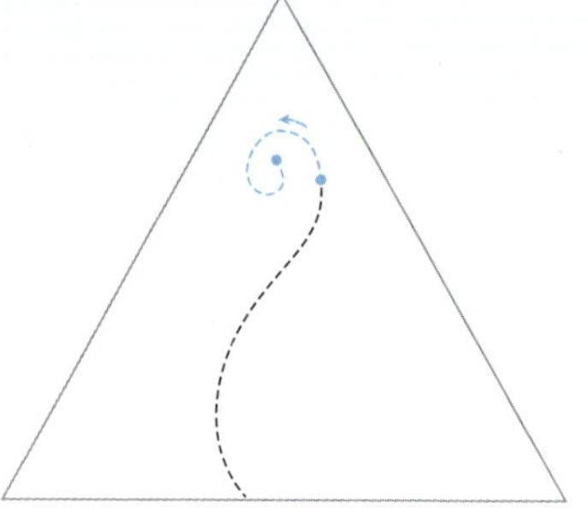

2. Before you reach the top, quilt the inside of a swirl.

3. Echo out of the swirl, heading toward the top of the quilting area.

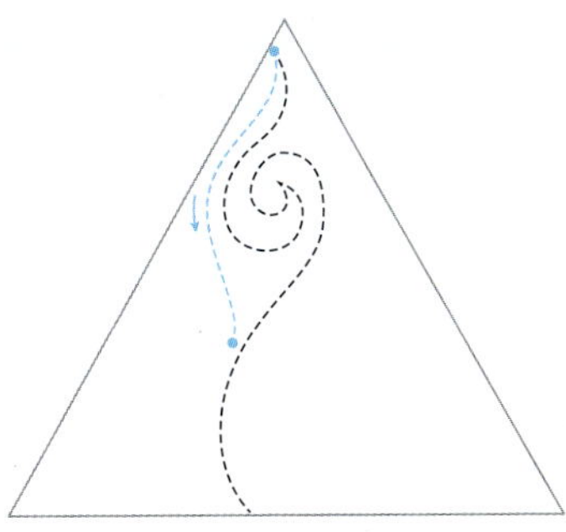

4. Echo the left side of the line, curving around the outside of the swirl and ending when you are touching the center line.

Note

As you approach the center line, angle down as if you were going to trace the center line. This will make the rest of your design fit better.

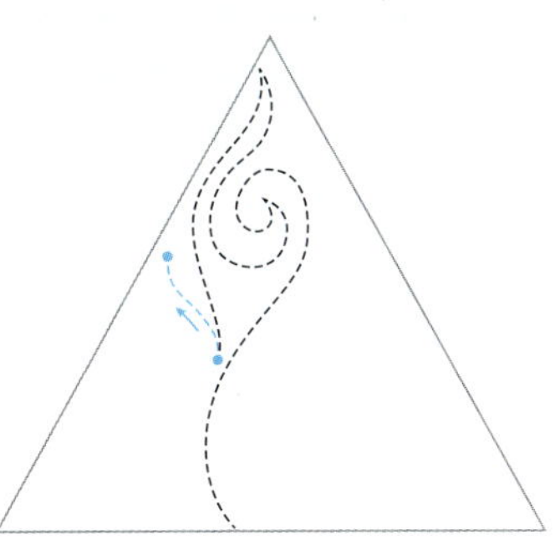

5. Echo the curve back toward the top, following the same curve. Stop when you reach the edge.

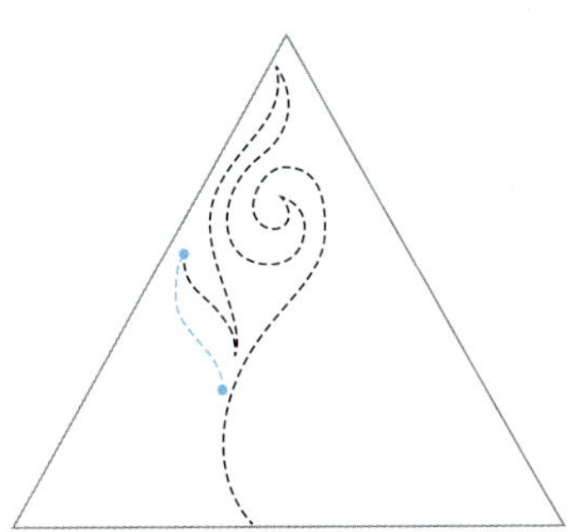

6. Echo back down toward the center line, touching it at the same angle as the line above.

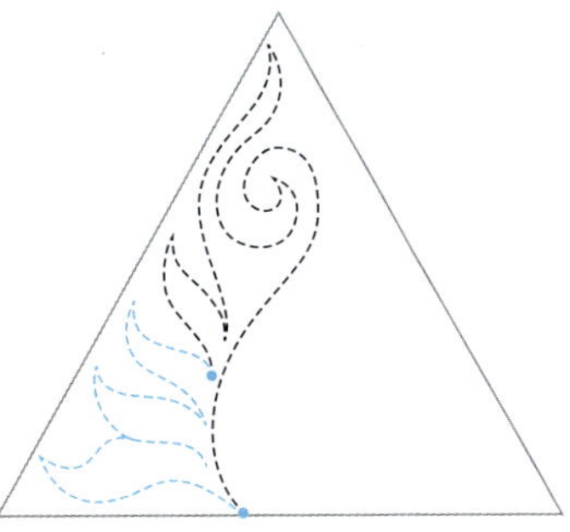

7. This is an individual leaf of the feather. Continue quilting the leaves, filling the space until you reach the bottom. End at the starting point.

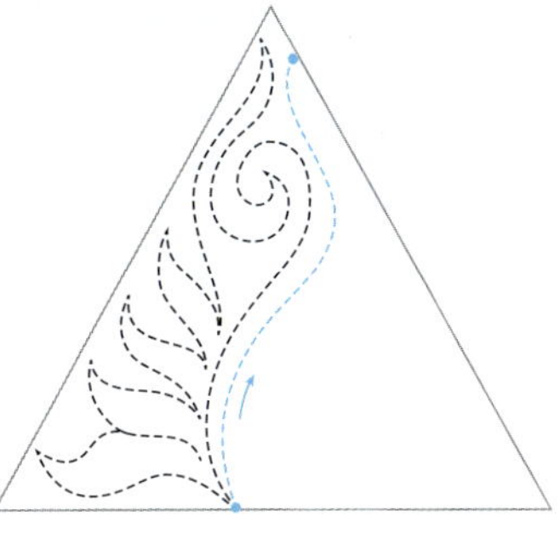

8. Echo the main stem until you are ¼″ from the top of the quilting area.

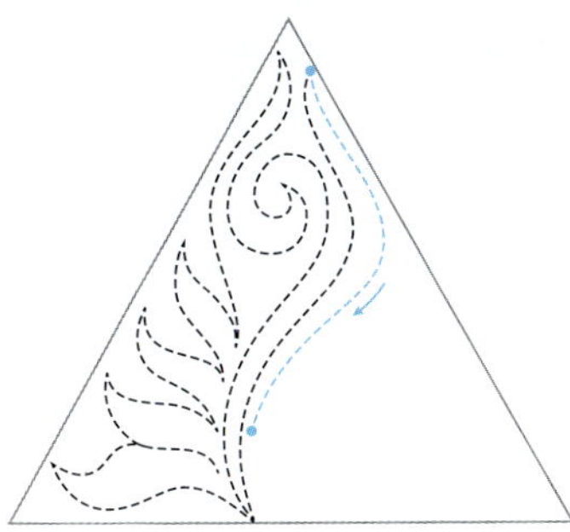

9. Echo the line you just quilted, curving out and back until you touch the center stem. Don't forget to come in at the same angle as the center line.

10. Quilt a leaf, echoing out and back to the center line.

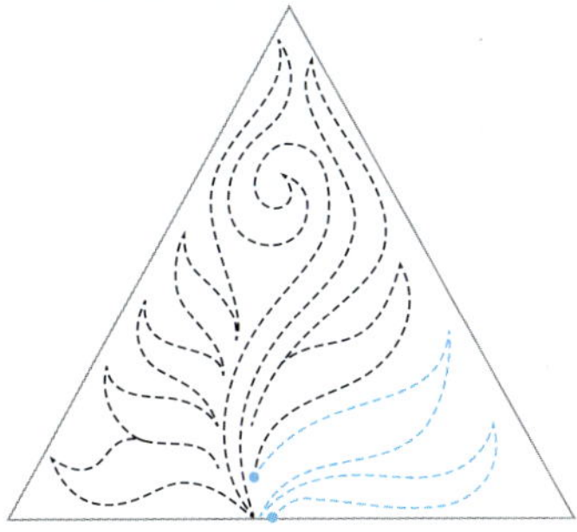

11. Continue quilting the leaves down the side of the design until you reach the bottom.

FEATHER MEANDER

Feathers are the one quilting design that I really, really wanted to learn when I first started quilting. It took a lot of practice, but I finally figured it out. This meander takes a feather quilting design and makes it a little more manageable by only quilting one side. Once you're comfortable quilting this design, you will practically be ready for quilting full feathers in all areas of your quilts.

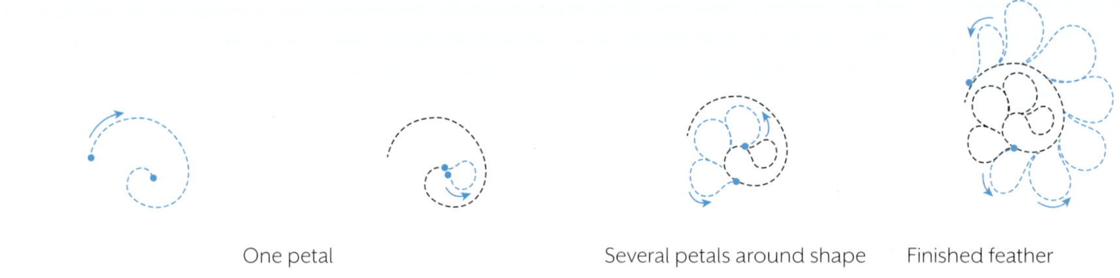

One petal

Several petals around shape

Finished feather

1. Start by quilting a swirl shape (page 120), leaving at least ½″ between the lines. The swirl doesn't have to be any particular size, just make sure that there is enough space in between the lines to add the petals.

2. From the center of the swirl, begin quilting petal shapes.

Continued on page 236

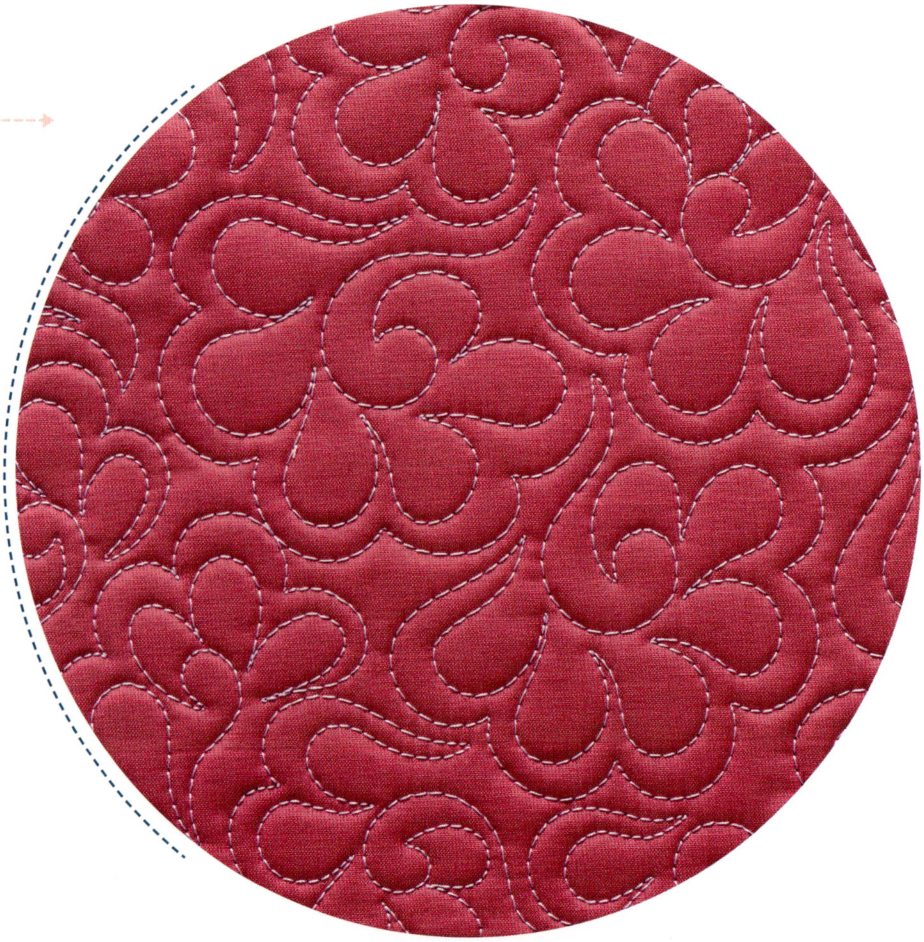

Note

The petal shape is similar to a "half-heart" shape if we were to stretch out the swirl and lay it straight.

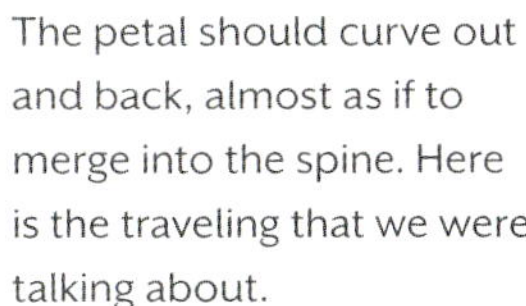

The petal should curve out and back, almost as if to merge into the spine. Here is the traveling that we were talking about.

Leave an area to quilt the next petal, so that it fits snuggly into the first petal.

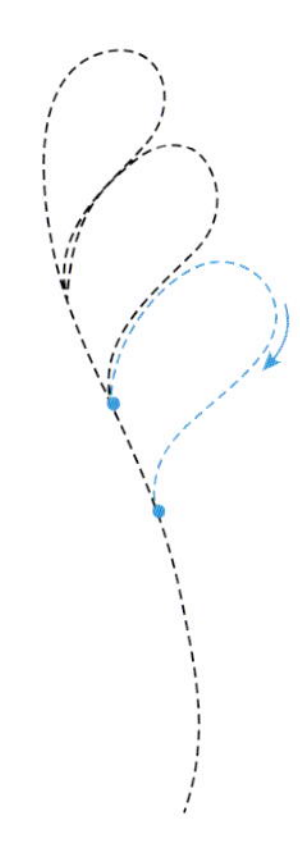

It helps me to think of it as though the bottom of the petal "merges" into the spine. It travels along the line, but just for a short time.

The petals can touch each other, or there can be a space.

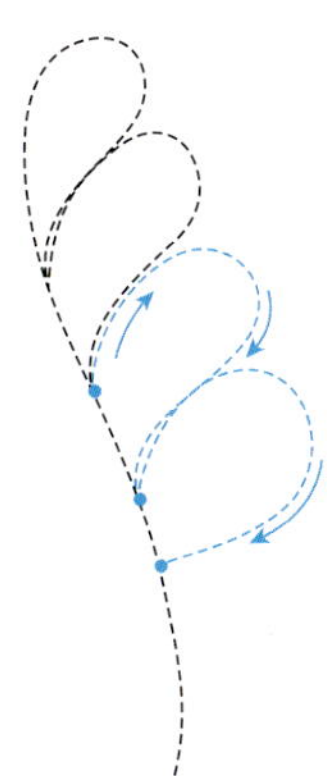

If the petal doesn't merge into the line, it will look like this.

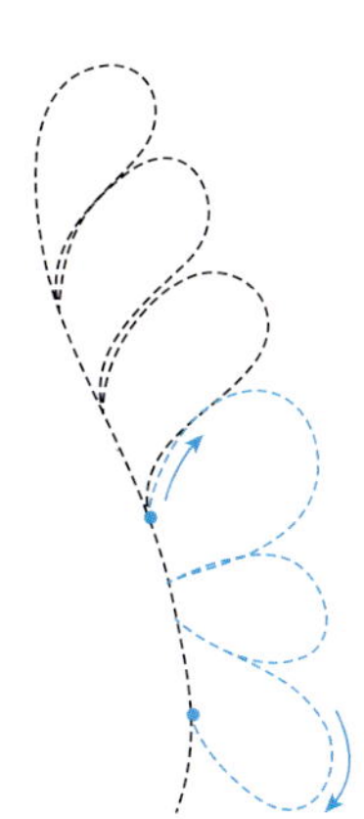

As you can see, it leaves no room for the next petal.

Soon your petals will be going the wrong direction.

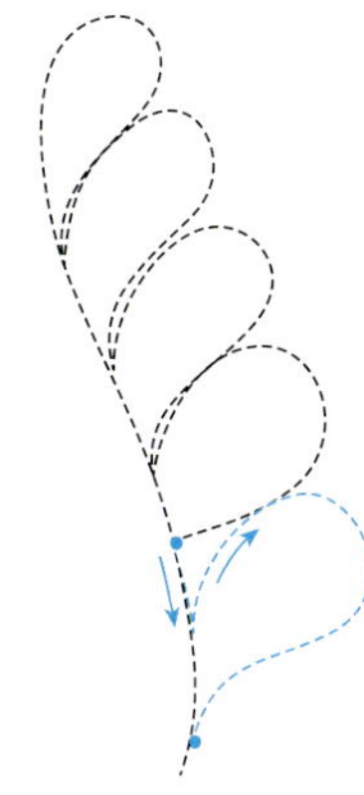

If you notice that your petal isn't merging into the spine, travel down then start the next one. It might look weird now, but it won't be as noticeable when the quilt is finished.

This has happened to me more than once. It's more important to keep going instead of stopping.

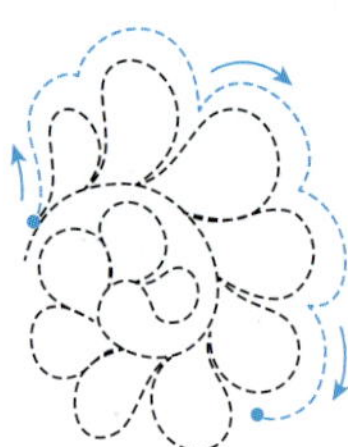

3. Once you are finished with the first swirl, echo around the feather until you get to where you would like to add your next feather.

This doesn't have to be any certain place, just pick a spot that looks good.

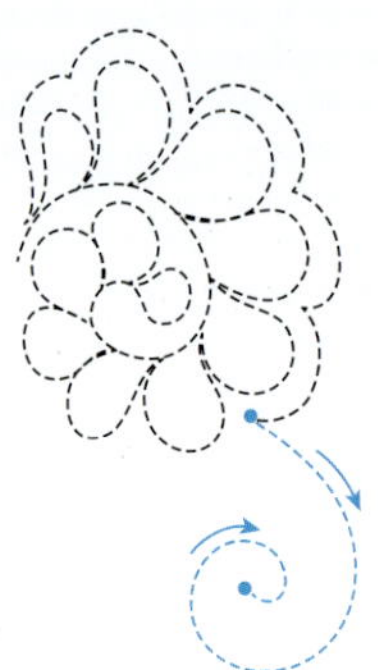

4. Quilt another swirl that extends from the first one. Don't be afraid to let it go out into the unquilted area.

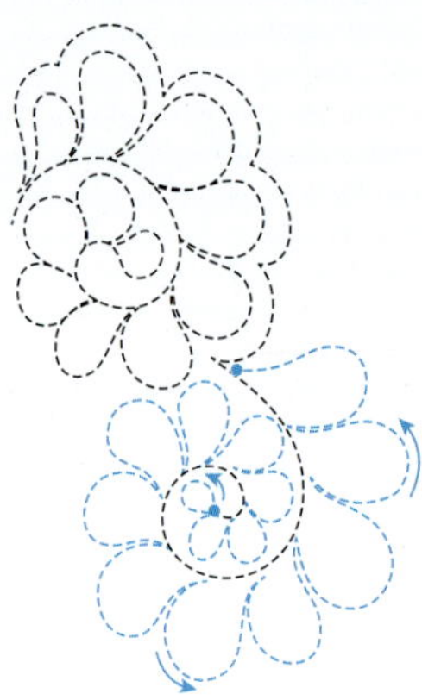

5. Add petals around the swirl, just as you did in the first feather.

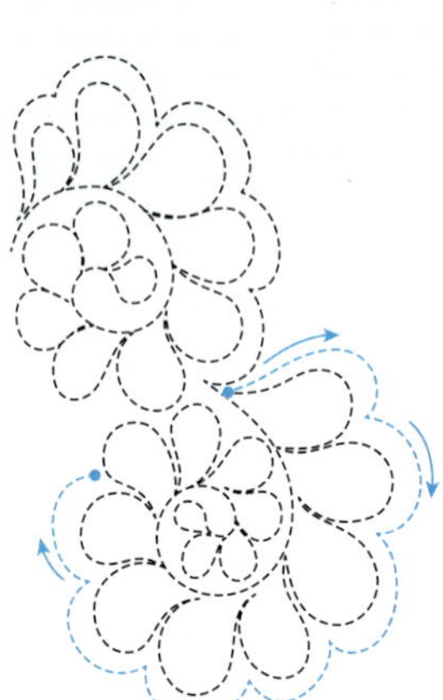

6. Echo around the feather to get to the area you would like to quilt your next feather.

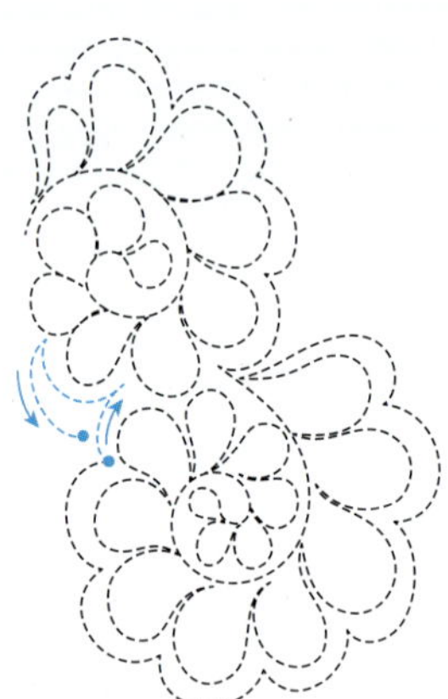

Echoing also helps you fill in any gaps between the feathers.

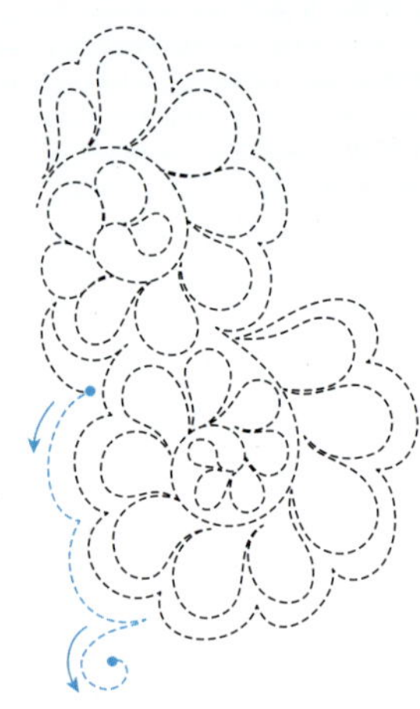

In the corners, if you can't fit another feather, just echo or add another swirl like I have.

Then, echo around until you have space to add your next one.

Fill in gaps between feathers with more echoing.

Note

You can also echo around a previously quilted feather.

7. Continue quilting until the whole area is filled.

FAUX ROPE

Faux Rope is a little fancy but could be perfect for the right kind of quilt. This design uses no markings, and it begins and ends in the same place, which makes it efficient as well as striking.

The Faux Rope is quilted in two sections, first the top and then the bottom. Before you start, determine where the top of your design will be. This might be the top of a block or a line you have marked on your quilt top.

Top of quilting area

Bottom of quilting area

1. From the middle of the bottom edge of your quilting area, quilt a gentle S curve, ending in the middle of the top edge.

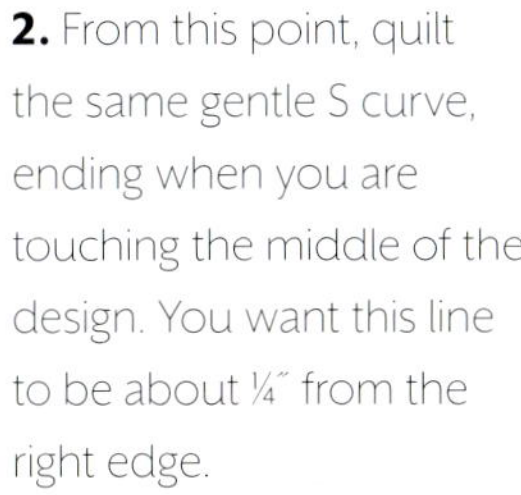

2. From this point, quilt the same gentle S curve, ending when you are touching the middle of the design. You want this line to be about ¼˝ from the right edge.

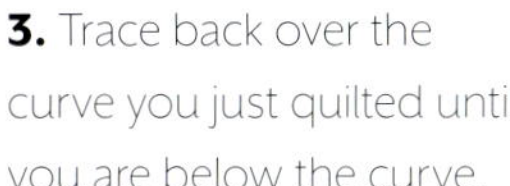

3. Trace back over the curve you just quilted until you are below the curve.

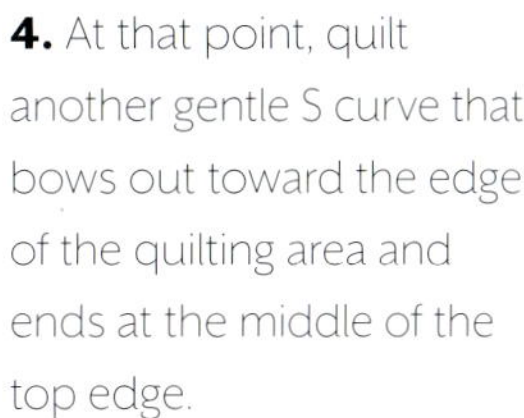

4. At that point, quilt another gentle S curve that bows out toward the edge of the quilting area and ends at the middle of the top edge.

5. Now that you have completed the top portion of the design, echo along the middle of the design, ending at the middle of the bottom edge.

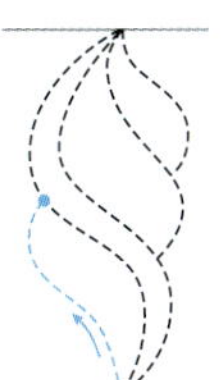

6. Quilt the bottom half of the rope the same as you quilted the top.

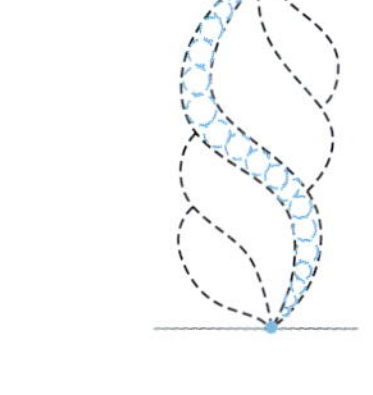

If you would like to make your faux rope stand out more, you can quilt Pebbles (page 116) up the center spine.

CIRCLE 1

Feathers, feathers, feathers—is there anything better? This design is a twist on the classic quilting feather.

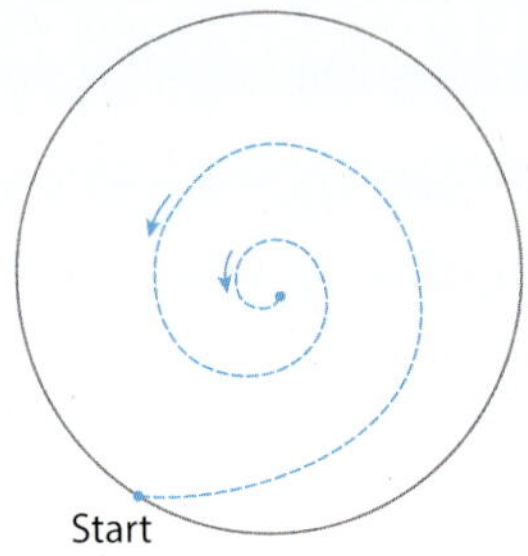

1. Starting from any point on the outside edge of the circle, quilt a spiral inside the circle, ending at the center.

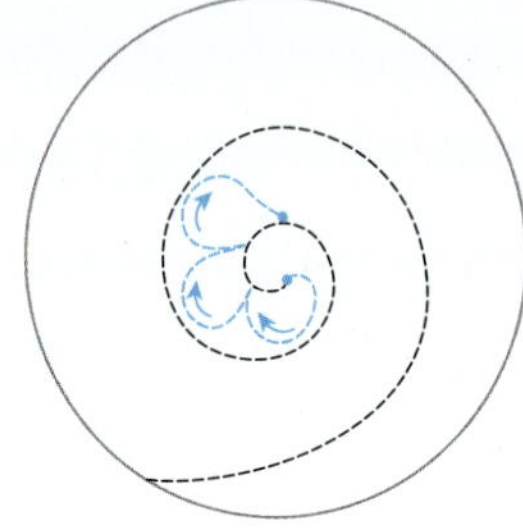

2. From the center of the circle, start adding petals along the spiral. For the petals, imagine that you are quilting a half heart shape.

Tip

Try to keep the lines at least 1˝ apart. This will ensure that you have room to quilt the petals in the next step.

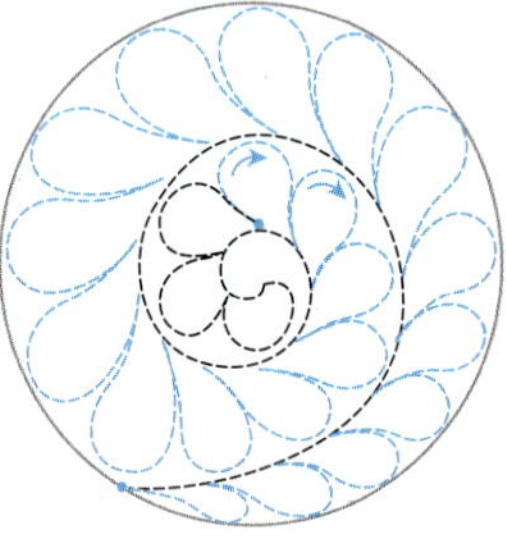

3. Continue adding the petals, filling in the space consistently until you end up where you started.

Variations

To quilt a variation of this design, echo inside each petal as you go. This is especially effective for larger circles or for circles where you want more quilting.

Try echoing the petals for a variation of the design.

SQUARE 1

This design fits the petals of a feather into a square shape. I like to use it in smaller squares, especially on irish chain quilts, or as a way to soften the corners of a complex block. You can use this block design as a great way to practice feather designs without committing to using them over the whole quilt.

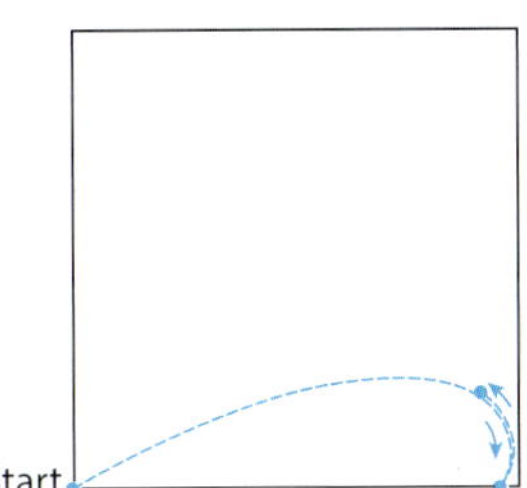

1. First, decide on a starting point. This will be your pivot corner, meaning that all of the lines will come back to this point. Quilt a softly curving line that makes a sharper curve toward the adjacent corner just before you reach the other side of the block. Travel back along the curve about ½".

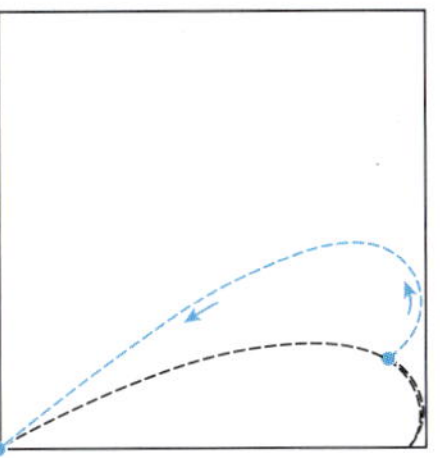

2. Quilt the next petal of the feather by stitching a line that curves out a bit and then returns to the starting corner.

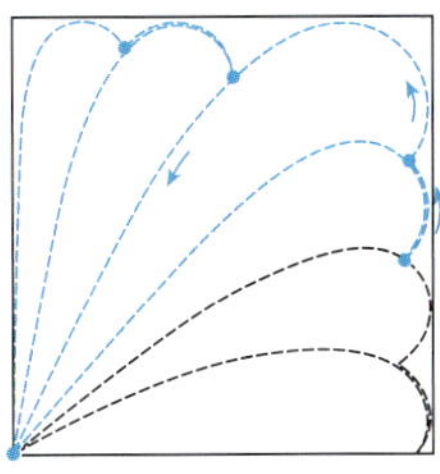

3. Continue quilting the petals, filling in the block as much as possible.

Note 

The petal that goes to the opposite corner from the starting point will be bigger than the rest.

4. To move on to the next block, travel along the block edges.

Variation

Quilting 4 blocks with the same pivot point will give you a design that looks like a feather wreath but is much easier to quilt!

Create a wreath design by quilting 4 blocks with the same pivot point.

BORDER: SERPENTINE CLUSTERS

One design that I love, love, love to use in borders is the serpentine line. It adds a bit of depth to the quilt but is a quick design to quilt (once you get the hang of it!). This variation of the serpentine line adds free-motion quilting motifs for an unusual look.

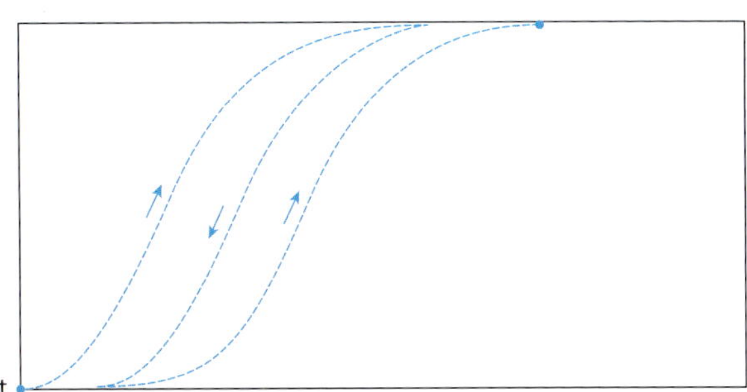

1. Quilt a serpentine line that goes from a long side of the border to the opposite side. Travel along the border edge and echo the line 2 more times.

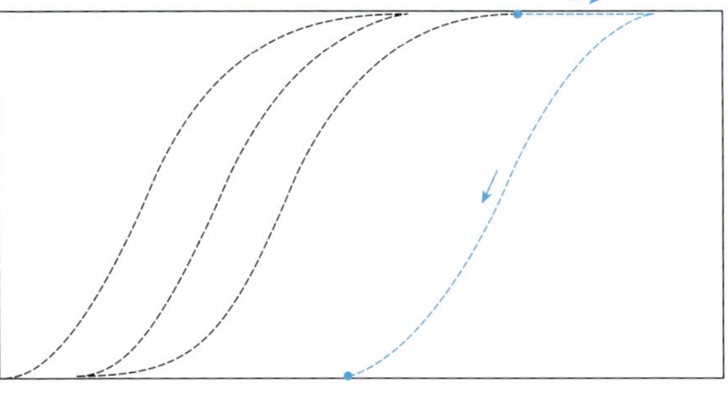

2. After quilting a group of serpentine lines, travel along the edge of the border for about 2″ and quilt another serpentine line.

Note

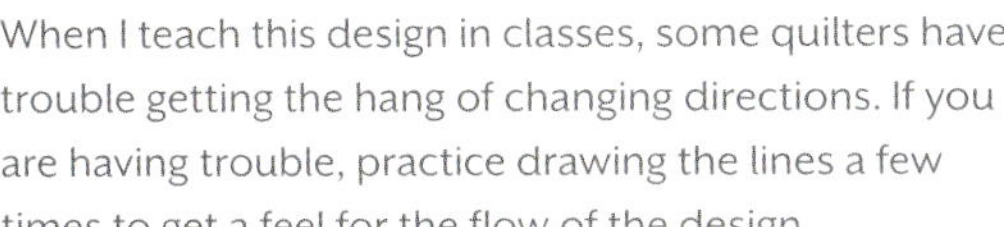

When I teach this design in classes, some quilters have trouble getting the hang of changing directions. If you are having trouble, practice drawing the lines a few times to get a feel for the flow of the design.

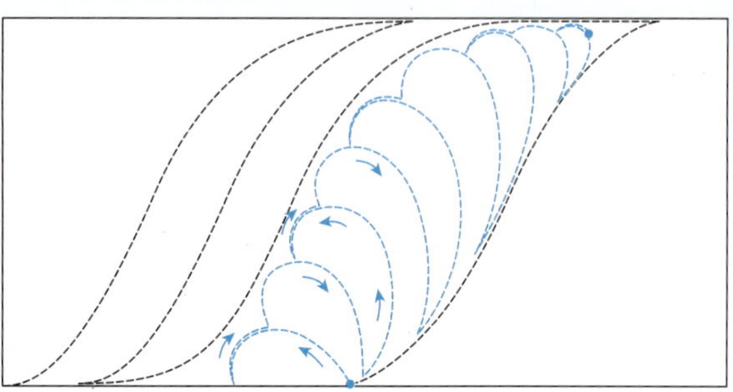

3. Before continuing with the serpentine lines, fill the gap with a different design. I quilted the sides of a feather, but you could quilt something different, such as a wishbone design.

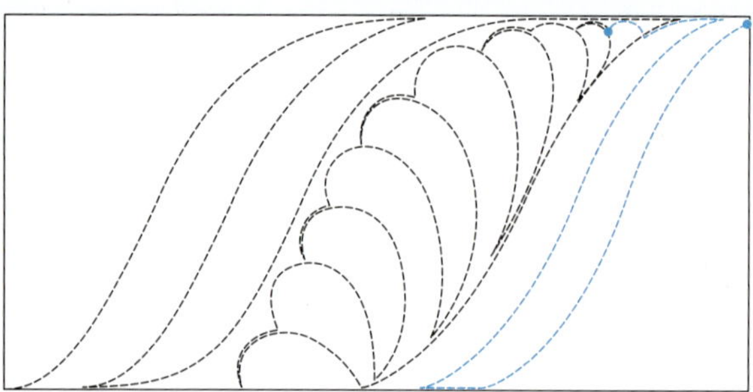

4. Continue quilting the design across the border, alternating between groups of serpentine lines and a filler design.

5. When you get to the corner of the border, quilt the lines so that they wrap around to the next side.

Use the inner border corner as a reference to wrap the serpentine lines around the corner.

Note

Even though I tend to quilt the serpentine lines in groups of three, you could have more or fewer lines in your group.

Variations

Switch up the design to make it work for you!

Instead of quilting all the serpentine lines in the same direction, you can alternate between directions to create a different texture. This gives the design a different look altogether.

Change the direction of every other set of lines to create a more open look.

Try experimenting with different fillers to find which one works best for you.

This wishbone filler makes the serpentine lines stand out more.

ARCS & POINTS

ARCS

This design is so easy that it can be underrated. But don't let the simplicity fool you. Arcs are one of my all-time favorite designs for thinner pieces on a quilt. Wedges, irregular strips, and borders are great places to quilt arcs.

Tip

Don't worry about measuring. Once you get in a rhythm, it will be easier to keep the spacing even.

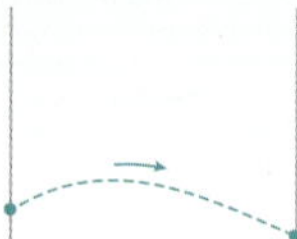

1. Starting at the bottom, quilt a gentle arc from one side to the other. Try to line up the points parallel to each other.

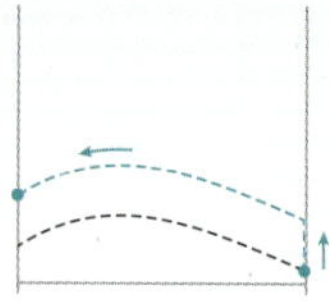

2. Travel up the side ¼″ and quilt an arc going back to the other side.

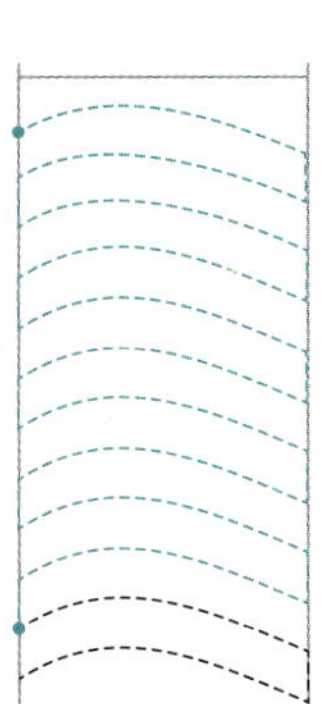

3. Repeat, quilting arcs until you reach the top of the area.

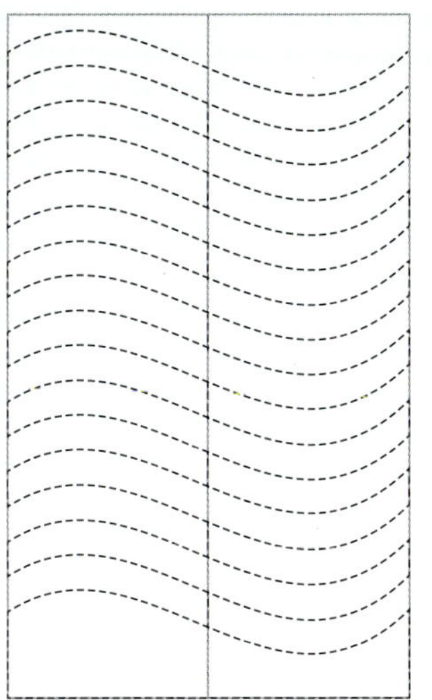

When you have 2 strips next to each other, you can quilt the second one with the arcs facing the opposite way. This gives the illusion of wavy lines.

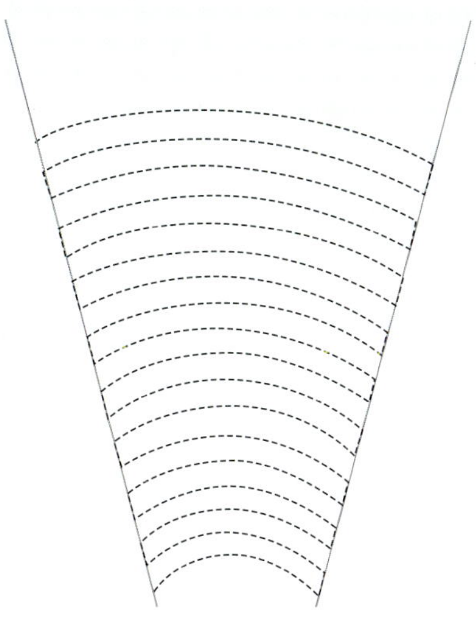

Quilting arcs in irregular shapes is just as easy if you use the sides of the block as your guide.

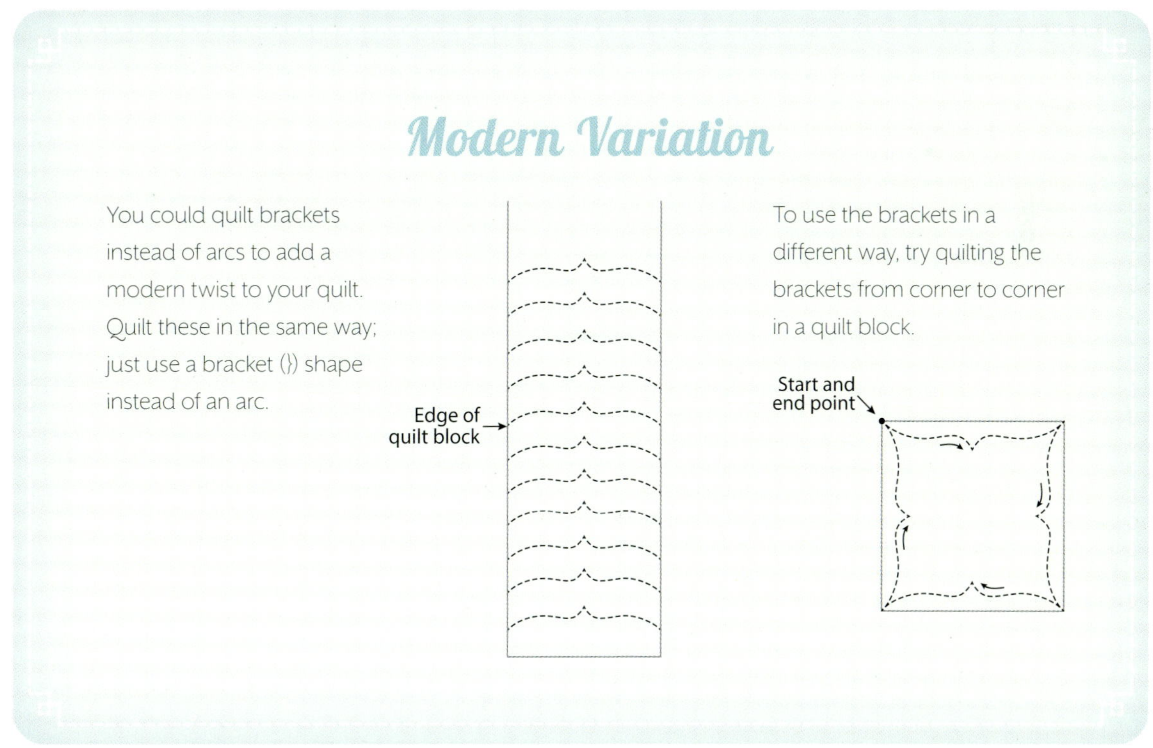

Modern Variation

You could quilt brackets instead of arcs to add a modern twist to your quilt. Quilt these in the same way; just use a bracket (}) shape instead of an arc.

To use the brackets in a different way, try quilting the brackets from corner to corner in a quilt block.

WOVEN ARCS

This filler is smaller and has a woven look to it. It takes the classic design, shrinks it down, and adds a bit of travel for a design that is big on texture.

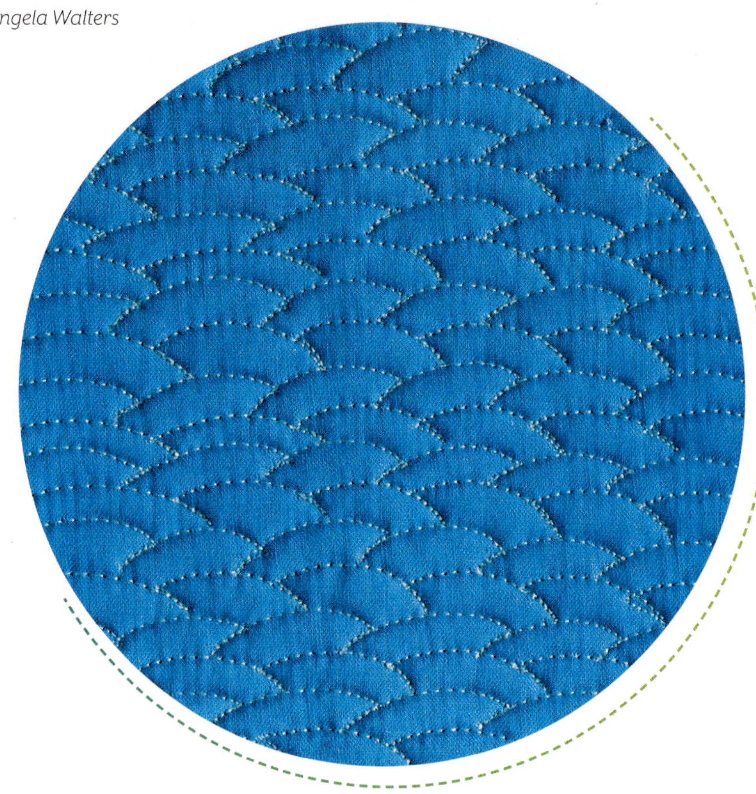

Tip

For this particular design, I like to keep my arc fairly small.

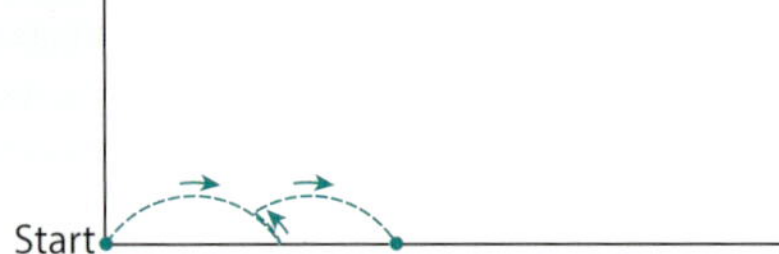

1. Starting at a lower corner of the quilting area, stitch a small arc, then travel back along the curve for about ¼″. Quilt another arc.

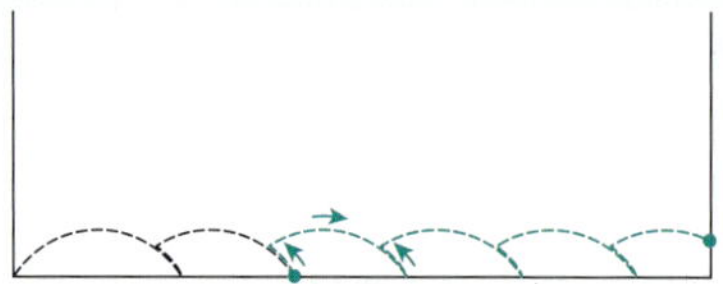

2. Work your way across the area, quilting arcs and traveling until you reach the opposite edge.

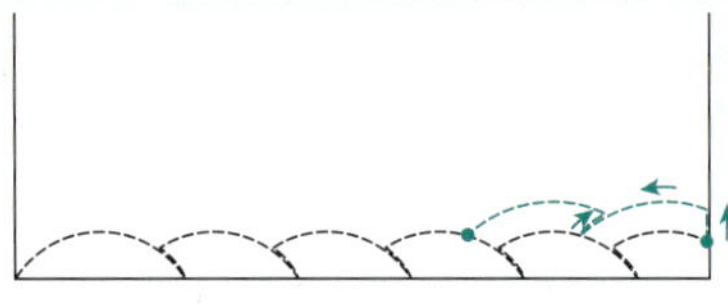

3. Travel up along the edge of the quilting area about ¼″, then echo the arc quilted underneath it. Travel back along the edge of the arc about ¼″ and quilt another arc.

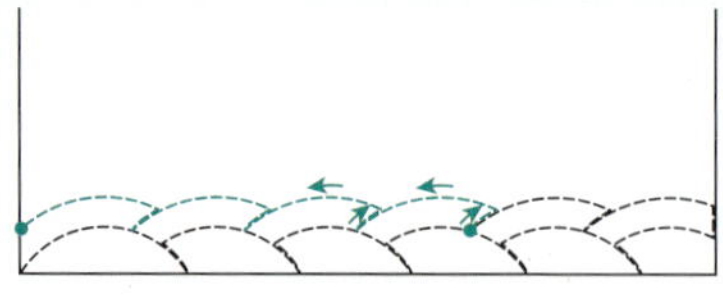

4. Continue quilting the second row of arcs until you reach the opposite side.

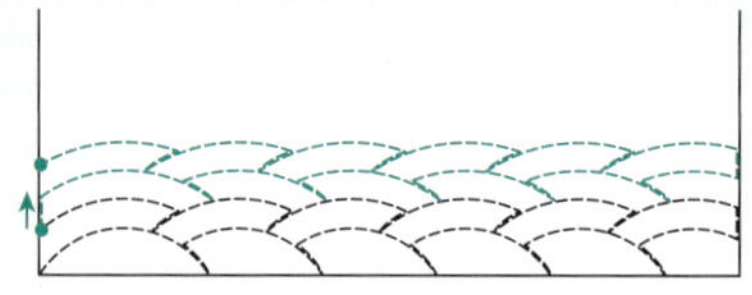

5. Continue quilting rows of the woven arcs until you fill the quilting area.

Variations

Don't limit the design to background quilting. Try it in borders for a striking effect.

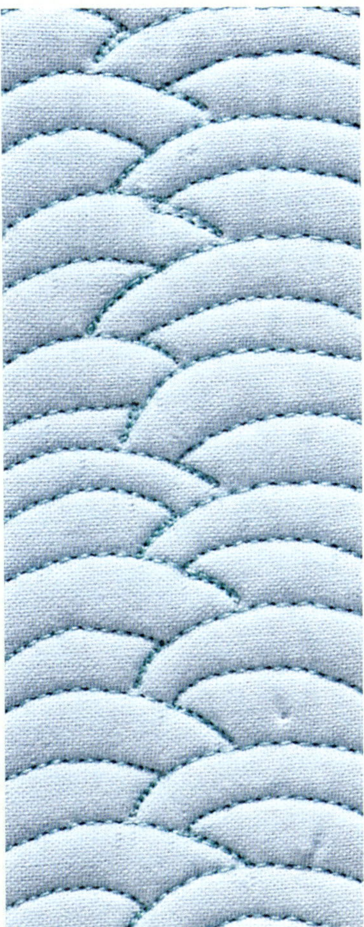

Stitch a narrow section of quilted arcs in a border.

As an alternative to straight lines, quilt the arcs so that they wrap around an element, such as a row of larger pebbles.

You could also quilt these a lot larger and fill in between the lines for a more complex looking design.

These Woven Arcs look lacy when enlarged and filled with Double Wishbones (page 228).

Quilt the first arc slightly larger and then quilt a filler design, working your way back to the starting point. Echo around the shape. Travel back along the previously quilted echo line and quilt the next arc.

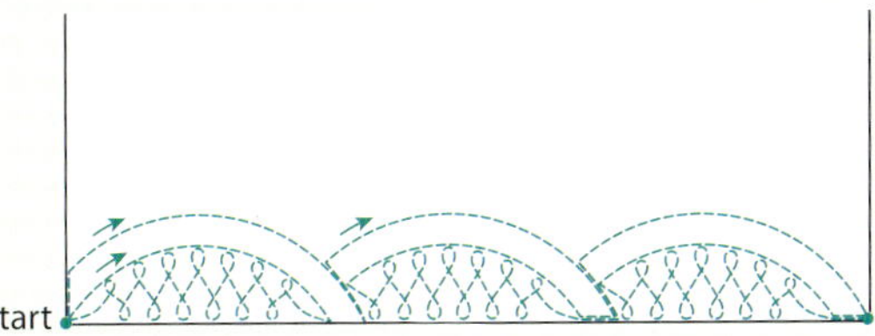

You can quilt larger arcs and fill them with a contrasting dense design.

CIRCLE 1

This is my default quilting design for small circles. It's quick and easy, but more interesting than just stitching in-the-ditch.

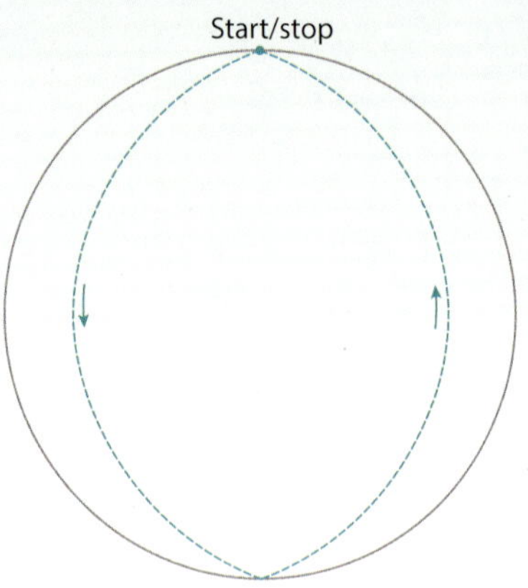

1. Starting from the top of the circle, quilt an arc going to the opposite side of the circle. Quilt another arc back up to the starting point.

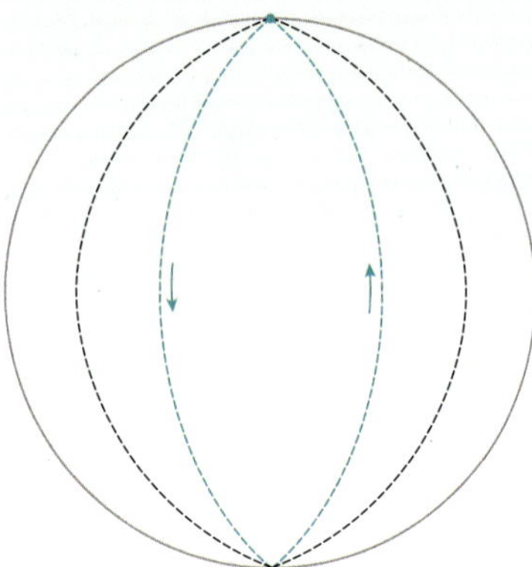

2. Repeat Step 1, echoing inside the arcs you just quilted. Return to the starting point.

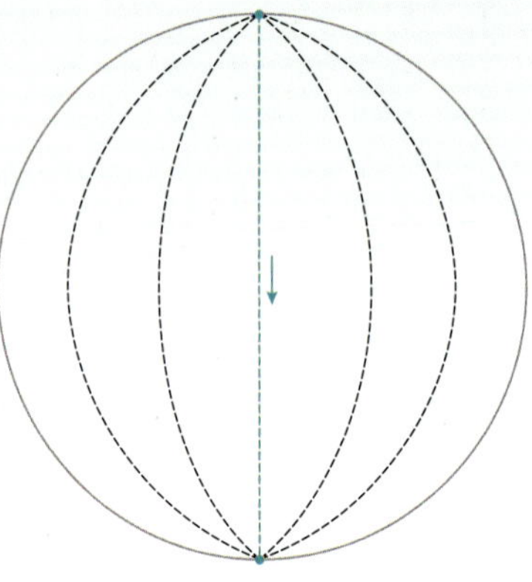

3. As an optional step, you can quilt a straight line down to the bottom of the circle.

Variations

I usually add another design in the center if I want to end up on the other side of the circle. However, instead of a straight line as done in Step 3, you could quilt a different design such as the ribbon candy inside the echoed curves.

CIRCLE 2

This curvy design adds a lot of detail to your circles, a plus for larger blocks. While marking isn't necessary, you could make small marks at the top, bottom, and the center sides of the blocks to help keep it symmetrical.

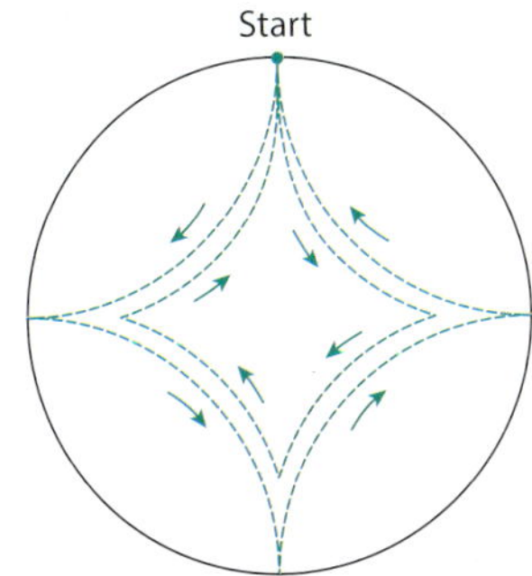

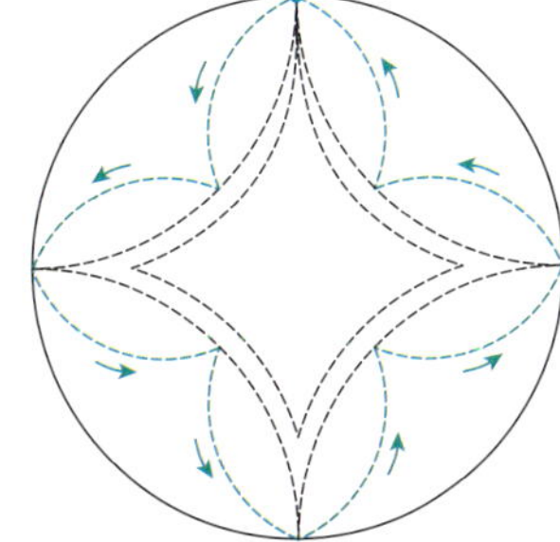

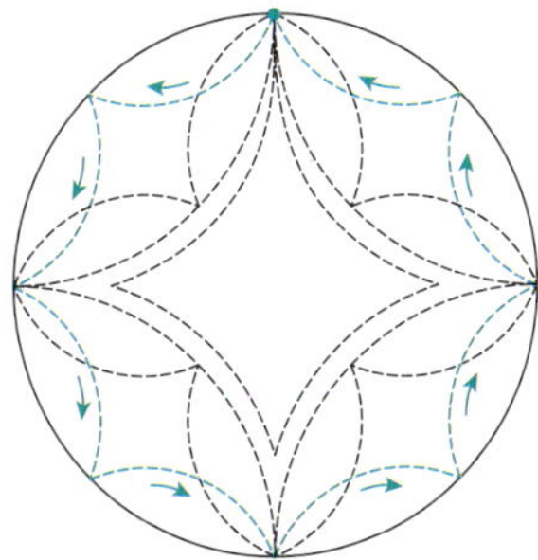

1. From the top, quilt a curved line that goes to the middle of the side, to the bottom, and to the next side, returning to the top. Echo inside of the design, returning to the starting point.

2. Quilt a curved line to the middle of the previously quilted curve, then on to the next point. Continue working around the quilt, quilting curved lines until you return to the starting point.

3. Work around the block again, repeating Step 2 but with the middle point touching the outside of the circle.

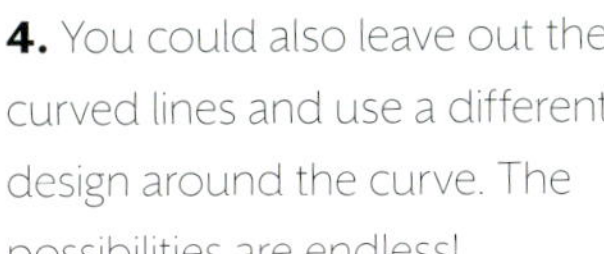

4. You could also leave out the curved lines and use a different design around the curve. The possibilities are endless!

Variations

Experiment with the fillers and echo lines to come up with your own variations.

This design works in square blocks as well.

TRIANGLE 1

This design takes arc-shaped lines and stacks them to give your triangle blocks a more rounded look.

Tip 

When quilting the curved lines, make sure to tuck the ends of the curve into the edges of the triangle. This will ensure that your curved lines stay curved and won't flatten.

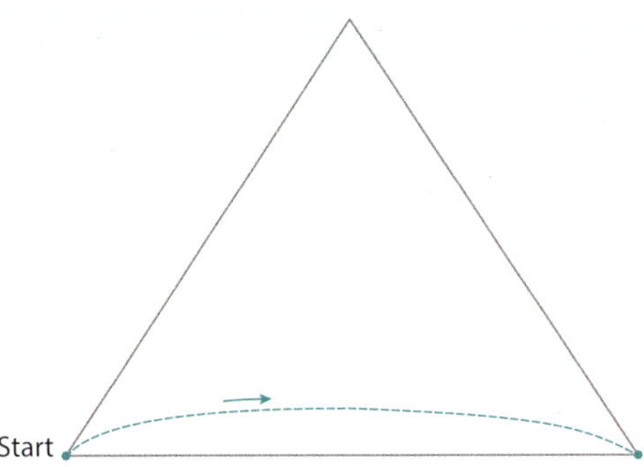

1. Starting from the base of the triangle, quilt a slightly curved line that goes from one point to the other.

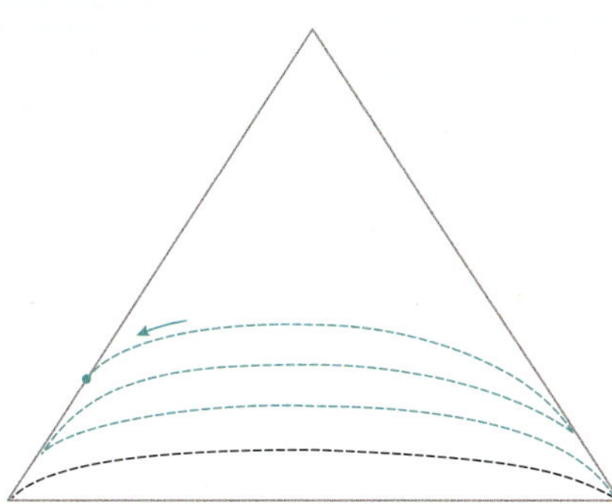

2. Echo the first curved line, alternating from side to side.

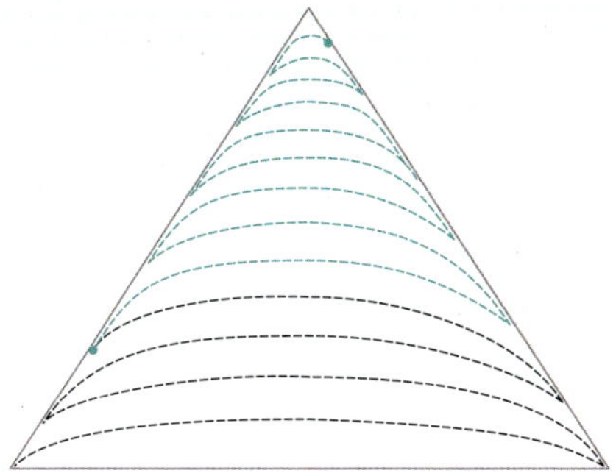

3. Continue quilting arcs until you reach the top of the triangle.

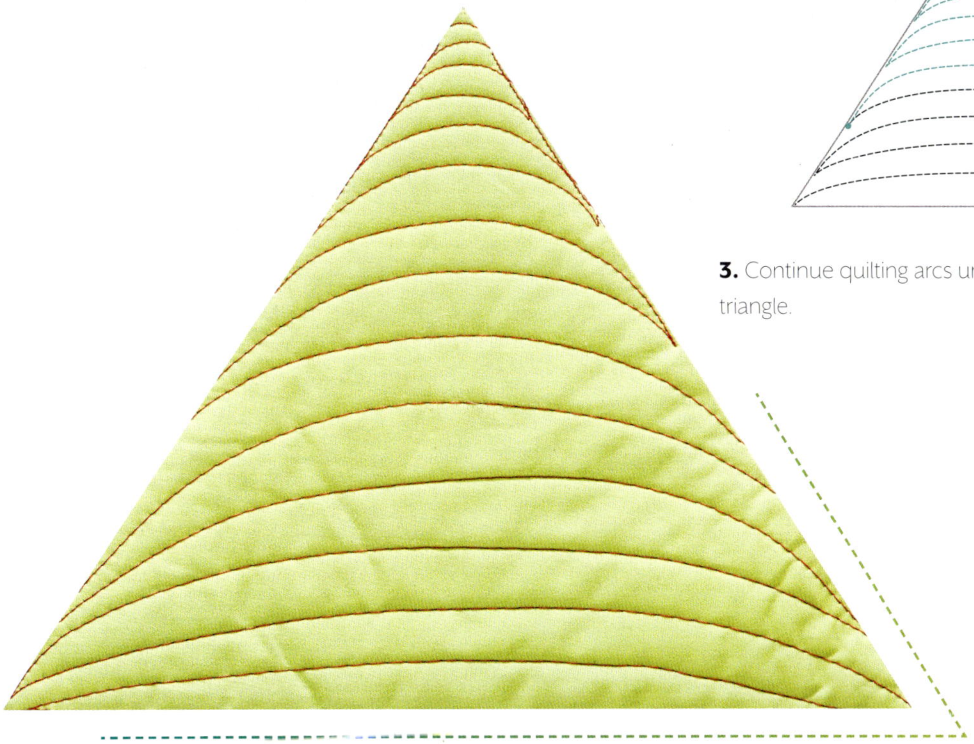

DIAMOND 1

I love, love, love how this design looks when it is used in star blocks. It really adds a secondary design to the quilt! Try it in diamonds of all sizes.

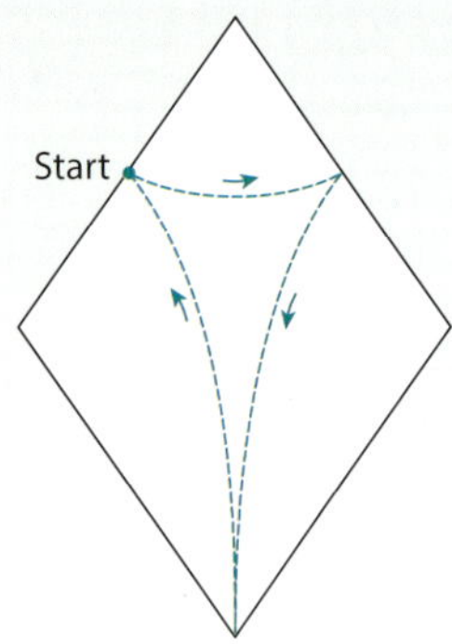

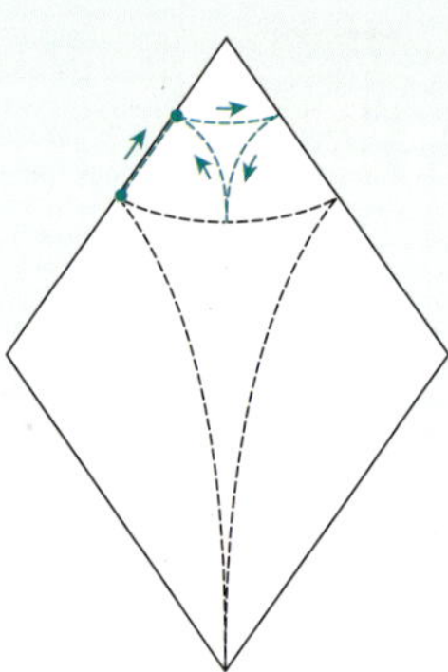

1. From halfway between the top corner and a side corner, quilt a line that curves across, stopping a couple inches away from the opposite side. Continue quilting a curvy line to the opposite side of the block and back to the starting point.

2. Travel along the side of the block, stopping about 1˝ away from the top corner. Quilt a line that curves to the opposite side, down to the previous quilting, and back to the starting point. Continue quilting along the edge of the block to move on to the next block.

Variation

This design can make a curvy starlike shape as well. Just travel to the opposite corner from where you started and repeat Step 1.

Stitch a star by repeating Step 1 from the opposite side.

Note

I don't mind traveling in the seams, but that's just my personal preference. If you want, you can leave that part out. Just stop in the middle of the top curve in Step 1, quilt the smaller shape, and then complete the design.

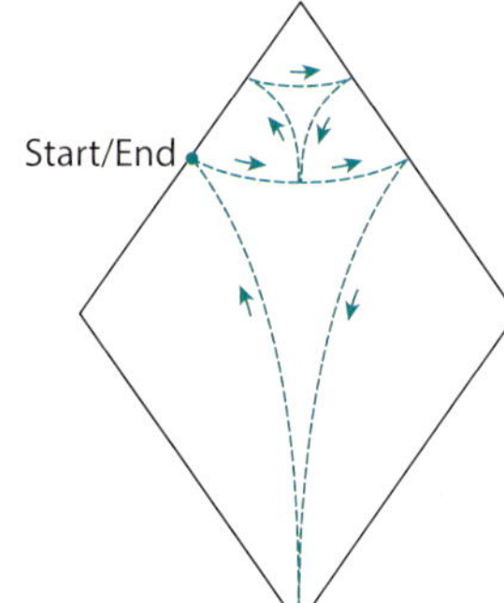

It's hard to get an idea of just how beautiful this design is when you can see only a single diamond! Here is what it would like when used in diamond blocks that are arranged in a star formation.

The design really shines in a pieced star.

HEXAGON 1

This design uses the corners of the block to make an intricate design. It may seem a little complex at first glance, but it's just a couple of steps repeated twice. Like most of the other designs in this section, it looks great in multiple blocks.

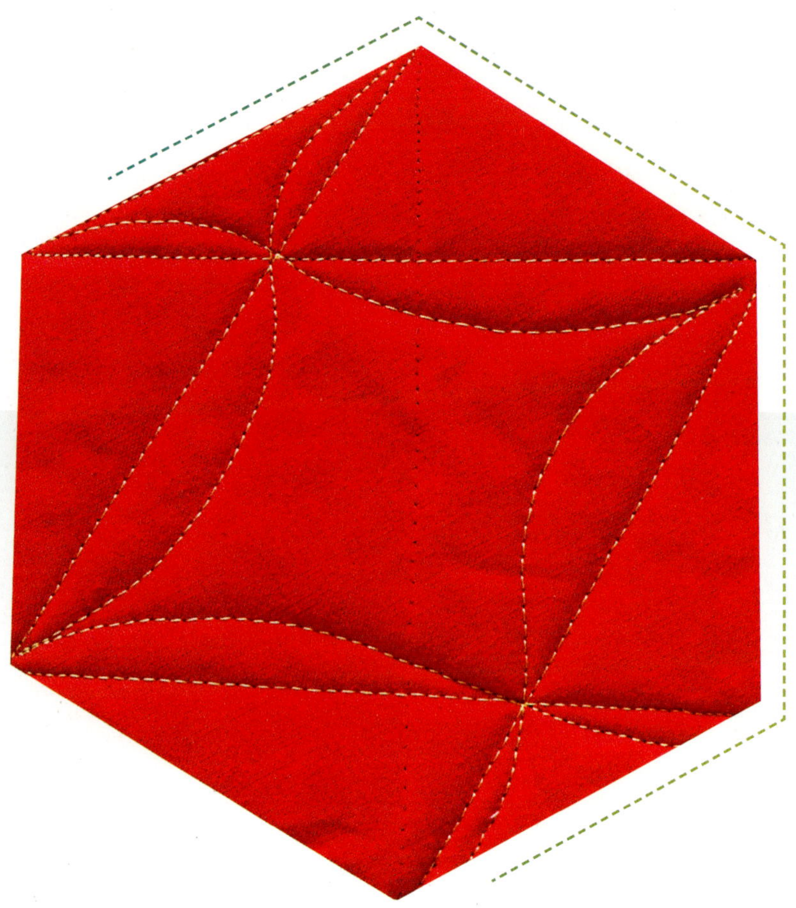

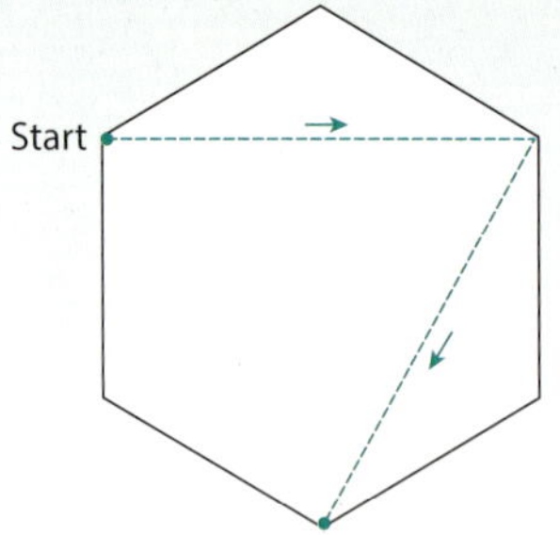

1. From any corner, quilt a horizontal line to the second corner from the starting point, then diagonally to the second corner away from that point.

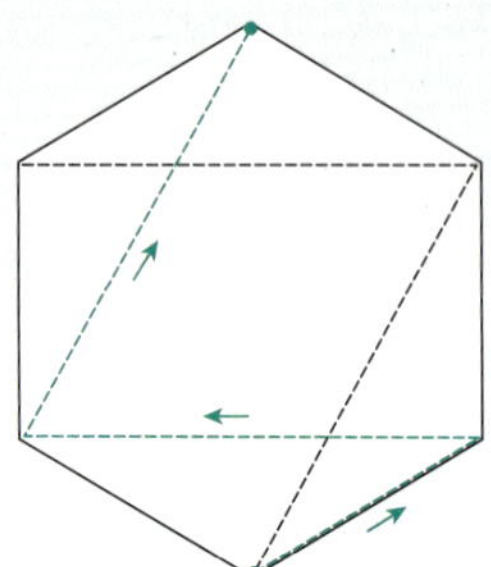

2. Travel back along the edge of the block to the corner between the last 2 points. Repeat Step 1 on the other side of the block.

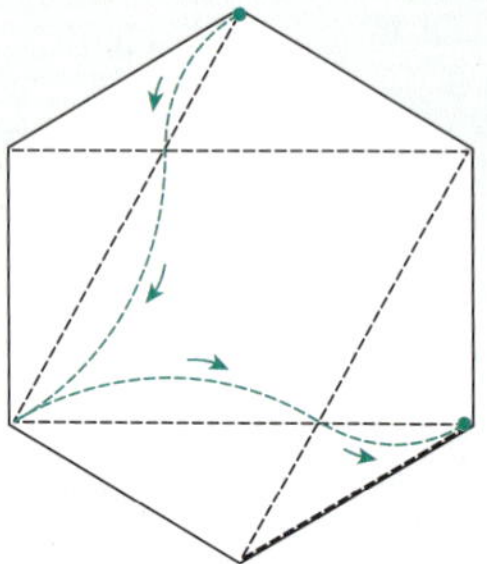

3. Follow the straight lines you stitched in Steps 1 and 2 to add curved lines to the design. Quilt a curved line from the last corner to the intersection of the straight lines, then change the direction of the curve as you stitch to the next corner. Repeat to work your way to the opposite side of the block.

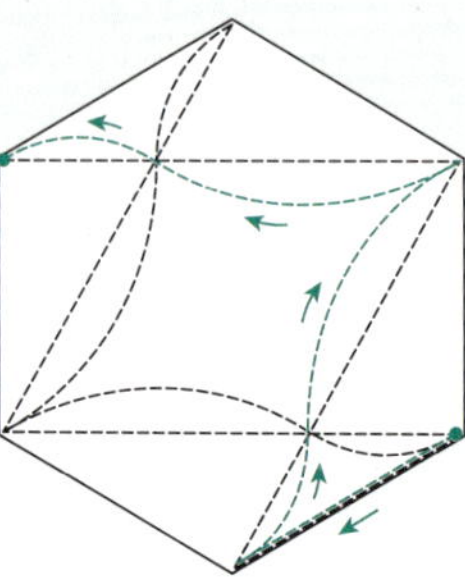

4. Travel back along the edge of the block to the next corner and repeat Step 3 to quilt the other side.

Variations

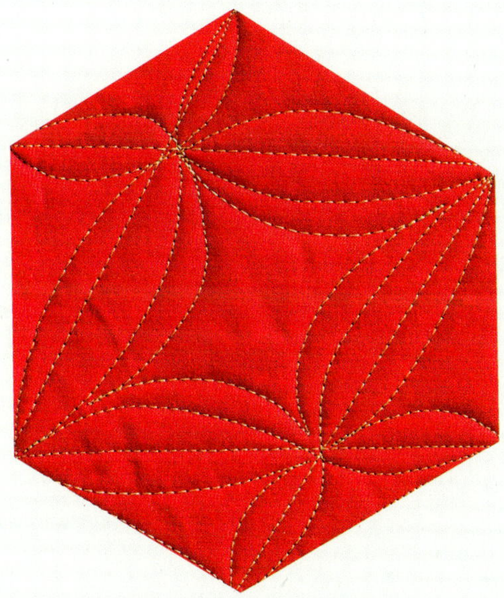

Echo the lines for a more complex look.

This pattern looks great quilted in a square.

Since you create diamonds and triangles in Steps 1 and 2, you can change up this design by filling them in with different patterns. Or just add more echo lines to the design for a more complex look to your blocks.

Experiment with differently shaped blocks, including squares.

BORDER: HALF BRACKETS

Sometimes, to come up with a new design, all you need to do is take a favorite design, divide it in half, and repeat with a mirror image. Sound confusing? I promise, it isn't. Soon you will be quilting half brackets on your favorite quilts. Try quilting this design in borders of all widths.

When I am quilting the half bracket design on my quilts, I don't mark the sections. Even if they aren't all the same exact size, this design still looks great!

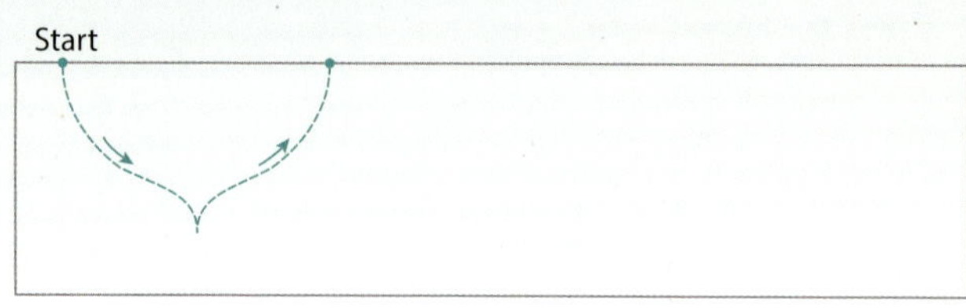

1. Starting from one corner of the border, travel along the edge about ½˝. Quilt a curved line that comes to a point and then curves back to the border.

Try to have the half bracket shape come to a point before you reach the other side of the border. I usually like to leave about 1˝ or so.

Variations

Just like the other designs in this book, you can think up fun variations for this quilting design. Try quilting skinnier or wider half brackets, or quilt the echoed lines closer together.

If you want denser quilting, or really want to draw attention to this design, you could make another pass to fill in between the half brackets with pebbles.

2. Travel along the edge of the border about ¼″ and echo inside the shape you just quilted. Keep traveling and echoing until you run out of space.

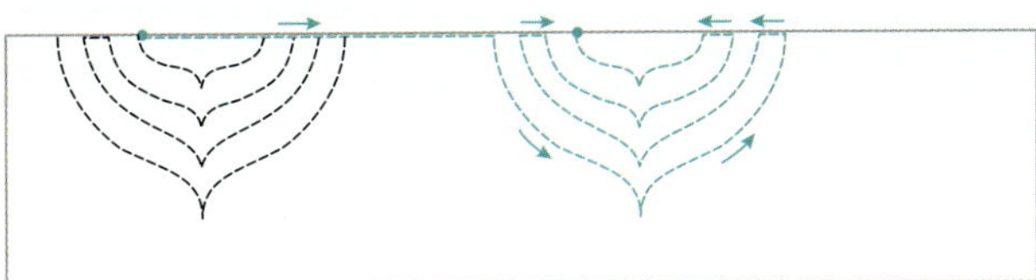

3. Travel along the edge of the border and leave a space about the same as the width of the half bracket. Repeat the technique in Steps 1 and 2 to create another set of half brackets.

Continue along the border, quilting the half brackets and spacing them evenly.

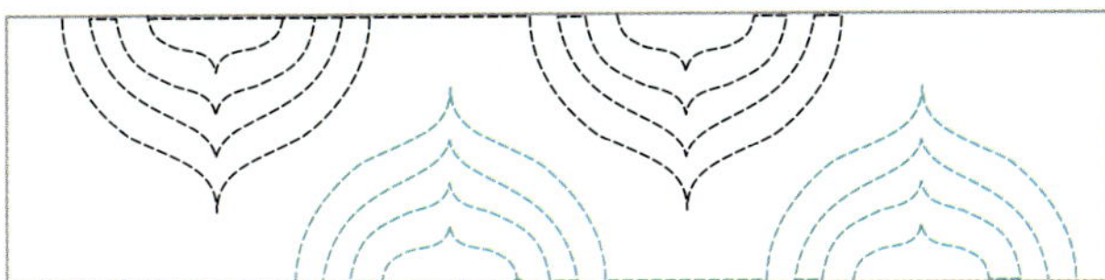

4. Starting from the opposite edge of the border, repeat the process so that the half brackets fit between the ones on the top row.

Tip 

You can change the size and spacing of the half brackets to make them fit your border.

ALLOVER LEAVES

This design has been around the machine quilting scene for quite a while, but it can still perform. The Allover Leaves design looks great on a masculine quilt and works best in open areas or as an allover design.

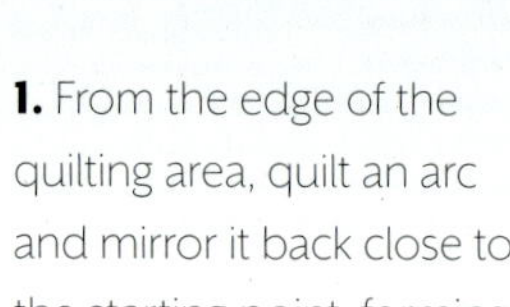

1. From the edge of the quilting area, quilt an arc and mirror it back close to the starting point, forming a leaf.

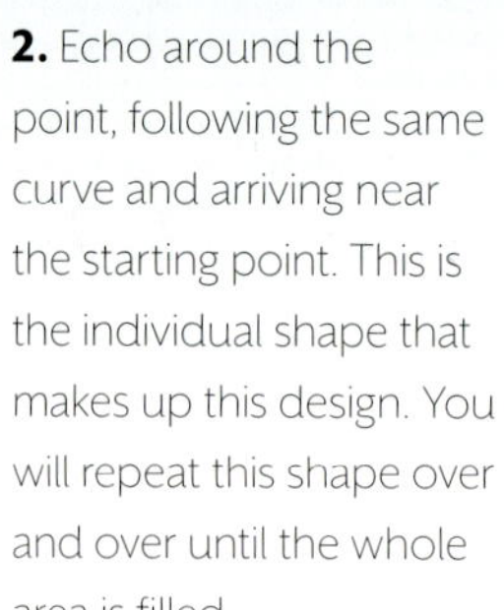

2. Echo around the point, following the same curve and arriving near the starting point. This is the individual shape that makes up this design. You will repeat this shape over and over until the whole area is filled.

3. From the ending point, curve out in a different direction and back.

4. Echo around the last point and stop when you are near the edge of the first leaf you quilted.

5. Quilt another leaf pointing up and echo it, ending when you are very close to a previously quilted line. You can echo around the leaves several times to move around the quilting area.

6. Continue quilting leaves and echoing them until the whole area is quilted.

Tip

You also can make the leaves different sizes so that you are able to fill in the whole area.

CIRCLE 1

This design shows that echoing can make all the difference. This flowery-looking design is centered in the circle, but don't feel compelled to mark the exact point. I find that eyeballing it is usually close enough.

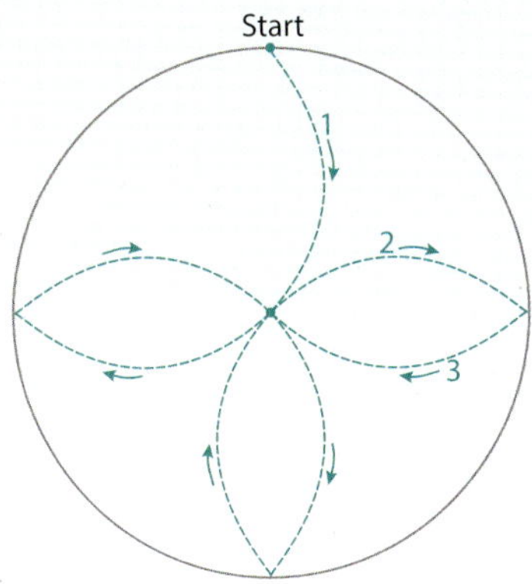

1. From the top of the circle, quilt a curved line ending at the center of the circle, forming a half petal. Visualize the circle divided into quarters and quilt 3 petals, stopping each time at the center of the circle.

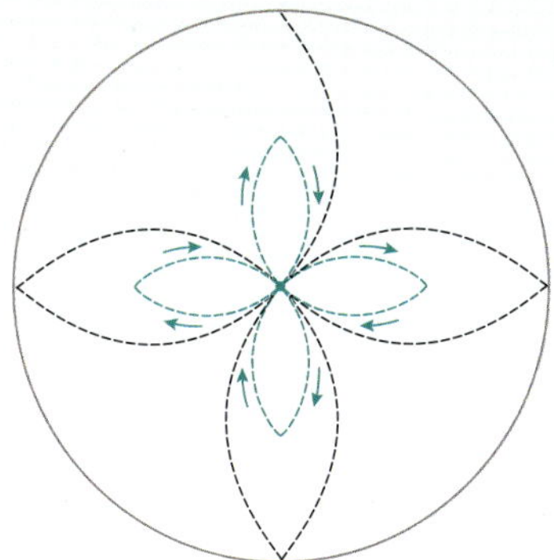

2. Before completing the last half petal, echo inside the petals you just quilted, including the half petal.

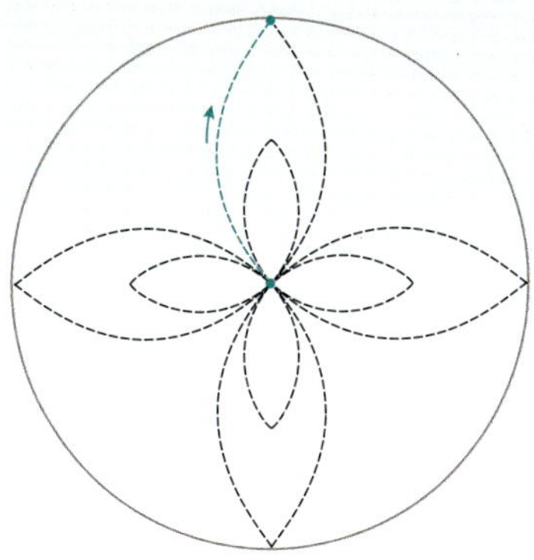

3. Finish the first petal, returning to the original starting point.

Variations

This design works best in smaller to medium-sized circles, but you can easily adapt it to fit larger circles by echoing around the outside of the petals. Simply quilt the petal design and then add echoes to it.

Echo the design to create a different look or to fill larger circles.

CIRCLE 2

This design makes me think of the spirograph that I used to play with as a child. Quilting it is actually kind of similar!

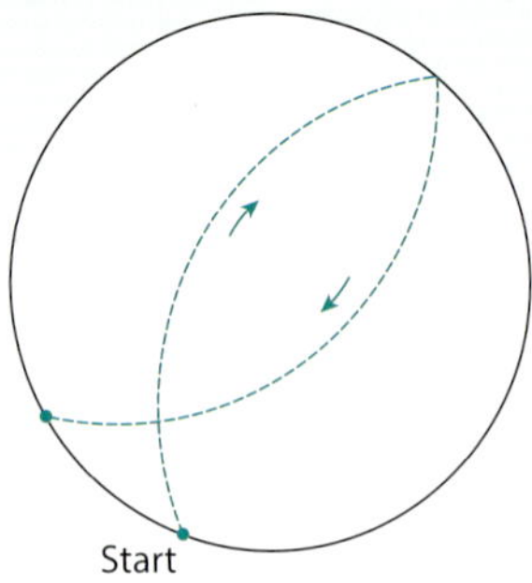

1. Quilt a curved line that reaches the other side of the circle and curves back about 1˝ away from the starting point.

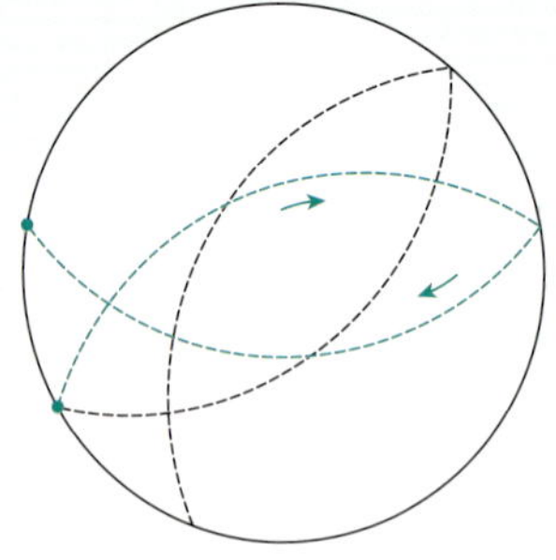

2. Quilt another curved line that touches the other side about 1˝ away from the previously quilted line. Curve back so that you are touching about 1˝ from where you started.

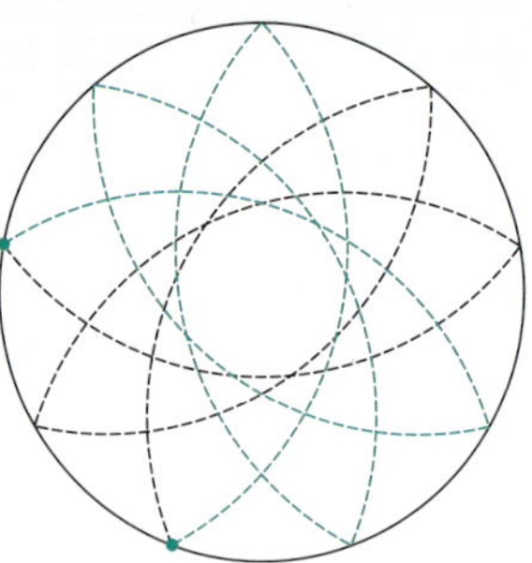

3. Continue working your way around the block, quilting petals about 1˝ apart.

Variations

You can change the look of the design by quilting the curves so that they are closer together or farther apart.

Change the spacing of the curves to vary the design.

SQUARE 1

This quilting design creates an interesting grid when used in adjacent squares. It combines both straight and curved lines and is so fast and easy to quilt. Another benefit of this design is that it works well in squares of all sizes.

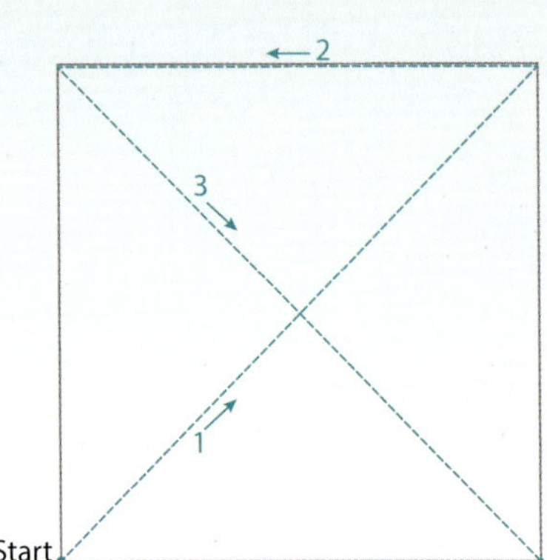

1. Starting from one corner, quilt a straight line diagonally to the opposite corner. Travel along the edge of the block until you reach the other corner. Quilt a line diagonally to the opposite corner.

Note 

Not only do the crossed quilting lines add to the design, but they easily mark the center of the block for the next step.

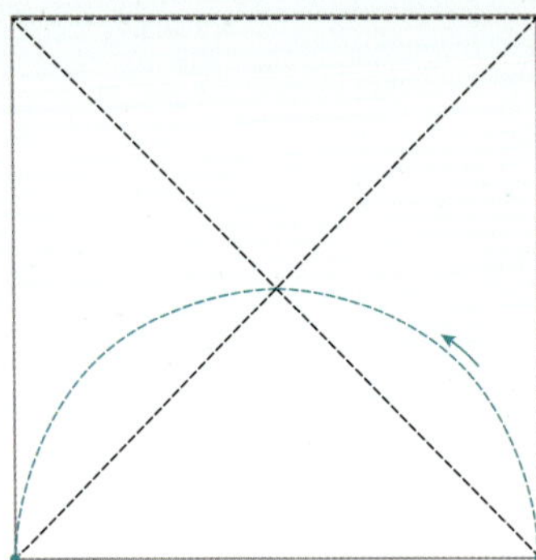

2. Quilt a curved line from the corner to the center of the block. Continue the curve to the next corner.

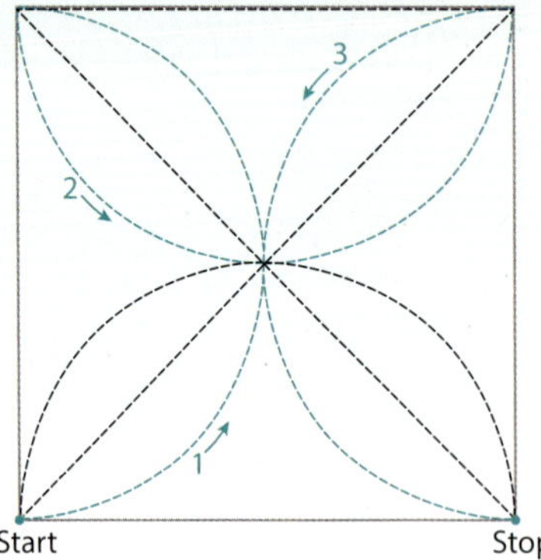

3. Continue working your way around the block until you return to the starting point.

Variations

For larger blocks, you can echo the curves to fill in the block even more.

This design can be easily enhanced by echoing the curves.

SQUARE 2

When working with larger squares, I often start by dividing the area to be quilted into smaller shapes. Not only does this make the quilting more interesting, but it also helps make it more manageable. This design takes a square block and breaks it up into a smaller, on-point square and four surrounding triangles. The block can be divided in a myriad of ways, so try tweaking the design to see what you can come up with!

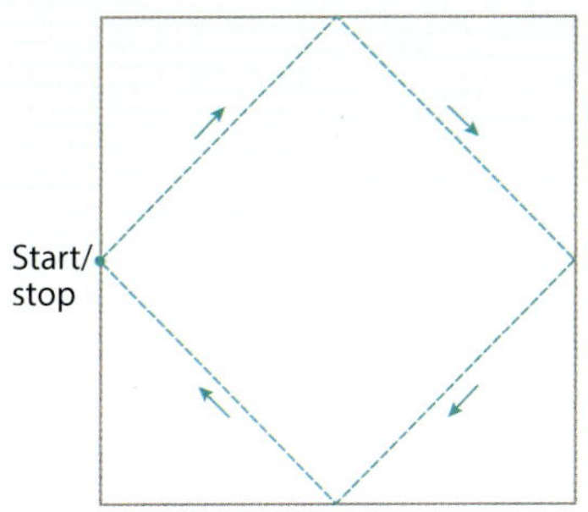

1. Starting from the midpoint of one side of the block, quilt a square on point. Try to place the points of the square at the midpoint of each side, ending at the starting point.

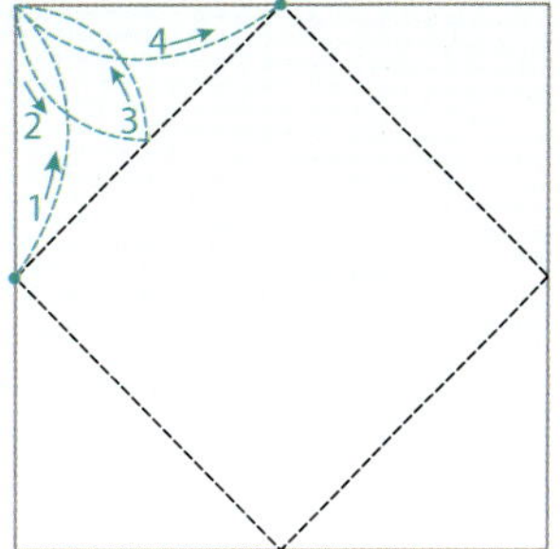

2. Fill in the first triangle section. Quilt a line curving to the corner of the block, out to the middle of the side of the on-point square, back to the corner, then to the midpoint of the next side.

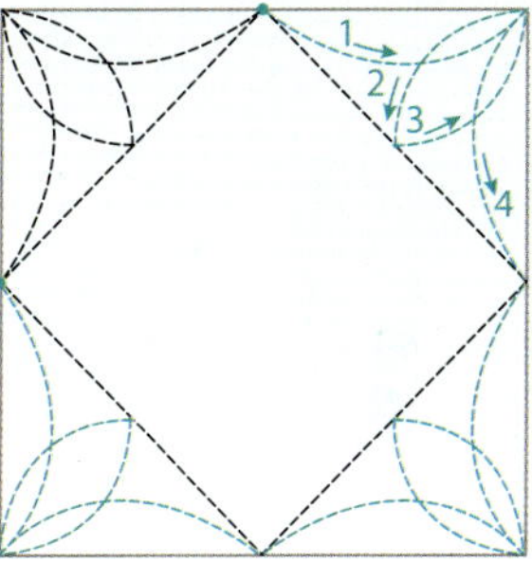

3. Repeat Step 2, filling in each of the "triangles" of the block, working your way around. You will end at the starting point.

Variations

To fill in larger blocks or to create more dense quilting, you can echo the inside of the square and add a filler. In the example below, I quilted the on-point square and then used the mitered corners design and filled inside with swirls before moving on to Step 2. I'm sure you can see that there are many different possibilities with this design.

When using this design in larger square blocks, try echoing inside the square and filling with swirls.

HEXAGON 1

This simple flower design is anything but boring. I use it often in blocks of different shapes, but I especially like it here because the flower looks like it's made for hexagons.

Tip

When quilting this design, I just aim for the center. But if you want, you could mark a dot in the center of the block, so it's symmetrical.

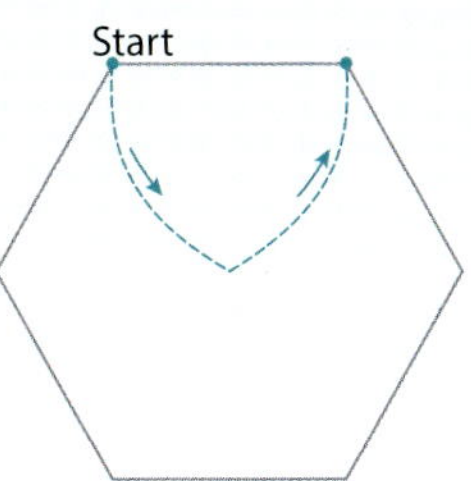

1. Starting from a corner, quilt a line that curves to the center. Quilt a curved line to the next point.

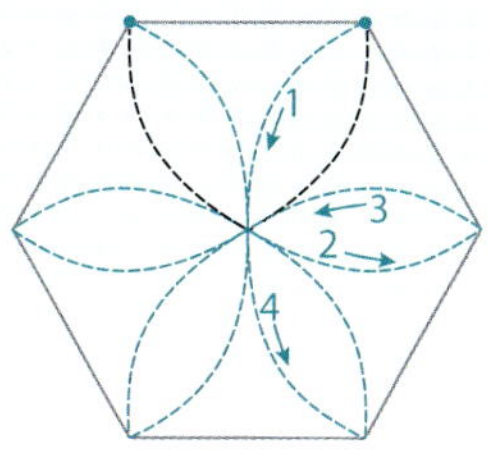

2. Continue working your way around the block, going from a point, to the center, on to the next point, and so on. Stop when you return to the starting point.

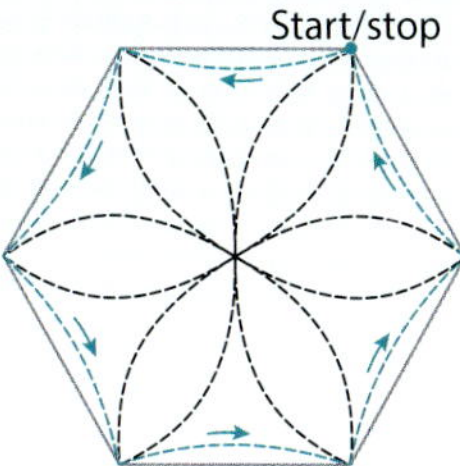

3. Quilt curved lines that go from corner to corner until you return to the starting point.

Variations

I think this design looks a little like a kaleidoscope, but you can change it up a bit for a more floral look. At Step 3, instead of quilting curved lines, echo the sides of the curves. It's a simple twist that completely brings out the floral aspect.

For an easy variation of this design, echo the curved lines instead of quilting the curves in Step 3.

You can also quilt this design in square or rectangle blocks.

FLOWER POWER

Small arcs quilted around a swirl, Flower Power will definitely add a punch to your quilts. This design is great when used in a row or in the middle of a square block. But like real flowers, they look best in a bunch.

1. From the edge, quilt a small swirl.

2. Once inside the swirl, quilt your way back out of the swirl, making small arcs that touch or come close to the swirl. These are the petals of your flower. Quilt all the way around the swirl.

3. When you reach your starting point, reverse direction and quilt arcs in another layer around the first row. Stop when you make it all the way around the flower.

Continued on next page

4. Continue going around the flower until it is the size you like.

5. When you are happy with the size of the flower, quilt more petals, stopping when you are halfway around the flower.

6. From that point, quilt another swirl extending from the first flower.

7. Quilt petals around the swirl until it is as big as you want.

Note 

When adding the rows of petals to the flowers, you will run into other flowers. When that happens, reverse direction and go back the other way. This will give the illusion that flowers are under each other.

8. Continue until you have filled the quilting area with flowers.

CIRCLE 1

I have used this flower design as a meander design more times than I can count. Now it's time to use it to highlight a circle block. This is a forgiving design, so jump right in and get started.

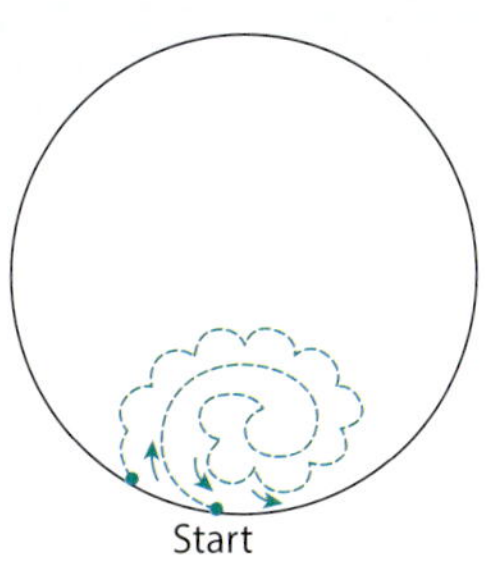

1. Quilt a small curl close to the edge of the circle block. Work your way back around the outside of the curl by quilting small arcs to resemble petals.

2. Echo back around the petals.

3. Once you get to the edge of the block, quilt another row of arc-shaped petals and echo your way back to the other side. Continue quilting rows until you reach the top of the block.

Note

Try to keep the arcs as consistent as possible. This will ensure that the texture of this design really shows up in your block.

Variations

Instead of quilting the rows all the way to the top of the block, you can stop halfway through and add a different design, such as leaves.

Add a different design in half of the block.

If you don't mind starting and stopping, you can start the flower in the center of the block. It will really add a focal point to your blocks.

Put the flower in the center of the circle.

Or, forget the flower altogether and turn those arcs into clamshells to give your larger circle blocks a textured look.

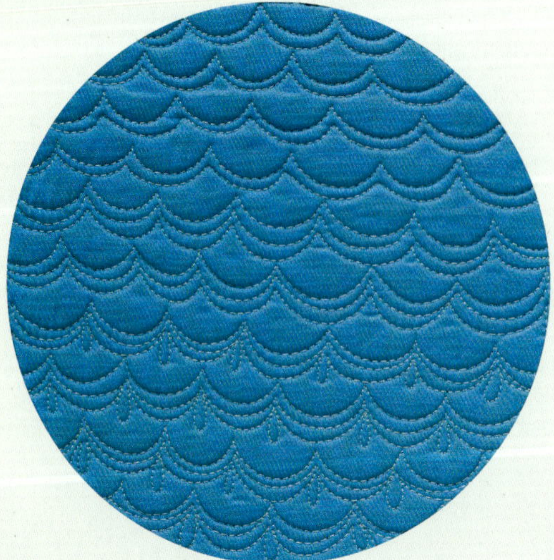

Stitch clamshells in larger circles.

HEXAGON 1

Sometimes I want certain blocks to really stand out, and this design makes that happen. Use it in areas that you want to highlight, or in the center of groups of hexagons. I like to start this design in the center of the block to help ensure that it's as symmetrical as possible.

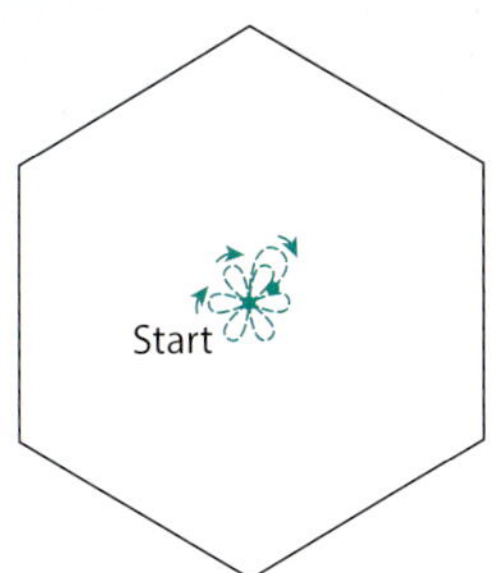

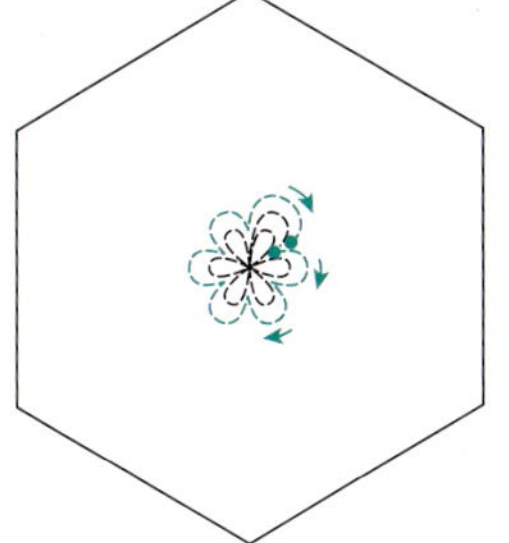

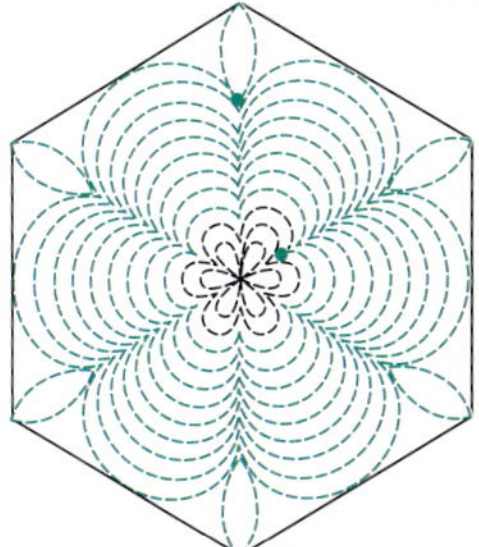

1. Starting in the center of the block, quilt a small flower shape with 6 petals. Try to stitch them so that each loop points to the center of a side.

2. Echo around each of the petals, continuing around and around until the outer petals are close to the block sides.

3. To fill in the corners, add a leaf shape on your last time around the petals.

Variations

For a slight variation, quilt 3 petals instead of 6. Start with the loop of each petal pointing toward a block corner.

For a different look, stop echoing the petals halfway through and fill in the rest of the space with a different pattern. This is what I do when the design isn't looking as even as I would like.

Switch it up by quilting 3 petals instead of 6.

Fill in the outer edge of the block with a different pattern.

WOOD GRAIN WITH KNOTS

When you want tons of quilting and a lot of texture on your quilt, Wood Grain is the design to use. It is quilted from side to side, adding line upon line of quilty goodness. This design works great in large, open areas or as an allover design.

More than with any other design, using a matching thread is key—you want to see texture, not thread.

Tip

You can quilt the lines closer together or farther apart, but don't spread them out too much or you will lose the wood grain effect.

KNOT

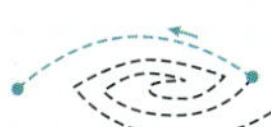

1. Start with a gentle arc.

2. Quilt another arc back, stopping ½″ from the top and ½″ from the side of the first arc.

3. Quilt 2 more arcs going in on themselves, leaving a space of about ½″ between the lines. Stop in the middle of the shape. At this point it resembles a swirl with pointed ends.

4. Echo back out, following the curve of the arcs. You will end on the opposite side of your starting point.

WOOD GRAIN

1. Quilt a wavy line from the left side toward the right side.

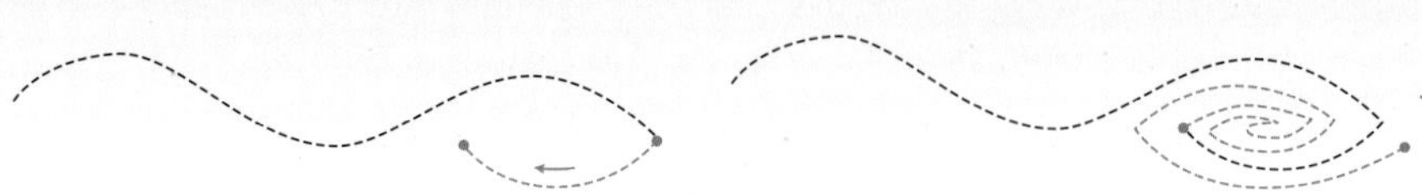

2. Without stopping, go right into quilting the knot.

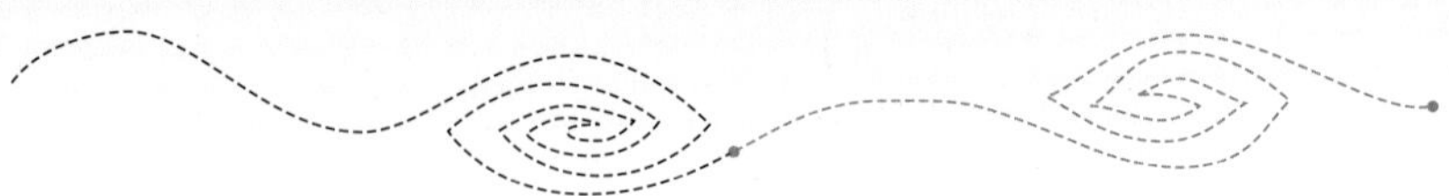

3. Continue quilting a wavy line, adding random knots. Stop when you reach the edge of the quilting area.

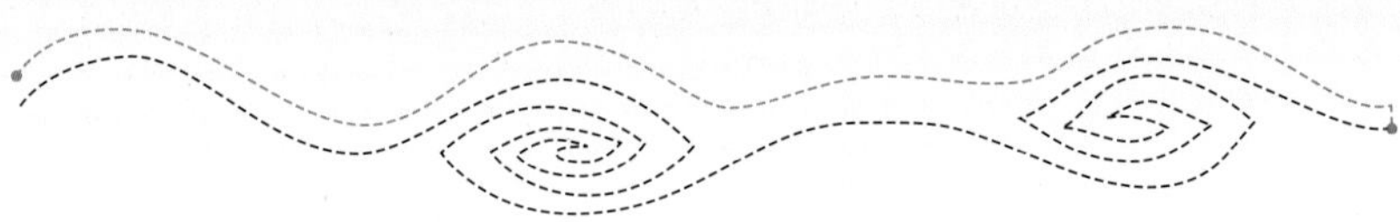

4. Travel up the side of the quilting area about ¼″ and quilt a wavy line echoing back to the left, following the curves of the line below it. Quilt all the way back to the left side.

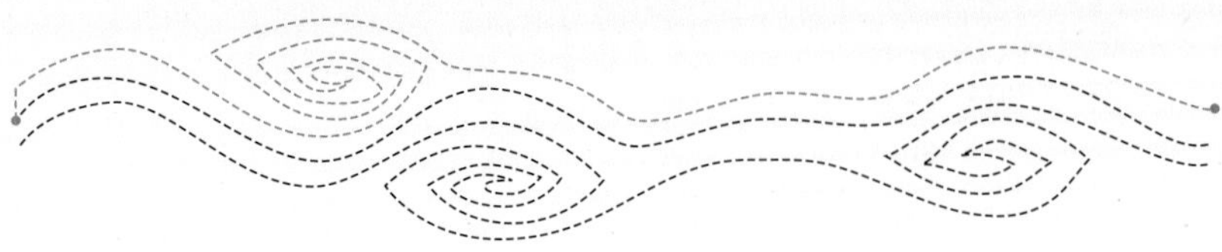

5. Travel up the left side ¼″ and start quilting toward the right, echoing about ½″. As you quilt, add knots in the places where the line below curves down. This makes them look as though they are ingrained in the design.

6. Continue quilting until the wood grain design has filled the whole area.

MOD CLAMSHELL

Clamshell quilting designs have been around almost as long as quilting has. But this classic design gets a modern makeover. Mod Clamshells will add a lot of interest and fun to your quilt, and they are easy to do. The best part: no marking!

Tip
Use one row in a narrow sashing, or stack rows on top of one another to fill larger areas. The possibilities are endless!

1. From the beginning of your quilting area, quilt an arc.

2. At the end of the arc, quilt 2 tiny zigzags. You don't need them to be perfect; you just want a little texture.

3. After you quilt the zigzag, quilt another arc, trying to keep it approximately the same size as the first one.

4. Continue quilting until the row is complete.

5. Stacking the rows on top of one another is easy and a great way to fill large areas. After you finish the first row, travel up the edge of the quilting area until you are approximately twice as high as the first row. From the edge of the quilting area, quilt a curved line that touches the middle of the clamshell below it.

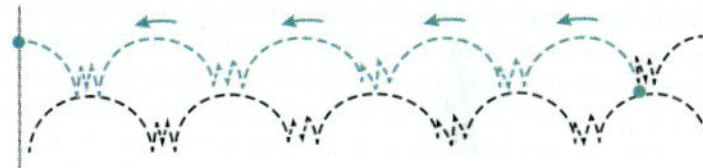

6. Quilt 2 tiny zigzags, and then quilt another arc, ending in the middle of the next clamshell. Continue across the row until you reach the beginning of the first row.

7. When you reach the beginning, you should have a row of clamshells with 2 half clamshells on each side. Continue stacking rows of clamshells until you reach the top of the quilting area.

LINKS

This design is made up of two basic shapes and is fast and easy to quilt. This can just as easily fit in blocks, borders, or even as an allover quilting design.

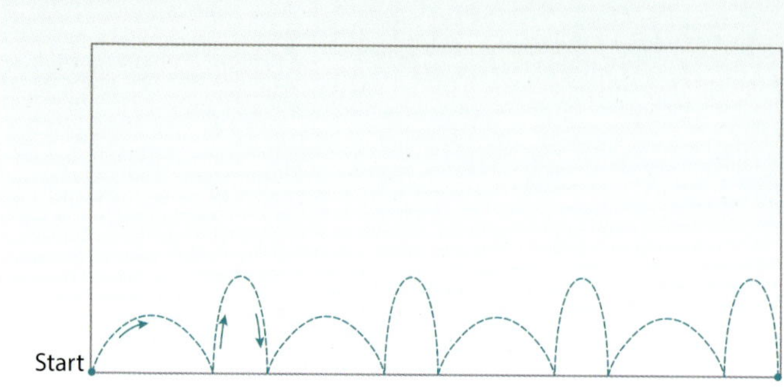

1. Starting at the bottom of the quilting area, quilt a row of arcs. Alternate between short, wide arcs and tall, skinny arcs. As a general guide, the shorter ones should be about twice as wide and half as tall. End when you get to the edge of the quilting area.

Note

Don't worry about making them perfect. As long as the quilting area is filled in, it will look great!

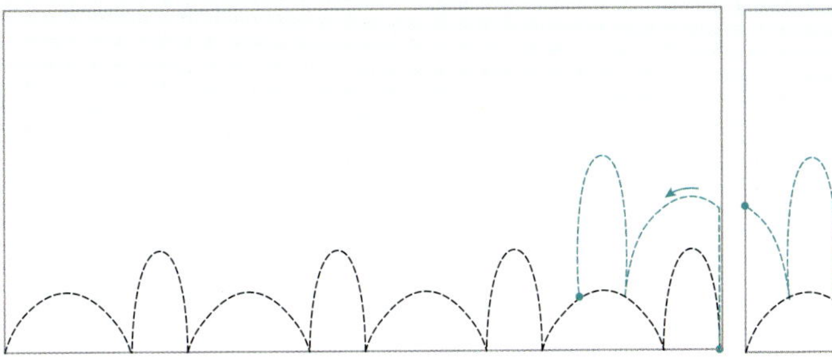

2. Travel up the edge of the quilting area and echo over the top of the skinny arc. Then quilt a skinny arc centered over the wider arc.

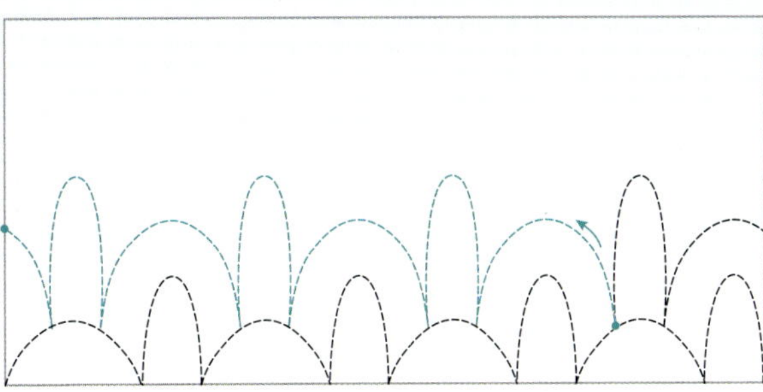

3. Work your way across the quilting area, echoing over the skinny arcs and quilting skinny arcs above the wider arcs. Make sure that the skinny arcs that you quilt on this row are taller than the echoed lines.

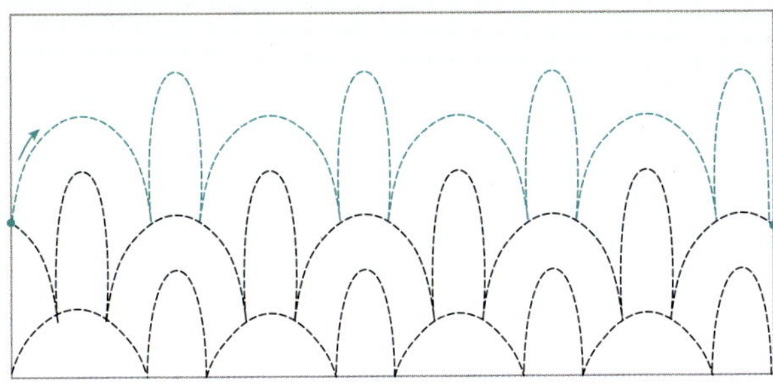

4. Continue quilting the rows by repeating the arcs and echoed lines.

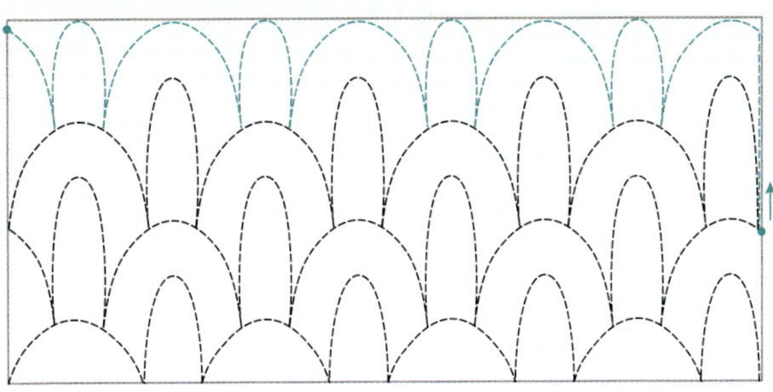

5. When you reach the top of the quilting area, make the skinny arcs short enough to fill in the top completely.

Tip 

Change up the size to quilt quicker! Making the design larger means that you can quilt more, faster.

COMBINATIONS

ALLOVER DESIGNS

SEAFOAM

Seafoam combines Concentric Circles (page 143) and Pebbles (page 116). I named this design Seafoam because the swirls (Concentric Circles) look like ocean waves, and the small circles (Pebbles) look like the bubbles made from the swirling water.

Tip

Like the Concentric Circles design, Seafoam is best used in large areas of the quilt. You can use it as an allover design, or to highlight certain areas.

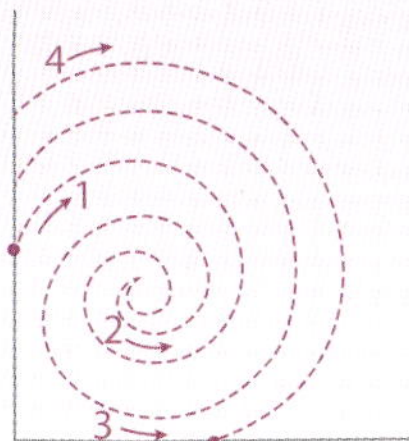

1. From the edge of the quilting area, quilt a Concentric Circle.

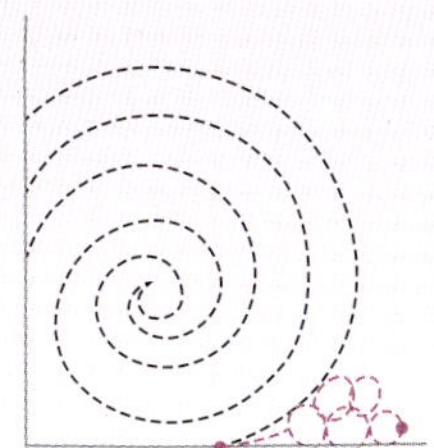

2. At the end of the first Concentric Circle, add a few Pebbles. In this illustration, I added 5, but you could add more or fewer, depending on your preference and the area to be filled.

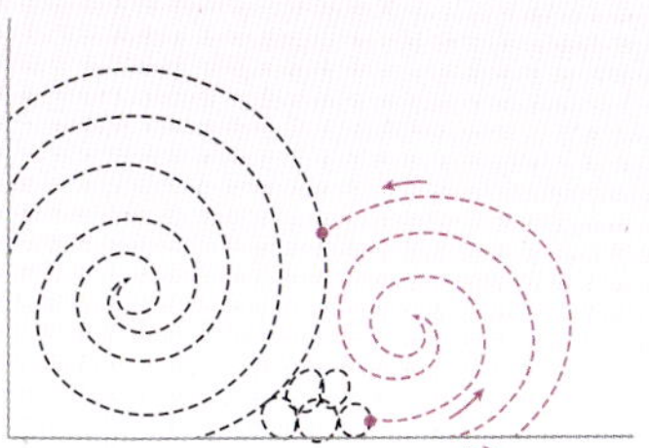

3. After quilting the last Pebble, quilt another Concentric Circle. Echo the outside of the circle until it is the size you want.

4. At the end of the second Concentric Circle, add more Pebbles. Quilt another Concentric Circle.

5. Continue alternating between Concentric Circles and Pebbles until the quilting area is filled.

Tip

Use the Pebbles to fill in the spaces between Concentric Circles; these are normally hard to quilt.

PEAPODS

Sometimes the easiest way to come up with a quilting design is to combine some of your favorite designs. Peapods does that by combining Pebbles (page 116) and Serpentine Lines (page 210). This design is fantastic because the quilting can be very small and dense or large and airy. It works well in smaller background areas of quilts and in larger negative space.

Tip

Since the peapods are larger than the pebbles, quilt peapods first and then fill around them with the pebbles.

Start/stop

1. Start by quilting a gentle serpentine line that goes out and echoes back to a point.

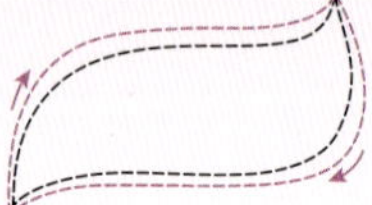

2. Echo the sides of the shape, touching the end point and returning to the starting point.

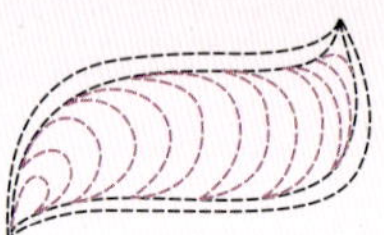

3. Fill inside the peapod shape with a filler. For this example I filled the pod with arcs. End at the opposite point.

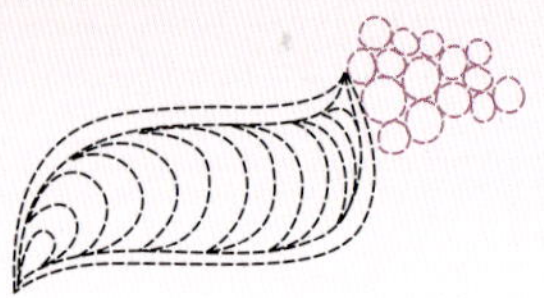

4. Fill around the peapod with pebbles.

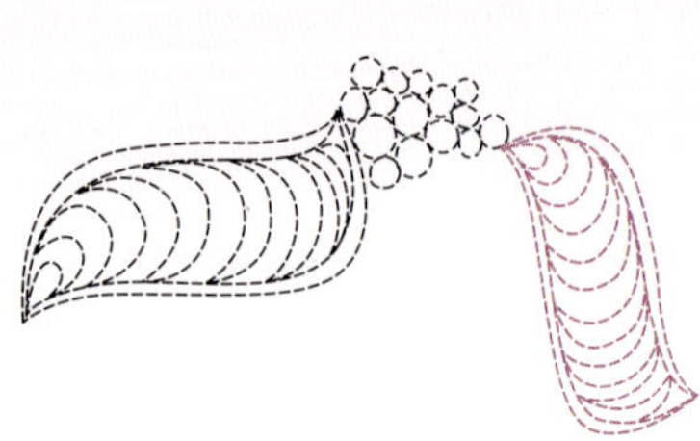

5. Once you have covered enough space, quilt another peapod.

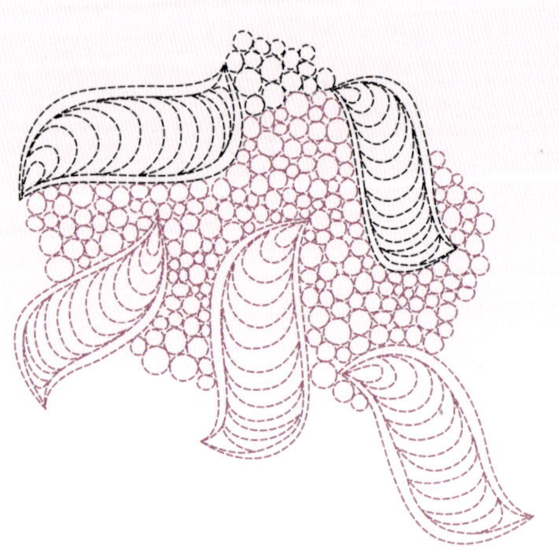

6. Continue quilting pods and your filler quilting design until the area is filled.

PEBBLED LEAVES

Do you want a design with a lot of texture and contrast? Then the Pebbled Leaves design is perfect for you.

Note 

This is a great way to practice quilting pebbles without committing to using them over the whole quilt. Try stitching a few. If you decide that you don't like quilting them, switch to regular leaves.

1. Quilt a leaf shape by quilting a curve that arcs out to a point and returns to the starting point. Make the shape 2″ or bigger so that you don't have to squeeze the pebbles into a small area.

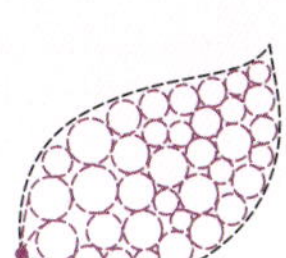

2. Fill the shape by quilting pebbles, ending at the original starting point.

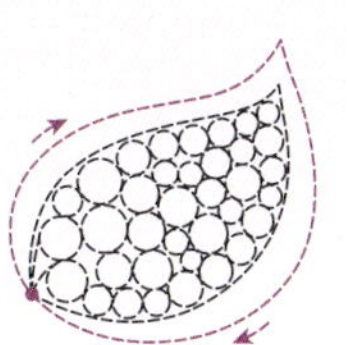

3. Echo around the outside of the leaf shape. It doesn't matter how many times you echo; the echoing just helps separate the pebbles from the rest of the quilting, making them stand out a bit more.

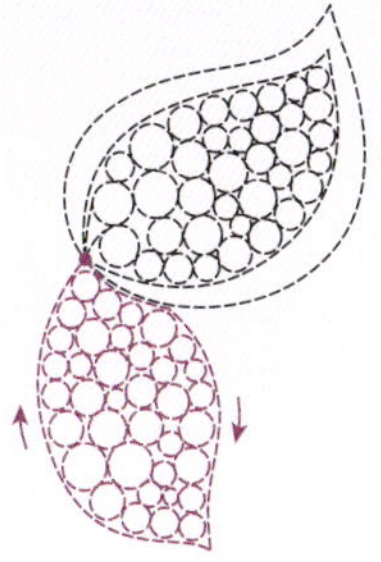

4. Start the next leaf by pointing the arc shape in a different direction than the first leaf.

5. Continue adding leaves and filling in with pebbles as you move around the quilting area, filling in as consistently as possible.

Note 

Stuck? If you are having trouble with your leafy meander, try these tips:

- Use echoing to help move around the area. You can echo what you have just quilted or leaves that you quilted previously.
- Try to make your leaves point in many different directions (unless, of course, you want them all facing the same way). This will help make them look more like an allover design.
- If you have any awkwardly shaped areas, just throw in a few more pebbles.

Variations

Frame a quilt block with Pebbled Leaves.

Note how the leaf shapes create a glow around the star block.

This design is stunning but can be time-consuming to stitch. If you don't have time to stitch it in a big filler area or just want to add a bit of interest to your quilt instead, use the pebbled leaves as a way

You can also quilt the leaves so that they add detail to other quilt blocks. In this example, I quilted leaves between quilt blocks.

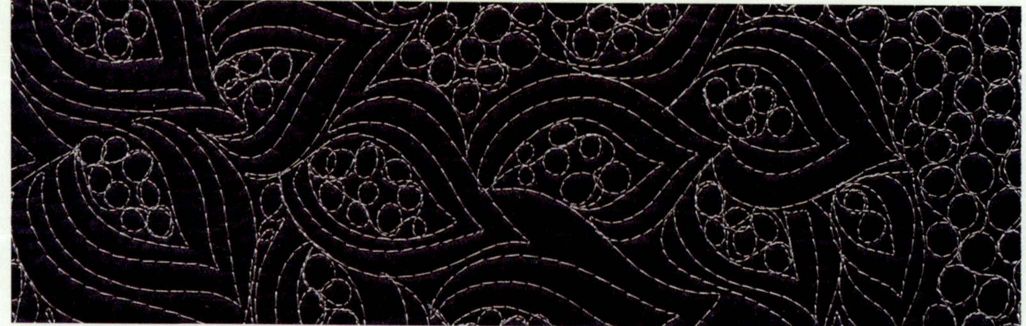

Or if you like pebbles, you can quilt more of them with leaves thrown in.

PAISLEY FEATHER

Love feathers and I love echoing, so it makes perfect sense that I would include a design that contains both! This design is perfect for quilt backgrounds because you can make the motifs as large or as small as you would like. It also adds a beautiful texture to your quilt.

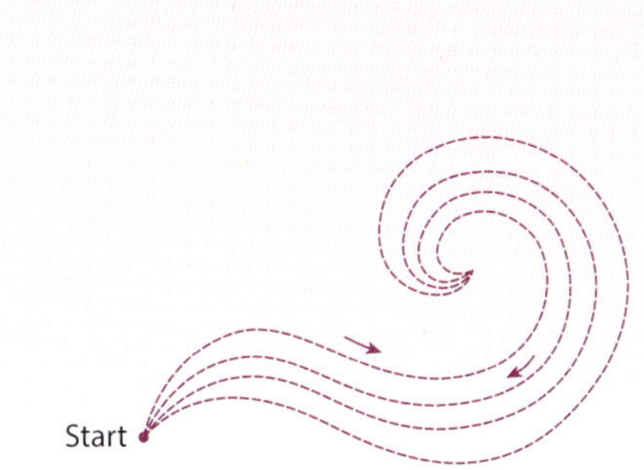

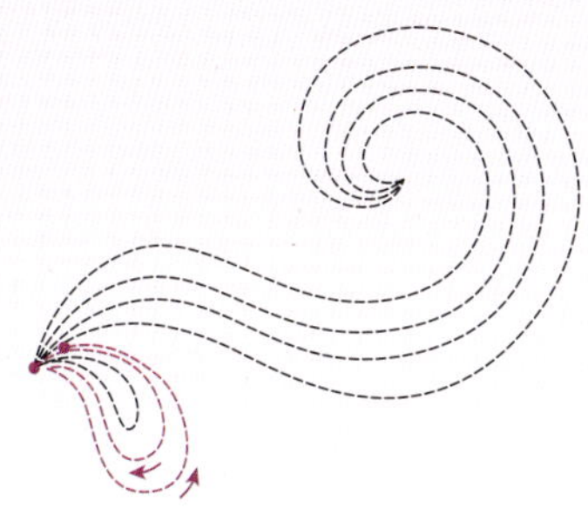

1. Quilt an elongated swirl and echo back to the starting point. Echo it twice more, ending at the same place you started.

2. At the bottom of the swirl, quilt a paisley that extends away from the swirl.

3. Echo around the paisley at least twice.

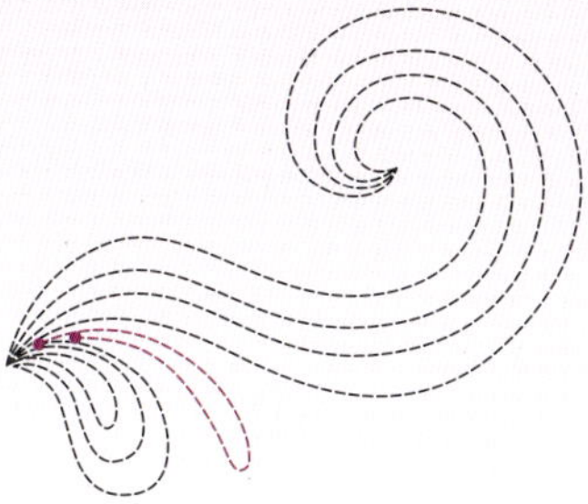

4. Add another paisley between the first paisley and the swirl.

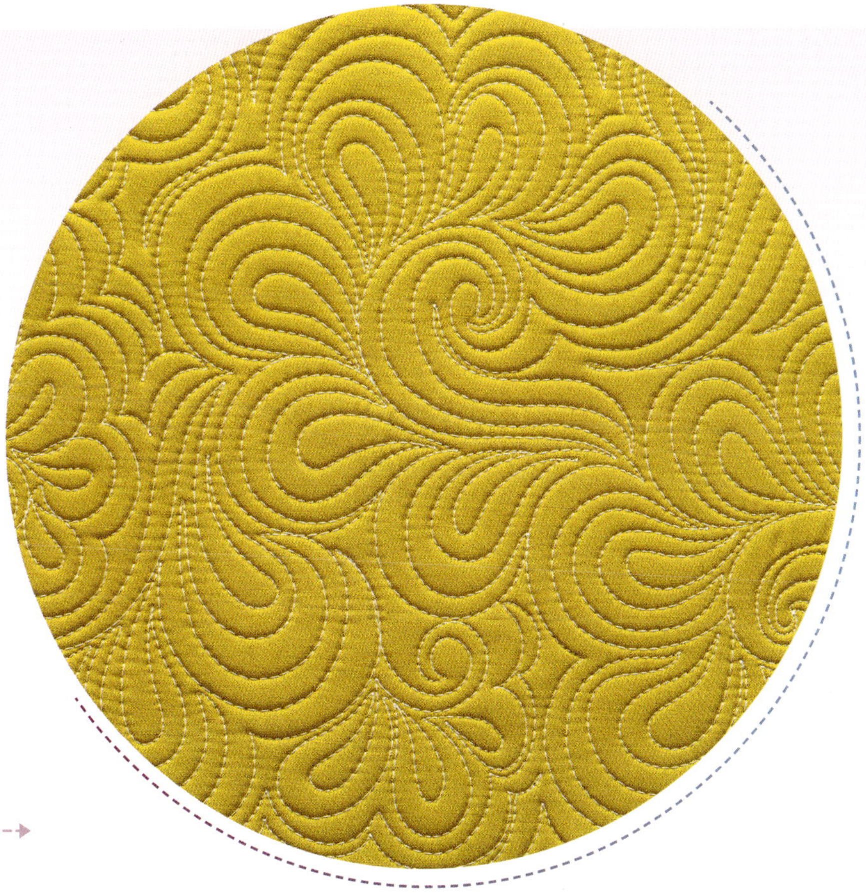

Continued on next page

5. Echo around the new paisley. Continue working your way around the swirl by quilting paisleys and echoing around them. As you work inside the swirl, the paisleys will become smaller.

6. To begin the next paisley feather, echo around the paisleys until you reach the point where you want to add the next one. Quilt an elongated swirl and continue quilting.

Tips

Beautiful Paisley Feathers

Don't be afraid to echo. Echoing around the paisleys is what really makes this design shine. Echoing also helps hide any mistakes. So, when in doubt ... echo!

If you have any spaces that are too small for a paisley feather, just add some paisleys by themselves. Or you can add a different design, such as pebbles.

Keep your paisleys skinny, almost like a finger. That will give you space to add more echoing around it.

Oh, and don't forget to echo. I know I have already said that, but it's important to remember!

Add single paisleys or pebbles to fill in small spaces.

IMPROV

The modern quilt movement is well known for improvisational piecing. But I think we can also apply that to machine quilting. One of my favorite things to do is "improv quilt," where I pick a few of my favorite quilting designs and throw them together. It may look completely random, but there is actually a method to my madness. Let me show you!

Tip

This is a great way to practice a new design. Throw it in with some designs that you are more comfortable with, and get quilting!

Before you start quilting, take a moment to think about the different quilting designs you want to use. I usually decide on 3 or 4 designs. At least one of them needs to work as a filler design that can be quilted in a smaller scale compared with the others.

Note

Don't worry about quilting the individual designs perfectly. It's more important that the quilting area is filled in completely.

Some of my favorite designs to use include these:

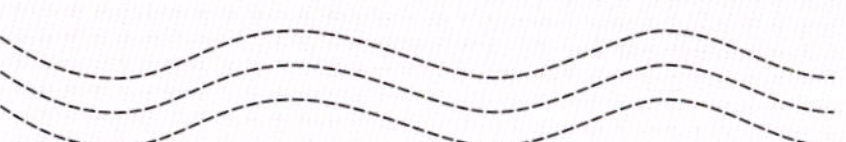

Wavy lines, useful for breaking up the quilting area into smaller sections

Flowers, easy to execute with this design, which can grow to fit various sizes

Swirl chain, which we learned earlier in this chapter

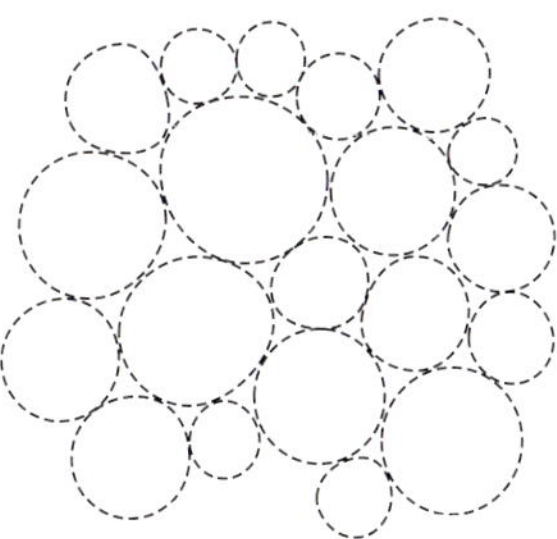

Pebbles, an ideal design to use as a filler

Continued on next page

When combining designs, I like to divide them into "bigger" designs and "filler" designs. The "bigger" designs aren't necessarily larger they just take up a little more space than the rest. These would include:

- Paisleys
- Leaves
- Feathers

The "filler" designs are ones that don't take up as much space, making them perfect for filling in the gaps between the other quilting designs. These would include the rest of the designs in the book:

- Meander
- Loopy Meander
- Swirl Meander
- Swirl Hook Meander

1. Start by quilting one or two bigger designs, a feather and some leaves for instance. Transitioning from one design to the next is as easy as finishing one then starting the next. If necessary, use echoing to work your way around a design until you reach the perfect area for the next one.

2. Use a "filler" design to fill in any spaces between the quilting and the edge of the area. The meander design is perfect for this.

Note  

If you aren't sure a design is going fit with another, take a moment and use your finger to trace it on the fabric. It will help your brain visualize where to go next.

Continued on page 290

Tip

I like to think of my quilting as a "blob." Keeping the quilting together helps prevent any gaps between the quilting designs.

Stringing out the designs may make it harder to fill the gaps later.

Keeping the quilting close together helps prevent gaps.

3. Quilt another "bigger" quilting design. How about a couple of swirls?

4. Add a few paisleys, then quilt the loopy meander to fill in between the other quilting.

5. Use the designs you want! There is no special order or frequency you have to follow. When a design pops into mind, quilt it!

6. The corners can be a little tricky, just remember to fill them in as much as possible.

7. Have fun with it!

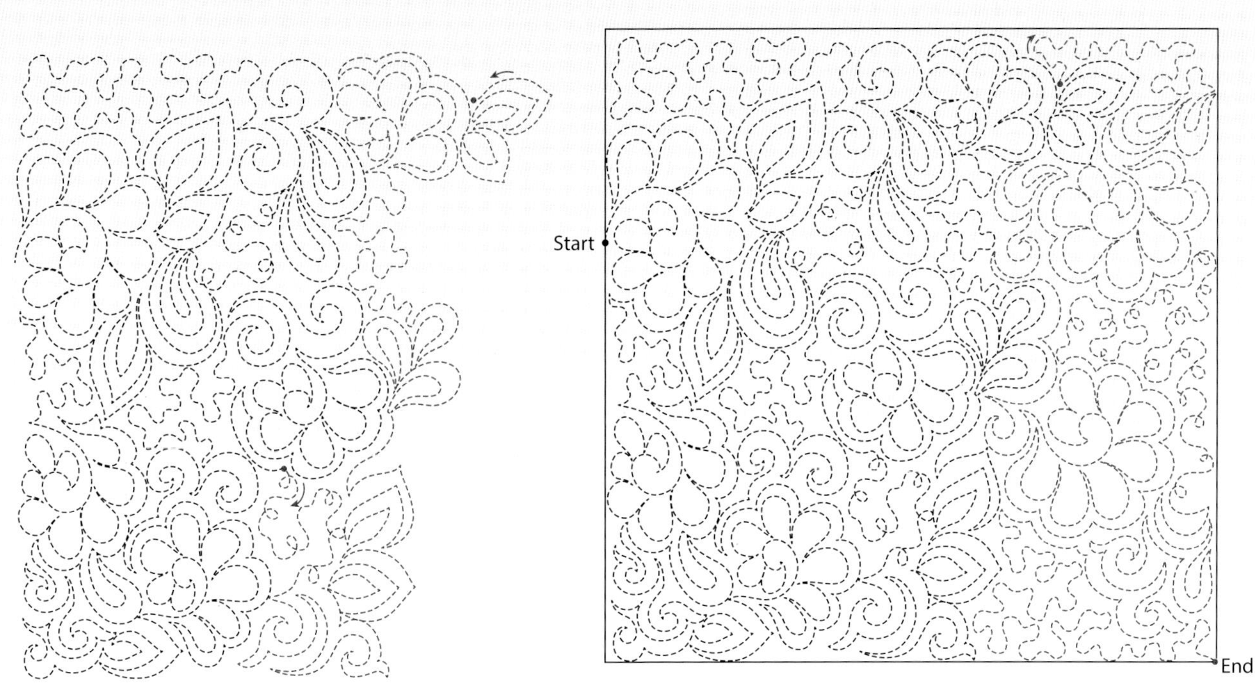

Hopefully by this point of the book, you are feeling more comfortable with the machine quilting process. Try to have fun with this technique. I love to let my mind wander while I quilt several fun designs.

OTHER WAYS TO USE IMPROV QUILTING

Organized Chaos

I like to mix up the designs because it plays right into my ADD style of machine quilting. But, if that seems like too much bouncing around, try quilting them in sections.

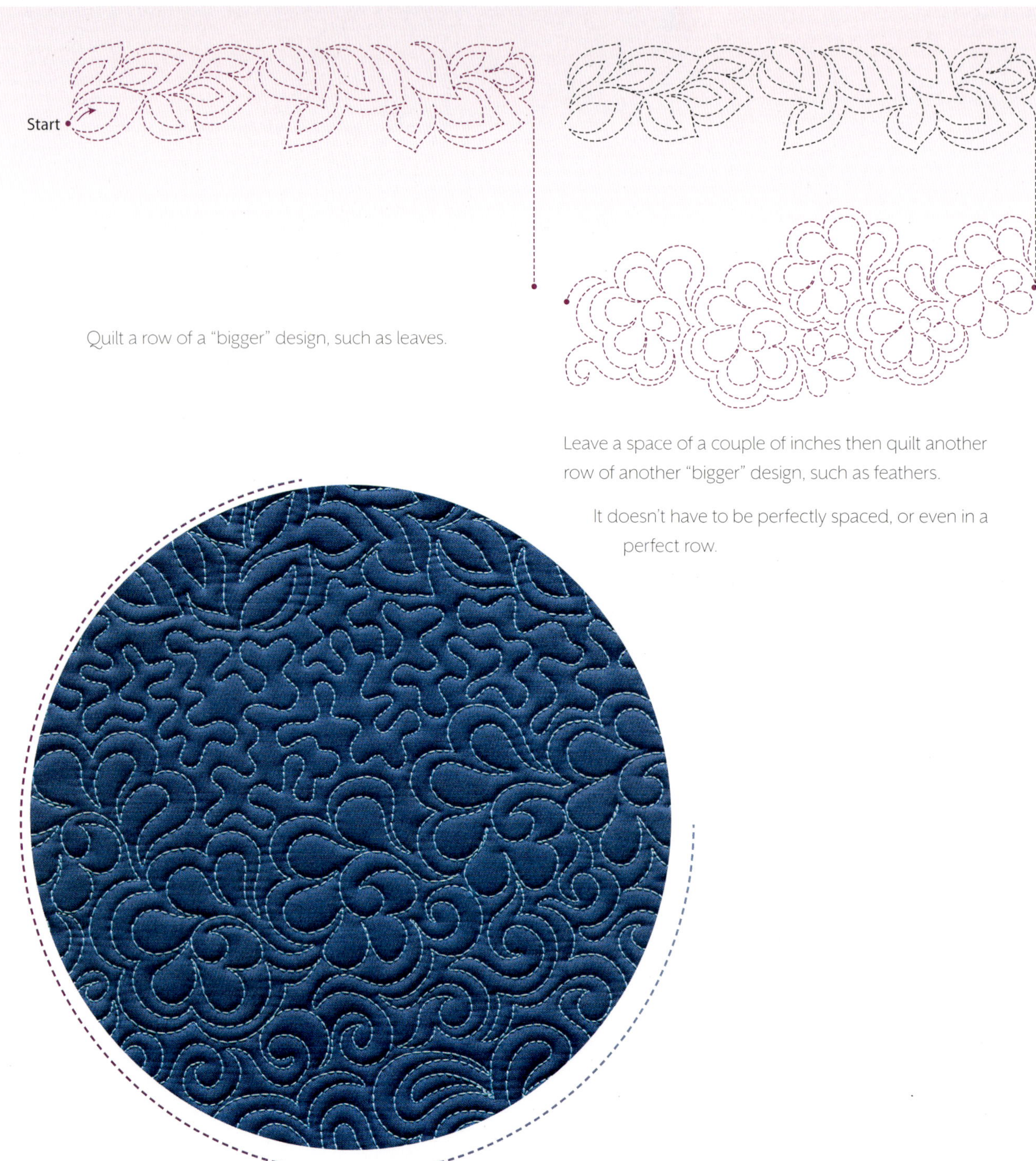

Quilt a row of a "bigger" design, such as leaves.

Leave a space of a couple of inches then quilt another row of another "bigger" design, such as feathers.

It doesn't have to be perfectly spaced, or even in a perfect row.

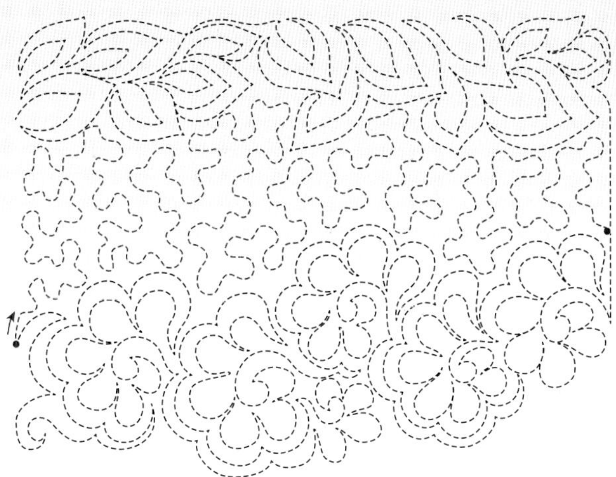

Next, quilt the spaces in between with a "filler" design, such as the basic meander.

Note

If you prefer, you can just quilt the rows without leaving a space in between them. Quilt the designs in the order that works for you!

Keep repeating until the whole area is filled in.

Continued on next page →

I am quilting the swirls in this illustration.

Start

I am echoing around the feathers as well.

Focal Point

Another easy way to use this technique on your quilt is to play with the scale of the quilting. Making some of the designs bigger (with more space between the lines) will make them show up more.

This is especially helpful if you want a particular design to be more prominent. For instance, let's pretend that you love quilting feathers. (I'm sure you love feathers, right? Even if you don't, you can still be friends!) Quilt them on a larger scale to show them off!

BORDER: HERRINGBONE

When it comes to quilting the borders of a quilt, I love any design that breaks it up into smaller sections; this includes the herringbone design. I love everything about it. It works in borders of all widths, and can add an intricate, custom-quilted look to your quilt.

To keep the individual sections the same width, you could mark the dividing lines. However, I find that eyeballing it will get you close enough!

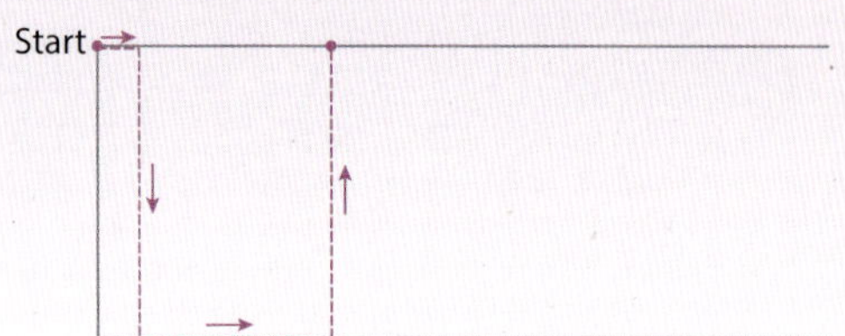

1. From the top corner of the border, travel along the edge approximately ½˝. Quilt a line down to the other side, travel along the bottom edge of the border, and quilt up to the top of the border.

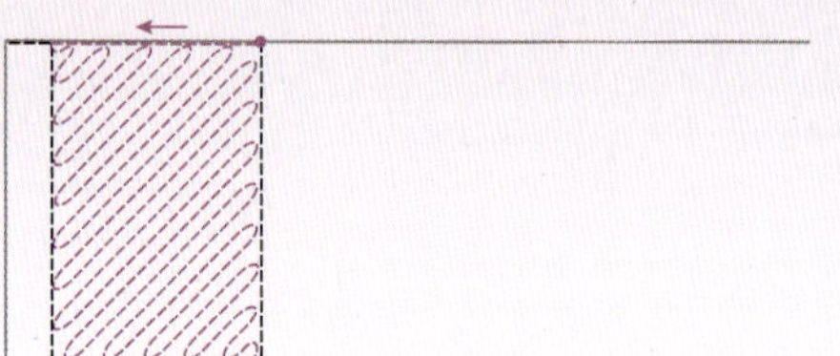

2. Travel along the top edge of the border, returning to the top left corner of the rectangle. Fill in the rectangle with a diagonal back-and-forth line, ending at the opposite bottom corner.

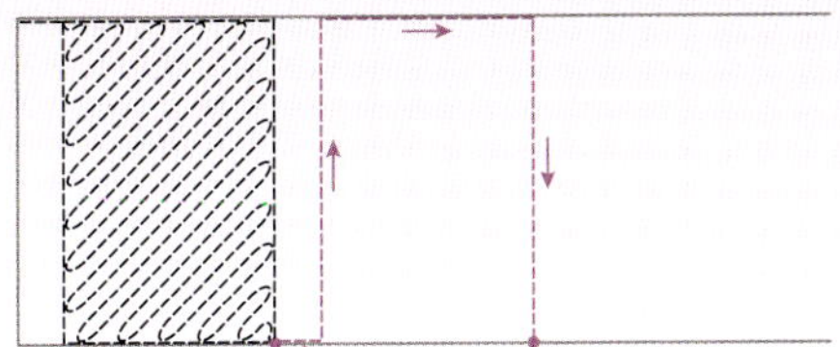

3. Travel along the bottom edge of the border about ½″ and quilt the outside of another section by quilting up, to the right, and then down again.

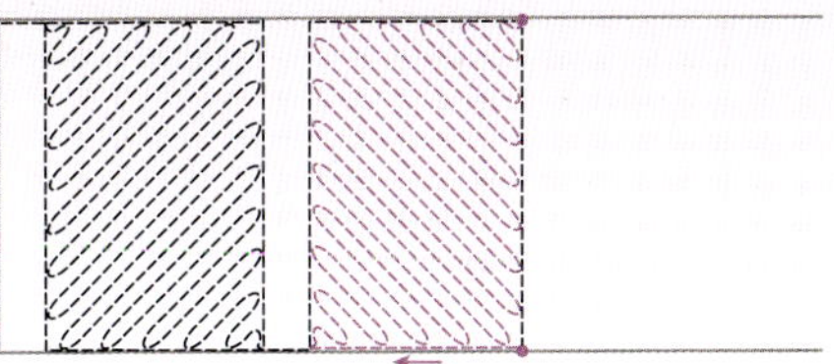

4. Travel along the bottom edge of the border, completing the section and filling in by quilting diagonal back-and-forth lines in the opposite direction of the first section.

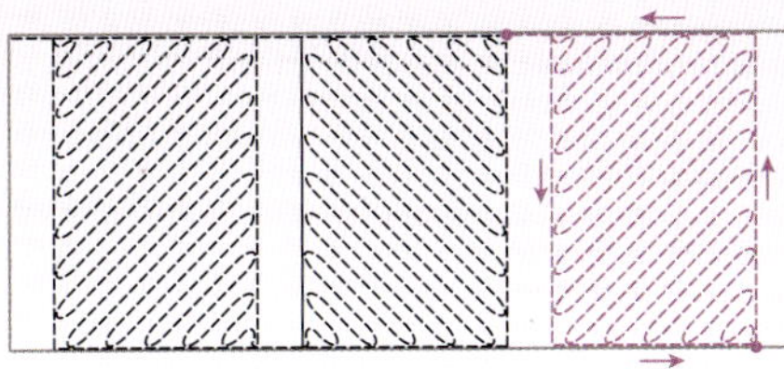

5. Repeat Steps 1–4 to fill the border with the sections to create the herringbone pattern.

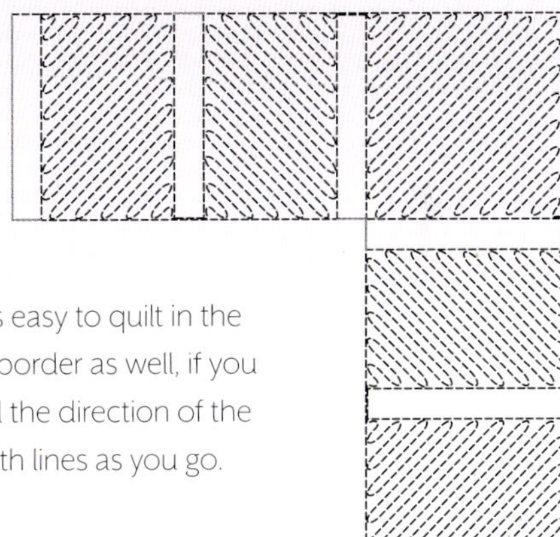

This design is easy to quilt in the corners of a border as well, if you keep in mind the direction of the back-and-forth lines as you go.

Variations

If you don't particularly like the diagonal lines on this design, or you need a different look, here are a couple of options:

Make the separating lines closer or farther apart, depending on how dense you want the quilting to be.

Instead of quilting diagonal lines, try using a different filler design, such as a figure-eight or ribbon candy design.

BORDER: BRACKETS

This design combines two of my go-to designs: brackets and back-and-forth lines. It's a quick and easy design that can pack quite a visual punch. This adaptable design fits in borders of all sizes and can also work in larger blocks and sashing. Try using it in the outer borders of a quilt to add a "framed" effect to the quilt.

Tip

This design is quilted in several passes, but it is easily broken down into chunks. Follow along and manage each simple chunk to get a complex result.

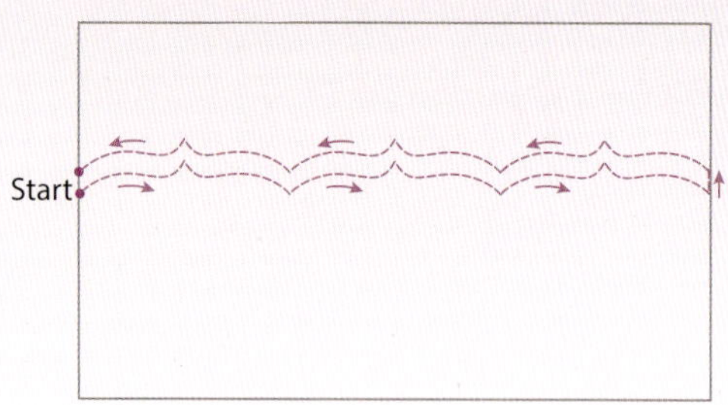

1. Start on one edge of the border, slightly above the middle. Quilt a repeating bracket shape until you reach the edge of the border. Travel along the edge of the border approximately ½″ and echo the brackets back to the beginning.

I don't mark the brackets; I just go for it. But you could consider marking a horizontal line along the border, so your line of brackets stays straight. You could also vary the spacing between the lines of brackets, depending on how dense you want the quilting.

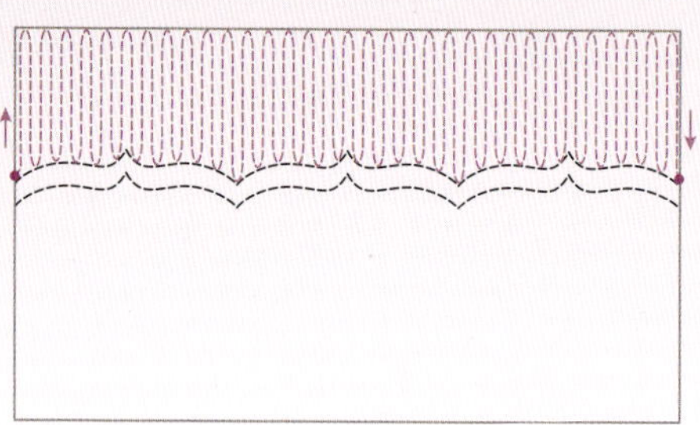

2. Quilt back-and-forth lines between the top of the brackets to the top of the border.

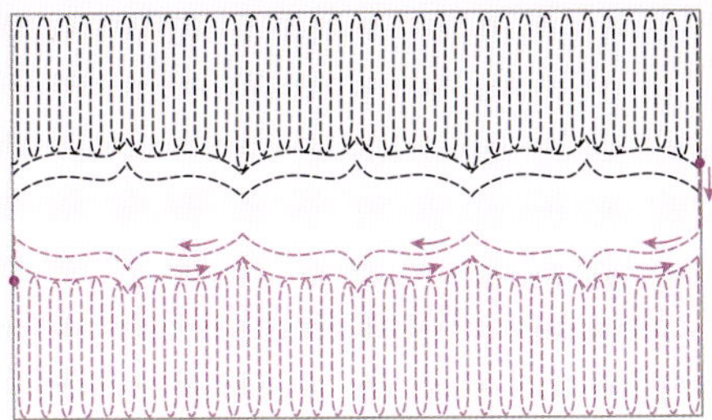

3. Once you reach the end of the border, travel along the edge until you are below the middle of the border. Repeat the technique in Steps 1 and 2 to quilt the bottom portion of the border.

I try to quilt the second row of brackets so they are a mirror image of the top row, but I don't stress out if it's not perfect!

Variations

This design is quilted using several passes over the whole border. Sometimes, that isn't the most convenient way to quilt the border. If that is the case, quilt the bracket lines so they span the width of the border instead of the length.

CORNERS

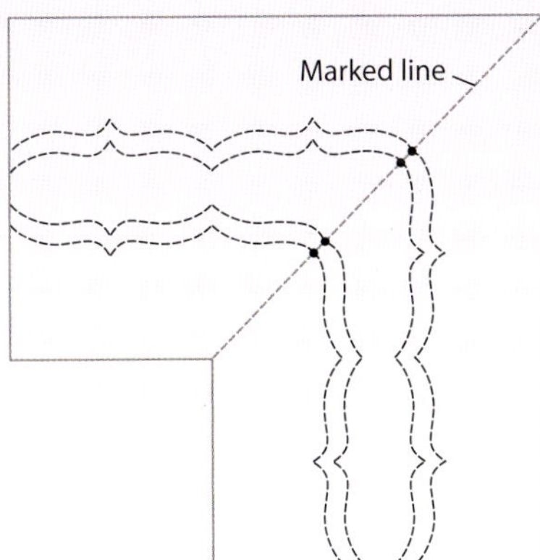

Quilting the brackets design so it wraps around a corner seamlessly is actually easier than it sounds. Before you start quilting, mark a line connecting the inner corner to the outer corner. When quilting the bracket lines, stop when you get to the marked line.

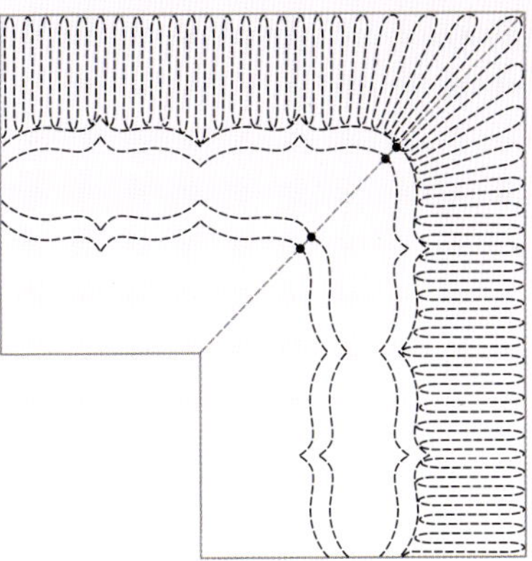

When quilting the back-and-forth lines, quilt them so they wrap around the corner.

PIECED SHAPES

SQUARE 1

This design is basic and straightforward. However, when multiple squares with this design are arranged, the diagonals create a secondary pattern that can add huge interest to your quilt! It first divides the square in half diagonally and then uses different quilting designs in each half. I love to use this design in larger squares, alternating the direction of the lines. It creates a grid-like look to the quilting that I just love!

Note 

When considering what designs to use in each section of the block, I try to pick designs that vary in style, line, or scale. This helps give the quilting contrast, which is something that I am particular about.

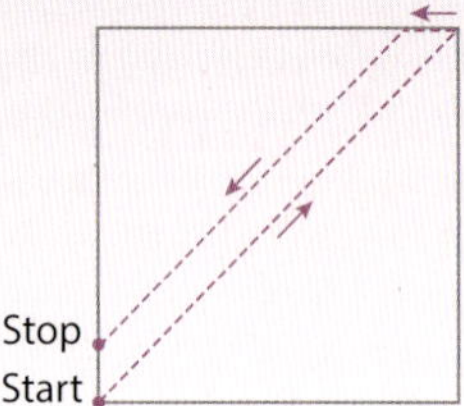

1. Quilt a straight line from one corner of a block to the opposite corner. Travel along the edge of the block approximately ¼˝ and echo the line you just quilted until you end on the other side of the block about ¼˝ from the starting point.

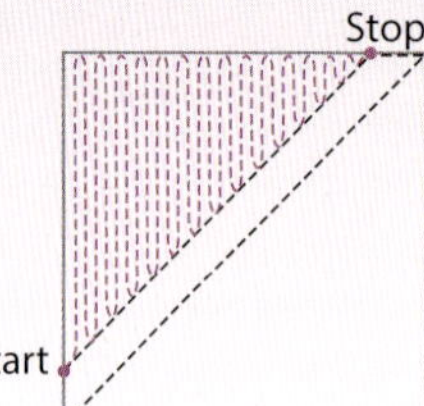

2. Quilt a dense back-and-forth line, filling in the top portion of the block.

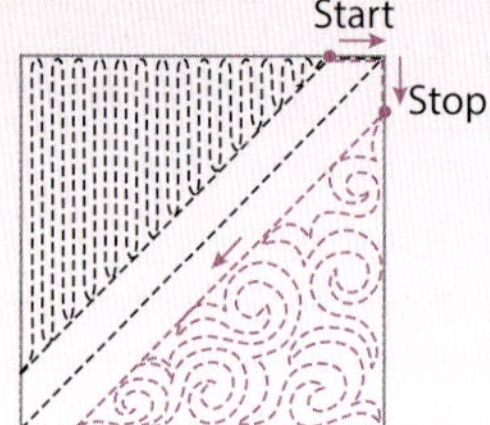

3. Travel around the corner of the block until you are about ¼˝ below the first line you quilted. Quilt a straight line to the opposite side of the block and fill in the area with a free-motion quilting design, such as swirls.

Variations

Experiment with this design by using different fillers in each side of the square. Pebbles and leaves are two great options.

Try using different quilting designs such as pebbles and leaves.

SQUARE 2

Instead of tackling one big square, use this design to make four smaller squares. breaking up the larger square is easy. For the smaller squares, I chose two designs that contrast well with each other: continuous-curve lines and dense back-and-forth lines. The clear contrast ensures that your quilting will get noticed!

This design works in blocks of all sizes, from small to large.

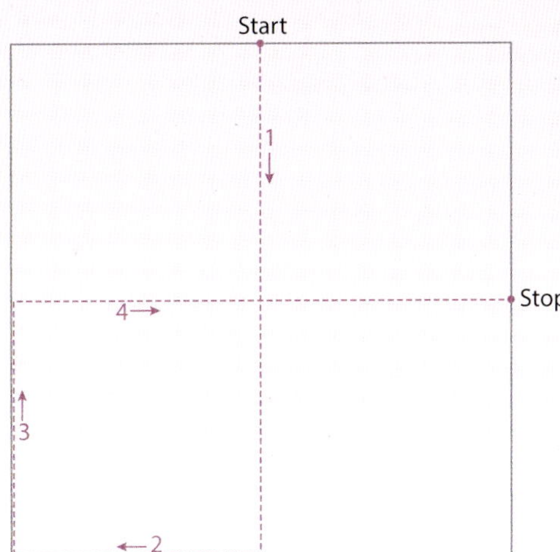

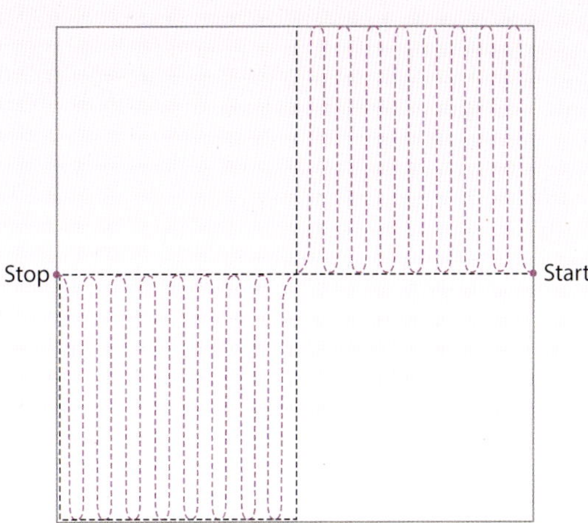

1. Starting from the middle of the top of the block, quilt a vertical line straight down to the opposite side. Travel along the edge, then around the corner to the midpoint of the next side. Quilt a straight line across to the middle of the opposite side. You've divided the block into four convenient sections.

2. Quilt back-and-forth lines, filling in one of the square sections. When the section is filled, cross over the center of the block and continue filling in the square section catty-cornered to the one you just quilted.

Continued on next page

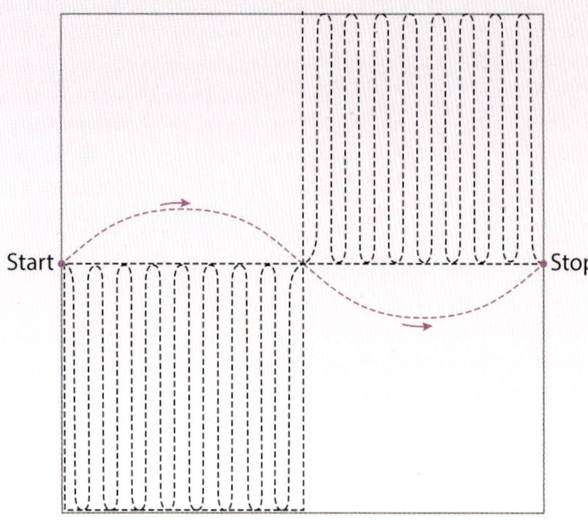

3. Quilt the remaining sections with a continuous-curve design. Start by quilting a curved line to the center of the block. From the center, quilt a curved line into the catty-cornered square.

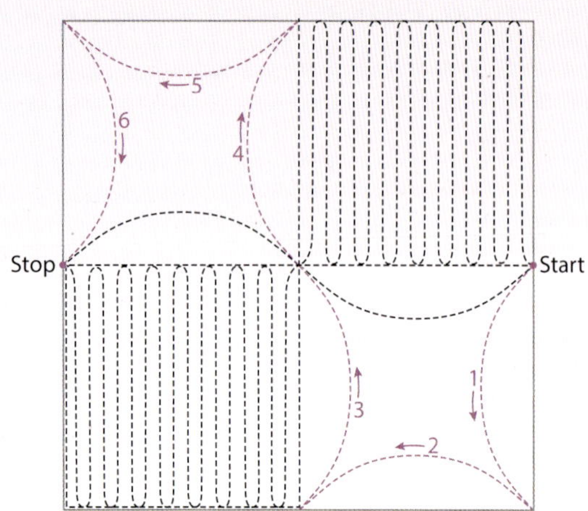

4. Quilt the remaining 3 curves for this square and then resume quilting the curves for the other square, ending at the starting point.

Variations

Sometimes when I am quilting this design, I like to switch things up just a bit by quilting the back-and-forth lines diagonally instead of horizontally.

You can also quilt this design with diagonal back-and-forth lines.

SQUARE 3

This design is a play on the continuous curve design. It's a quick and easy design to quilt, and the variations are endless. You will need to do a little traveling along the edge of the block, but the result is well worth it!

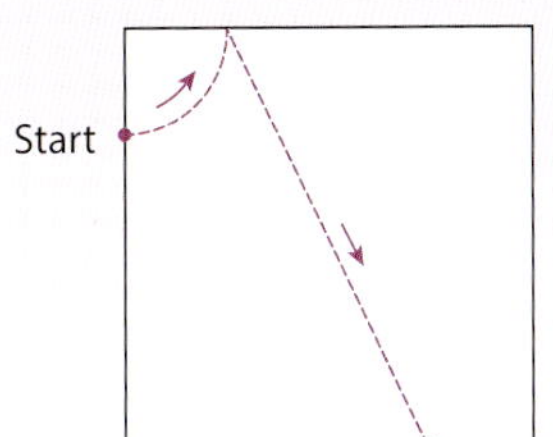

1. Starting about 2˝ away from any corner, quilt a curved line that ends about 2˝ on the adjacent side. Quilt a diagonal line to approximately 2˝ away from the opposite corner.

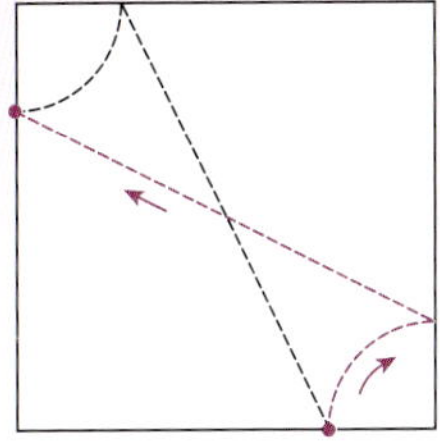

2. Quilt a curved line that ends about 2˝ away from the new corner's adjacent side, then quilt a diagonal line that ends at the original starting point.

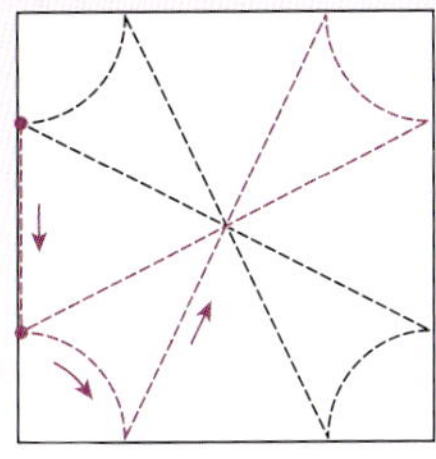

3. Travel along the edge of the block until you are about 2˝ away from the next corner. Repeat Steps 1 and 2 to fill in the design in the remaining corners.

Note

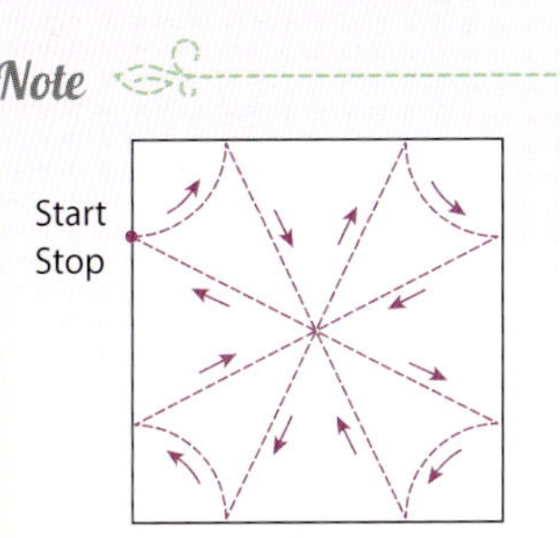

I prefer traveling along the block edge to start the next shape because I can ensure that the lines cross in the center. If you prefer to omit the traveling, try this alternative option. Stitch from the first corner to the center of the block, then on to the next corner. A benefit of this technique is that it starts and ends at the same place.

Variations

For a more geometric look, use straight lines instead of curved lines.

Use straight lines instead of curves.

Try it in a Four-Patch block as a way to connect the squares. It's also helpful to have the corners as a reference.

Stitching this design over a Four-Patch block will pull the block together.

TRIANGLE 1

When it comes to choosing quilting designs, I tend to think, "the more, the merrier." In this design, I've combined a few basic quilting designs to create a pattern that really brings attention to the block. It's especially great for larger blocks, such as setting triangles, since you can divide the quilting into smaller sections.

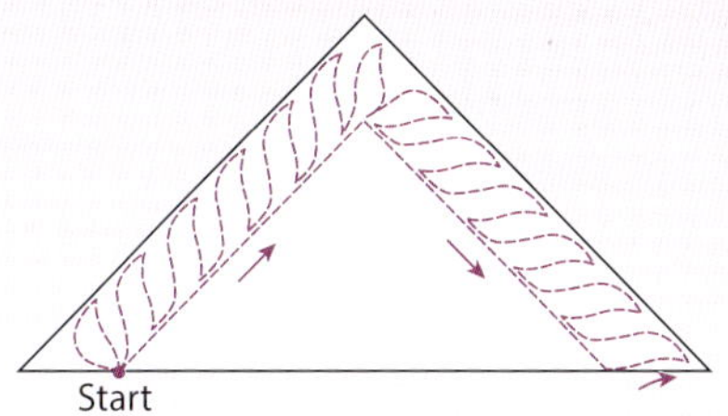

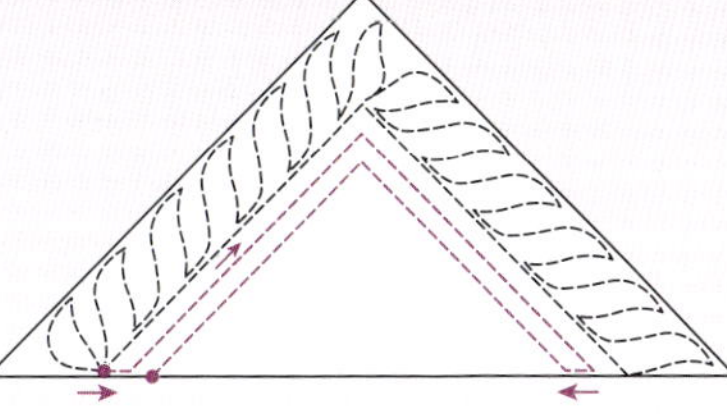

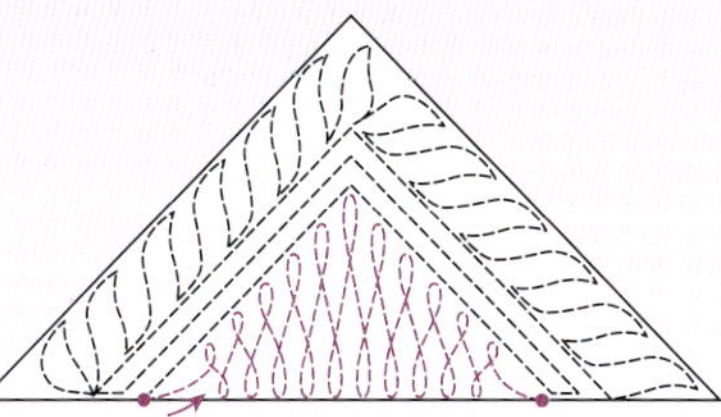

1. Starting about 1″–2″ away from the bottom corner of the triangle, quilt a line that echoes the top sides of the triangle. Fill in the space between the edge of the block and the quilted line with a serpentine quilting line, returning to the starting point.

2. Travel along the bottom of the triangle about ¼″ and echo the first line from Step 1. Travel back ¼″ along the bottom of the triangle and echo the line again.

3. Fill in the resulting smaller triangle with the quilting design of your choice. I used a wishbone quilting design, one of my favorites. I love how it easily fills the triangle and contrasts with the serpentine pattern at the top of the triangle.

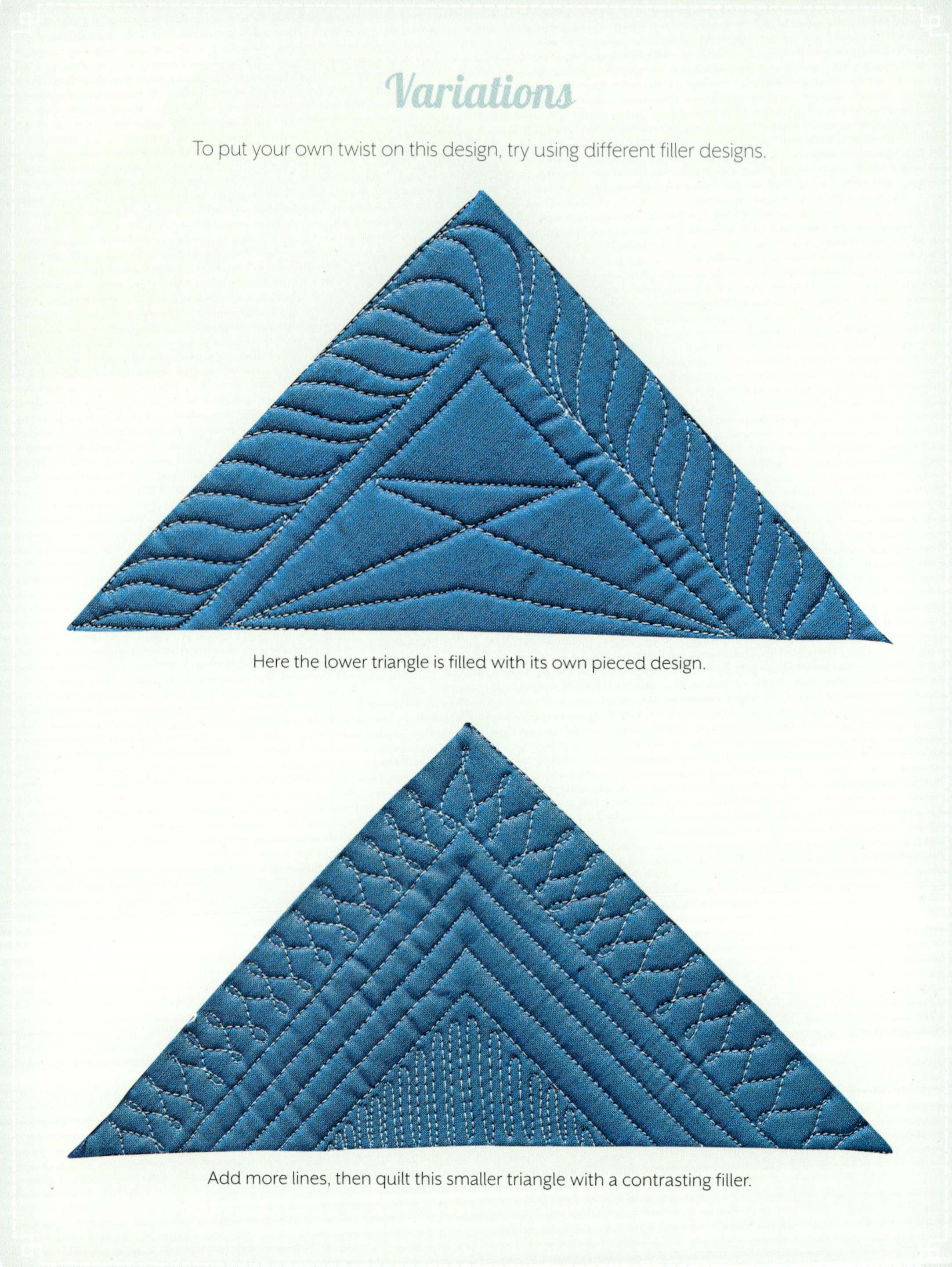

Variations

To put your own twist on this design, try using different filler designs.

Here the lower triangle is filled with its own pieced design.

Add more lines, then quilt this smaller triangle with a contrasting filler.

TRIANGLE 2

I like to use quilting to divide blocks into other shapes. This design is a great example of that. It's basic, but quick, and great for triangles of most sizes.

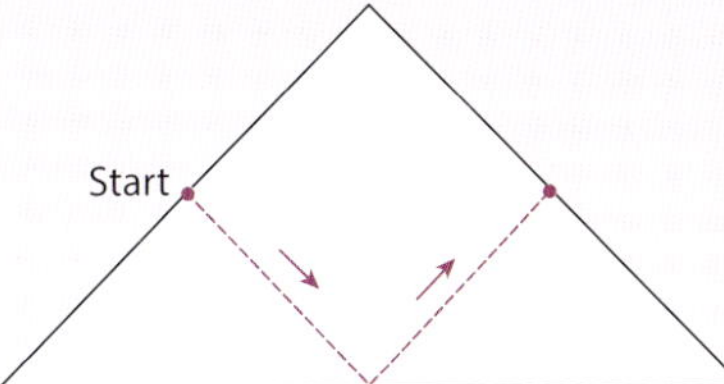

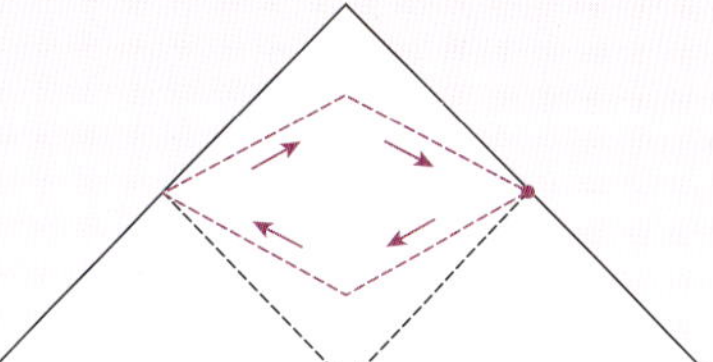

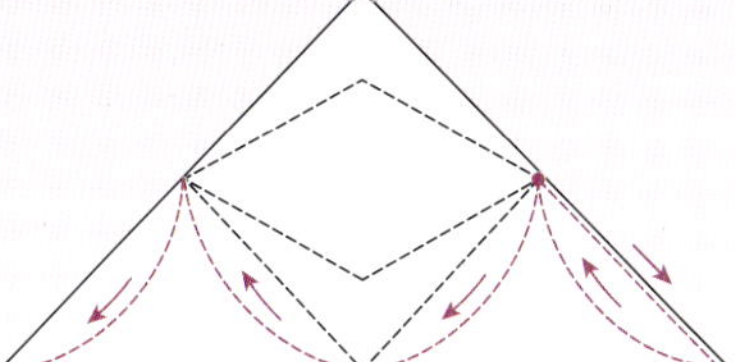

1. Start halfway between the points of a short side and quilt a diagonal line ending halfway between the points of the long side. Quilt another diagonal line ending halfway between the points of the other short side of the triangle.

2. Now that you have 3 little sections—2 triangles and a square—it's time to fill them in! In the square, quilt a diamond shape that touches the first starting point in Step 1 and returns to the starting point on the right side of the block.

3. Travel along the side of the triangle until you are at the nearest bottom point. Quilt a continuous curved line that goes from point to point, ending at the bottom of the square you just quilted. Quilt the remaining triangle the same way, ending on the opposite point from which you started.

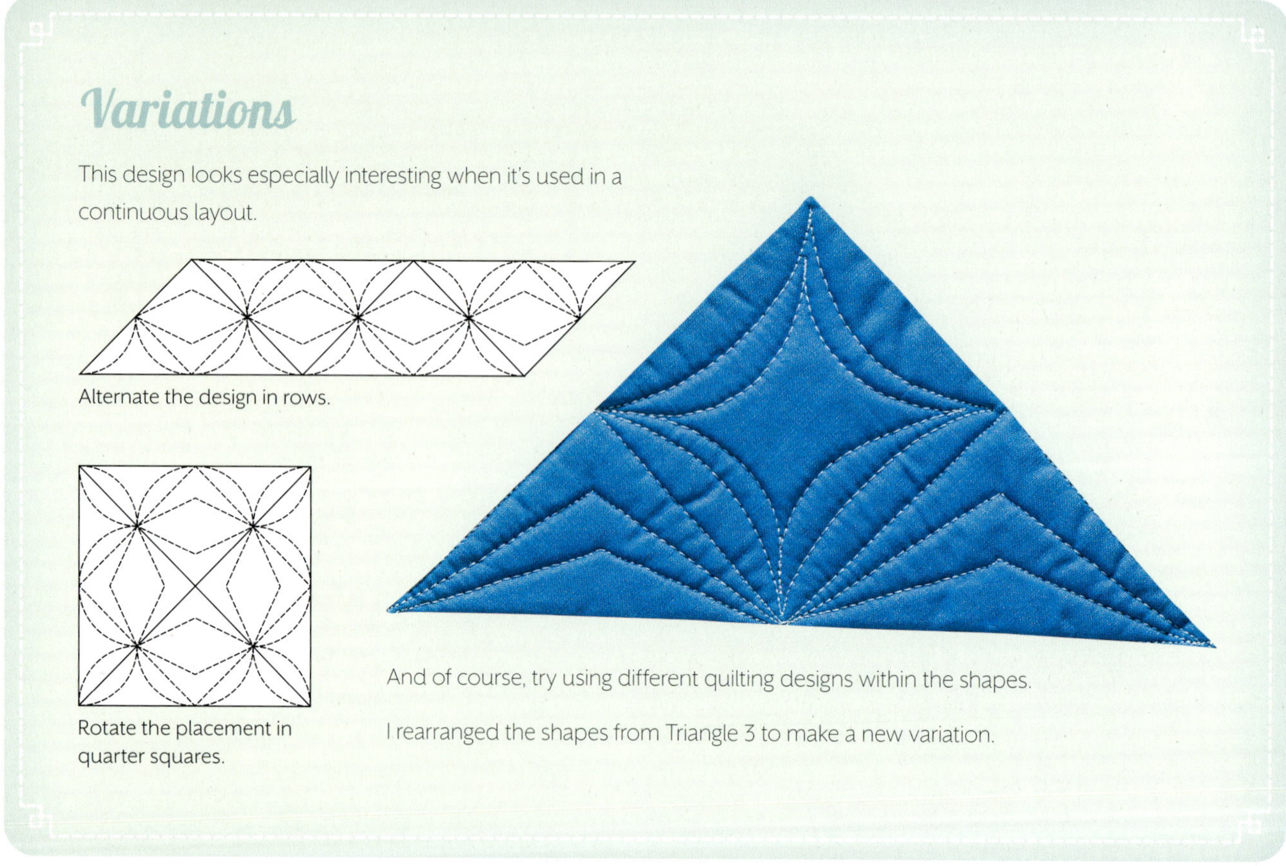

Variations

This design looks especially interesting when it's used in a continuous layout.

Alternate the design in rows.

Rotate the placement in quarter squares.

And of course, try using different quilting designs within the shapes.

I rearranged the shapes from Triangle 3 to make a new variation.

DIAMOND 1

Surely you didn't think I was done with the brackets design? I've said it before and I will say it again: this handy design is so versatile. For this design, I am combining it with dense back-and-forth lines to create a stunning visual. you can easily modify it to fit quilt blocks of all sizes and shapes.

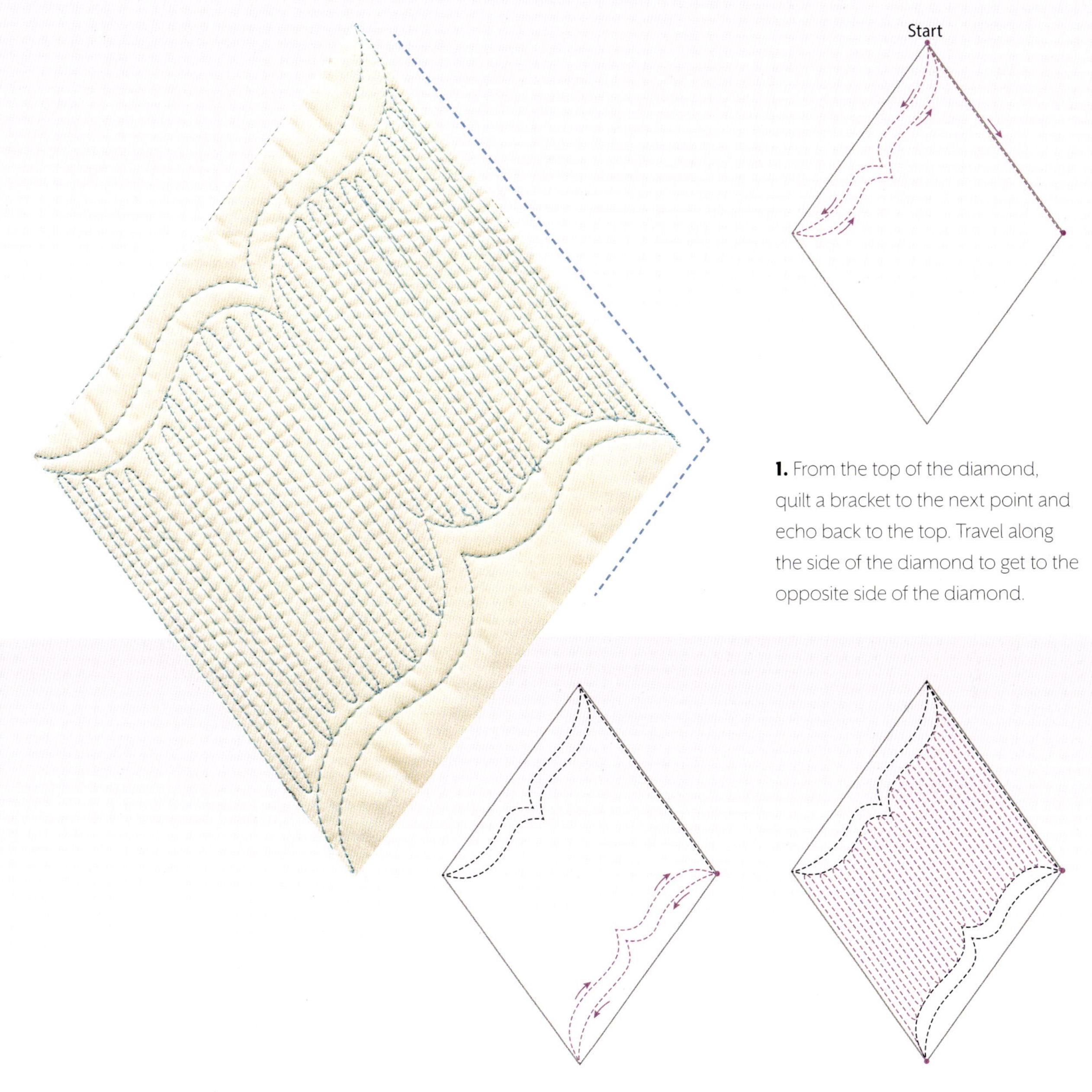

1. From the top of the diamond, quilt a bracket to the next point and echo back to the top. Travel along the side of the diamond to get to the opposite side of the diamond.

2. Quilt a bracket to the bottom of the diamond and echo back.

3. Using a dense back-and-forth line, fill in the area between the brackets, working your way to the other side of the diamond.

DIAMOND 2

I first worked with this design on a quilt with gothic arches. I love how the play on a basic wishbone design jazzes up the whole block. Since this design has several elements, I prefer to use it in larger diamond shapes. But don't let all the steps keep you from trying the design; it's just curved lines and wishbones!

> **Note**
> Of course, if you don't like the wishbone design, you can substitute with any filler design. The most important thing is that you end up at the bottom!

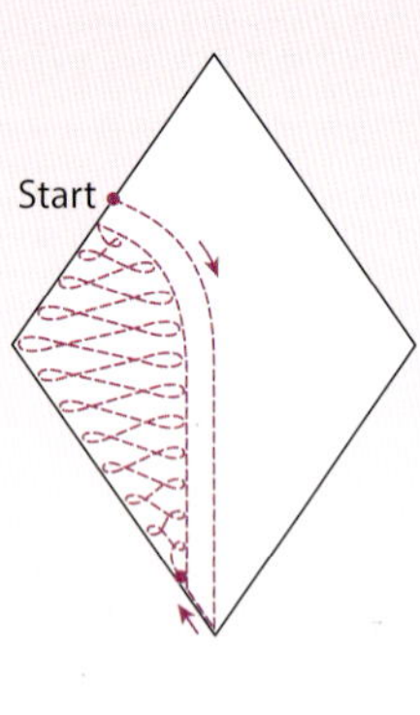

1. Starting halfway between the top corner and a side corner, quilt a line that curves out and then down the center of the block, stopping at the bottom corner. Travel ¼˝ along the edge and echo the side of the line. Work your way back toward the bottom corner, filling in between the echoed line and the edge of the block with a wishbone design.

2. Quilt a line that travels up the center line and curves to the opposite side of the block. Echo the side of the line and quilt the wishbone design so that you end up near the top of the block.

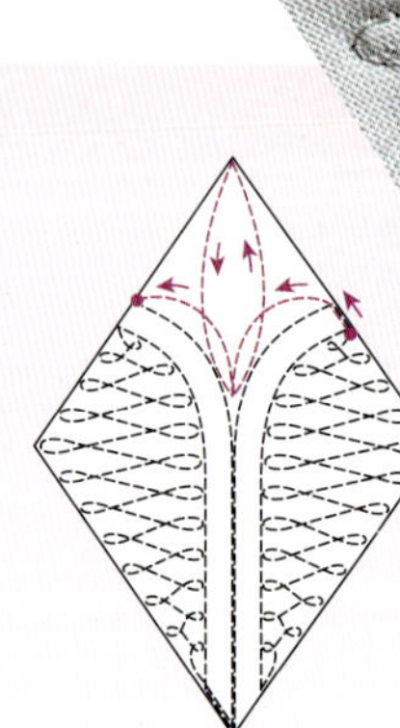

3. Fill in the top of the block by quilting a continuous curve design.

DIAMOND 3

This design can soften the angular sides of a diamond block by adding a "ray" effect to the quilt. It's another example of how basic shapes can make an impact on your quilts.

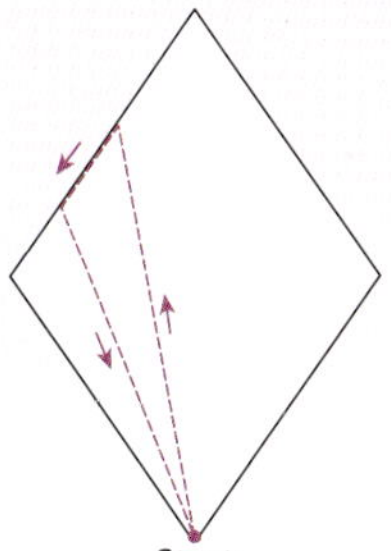

Start

1. Starting from the bottom corner of the block, quilt a straight line that angles out to about 1˝ away from an adjacent corner. Travel along the edge of the block about 1˝ and stitch a straight line back to the starting point.

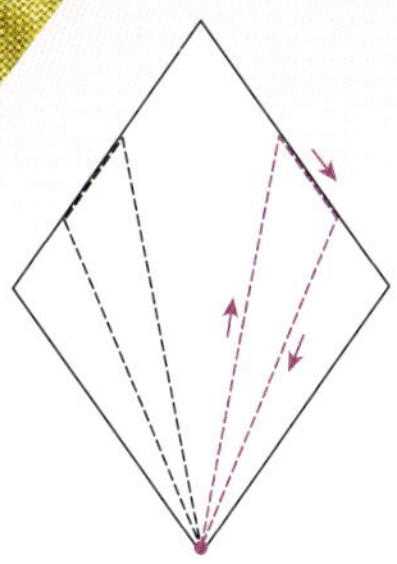

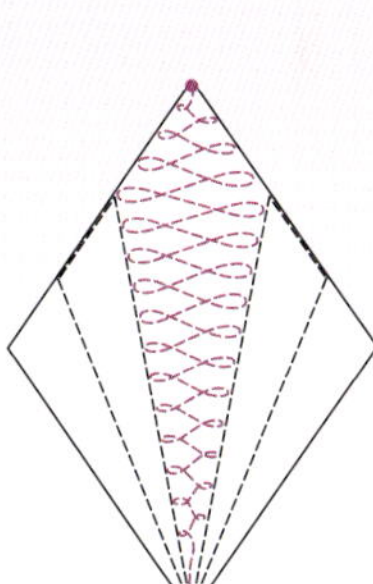

2. Repeat Step 1 on the other side of the block.

3. Quilt your way to the top corner using the design of your choice.

Variations

A really easy way to quilt an interesting variation of this design is to switch up the lines and the fillers.

Switch the placement of the lines and the fillers for a different look.

Try it in adjacent diamond blocks.

Alternate the placement of straight lines and fillers in adjacent blocks.

DIAMOND 4

This design might appear complex because of the number of steps required, but it isn't hard at all. It's best for larger blocks.

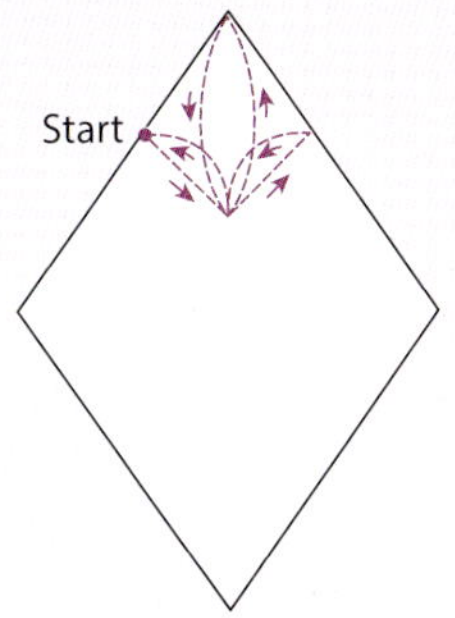

1. Starting 1″–2″ from a top corner, quilt a line that angles down toward the middle and back up to the opposite side. Fill in the space above with a continuous curve flower.

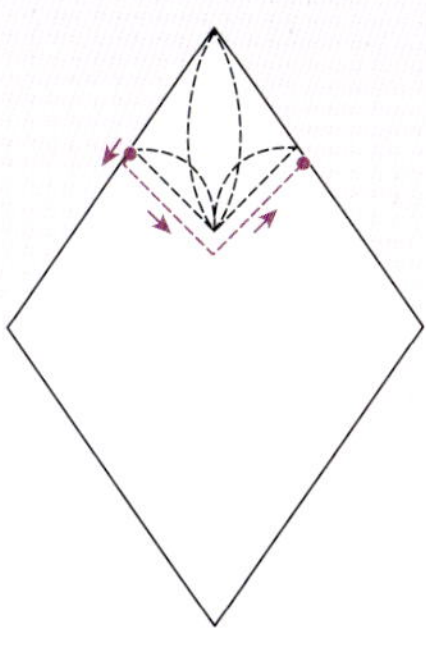

2. Travel along the edge and echo underneath the first line you quilted.

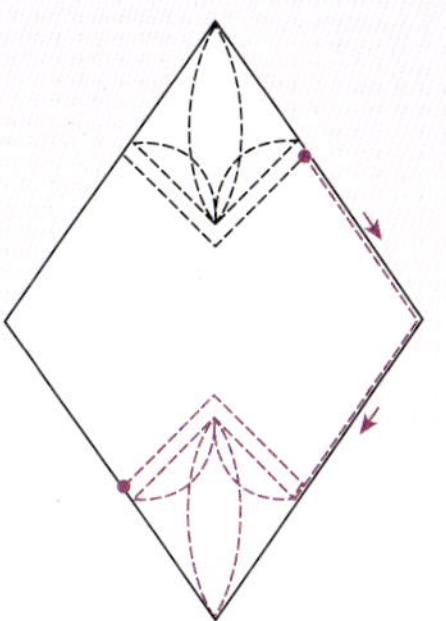

3. Travel along the edge of the block and repeat Steps 1 and 2 on the opposite corner of the block.

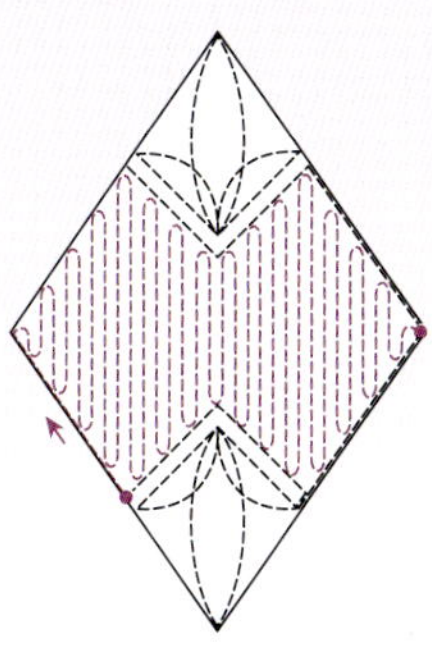

4. Travel to a side corner and fill in the area from side to side with a design.

HEXAGON 1

Even though I like how this design looks on its own, I think it looks especially wonderful when used in hexagons in rows. You can quickly quilt a whole section at once. Now that's my kind of quilting!

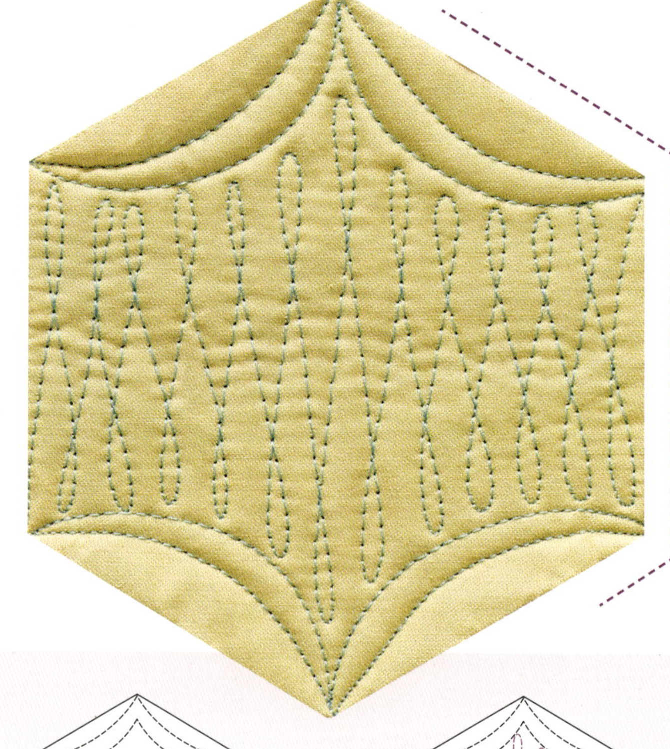

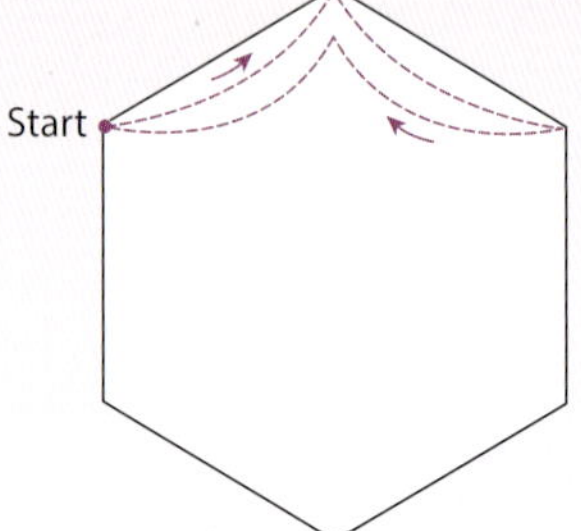

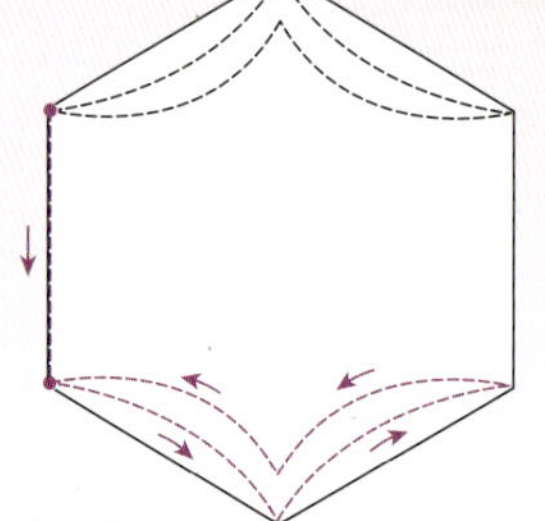

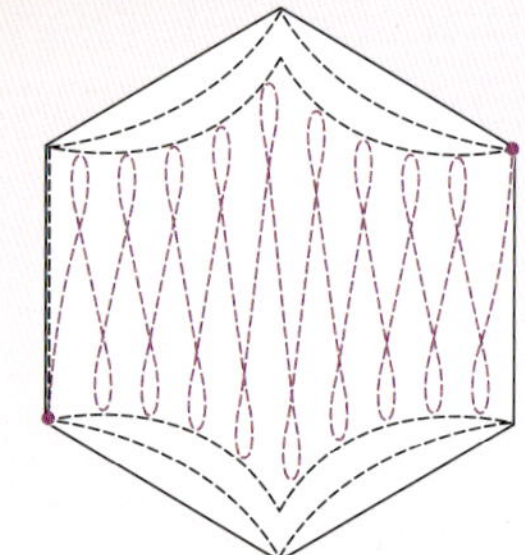

1. Starting from any corner, quilt a line that curves to the next corner and again to the next adjacent corner. Echo the line that you just quilted, returning to the starting point.

2. Travel down the edge of the block and repeat Step 1, quilting the bottom of the hexagon the same as the top.

3. Fill the area in between with the filler of your choice.

This design makes a cool secondary pattern when quilted in a group of hexagons.

Tip

If you are working on a straight row of hexagons, you could repeat Step 1 to quilt all the tops before moving on to the next step.

Variations

Add some more echo lines and change out the fillers for a slightly different look.

Change the look with more echoes and different fillers.

HEXAGON 2

This design combines a basic continuous curve with a filler to create a more complex-looking design. Use this in areas of the quilt that you want to shine. It will definitely get attention!

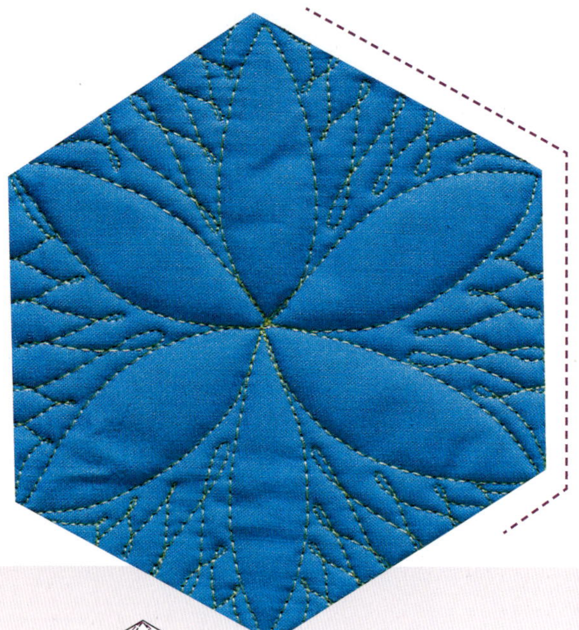

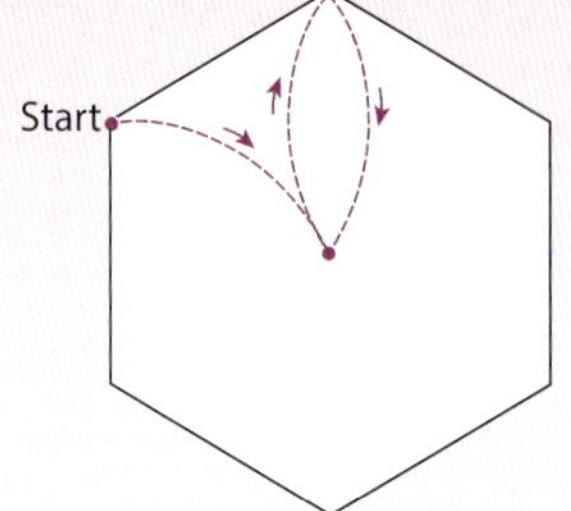

1. Starting from any corner, quilt a line that arcs to the center of the block, up to the next corner, and back to the center.

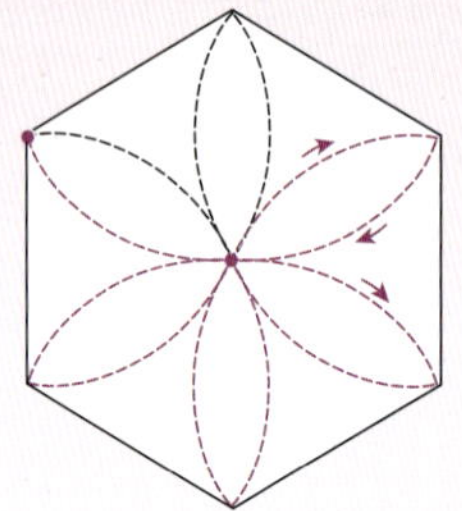

2. Continue quilting your way around the block, arcing to each corner and back to the center, until you return to the starting point.

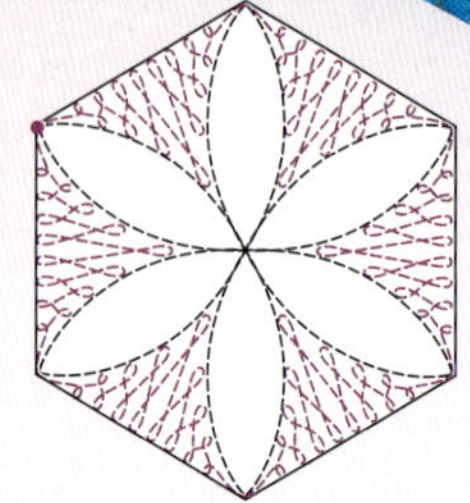

3. Fill in the spaces between the edge of the block and the quilting with the design of your choice, working your way around the block until you return to the starting point.

Tip

If you are quilting a large block or working with a smaller sewing machine, you can quilt the design in a different order to make it easier.

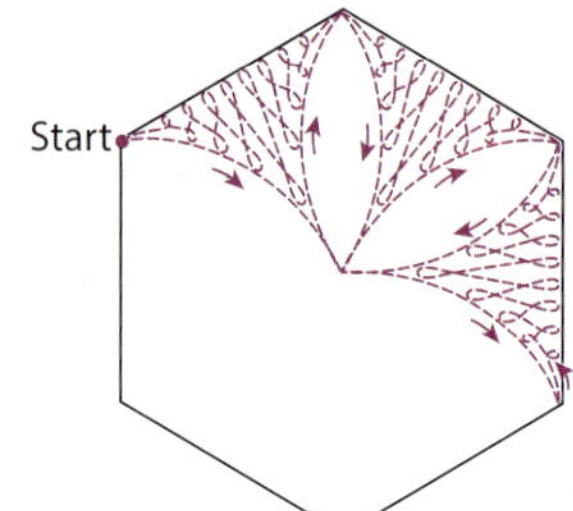

Quilt half of the block with curved lines, and then fill in the top, returning to the starting point.

Repeat with the bottom half of the block.

Variations

Try using this design in blocks of several different shapes, such as squares.

Try the design in other shapes, such as this 4-petal pattern in a square.

HEXAGON 3

Combining straight lines, curved lines, and some free-motion quilting results in a unique design. If you admire Mid Century Modern design, you will love this one. Try it in medium and larger blocks.

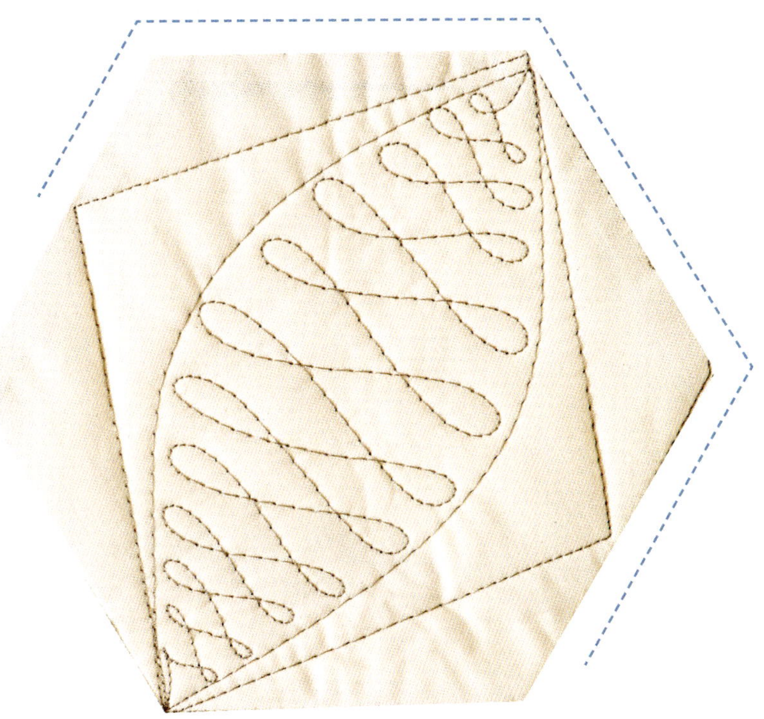

Tip

I show this design starting at the top right corner of the block, but you can start from any corner.

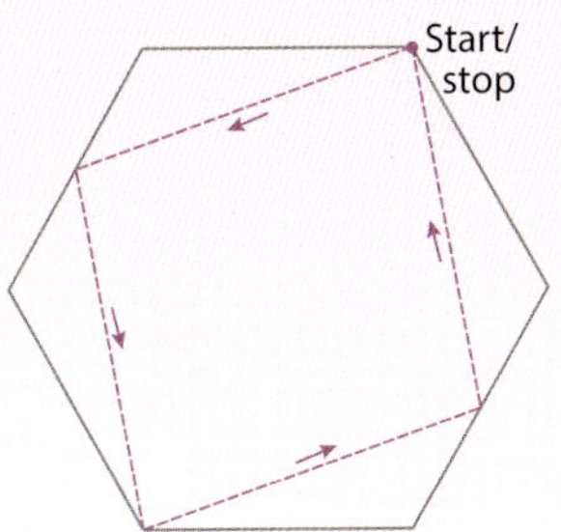

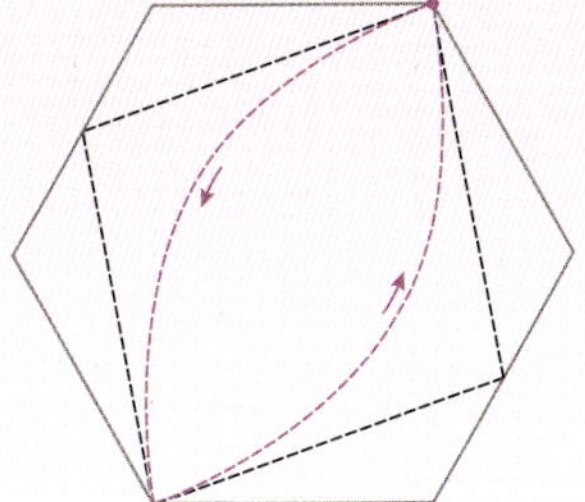

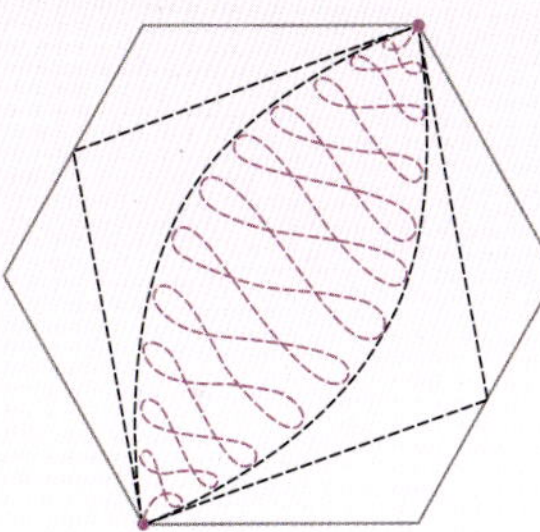

1. Starting at a corner of the hexagon block, quilt a diagonal line to the midpoint of the next side of the block. Quilt diagonally to the bottom corner, then diagonally to the midpoint of the next side. Quilt a fourth line that returns to the starting point.

2. Quilt a curved line to the opposite corner and another line curving back to the starting point.

3. Fill inside the curves with a figure-eight design, working your way from the top corner to the bottom corner.

Variations

This is one of those "moving on" designs. It starts and ends in different places. If you need a design that starts and ends in the same place, instead of quilting a figure-eight design in Step 3, you can echo the curved lines. It fills in the space but also brings you back to where you started.

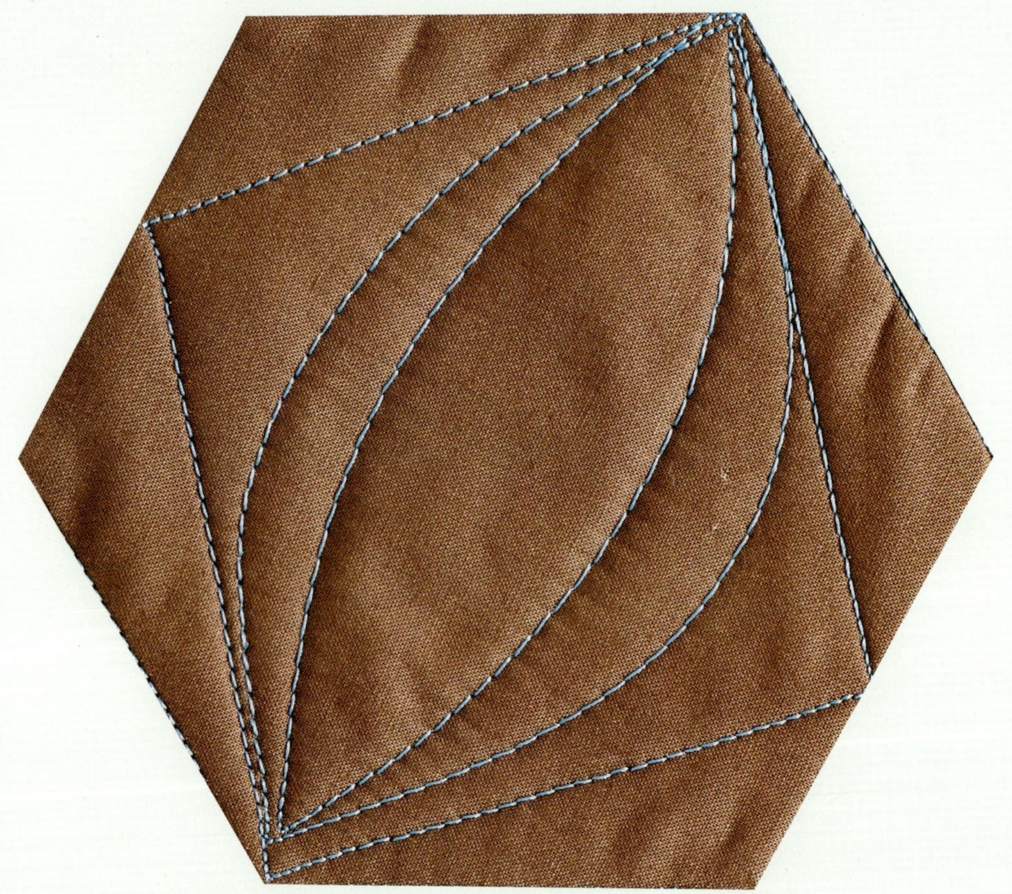

Replace the figure-eight design with echoed lines to end where you started.

About the AUTHOR

Angela Walters is a machine quilter and author who loves to teach others to use quilting to bring out the best in their quilts. Her work has been published in numerous magazines and books. She shares tips and finished quilts on her blog, quiltingismytherapy.com, and believes that "quilting is the funnest part!"